Lecture Notes in Computer Science 16204

Founding Editors

Gerhard Goos
Juris Hartmanis

Editorial Board Members

Elisa Bertino, *Purdue University, West Lafayette, IN, USA*
Wen Gao, *Peking University, Beijing, China*
Bernhard Steffen, *TU Dortmund University, Dortmund, Germany*
Moti Yung, *Columbia University, New York, NY, USA*

The series Lecture Notes in Computer Science (LNCS), including its subseries Lecture Notes in Artificial Intelligence (LNAI) and Lecture Notes in Bioinformatics (LNBI), has established itself as a medium for the publication of new developments in computer science and information technology research, teaching, and education.

LNCS enjoys close cooperation with the computer science R & D community, the series counts many renowned academics among its volume editors and paper authors, and collaborates with prestigious societies. Its mission is to serve this international community by providing an invaluable service, mainly focused on the publication of conference and workshop proceedings and postproceedings. LNCS commenced publication in 1973.

Irene-Angelica Chounta · Hironori Egi ·
Ari Nugraha · Harry Budi Santoso ·
Tomoo Inoue · Tamara Adriani Salim
Editors

Collaboration Technologies and Social Computing

31st International Conference, CollabTech 2025
Jakarta, Indonesia, November 4–7, 2025
Proceedings

Editors
Irene-Angelica Chounta ⓘ
University of Duisburg-Essen
Essen, Germany

Hironori Egi ⓘ
The University of Electro-Communications
Tokyo, Japan

Ari Nugraha ⓘ
Universitas Indonesia
Depok, Indonesia

Harry Budi Santoso ⓘ
Universitas Indonesia
Depok, Indonesia

Tomoo Inoue ⓘ
University of Tsukuba
Tsukuba, Japan

Tamara Adriani Salim ⓘ
Universitas Indonesia
Depok, Indonesia

ISSN 0302-9743   ISSN 1611-3349 (electronic)
Lecture Notes in Computer Science
ISBN 978-3-032-10155-6   ISBN 978-3-032-10156-3 (eBook)
https://doi.org/10.1007/978-3-032-10156-3

© The Editor(s) (if applicable) and The Author(s), under exclusive license
to Springer Nature Switzerland AG 2026

This work is subject to copyright. All rights are solely and exclusively licensed by the Publisher, whether the whole or part of the material is concerned, specifically the rights of translation, reprinting, reuse of illustrations, recitation, broadcasting, reproduction on microfilms or in any other physical way, and transmission or information storage and retrieval, electronic adaptation, computer software, or by similar or dissimilar methodology now known or hereafter developed.
The use of general descriptive names, registered names, trademarks, service marks, etc. in this publication does not imply, even in the absence of a specific statement, that such names are exempt from the relevant protective laws and regulations and therefore free for general use.
The publisher, the authors and the editors are safe to assume that the advice and information in this book are believed to be true and accurate at the date of publication. Neither the publisher nor the authors or the editors give a warranty, expressed or implied, with respect to the material contained herein or for any errors or omissions that may have been made. The publisher remains neutral with regard to jurisdictional claims in published maps and institutional affiliations.

This Springer imprint is published by the registered company Springer Nature Switzerland AG
The registered company address is: Gewerbestrasse 11, 6330 Cham, Switzerland

If disposing of this product, please recycle the paper.

Preface

This volume contains the papers presented at the 31st International Conference on Collaboration Technologies and Social Computing, CollabTech 2025. This year, the conference was hosted by Universitas Indonesia, in Indonesia, from November 4 to November 7, 2025. The conference invited contributions covering theoretical foundations, models, methodologies, and case studies that explore the complex interplay between collaboration and technology. The topics of interest included innovative technical + human + organizational approaches to expand collaboration support with an interdisciplinary perspective including computer science, management science, design science, cognitive science, and social science.

CollabTech 2025 received 50 submissions, each of which was carefully double-blindly reviewed by at least three program committee members. As a result, the committee decided to accept 12 full and 8 work-in-progress papers. The accepted papers present relevant, timely, and rigorous research related to theory, models, design principles, methodologies, and case studies that contribute to better understanding of the complex interaction between collaboration and technology.

As editors, we would like to thank the authors of all CollabTech 2025 submissions and the members of the Program Committee for carefully reviewing the submissions. Our thanks also go to our sponsors who allowed us to make CollabTech 2025 attractive to participants. Our special thanks go to the Information Processing Society of Japan (IPSJ), for their sponsorship.

Last, but not least, we would like to acknowledge the effort of the organizers of the conference, and thank the Steering Committee for the opportunity, trust and guidance they provided during the whole process.

November 2025

Irene-Angelica Chounta
Hironori Egi
Ari Nugraha
Harry Budi Santoso
Tomoo Inoue
Tamara Adriani Salim

Organization

General Chairs

Tomoo Inoue — University of Tsukuba, Japan
Tamara Adriani Salim — Universitas Indonesia, Indonesia

Program Committee Chairs

Irene-Angelica Chounta — University of Duisburg-Essen, Germany
Hironori Egi — University of Electro-Communications, Japan
Ari Nugraha — Universitas Indonesia, Indonesia
Harry Budi Santoso — Universitas Indonesia, Indonesia

Steering Committee

Nelson Baloian — Universidad de Chile, Chile
Ulrich Hoppe — University of Duisburg-Essen, Germany
Minoru Kobayashi — Meiji University, Japan
Hideaki Kuzuoka — University of Tokyo, Japan
Hiroaki Ogata — Kyoto University, Japan
Tomoo Inoue — University of Tsukuba, Japan

Program Committee

Mubarik Ahmad — YARSI University, Indonesia
Baginda Anggun Nan Cenka — Universitas Indonesia, Indonesia
Ati Suci Dian Martha — Telkom University, Indonesia
Yannis Dimitriadis — University of Valladolid, Spain
Micaela Dinis Esteves — Politécnico de Leiria, Portugal
Kinya Fujita — Tokyo University of Agrculture and Technology, Japan
Cédric Grueau — Instituto Politécnico de Setubal, Portugal
Naoko Hayashida — Fujitsu Laboratories Ltd., Japan
Atsuo Hazeyama — Tokyo Gakugei Unversity, Japan
Davinia Hernández-Leo — Universitat Pompeu Fabra, Spain

H. Ulrich Hoppe	University Duisburg-Essen/RIAS Institute Duisburg, Germany
Satoshi Ichimura	Otsuma Women's University, Japan
Marc Jansen	University of Applied Sciences Ruhr West, Germany
Thomas Largillier	GREYC, France
Liang-Yi Li	National Taiwan Normal University, Taiwan
Bibeg Limbu	University of Duisburg-Essen, Germany
Rene Lobo	Universitat Pompeu Fabra, Spain
Rwitajit Majumdar	Kumamoto University, Japan
Sonia Mendoza	CINVESTAV, Mexico
Cláudio Miguel Sapateiro	EST-IPS, Portugal
Marcelo Milrad	Linnaeus University, Sweden
Mamoun Nawahdah	Birzeit University, Palestine
Masayuki Okamoto	Toyota Motor Corporation, Japan
Masaki Omata	University of Yamanashi, Japan
Amalia Rahmah	STT Terpadu Nurul Fikri, Indonesia
Matías Recabarren	Universidad de los Andes, Colombia
Armanda Rodrigues	Universidade NOVA de Lisboa, Portugal
Flavia Santoro	Universidade do Estado do Rio de Janeiro, Brazil
Hideyuki Takada	Ritsumeikan University, Japan
Muhamad Prabu Wibowo	Universitas Indonesia, Indonesia
Takaya Yuizono	Japan Advanced Institute of Science and Technology, Japan
Alejandro Zunino	UNICEN, Argentina
Gustavo Zurita	Universidad de Chile, Chile

Contents

Collaborative Learning and Group Interaction

Facilitating Smooth Rejoining in Face-to-Face Group Chats by Sharing
Common Conversational Information after Temporary Absence 3
   Jotaro Hori, Masayuki Ando, Kouyou Otsu, and Tomoko Izumi

Research on Switching Learning Tasks According to Fatigue Levels
to Accommodate Possibility of Interaction 20
   Ryohei Shimizu, Masaki Kodaira, and Hironori Egi

Social Interactions and Online Engagement in CSCL Environments:
Examining a Measurement Scale 29
   J. Roberto Sánchez-Reina, Emily Theophilou,
   and Davinia Hernández-Leo

Estimating Discussion State from Head Movements in Collaborative
Learning Environments 39
   Hayato Kawashima, Ryosuke Nakamura, Ryunosuke Nishimura,
   and Hironori Egi

Self-selected Groups vs. Random Groups: An Analysis of Student
Engagement, Achievement, and Preferences in Collaborative Learning 55
   Ati Suci Dian Martha, Sri Widowati, Arinza Aurelvia,
   Soraya Haidar Salma, and Muhammad Dias Adani

Technology-Mediated Communication and Online Environments

What Makes Turn-Taking Smooth? Analysis of Gaze Behavior During
a Multitasking Videoconference 73
   Taketo Imagawa, Atsuto Kurokochi, Koki Yanagii, Kazuyuki Iso,
   Masayuki Ihara, and Minoru Kobayashi

A Proposal and Evaluation for Externalizing Thoughts of Passive Speakers
in Three-Party Video Conferences with Gaze Tracking Functionality 90
   Hiroya Miura, Kimitaka Yamamoto, Yoshinari Takegawa, and Keiji Hirata

Temporal Analysis of User Engagement, Technology Trends
and Emotional Dynamics on Stack Overflow 107
   Linda Okpanachi, Gema Rodríguez-Pérez, and Ifeoma Adaji

Do You See What I See? Vocal Cues to Visual Acuity Discrepancies
in VR-Based Stargazing 123
   Sora Iida and Satoshi Nakamura

AI in Education: LLMs and Content Generation

Simulating Collaborative Learning with Data-Driven LLM-Agents 135
   Yu Yan, Changhao Liang, and Hiroaki Ogata

Evaluation of LLM-Based Feedback Generation for Distance
Project-Based Learning 144
   Kosuke Sasaki and Tomoo Inoue

Generating Vicarious Dialogue for Online Learning Using Knowledge
Graph-Based Retrieval-Augmented Generation 161
   Yaofei Ding and Tomoo Inoue

Social Interaction, Community and Public Spaces

Dynamic Analysis of Social Capital in Commercial Areas Using
Connection Networks 179
   Yuya Ieiri, Ryo Okutani, Hiroshige Dan, and Osamu Yoshie

Emotional Analysis of Excluded Person Using Review Texts 195
   Megumi Yasuo, Kaito Shingu, Junjie Shan, Kazuho Yamaura,
   and Yoko Nishihara

Public Quest: A Communication Game to Foster Understanding
and Relationships in Public Space 204
   Shinya Nishide and Takeshi Nishida

How Do People Use Others' and Their Own Traces in Free Exploration? 212
   Ayaka Negishi, Hiroki Echigo, Kazuyuki Iso, Masayuki Ihara,
   and Minoru Kobayashi

Systems for Supporting Discourse and Understanding

A System for Extracting Discussion Topics Worth Deeper Exploration 231
   Yoko Nishihara, Kosuke Fujishima, Megumi Yasuo, Junjie Shan,
   and Tetsuo Yoshimoto

Exploring the Potential of Hackathons as a Means to Promote
Understanding of AI Literacy: A Case Study 244
   *Cleo Schulten, Li Yuan, Kiev Gama, Alexander Nolte,
   and Irene-Angelica Chounta*

Supporting Time-Constrained Student Sports Journalists: Smartwatch
Flagging and Match Visualization for Better Interview Questions 252
   Ai Hagihara and Satoshi Nakamura

Structural Analysis of Rebuttals to Evaluate Argumentative Interaction
in Parliamentary Debates 268
   Masahiro Fukui and Satoshi Nakamura

Author Index 277

Exploring the Potential of Hackathons as a Means to Promote
Understanding of AI Literacy: A Case Study 244
   *Cleo Schulten, Li Yuan, Kiev Gama, Alexander Nolte,
   and Irene-Angelica Chounta*

Supporting Time-Constrained Student Sports Journalists: Smartwatch
Flagging and Match Visualization for Better Interview Questions 252
   Ai Hagihara and Satoshi Nakamura

Structural Analysis of Rebuttals to Evaluate Argumentative Interaction
in Parliamentary Debates 268
   Masahiro Fukui and Satoshi Nakamura

Author Index 277

Collaborative Learning and Group Interaction

Facilitating Smooth Rejoining in Face-to-Face Group Chats by Sharing Common Conversational Information after Temporary Absence

Jotaro Hori[1(✉)], Masayuki Ando[1], Kouyou Otsu[2], and Tomoko Izumi[1]

[1] Ritsumeikan University, Ibaraki Osaka 567-8570, Japan
is0578iv@ed.ritsumei.ac.jp, {mandou,izumi-t}@fc.ritsumei.ac.jp
[2] Aoyama Gakuin University, Sagamihara Kanagawa 252-5258, Japan
otsu.kouyou@it.aoyama.ac.jp

Abstract. This study proposes a method via which to support smooth rejoining in a face-to-face group chat for a participant (the leaver) after they have temporarily left, without interrupting the conversation. A previous study demonstrated that presenting a summary containing much of the recent conversational content to the leaver immediately before their return facilitates smoother rejoining for the leaver. However, because the conversation involves all participants, the issue of rejoining concerns not only the leaver but also those who continued the conversation (the conversers), who should be supported in continuing their conversation smoothly, without disruption. Therefore, in this study, we attempt to support smooth rejoining for both the leaver and the conversers. We propose a method of sharing common conventional information with both parties and discuss the effective types of information to share: a summary and keywords. An evaluation experiment suggested that sharing a summary enhances the leaver's sense of being able to rejoin early and their ease of understanding the conversational content. Furthermore, sharing the summary reduced the conversers' sense of the time required to explain the conversational content to the leaver. However, we could not confirm the effectiveness of sharing keywords in facilitating smooth rejoining. These findings suggest that when sharing common information before the leaver returns, it is important to share information that allows both parties to grasp the conversational content with the same level of detail and ease.

Keywords: Conversation Rejoining · Face-to-Face Communication · Shared Understanding · Group interaction

1 Introduction

Face-to-face communication, including casual chatting, plays a crucial role in building good interpersonal relationships and forming cohesive organizations. In the workplace, casual chatting has been reported to enhance team performance [1] and increase productivity by increasing positive social emotions [2]. In this study, we address the communication issues that occur when a member of a face-to-face group chat temporarily leaves a conversation. In such informal chats, topics tend to change incidentally and frequently. Therefore, when a member, hereinafter referred to as the "leaver," temporarily steps away, for example, to take a phone call, use the restroom, or attend to another minor matter, the topic often changes by the time they return. In these situations, the leaver typically attempts to catch up by observing the ongoing conversation or asking another participant who remained in the conversation, hereinafter referred to as the "converser," about the current topic. However, it is often difficult for the leaver to grasp the conversation flow because they may hesitate to take such actions for fear of interrupting it. Conversely, the conversers may also feel that the flow of the conversation is disrupted or its liveliness is diminished. Therefore, we examine a way to support the smooth rejoining of a conversation for both the leaver and the conversers.

In the field of Human–Computer Interaction, particularly in the context of online communication, there is research on supporting participation in the middle of an ongoing communication. For example, Matsuo et al. [3] proposed an approach that characterizes messages on electronic message boards and a summarization system using it. Furthermore, Yamashita et al. [4] investigated how different types of dialogue summaries can facilitate the handover from a dialog system to a human operator in a call center. While these studies help new participants understand the content of a conversation, they do not address face-to-face chats or cases where participants rejoin with prior knowledge about the conversation before leaving. In face-to-face conversations, it is difficult to review dialogue while the interaction is in progress, and the requirements for smooth communication are assumed to differ from those in online settings. Therefore, this study explores ways to support rejoining conversations in face-to-face settings.

Our previous study [5] partially addressed this issue and proposed a system that provides the leaver with a summary of the conversation that took place during their absence. The system provides the leaver with a "recent conversation summary" that focuses on the content of the conversation immediately before their return, offering cues to facilitate rejoining. The results of the evaluation show that presenting the recent conversation summary to the leaver was effective in improving their sense of being able to rejoin the conversation early and enhancing their understanding of the conversation.

However, because a conversation involves all its participants, the issue of rejoining concerns not only the leaver but also the conversers, who should be supported in continuing their conversation smoothly, without disruption. In our previous study [5], we did not focus on the support provided to the conversers. In fact, with our method, the conversational summary was provided only to the leaver, so the conversers may be unaware of what the leaver had already grasped upon returning. This may have caused confusion for the conversers and a sense of disruption in the conversation, potentially hindering smooth rejoining for both parties. In communication, the importance of establishing common ground between participants is widely recognized. Common ground refers to not only the knowledge shared between conversational partners but also their mutual belief that this knowledge is, indeed, shared [6]. Therefore, it is necessary to have a mechanism that supports the formation of a shared understanding between the leaver and the conversers when the leaver returns after a temporary absence.

In this study, we extend the method proposed in our previous study [5] by proposing that information be provided not only to the leaver but also to the conversers in advance in order to support the smoother rejoining of the conversation for both parties. However, if the conversers are given sufficient, detailed information about the conversation, they may take time to review it, potentially interrupting the their conversation flow. Because the conversers have already experienced the full conversation, they may not require detailed information to understand what the leaver received. Therefore, in this study, we consider two types of information that could be presented to the conversers: summary sentences, which provided detailed information, and keywords, which provided brief information. In this paper, we present a proposal regarding sharing information design and the results of an experiment intended to investigate the effects of these information types on conversation progression and the rejoining process.

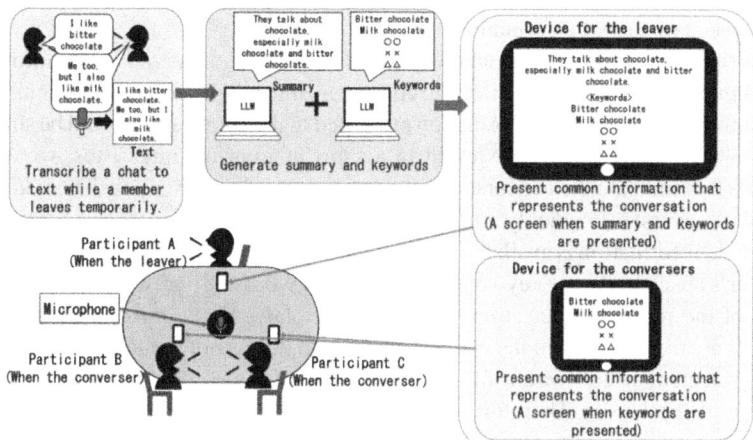

Fig. 1. Overview of the proposed system and processing flow

2 Proposed Method

2.1 Proposed Concept

We propose a system that supports rejoining a face-to-face group chat when a leaver returns. Figure 1 shows the usage flow for the proposed system. First, when the leaver leaves a conversation, a microphone installed on the table begins recording and transcribing the conversation in real time. Directly before the leaver returns, information representing the content of the conversation during their absence is generated from the transcription. This information is then presented to both the leaver and the conversers and reviewed by them before the leaver returns to the conversation.

By using this system, the leaver can rejoin after confirming the conversation content. At the same time, the conversers can review the same information while continuing their conversation, allowing them to understand in advance what the leaver knows. By presenting shared information to both parties in advance, it is expected that the leaver will be able to rejoin the conversation more easily, and the conversers will be able to identify which parts of the conversation are known to the leaver. This can lead to a smoother rejoining process for both parties and reduce the sense of stagnation.

2.2 Providing Information to the Leaver and the Conversers

In this study, we consider two types of information that can be provided to the leaver and the conversers in order to form a shared understanding: the recent conversation summary and the keywords extracted from the summary. The recent conversation summary is a summary that focuses primarily on the content of the conversation immediately before the leaver returns, unlike a typical summary, which covers the entire conversation evenly. In our previous study [5], we suggest that leavers were more easily able to grasp the content of a conversation that took place during their absence when a recent conversation summary was presented as compared to when a normal summary was used. Therefore, in this study as well, which is intended to share conversational information between the leaver and the conversers, the recent conversation summary is provided to both parties as a key piece of shared information.

However, unlike the leaver, who can take time to review the provided information before returning to the conversation, the conversers must review it while continuing their conversation. Therefore, the information presented to the conversers should be structured in such a way that it can be reviewed in a short amount of time. Thus, we consider keywords that indicate the conversation content to be such information. These keywords enable the conversers to quickly infer the content being presented to the leaver, even when only limited information is available, because they participated in the conversation during the leaver's absence. These keywords are important words or phrases extracted from the portion of the recent conversation summary that relates to the most recent content. If keywords are extracted from the entire conversation, terms not included in the summary may be selected, which would fail to serve as shared information with the summary presented to the leaver. Therefore, in this method, keywords are extracted only from the summary, using a generative AI model based on a large-scale language model. The extracted keywords are also presented to the leaver along with the recent conversation summary so that both parties can grasp the shared conversational information.

3 Prototype System

To evaluate the proposed method, we developed a prototype system that presents a conversation summary or keywords to both the leaver and the conversers.

3.1 Overall Design

This system consists of four main functions: voice recording, recent conversation summary generation, keyword extraction, and information presentation. The first three functions are implemented on the main PC, while the last is implemented as a web application on the participants' smartphones, with an interface for operation.

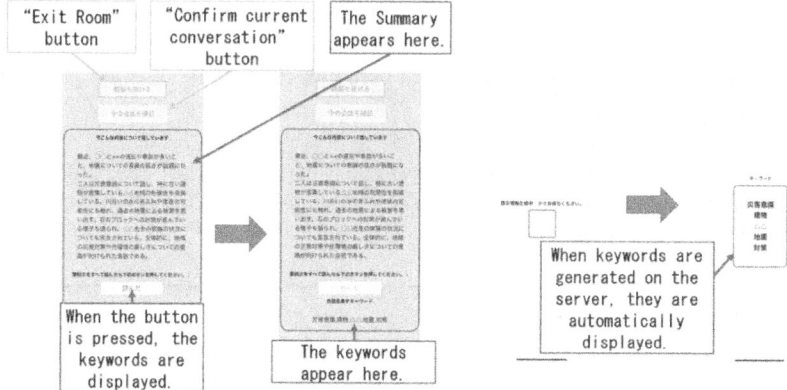

Fig. 2. Example of display of system screen for leaver (left two screens) and system screen for converser (right two screens). (in the figures, all text displayed on the screen is in Japanese because we conducted the experiment with Japanese students)

Figure 1 shows the system processing flow and Fig. 2 shows the example screens presented to the leaver and the conversers. In the leaver's interface (left section of Fig. 2), only the "Exit Room" button is initially enabled. When the leaver presses this button on their smartphone, the system begins recording the conversation using the microphone on the table and transcribes the conversation in real time. Then, when the leaver is ready to return to the conversation and presses the "Confirm current conversation" button, the system on the web server generates a summary sentence from the transcribed text and extracts the keywords. On the converser's smartphone, the message "Information is being generated. Please wait a moment" is initially displayed (right section of Fig. 2). After the summary text and keywords are generated, they are sent from the server to the respective terminals and then automatically displayed on the screens, accompanied by notification sounds. On the leaver's terminal, a "Read" button appears with the summary text, and when the leaver finishes reading the summary and presses it, the keywords are displayed. In this prototype system, all of these operations can be performed on the interface on the leaver's smartphone.

3.2 Generating the Recent Conversation Summary

The generation of the recent conversation summary was based on the method proposed in our previous study [5], with improvements having been made to the language model and prompt design. For real-time transcription, we used faster-whisper [7], a reimplementation of OpenAI's speech recognition model Whisper that uses CTranslate2. The transcription process segments the ongoing conversation every five seconds, converting the speech into a text file in which each line corresponds to a five-second segment. This text file is then divided into two parts: the first 70% (the front part) and the remaining 30% (the recent part). A summary sentence is generated for each part using the ChatGPT [8] application programing interface (API). In this phase, the recent part of the summary is designed to be at least 40 Japanese characters longer than the front part to ensure that it includes more details from the most recent portion of the conversation. The generation is repeated until this condition is satisfied, and the two summaries are then combined. We used the gpt-4o-mini-2024-07-18 model, hereafter referred to as.

Table 1. Prompts for generating the recent conversation summary (When generating the front part of the summary, we replaced inputs such as specified num-ber of characters and "recent part" in the prompt with the inputs in "()". All prompts in the system are written in Japanese.)

Basic Generation Prompt
{"role": "system", "content": "You are a reporter who is good at summarizing."},
{"role": "user", "content":f"""{[recent part (front part) sentence]}
###
Please summarize the conversation between these two people in a sentence of 150 or more (50 words or less).
The following rules must be followed when generating the text.
Do not include any sentences other than the summary sentence."""}

If the result does not meet the specified rules: add the following and regenerate
{"role": "assistant", "content":{[Unsuitable summary of recent part (front part)]},
{"role": "user", "content": "Less than (More than) 150 characters (100 characters). Please make it longer (shorter)."}

GPT-API, to generate the summary. Table 1 shows the prompts used in the system.

3.3 Extracting Keywords

During keyword extraction, five contextually important words are extracted from the recent part of the recent conversation summary. However, because the summary text is already a condensed version of the conversation, simple frequency-based extraction may fail to capture contextual importance information. Therefore, in order to extract context-aware keywords, the GPT-API is used based on the prompts shown in Table 2.

Table 2. Prompts for keyword extraction

Basic Generation Prompt
{"role": "user", "content":f"""{[recent part of the summary text]}
\#\#\#
This sentence is a summary of a conversation. Please select five keywords from this summary sentence.
\#\#\#
Rules for generation
・ Be sure to include five keywords in the output result.
・ The format of the output should be as follows. [Keyword 1, Keyword 2, Keyword 3, Keyword 4, Keyword 5]
・ For the keywords, select only the words included in the summary text.
"""}

If the result does not meet the specified rules: add the following and regenerate
{"role": "assistant", "content":{[unsuitable output result]}},
{"role": "user", "content":"""The specified rules are not followed. Please output keywords from the summary text again according to the rules at the time of generation.
\#\#\#
Rules for generation
・ Be sure to include five keywords in the output result.
・ The format of the output should be as follows. [Keyword 1, Keyword 2, Keyword 3, Keyword 4, Keyword 5]
・ For the keywords, select only the words included in the summary text.
"""}

These prompts are designed to extract keywords with the recognition that the input is a summary of a conversation. Specifically, it instructs the model to extract exactly five keywords and specifies the required output format. In addition, constraints are imposed to ensure that only words appearing in the summary text are selected. The extracted keywords are sent to each terminal only when the output satisfies the specified format. If the output does not satisfy the format, the extraction process is repeated.

4 Experiment

4.1 Purpose and Hypotheses

The purpose of this experiment is to verify the effect of presenting information related to the conversation that occurred during the leaver's temporary absence to both the leaver and the conversers in terms of facilitating the smooth rejoining of the conversation. In addition, we compare the effects of presenting either a summary or keywords extracted from the summary to the conversers, focusing on how each affects their conversational experience. Based on these objectives, we test the following hypotheses:

- **H1:** Effect of sharing conversational summaries during the leaver's absence in advance.

    - **H1–1 (for the leaver):** Reviewing the shared conversational summary in advance makes it easier for the leaver to smoothly rejoin the conversation than not sharing information.
    - **H1–2 (for the converser):** Reviewing the shared conversational summary in advance reduces the likelihood that the converser will feel inhibited in the flow of the conversation.

- **H2:** Effect of presenting keywords as shared information for the conversers.

    - **H2–1 (smoothness of rejoining):** Presenting only keywords facilitates the smooth rejoining of the conversation for both the leaver and the conversers as effectively as presenting a full summary.
    - **H2–2 (progress of the conversation):** Presenting keywords reduces the likelihood that the converser will feel inhibited in the flow of the conversation when reviewing information as compared to when a full summary is presented.

H1 tests the impact of sharing a common summary on both the leaver and the conversers. For H1–1, which concerns the leaver, the smoothness of rejoining the conversation is evaluated based on the following factors: the ease of understanding the explanation of the conversation, the sense of early rejoining, and the sense of conversational interruption. For H1–2, which concerns the conversers, the smoothness of rejoining is evaluated from the perspective of the ease of explaining the conversation to the leaver and the sense of conversational interruption. H2 examines the effect of presenting keywords to the conversers as compared to presenting a summary. H2–1 focuses on the experience at the time of rejoining and evaluates it based on the same factors as H1–1 and H1–2. H2–2 is used to verify the potential advantages of presenting keywords in terms of the ease of grasping information during an ongoing conversation.

4.2 Experimental Conditions

In this experiment, a group of three participants was asked to chat freely. In each trial, one participant was assigned the role of leaver, and the other two were assigned the role of converser. Each participant experienced our prototype system according to their assigned role.

We defined three experimental conditions by varying the information presented to the leaver and the conversers. Figure 3 shows the system used in each condition.

1. **Presenting-summary-to-leaver condition**

    - Converser: No information is provided before the leaver returns.
    - Leaver: The recent conversation summary is provided before returning (Fig. 3-a).

2. **Sharing-summary condition**

- Converser: The recent conversation summary is provided before the leaver returns (Fig. 3-c).
- Leaver: The recent conversation summary is provided before returning (Fig. 3-a).

3. **Sharing-keywords condition**

- Conversers: Keywords are provided before the leaver returns (Fig. 3–d).
- Leaver: Both the recent conversation summary and keywords are provided before returning (Fig. 3–b).

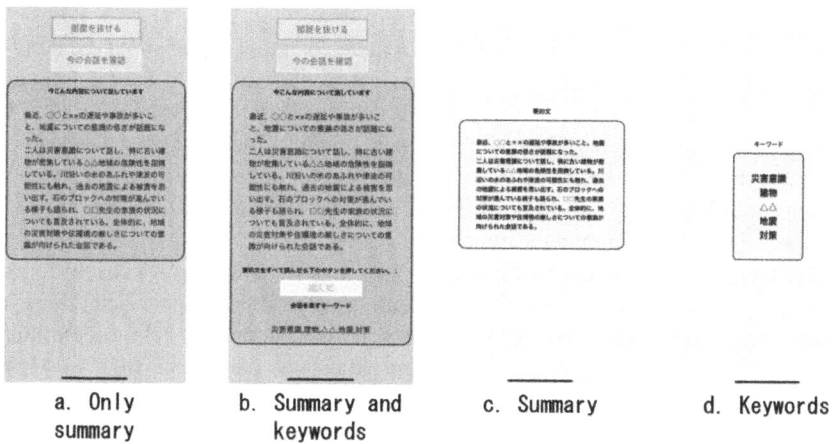

a. Only summary   b. Summary and keywords   c. Summary   d. Keywords

Fig. 3. Example of system screen used for each condition (the summary and keywords are written in Japanese because we conducted the experiment for Japanese students)

The presenting-summary-to-leaver condition was similar in terms of setting to our previous study [5], reproducing a situation in which only the leaver can review a summary of the conversation content. The sharing-summary condition examines the effect of forming a shared understanding by having both the leaver and the conversers review the same summary sentence. The sharing-keywords condition, in which the conversers review only the keywords but the leaver reviews both the summary and keywords, examines the effect of providing simple and easily readable information to the conversers. H1–1 and H1–2 are tested by comparing the presenting-summary-to-leaver condition and the sharing-summary condition. H2–1 and H2–2 are tested by comparing the sharing-keywords condition with the sharing-summary condition.

4.3 Experimental Environment

The experiment was conducted in a university laboratory. As shown in the bottom left of Fig. 1, the three participants were seated around an elliptical table, with a microphone placed at the center to record the conversation. In addition, each participant was provided with a smartphone running the experimental system. In this experiment, system operations, such as starting transcription and the generation of summaries and keywords, were controlled by the experimenter. The participants only viewed the information displayed on their smartphones. A video camera recorded the interior of the laboratory.

4.4 Experimental Procedure

In this experiment, all three members of each group experienced both the leaver and converser roles across the three conditions. The experiment was conducted over three days, with each group experiencing one condition per day to minimize the effects of fatigue and habituation. The order of the conditions was counterbalanced across groups to control for order effects.

On the first day of the experiment, the participants were informed about the purpose and procedure of the study and gave their consent to participate. At the beginning of each day, the detailed experimental procedure and the system to be used on that day were explained. In each condition, all participants received individual instructions on how to use the system; the types of information that would be displayed; and what shared information, if any, would be provided. Each participant was then provided with a smartphone for reviewing the information provided.

Next, the three participants in each group were instructed to begin a casual conversation. To facilitate the start of the conversation, topic cards were provided. However, the participants were free to change topics at any time. Approximately three minutes after the conversation began, the experimenter called one participant (the leaver) via their smartphone and asked them to step out of the room. The experimenter collected the leaver's smartphone and began the transcription of the ongoing conversation inside the lab. The leaver was then escorted to a separate location by the experimenter and asked to complete a simple arithmetic task.

Approximately three minutes after the leaver exited the laboratory, the experimenter explained the system usage again and accompanied them back to the front of the laboratory. Approximately five minutes after the leaver had left the laboratory, the experimenter operated the system to begin generating a summary and keywords and handed the smartphone to the leaver when the information was displayed. The leaver returned to the laboratory after reviewing the information. Before starting the experiment, we asked the conversers to briefly explain the topic of the ongoing conversation to the leaver upon their return and then continue talking about that topic until it naturally shifted. Approximately two minutes after the leaver returned to the laboratory, the experimenter entered the lab and asked both the leaver and the conversers to complete their respective online questionnaires on their personal mobile devices.

The procedure described above was repeated until all three participants experienced the role of leaver. The same experimental procedure was also conducted over three days under different experimental conditions. The order in which the participants were assigned the role of leaver was kept the same across all conditions (i.e., across all days) to ensure consistency in terms of their experience with the system.

4.5 Evaluation Items

The questionnaires given to the leavers and the conversers are shown in Table 3 and 4, respectively. These questions were based on a 7-point Likert scale, with 7 being the highest score. The items in the leaver's questionnaire relate to H1–1 and H2–1 and ask about the ease of understanding the explanation offered by the conversers, the sense of early rejoining, and the sense of conversational interruption. In the questionnaires for conversers, Q1-Q5 relate to H1–2 and H2–1, which are about the ease of explaining the conversation to the leaver and the sense of conversational interruption. Q6-Q8 relate to H2–2 and ask about the ease of grasping information and the costs of reviewing it. Because Q6-Q8 pertain to the experience of the conversers using the systems, they were asked only in the sharing-summary and sharing-keywords conditions.

4.6 Results

In the experiment, six groups of three undergraduate or graduate students participated, yielding a total of 18 students. The members of each group were familiar with one another and able to engage in natural one-on-one conversations with any other members. In this section, we present the results derived from the questionnaires for the leaver and the converser. In this experiment, for each condition, each participant took on the role of leaver once and the role of converser twice. Therefore, for each condition, data derived from 18 leavers and 36 conversers (18×2) were included in the analysis.

Table 3. Questionnaire items for the leavers.

No	Questionnaire items	Hypothesis
1	The information I saw beforehand made it easier to understand the ongoing conversation when I returned to the conversation.	
2	I felt I interrupted an ongoing conversation when I returned to the conversation.	
3	It was easy to understand the explanation of the conversation from the other participants when I returned to the conversation.	H1-1/H2-1
4	It was necessary to ask for more details in order to understand the content of the conversation when I returned to the conversation.	
5	I felt no need for the other participants to explain the content of the conversation when I returned to the conversation.	
6	I felt I could rejoin into the conversation early after returning to room.	

Table 4. Questionnaire items for the conversers.

No	Questionnaire items	Hypothesis
1	When the person who temporarily left the room returned to the conversation, I felt the flow of the conversation stopped.	
2	When the person who temporarily left the room returned to the conversation, I felt an interruption of our own conversation.	
3	It took time to get the person who temporarily left the room to understand the content of the conversation.	H1-2/2-1
4	It was easy to explain the content of the conversation to the person who temporarily left the room.	
5	When explaining the content of a conversation to the person who temporarily left the room, I wondered what to tell them.	
6	The information displayed on the device during the conversation was easy to grasp.	
7	During the conversation, I felt that the progress of the conversation was stopped by the information presented by the device.	H2-2
8	During the conversation, I was distracted by the information presented by the device.	

4.6.1 Questionnaire Results for Leavers

The questionnaire results for the leavers are shown in Fig. 4. A one-way Analysis of Variance (ANOVA) with for each item revealed no significant differences in any of the items. Comparing the average values for Q2, "Sense of conversational interruption,"

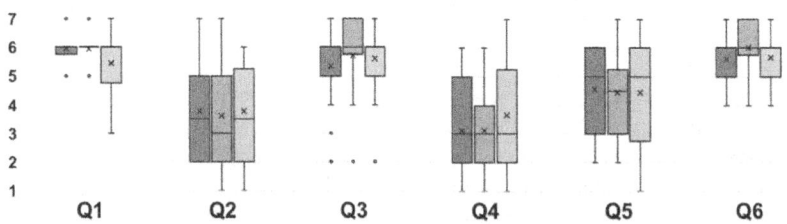

■ **Presenting-summary-to-leaver condition** ■ **Sharing-summary condition**
▫ **Sharing-keywords condition**

Fig. 4. Box and whisker plots for Q1~6 asked to the leavers (N = 18)

Table 5. Results of equivalence tests for the leaver.

	Q1	Q2	Q3	Q4	Q5	Q6
p-value	0.2758	0.1850	0.1101	0.4038	0.1068	0.0996

the presenting-summary-to-leaver and sharing-keywords conditions had the same average value, which was higher than that of the sharing-summary condition. For Q3, "Ease of understanding the explanation," and Q6, "Sense of early rejoining the conversation," the sharing-summary condition had higher average values, indicating more positive evaluations, than the other two conditions. For Q1, "Ease of understanding the conversation," and Q4, "Need for additional questions," the sharing-keywords condition scored lower for Q1 and higher for Q4 than the other two conditions. For these items, the average values for the presenting-summary-to-leaver condition and the sharing-summary condition were the same, with both conditions receiving equally positive ratings. The results for Q5 are omitted from the discussion because a high score does not necessarily indicate a positive outcome. When the explanation from the conversers contained only necessary content, a low score can be positive.

To verify H2–1, equivalence tests between the sharing-summary and sharing-keywords conditions were conducted using the Two One-sided Test (TOST)[9], with equivalence being defined as the 95% confidence interval of the mean difference falling within ± 0.7. The p-values of the TOST are shown in Table 5. Among the tested items, Q6 showed marginally significant equivalence ($p = .0996$).

4.6.2 Questionnaire Results for the Conversers

The questionnaire results for the conversers are shown in Fig. 5. A repeated measures one-way ANOVA was used for Q1-Q5, and t-tests were conducted for Q6-Q8 to compare the sharing-summary and sharing-keywords conditions. The results of the ANOVA were significant for Q3, "Sense of time spent on explanation" ($p = .001$), and Q5, "Difficulty in making a choice of explanatory content" ($p = .002$). Multiple comparisons using the Holm method revealed that the sharing-keywords condition scored significantly higher than the sharing-summary condition for Q3 ($p < .001$). In addition, for Q3, a significant trend was identified between the presenting-summary-to-leaver and sharing-summary conditions, with the latter having a lower average value. For Q5, the sharing-keywords condition scored significantly higher than both the presenting-summary-to-leaver ($p = .040$) and the sharing-summary condition ($p = .001$). In terms of average values, the sharing-summary condition had the lowest score for both Q3 and Q5.

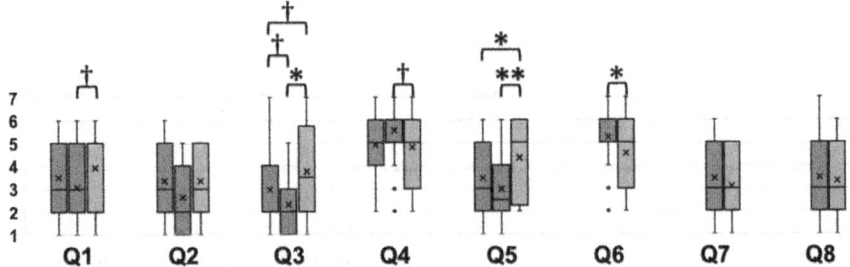

Fig. 5. Box and whisker plots for Q1–8 asked to the conversers (N = 36, †: p < 0.1, *: p < 0.05, **: p < 0.01)

The results of the ANOVA indicate a significant trend for Q1, "Sense of stagnation in conversation flow" (p = .083), Q2, "Sense of conversation interruption" (p = .062), and Q4, "Ease of explanation" (p = .065). The multiple comparison tests showed a significant trend in the differences between the sharing-summary and sharing-keywords conditions for Q1 and Q4. Moreover, the sharing-summary condition had a lower average for Q1, and the sharing-keywords condition had a lower average for Q4. The multiple comparisons for Q2 showed no significant differences between the conditions. The average values for Q2 were the same in the presenting-summary-to-leaver and sharing-keywords conditions, while the sharing-summary condition had a lower score than the other two conditions. The equivalence test (TOST) for Q2 between the sharing-summary and sharing-keywords conditions did not confirm equivalence (p = .53).

A t-test for Q6, "Ease of grasping information," indicated that the sharing-summary condition scored significantly higher than the sharing-keywords condition (p = .028). No significant differences were found for Q7, "Stagnation in conversation due to information presentation," and Q8, "Distraction during information presentation." However, the sharing-summary condition had higher average values for both.

4.7 Discussion

4.7.1 Effects of Sharing Summary

First, we discuss Hypothesis H1, "Effect of sharing conversational summaries during the leaver's absence in advance," from the perspectives of both the leaver (H1–1) and the conversers (H1–2). Regarding H1–1, we discuss the effects of sharing the summary on smoothly rejoining the conversation, based on the leavers' responses. Comparing the scores for the sharing-summary and presenting-summary-to-leaver conditions, no statistically significant differences were confirmed, and thus, H1–1 was not supported.

Therefore, regarding H1–1, we discuss the effect of sharing the summary based on the trends in the average scores. The sharing-summary condition received the most positive scores for Q2, "Sense of conversational interruption"; Q3, "Ease of understanding the explanation"; and Q6, "Sense of early rejoining the conversation." In particular, for Q3 and Q6, the order of average scores was sharing summary > sharing keywords >

presenting-summary-to-leaver. These results suggest that presenting the conversational summary to both the conversers and the leavers may improve the leaver's understanding of the conversation and their sense of early rejoining. Sharing common information beforehand appears to establish common ground, making it easier for the leaver to comprehend the topic and return to the conversation without disrupting its flow.

Next, we discuss H1–2, which concerns the effects on the conversers, by comparing the scores for Q1-Q5 based on the conversers' questionnaire. The sharing-summary condition was evaluated more positively than the presenting-summary-to-leaver condition for Q3, "Sense of time spent on explanation," and a significant trend was confirmed for the difference between the two conditions. These results suggest that sharing summaries was evaluated by the conversers as effective in reducing the perceived time spent explaining. Although no significant differences were observed, the average values for Q1, Q2, Q4, and Q5 were more positive in the sharing-summary condition than in the presenting-summary-to-leaver condition. This suggests that reviewing the summary helps conversers feel they can explain the content more easily, without perceiving interruptions in the conversation or feeling unsure what to explain. This is likely because the summary contains contextual information about the conversation, allowing the conversers to more accurately estimate the leaver's level of grasping and more easily judge which parts of the conversation need to be explained and which parts can be omitted. As a result, the burden of explanation is reduced. Therefore, H1–2 was partially supported, but only in terms of the time required for explanation.

4.7.2 Effects of Presenting Keywords as Shared Information

In this section, we discuss H2, which concerns the effect of presenting keywords as shared information to the conversers, by comparing the scores in the sharing-keywords condition with those in the sharing-summary condition. Regarding H2–1, "Presenting only keywords facilitates the smooth rejoining of the conversation for both the leaver and the conversers as effectively as presenting a full summary," the equivalence test for the leaver's questionnaire confirmed an equivalent trend only for Q6. Based on the conversers' questionnaire, significant or marginal differences were observed in Q1,3–5. Therefore, H2–1 was not supported for both parties.

We now discuss the results for the leavers. Although equivalence was not confirmed for Q3, "Ease of understanding the explanation" ($p = 0.1101$), the p-value approached marginal significance ($p < .10$). In addition, Q6, "Sense of early rejoining the conversation," showed an equivalent trend. This suggests that the leavers may not have perceived clear differences in comprehension or sense of rejoining the conversation early between the two conditions. However, in Q1, "Ease of understanding the conversation," and Q4, "Need for additional questions," the sharing-keywords condition had the most negative average scores. This may be because, although the leaver viewed the summary in all conditions, the conversers only saw the keywords in that condition. As a result, the conversers may not have been able to accurately judge what the leaver didn't know, and the leaver may have struggled with the conversers' fragmented explanation.

These facts can also be inferred from the conversers' responses. For Q3, "Sense of time spent on explanation," and Q5, "Difficulty in making a choice of explanatory content," the sharing-keywords condition was evaluated more negatively than even the presenting-summary-to-leaver condition, with a significant trend in Q3 and a significant difference in Q5. Compared to the sharing-summary condition, the sharing-keywords condition was also significantly worse for Q3 and Q5, and significant trends were also confirmed for Q1, "Sense of stagnation in conversation flow," and Q4, "Ease of explanation." While the sharing-summary condition had the most positive average values overall, the sharing-keywords condition had the most negative results for Q1, 3, 4, and 5. The results suggest that the conversers cannot grasp what the leaver has already understood from the limited keyword information, even if they themselves know all of the conversational content. As a result, it becomes difficult for them to decide what to explain, and their sense of the explanation time required increases, indicating the possibility of hindering the smooth rejoining. In other words, it may be important to provide information with both parties with equally detailed information that is easy to grasp the conversational context.

Finally, we discuss the results for Q6-Q8 for the conversers, which relate to H2–2, "Presenting keywords reduces the likelihood that the converser will feel inhibited in the flow of the conversation when reviewing information as compared to when a full summary is presented." The result show that the sharing-keywords condition did not have statistically significant positive scores for any of the items, and H2–2 was not supported. In particular, for Q6, "Ease of grasping information," the sharing-keywords condition was rated significantly more negatively than the sharing-summary condition. This indicates that even conversers who understood all of the conversational content had difficulty grasping the information presented as keywords. On the other hand, in Q7, "Stagnation in conversation due to information presentation," and Q8, "Distraction during information presentation," although statistically significant differences were not confirmed, positive results were observed for the sharing-keywords condition. This result may be attributed to the fact that the keywords were less informative and required less time for review as compared to the summary, whereas it may have been difficult for the conversers to check the summary text while continuing the conversation.

5 Conclusions

In this study, we examined support for the smooth rejoining of a conversation after a temporary absence, focusing on both the leaver and the conversers who remained in the conversation. We proposed a method of sharing information about the conversation content that occurred during the leaver's absence with both parties before the leaver returns. Regarding the information to present about the conversational content, we considered a recent conversation summary, which focused on the content immediately before the leaver's return, and keywords extracted from this summary.

In the experiment, we compared the effects of the presence or absence of shared information and differences in the information presented. The results did not confirm statistically significant differences among the conditions for the leavers. However, it was confirmed that sharing summary sentences may enhance the leaver's sense of early rejoining and ease of understanding the conversational content. For the conversers, it was shown that sharing a summary with the leaver also reduced their sense of the time required to explain the content. However, when only keywords were presented to the conversers, this was evaluated even more negatively than when no information was shared. These results suggest that any common information should provide easily graspable context, such as a summary, and be equally detailed for both the leaver and the conversers. In the future, it will be necessary to consider information that is easy for the conversers to review and that helps both the leavers and the conversers establish a shared understanding, even in the situations where the conversation is ongoing. Additionally, verifying the impact of different leaving times (set to five minutes in this experiment) and assessing the quality and appropriateness of summaries generated by ChatGPT remain important challenges.

Disclosure of Interests. The authors have no competing interests to declare that are relevant to the content of this article.

References

1. Watanabe, J.I., Fujita, M., Yano, K., Kanesaka, H., Hasegawa, T.: Resting time activeness determines team performance in call centers. In: 2012 International Conference on Social Informatics, pp. 26–31. IEEE (2012)
2. Methot, J.R., Rosado-Solomon, E.H., Downes, P.E., Gabriel, A.S.: Office chitchat as a social ritual: the uplifting yet distracting effects of daily small talk at work. Acad. Manag. J. **64**(5), 1445–1471 (2021)
3. Matsuo, Y., Ohsawa, Y., Ishizuka, M.: Mining messages in an electronic message board by repetition of words. In: The Second International Workshop on Chance Discovery, Pacific Rim International Conference on AI (2002)
4. Yamashita, S., Higashinaka, R.: Optimal summaries for enabling a smooth handover in chat-oriented dialogue. In: Proceedings of the 2nd Conference of the Asia-Pacific Chapter of the Association for Computational Linguistics and the 12th International Joint Conference on Natural Language Processing: Student Research Workshop, pp. 25–31 (2022)
5. Hori, J., Ando, M., Otsu, K., Izumi, T.: Conversation summarization system emphasizing recent context for supporting seamless rejoining of a group chat after temporary absence. In: Kurosu, M., Hashizume, A. (eds) Human-Computer Interaction. HCII 2024. Lecture Notes in Computer Science, vol. 14688, pp. 35-50. Springer, Cham (2024). https://doi.org/10.1007/978-3-031-60449-2_3
6. Clark, H.H., Brennan, S.E.: Grounding in Communication, Perspectives on Socially Shared Cognition, pp.127–149 (1991)
7. faster-whisper. https://github.com/SYSTRAN/faster-whisper. Accessed 29 Apr 2025
8. ChatGPT. https://chatgpt.com/. Accessed 29 Apr 2025
9. Lakens, D., Scheel, A.M., Isager, P.M.: Equivalence testing for psychological research: a tutorial. Adv. Methods Pract. Psychol. Sci. **1**(2), 259–269 (2018)

Research on Switching Learning Tasks According to Fatigue Levels to Accommodate Possibility of Interaction

Ryohei Shimizu[✉], Masaki Kodaira, and Hironori Egi

Department of Informatics, Graduate School of Informatics and Engineering,
The University of Electro-Communications, Chofu, Japan
s2530069@edu.cc.uec.ac.jp

Abstract. In educational settings, the trend of providing students with tablets for use during class is increasing. This shift is expected to encouraging encourage a transition toward active learning. However, fatigue hinders active learning. Interleaved learning has been proposed to reduce fatigue during learning sessions, but previous studies on interleaved learning did not control for the timing of task switching, possibly causing students to continue the same learning activity even when fatigued. In the current study, we hypothesized that switching tasks at the moment of fatigue can further help reduce fatigue. We developed a system that switches learning tasks based on fatigue levels (which are estimated by measuring leg movement) and examined changes in learner fatigue during its use. Evaluation experiment results indicated that the proposed method helped reduce fatigue, but the high frequency of task switching disrupted participant concentration immediately after each switch. In future work, we plan to investigate changes in learner fatigue when the system is used in group learning environments.

Keywords: Interleaved learning · Fatigue · Leg movement measurement

1 Introduction

In educational settings, the practice of providing students with tablets for use during class is becoming increasingly common. This trend is expected to transform lessons into active learning sessions [1]. Active learning requires motivating students to participate in the learning process. However, fatigue hinders active learning [2]. Interleaved learning has been proposed to reduce fatigue during learning [3]. In this learning method, multiple types of tasks are alternated during a learning session, thus reducing subjective cognitive loads. However, previous studies on interleaved did not control for the timing of task switching. Thus, learners may continue the same type of task even when fatigued. Switching tasks at the point of fatigue may further help reduce fatigue.

Fatigue estimation methods include those based on heart rate variability and eye blinks [4,5]. However, these methods require the attachment of devices to the body or the filming of learners using cameras, which may impose a psychological burden.

An approach using leg movement has been proposed as a method for estimating fatigue without these demands [6]. In this method, a device for measuring leg movement is installed under the learner's desk, so it is not attached to the body and remains out of the learner's line of sight.

In this study, we develop a system that switches learning tasks based on fatigue, and investigate fatigue changes caused by system use during learning.

2 Related Works

Kodaira et al. explored a system that recommends breaks based on students' perceived fatigue [6]. This system estimates fatigue from leg movement and provides rest recommendations accordingly. In their pilot study, the authors analyzed the relationship between rest timing and leg movement and found that performance decline due to fatigue can be predicted and prevented by measuring leg movement. Unlike the work of Kodaira et al., which aimed to reduce student fatigue through rest breaks, the present study aims to mitigate student fatigue through interleaved learning.

3 Proposed Method

3.1 Learning Tasks

Two types of learning tasks are used in this study: the advanced trail making test (ATMT) [7] and e-Learning. In the ATMT, the learner searches for and clicks on numbers displayed on a screen in ascending order. E-Learning involves watching a lecture video for Diet Advisor qualification.

3.2 Task Switching Proposal

The learning session consists of the ATMT and then e-Learning. Task switching based on fatigue estimated from leg movement is applied only during the ATMT. During e-Learning, learners study for the same duration as in the preceding ATMT session.

3.3 Leg Movement Measurement

As shown in Fig. 1, leg movement is measured using an infrared sensor installed under the desk. The standard deviation of the leg displacement within 1 s, calculated from the data obtained by the infrared sensor, is defined as the leg movement amount. A leg movement amount exceeding 40 means the leg is in motion. The duration wherein the leg is considered moving using this method is called the leg movement time.

Fig. 1. Infrared Sensor for Leg Movement Measurement

3.4 Fatigue Estimation

A 10 min preliminary measurement is performed before interleaving. The leg movement time measured during this 10 min period is called the preliminary leg movement time.

During the ATMT phase of interleaved learning, the leg movement time over the most recent 1 min is calculated every 20 ms. This leg movement time is then divided by the preliminary leg movement time to obtain the leg movement ratio. A leg movement ratio of 1.5 indicates learner fatigue.

The number of leg movements correlates with subjective fatigue levels [8]. Therefore, the state deemed fatigued using the proposed method is 1.5 times greater than the fatigue level before learning.

4 Evaluation Experiment

4.1 Experimental Conditions

An evaluation experiment was conducted with 16 science and engineering university or graduate students to evaluate fatigue changes caused by system use. Each participant performed interleaved learning under two conditions: the proposed and regular methods. Under the proposed method, fatigue during the ATMT was determined using leg movement measurement, and task switching was triggered based on the fatigue state. Under the regular method, the ATMT was completed before e-Learning. The order of the two learning conditions was determined randomly. The second condition was performed at the same time of day exactly one week after the first condition. Under both conditions, the ATMT and e-Learning were approximately 25 min each.

The participants performed a practice session before the actual learning phase. In the practice session, each participant performed the ATMT for approximately 10 min and then watched 1 slide (43 s) of the e-Learning video, after which the session ended. Preliminary leg movement measurement was conducted during the first 10 min of the ATMT in the practice session. Pre- and posttests for the e-Learning content were administered before and after the learning session, respectively. In addition, subjective fatigue was assessed using a visual analog scale (VAS) after the pretest and before the posttest. A questionnaire was administered after the posttest.

4.2 Questionnaire Content

The questionnaire was administered using Google Forms. The survey questions are listed in Table 1. Q1, Q4-2, and Q7 were answered in free-text format, and the remaining questions, were answered using a five-point Likert scale (1: strongly disagree, 2: disagree, 3: neutral, 4: agree, and 5: strongly agree).

Table 1. Questionnaire Content

Question No.	Question Text
Q1	Name
Q2	This question concerns the number search task throughout the learning session
Q2-1	I experienced fatigue partway through the task
Q2-2	I did not lose focus until the end
Q3	This question concerns the viewing of the e-Learning video throughout the learning session
Q3-1	I experienced fatigue partway through the task
Q3-2	I did not lose focus until the end
Q4-1	The intervals between learning task switches were short throughout the learning session
Q4-2	Please explain the reason for your response to Q4-1
Q5	I was able to refresh myself through the switching of learning tasks
Q6	My concentration on the task was diminished through the switching of learning tasks
Q7	Please describe your physical condition today

5 Results

IDs were assigned to the 16 experiment participants. Due to scheduling difficulties for one participant (ID 8), whose availability did not allow for consistent timing and intervals between sessions, this participant was excluded from analysis. Therefore, the following analysis and discussion are based on the data of the 15 remaining participants.

Additionally, responses to Q4-1 and Q4-2 were excluded from the analysis because the wording of these questions allowed for multiple interpretations.

Finally, due to communication delays and data loss, discrepancies existed between the leg movement calculated by the system in real time and the leg movement computed from the recorded data in the evaluation experiment.

5.1 Questionnaire Results

The responses to Q2, Q3, Q5, and Q6 are summarized in Table 2.

A t-test on Q3-1 between the proposed and regular methods showed a significant difference ($p = 0.022$). The mean and variance of Q3-1 under the proposed method were 3.5 and 1.1, respectively, whereas those under the regular method were 4.3 and 0.4, respectively. Therefore, the participants experienced greater fatigue during the e-Learning video under the regular method.

Table 2. Questionnaire Results

Question No.	Proposed Method		Regular Method	
	Mean Score	Standard Deviation	Mean Score	Standard Deviation
Q2-1	3.9	0.9	4.2	1.0
Q2-2	2.5	1.1	1.9	1.1
Q3-1	3.5	1.1	4.3	0.6
Q3-2	2.3	1.0	1.7	0.9
Q5	3.5	1.1	3.1	1.4
Q6	3.0	1.2	2.1	1.0

A t-test on Q6 also yielded a significant difference ($p = 0.025$) between the proposed and regular methods. The mean and variance of Q6 under the proposed method were 3.0 and 1.4, respectively, whereas those under the regular method were 2.1 and 0.9, respectively. Thus, the participants experienced more disruption in concentration due to task switching under the proposed method.

5.2 Leg Movement Data

The average leg movement times during the ATMT under the proposed and regular methods are shown in Table 3.

Table 3. Average Leg Movement Time during ATMT

ID	Proposed Method		Regular Method	
	Session Start (1 min)	Other	Session Start (1 min)	Other
1	0.071	0.082	0.000	0.058
2	0.057	0.035	0.083	0.139
3	0.042	0.028	0.000	0.035
4	0.046	0.011	0.000	0.048
5	0.058	0.016	0.000	0.012
6	0.051	0.008	0.000	0.013
7	0.004	0.000	0.000	0.001
9	0.000	0.000	0.006	0.072
10	0.068	0.023	0.050	0.085
11	0.021	0.035	0.000	0.000
12	0.143	0.062	0.077	0.047
13	0.054	0.009	0.000	0.080
14	0.224	0.077	0.064	0.147
15	0.040	0.011	0.038	0.004
16	0.000	0.002	0.000	0.016

A t-test was conducted on the average leg movement time during the first minute of each ATMT session under the proposed and regular methods, revealing a significant difference ($p = 0.006$). The mean and variance under the proposed method were 0.059 and 0.0033, respectively, and those under the regular method were 0.021 and 0.0010, respectively. Thus, the participants exhibited more leg movement under the proposed method.

A t-test on the average leg movement time excluding the first minute of each ATMT session under the proposed and regular methods, also revealed a significant difference ($p = 0.047$). The mean and variance under the proposed method were 0.027 and 0.0007, respectively, whereas those under the regular method were 0.050 and 0.0022, respectively. Hence, the participants exhibited more leg movement under the regular method.

Likewise, a t-test on the average leg movement time between the first minute of the ATMT and the remaining period under the proposed method revealed a significant difference ($p = 0.009$). The mean and variance for the first minute were 0.059 and 0.0033, respectively, whereas those for the remaining period were 0.027 and 0.0007, respectively. Thus, the participants exhibited more leg movement during the first minute.

Finally, a t-test showed a significant difference ($p = 0.008$) in average leg movement time between the first minute of the ATMT and the remaining period under the regular method. The mean and variance for the first minute were 0.021 and 0.0010, respectively, whereas those for the remaining period were 0.050 and 0.0022, respectively. Therefore, the participants exhibited more leg movement during the remaining period.

5.3 Number of Task Switches

The numbers of task switches under the proposed method are shown in Table 4. Only one task switch was done under the regular method.

6 Discussion

6.1 Comparison of Fatigue Between Conditions

According to their Q3-1 responses, the participants experienced greater fatigue during the e-Learning session under the regular method than under the proposed method. This finding was supported by the analysis of the average leg movement time: excluding the first minute of each ATMT session, the regular method showed higher levels of fatigue than the proposed method. Therefore, the participants experienced greater fatigue under the regular method than under the proposed method.

One possible reason for this was that fatigue was estimated through leg movement measurement under the proposed method, enabling the system to switch from the ATMT to e-Learning at appropriate moments of fatigue. This interpretation was further supported by the analysis of the leg movement time between the first minute of each ATMT session and the remaining period.

Table 4. Number of Task Switches under Proposed Method

ID	Number of Task Switches
1	31
2	13
3	15
4	3
5	17
6	13
7	3
9	1
10	13
11	17
12	25
13	1
14	25
15	9
16	1

Under the proposed method, the participants exhibited more leg movement during the first minute of each ATMT session than in the remaining period, indicating higher fatigue levels at the beginning. By contrast, under the regular method, more leg movement occurred during the remaining period than in the first minute, indicating an increase in fatigue as the ATMT continued.

Thus, under the regular method, the participants became fatigued as they continued the ATMT task. Under the proposed method, task switching to e-Learning likely occurred before substantial fatigue accumulated during the ATMT.

6.2 Comparison of Concentration Between Conditions

According to their Q6 responses, the participants experienced greater disruption in concentration due to task switching under the proposed method than under the regular method. Additionally, during the first minute of each ATMT session, the average leg movement time was longer under the proposed method than under the regular method. The number of leg posture changes is negatively correlated with concentration [9]. Therefore, concentration was more disrupted by task switching under the proposed method than under the regular method.

Under the regular method, all participants experienced only one task switch. Under the proposed method, the average number of task switches was 12.5. The high frequency of task switching may have disrupted their concentration.

7 Conclusion

This study was based on the assumption that switching learning tasks according to fatigue, as estimated through leg movement measurement can help reduce learner fatigue. A system that switches tasks based on fatigue levels was developed, and fatigue changes during its use were examined. In the evaluation experiment, each participant performed interleaved learning under the proposed and regular methods.

The evaluation experiment results demonstrated that the proposed method effectively reduced fatigue during interleaved learning. However, the proposed method involved a high frequency of task switching, which disrupted concentration immediately after each switch.

This system can be used in tablet-based classrooms to support the switch between periods of listening to the teacher and using the tablet. However, in this study, the system was applied to individual learners, not groups. Therefore, future work will investigate changes in learner fatigue when the system is used in group-based settings.

Acknowledgements. This work has been partly supported by the Grants-in-Aid for Scientific Research (No. 24K21451) by MEXT (Ministry of Education, Culture, Sports, Science and Technology) in Japan.

References

1. Varier, D., Dumke, E.K., Abrams, L.M., Conklin, S.B., Barnes, J.S., Hoover, N.R.: Potential of one-to-one technologies in the classroom: teachers and students weigh in. Educ. Tech. Res. Dev. **65**(4), 967–992 (2017). https://doi.org/10.1007/s11423-017-9509-2
2. Dacillo, M.J.F., Dizon, J.K.M., Ong, E.J.T., Pingol, A.M.L., Cleofas J.V.: Videoconferencing fatigue and online student engagement among Filipino senior high school students: a mixed methods study. Front. Educ. **7** (2022)
3. Chen, W., Chen, C., Li, B., Zhang, J.: Applying interleaving strategy of learning materials and perceptual modality to address secondary students' need to restore cognitive capacity. Int. J. Environ. Res. Public Health **19**(12) (2022)
4. Ni, Z., Sun, F., Li, Y.: Heart rate variability-based subjective physical fatigue assessment. Sensors **22**(9), 2022 (2022)
5. Akin, A., Kalkan, H.: Detecting driver fatigue with eye blink behavior, arXiv, arXiv:2407.02222 (2024)
6. Kodaira, M., Shimizu, R., Egi, H.: Adaptive learning system to suggest break timing based on multimodal data by measuring leg movement. In: The 15th International Conference on Learning Analytics and Knowledge Companion Proceedings, pp. 135–137 (2025)
7. Kajimoto, O.: Development of a method of evaluation of fatigue and its economic impacts. In: Fatigue Science for Human Health, pp. 33–46 (2008)

8. Aikawa, D., Asai, Y., Egi, H.: Proposing an estimation method of mental fatigue by measuring learner's leg movement. In: Zaphiris, P., Ioannou, A. (eds.) HCII 2019. LNCS, vol. 11590, pp. 227–236. Springer, Cham (2019). https://doi.org/10.1007/978-3-030-21814-0_17
9. Aikawa, D., Asai, Y., Egi, H.: A method to estimate interest of learner based on leg condition. In: The 18th International Conference on Information Technology Based Higher Education and Training, no. 127, pp. 1–6 (2019)

Social Interactions and Online Engagement in CSCL Environments: Examining a Measurement Scale

J. Roberto Sánchez-Reina(✉), Emily Theophilou, and Davinia Hernández-Leo

TIDE Research Group, ICT Department, Universitat Pompeu Fabra, Barcelona, Spain
roberto.sanchez@upf.edu

Abstract. Social interactions are key to promote effective coordination and participation in Computer-Supported Collaborative Learning (CSCL) environments. While current research examines how structural and technological features can enhance collaboration, there is still the need for validated instruments to assess learners' social Interaction and Online Engagement during online collaborative activities. This study presents an exploratory validation of a scale aimed at assessing learners' perceptions of social interaction and online engagement after CSCL activities. The scale was piloted within a questionnaire assessing online learning and collaboration, administered in the context of a standard Higher Education course. Data were collected from 68 undergraduate students who completed a synchronous task in the environment of the CSCL tool PyramidApp. The exploratory factor analysis showed three interpretable factors that mediate social interaction in the tool: *Cognitive Engagement, Social Engagement and Perception Value of the Experience* with satisfactory internal consistency for each subscale. Further research is needed to confirm the factor structure.

Keywords: CSCL platforms · Online Learning · Social Interaction · Student Engagement · Measurement Scale

1 Introduction

Social interactions are key to promote effective cooperation, enhance participation, and enrich knowledge building in Computer-Supported Collaborative Learning (CSCL) environments [1–3]. Although advances in learning technologies have improved the quality of social interaction [4, 5], successful collaboration still hinges on individual factors such as student engagement – cognitive and emotional attitudes that motivate social presence and interaction [2].

With most existing research instruments focused on assessing cognitive engagement or general learning outcomes [6, 7], the social-emotional and interactional dimensions of engagement within CSCL contexts remain relatively underexplored, limiting our understanding of how collaborative dynamics and emotional experiences influence both learning processes and outcomes.

This paper addresses the need for reliable instruments to capture the social dimensions of learner engagement in CSCL. Drawing on established frameworks in social presence theory, collaborative learning, and online engagement [4, 8, 9], we refined and examined a measurement scale designed to assess students' perceptions of social interaction following the completion of synchronous collaborative learning activities. Our objective was to redesign the scale and confirm its structure and internal consistency through statistical analysis. The manufactured scale offers a valuable resource for CSCL researchers seeking to evaluate and enhance the social effectiveness of collaborative learning environments.

1.1 Measuring Social Interaction and Online Engagement in CSCL

Research on CSCL engagement has expanded beyond cognitive and behavioral aspects to encompass emotional and interpersonal dynamics, linking online behaviors to social interactions and underscoring emotional involvement as essential to collaboration in virtual environments [2, 3, 10]. Despite growing interest in social interaction, most assessment tools still focus on primary outcomes (e.g. task completion, online behavior, participation) overlooking the mediation of factors like group regulation, emotional atmosphere, and ease of interaction [12–14].

While some studies have called for models that integrate emotional, behavioral, and social indicators [3, 9], others have applied frameworks such as Intrinsic Motivation Theory [15, 16] to explain how and why learners participate in collaborative online activities. In this context, Velamazán et al. [2] developed an engagement questionnaire to compare students' perceived experiences in online learning with their actual online behavior. Grounded in theories of social presence, online collaboration, and engagement [4, 8, 9], their proposed instrument was designed to examine interactions in both anonymous and identified online contexts. Although initially created for exploratory research, the instrument informed a subsequent methodological iteration adapted to a Likert-scale for this study.

The adapted scale (Table 1) was organized around two dimensions: (a) *Cognitive Engagement*, which assesses students' perceptions of task-oriented interactions requiring cognitive effort (e.g., task completion, brainstorming, providing feedback). This dimension included five items (Co1–Co5) addressing contributions to discussions, ease of communication, and idea exchange; and (b) *Social Engagement*, which captures students' perceptions of social connections and group dynamics while maintaining task focus (e.g., social climate and perceived engagement). This dimension comprised seven items (So1–So7).

Consistent with Velamazán et al. [2], the decision to use a concise 12-item scale was both theoretical and practical. In CSCL settings, especially during real-time or post-activity reflections, lengthy instruments risk participant fatigue, reduced accuracy, and disruption of engagement. A shorter scale is therefore beneficial in minimizing this burden while still capturing the essential dimensions of social and cognitive engagement [17, 18]. Psychometric evidence also shows that brief, well-designed instruments can provide reliable and valid measurements when items are clearly focused [19]. Moreover, concise instruments are especially valuable when paired with complementary data sources such as behavioral traces or open-ended feedback. Taken together, the 12-item scale offers a balanced solution: comprehensive enough to measure key aspects of engagement, yet efficient enough to avoid unnecessary cognitive or time demands.

2 Method

2.1 Study Design and Participants

We designed a pilot study in a Public Relations and Marketing course with 68 students. Participants engaged in a structured CSCL activity using the Pyramid App, a web-based application designed to promote discussion and knowledge building following the Pyramid collaborative learning flow pattern [20]. All participants had prior experience with online collaborative tools and had used the PyramidApp before the pilot study. Participation in the activity was required but completion of the questionnaire was voluntary. Nevertheless, all participants consented to join the study.

2.2 Scale Design

The redesigned scale was subjected to exploratory validation in an experimental context focused on learners' engagement in CSCL activities supported by an AI chatbot [21]. To establish a baseline, data were gathered during a pre-experimental phase in which respondents were not assisted by an AI chatbot, thereby focusing exclusively on human-to-human interaction. A preliminary version of the scale was reviewed by two educational technology experts to ensure content validity in a pilot group of 15 students to evaluate clarity and to improve item phrasing and thematic coherence. After revision, items were rated on a 5-point Likert scale ranging from 1 (*Strongly disagree*) to 5 (*Strongly agree*) to ensure clarity, facilitate respondent understanding, and enhance the reliability and comparability of responses while minimizing cognitive load and response bias [22].

Table 1. Scale Dimensions and Items.

Measurement of perceived interactions related with Cognitive Engagement	Perceived Contribution Quality	Co1. My contributions were of high-quality
		Co2. I was comfortable in writing my contributions
	Perception of Communication	Co3. It was easy to share ideas or proposal
		Co4. It was easy to give feedback and formulate answers
		Co5. I was able to make questions and solve doubts
Measurement of perceived interactions related with interactions Oriented to Social Engagement	Perception of Social Climate	So1. The chat activity provided me with good atmosphere

(*continued*)

Table 1. (*continued*)

Measurement of perceived interactions related with Cognitive Engagement	Perceived Contribution Quality	Co1. My contributions were of high-quality
		Co2. I was comfortable in writing my contributions
	Perception of Communication	Co3. It was easy to share ideas or proposal
		Co4. It was easy to give feedback and formulate answers
		Co5. I was able to make questions and solve doubts
		So2. I was feeling sociable
		So3. I made jokes during the activity
		So4. The chat helped me to break the ice and express my opinion
	Perceived Engagement in Platform and Task	So5. I feel that I wasted my time
		So6. I saw others wasting their time
		So7. I have gained a better understanding of the topic

2.3 Data Collection

The setting of the study was a Public Relations lesson on "Food Marketing". As part of the experiment, a warm-up activity within PyramidApp introduced students to online discussion. During the activity, students followed the PyramidApp phases [21] to complete the 20-min activity. Afterwards, students were invited to complete a self-report questionnaire via Google Forms. Although self-report questionnaires are often criticized for being overly positive and less accurate than objective measures, in CSCL settings they are valued as reflective tools, integrated into online learning processes and used as proxies for situated learning practices [23].

3 Results

To examine the scale structure, an Exploratory Factor Analysis (EFA) using Principal Component extraction with Varimax rotation was conducted in SPSS 29. Data suitability was confirmed by the Kaiser–Meyer–Olkin (KMO = 0.805) and Bartlett's test of sphericity ($\chi2 = 417.486$, df $= 66$, p $< .001$), both exceeding recommended thresholds for structure detection [24]. Items with loadings above .40 were retained, and factors were extracted based on eigenvalues greater than 1.0 and interpretability. The analysis revealed three factors *Cognitive Engagement, Social Engagement, and Perceived Value of the Experience*, accounting for 67.025% of the total variance. Internal consistency was evaluated using Cronbach's alpha, which exceeded .70 for all three factors, indicating satisfactory reliability [25].

When compared with the initial item categorization based on Velamazán et al. [2], it was observed that the item structure showed some slight changes after the EFA. While the original categorization grouped items under dimensions such as Perceived Contribution Quality, Perception of Social Climate, and Perceived Engagement in Platform and Task, the factor analysis yielded a three-factor structure (Table 2).

Cognitive Engagement emerged as the strongest factor, accounting for 44.46% of the total variance. The items aligned well with the original subdimensions of *Perceived Contribution Quality* and *Perception of Communication*. Items such as "My contributions were of high quality" and "It was easy to share ideas or proposals" loaded strongly on this factor, indicating a stable and coherent conceptual grouping centered on participants' cognitive involvement in the activity. The internal consistency for this factor was satisfactory, with a Cronbach's alpha of $\alpha = 0.79$.

Social Engagement accounted for 12.59% of the variance and included items related to affective and interpersonal dimensions of collaboration. Items such as "I made jokes during the activity" and "I was feeling sociable" indicate the relevance of informal and affective interactions, even within task-focused environments. However, some items originally categorized under cognitive or environmental aspects like "It was easy to give feedback" were reclassified, suggesting an interpersonal interpretation of feedback processes in this context. The internal consistency for this factor was satisfactory, with a Cronbach's alpha of $\alpha = 0.73$.

Perceived Value of the Experience explained 9.97% of the variance and encompassed items assessing students' perceived value of the collaborative experience and its effectiveness. Interestingly, this factor includes both positive and negative perceptions, such as the sense of having gained knowledge and the feeling of time being wasted. The strong loadings of both "The chat activity provided me with a good atmosphere" and "I feel that I wasted my time" suggest that learners make evaluative judgments not only about task outcomes but also about the affective and contextual capabilities of the CSCL environment. The internal consistency for this factor was satisfactory, with a Cronbach's alpha of $\alpha = 0.75$.

Table 2. Exploratory Factor Analysis of the Social Interaction Scale.

Factors (Items of the scale)	Factor Loadings	Eigen-value	Explained variance	α
Factor 1: Cognitive Engagement		5.336	44.46%	0.799

(*continued*)

Table 2. (*continued*)

Factors (Items of the scale)	Factor Loadings	Eigen-value	Explained variance	α
I was comfortable in writing my contributions	0.862			
My contributions were of high-quality	0.836			
It was easy to share ideas or proposal	0.674			
I have gained a better understanding of the topic	0.543			
Factor 2: Social Engagement		1.511	12.59%	0.735
The chat helped me to break the ice and express my opinion	0.417			
I was able to make questions and solve doubts	0.547			
I made jokes during the activity	0.710			
I was feeling sociable	0.703			
It was easy to give feedback and formulate answers	0.655			
Factor 3: Perceived Value of the Experience		1.197	9.973%	0.754
The chat activity provided me with good atmosphere	0.903			
I feel that I wasted my time [R]*	0.897			
I saw others wasting their time [R]*	0.438			

* [R] *Items reversed for statistical analysis.*

4 Discussion and Conclusion

The findings from the EFA provide evidence for the validity and internal consistency of the proposed Social Interaction and Engagement Scale. While the EFA broadly supports the conceptual structure proposed by Velamazán et al. [2], participants' perceptions during the activity led to a reorganization of certain constructs, particularly in how they appraised the environment and differentiated between cognitive and social elements of engagement. The three-factor solution provided in the analysis was consistent with theoretical frameworks highlighting the multidimensional nature of learner engagement in online collaboration [12–16].

Cognitive Engagement, which explained the largest portion of variance, aligned closely with literature on knowledge construction and individual cognitive investment in CSCL [3, 4]. Items such as perceived participation and contribution informed learners' sense of involvement in the co-construction of meaning, reflecting their active processing of content, articulation of ideas, and critical engagement with peers' input during the collaborative task. On the other hand, *Social Engagement* maintained a consistent structure highlighting the importance of social presence, emotional climate, and interpersonal interaction in fostering deeper engagement and sustained participation. The validation of the subscale reaffirms the role of emotional and social processes in collaborative learning environments [2, 16]. Ultimately, the *Perceived Value of the Experience* which showed a structural shift from the original scale aligned with studies that argue that learners' engagement is influenced not only by social dynamics but also by the perceived value and productivity of the experience as a whole [2, 23]. The structure of items in this factor appear to reflect participants' broader evaluative judgments about the usefulness and atmosphere of the chat activity, rather than purely social climate. This reinterpretation suggests a more holistic assessment of the learning environment.

The three-factor solution can also be interpreted through the lens of the Community of Inquiry (CoI) framework [9]. Cognitive Engagement aligns with Cognitive Presence, reflecting processes of meaning-making, idea exchange, and content-focused contributions. Social Engagement corresponds to Social Presence, emphasizing the affective and interpersonal dimensions of collaboration, such as sociability and humor. Perceived Value of the Experience complements both Cognitive and Social Presence, since students' judgments about atmosphere and usefulness often span task-focused and relational aspects.

Overall, the results highlight the importance of considering both cognitive and socio-emotional aspects when evaluating learner engagement in CSCL environments. While cognitive engagement remains central to task performance and knowledge acquisition, the quality of social interactions and the perceived usefulness of the environment significantly shape learners' willingness to participate and their overall satisfaction with the activity [2, 4]. A key distinction is that interaction refers to observable acts (e.g., jokes, feedback), while engagement reflects psychological investment (e.g., feeling sociable, valuing the activity). Keeping these constructs separate avoids conceptual mixing.

Several limitations must be acknowledged. The sample size of the study was intentionally limited for the purpose of the pilot. Moreover, the testing of the scale should consider other students' background and disciplines to validate its broader applicability. Future work should test the scale across different disciplines, platforms, and cultural contexts, as the present pilot was limited to a Public Relations course using PyramidApp. Additionally, integrating self-report data with behavioral analytics (e.g., participation logs, message frequency, response times) is recommended to better understand engagement patterns and support adaptive learning interventions [2, 16]. Triangulating self-report measurements with behavioral data from CSCL platforms can provide valuable insights into the alignment (or discrepancy) between perceived and observed engagement, enriching the interpretability and practical relevance of the scale. Future studies should also conduct confirmatory factor analysis with larger and more diverse samples to validate the factor structure.

Our study introduced a Social Interaction and Engagement Scale to assess students' perceived experiences in CSCL environments, with specific application to the PyramidApp collaborative learning tool. The study provides preliminary validation evidence. Larger and more diverse samples are needed before the scale can be considered fully validated. The scale offers a practical, theoretically grounded instrument for educators and researchers aiming to assess and enhance student engagement in CSCL. The study contributes to ongoing efforts to develop validated tools that capture the richness of student engagement in CSCL. By distinguishing between dimensions of Cognitive and Social engagement, the scale can inform educators and researchers on how students experience collaboration and where interventions might be targeted whether to enhance cognitive challenge, foster social connection, or improve platform usability and satisfaction.

Acknowledgments. This work has been supported by PID2023-146692OB-C33 and CEX2021–001195-M granted by MICIU/AEI/https://doi.org/10.13039/501100011033. D. Hernández-Leo (Serra Húnter) also acknowledges the support of ICREA through the ICREA Academia programme.

References

1. Zha, S., Tang, Y., Gong, J., Xu, Y.: COLP: scaffolding children's online long-term collaborative learning. Int. J. Hum. Comput. Interaction **1–23** (2025). https://doi.org/10.1080/10447318.2025.2498492
2. Velamazán, M., Santos, P., Sánchez-Reina, J.R., Hernández-Leo, D.: Optimising anonymity in CSCL: comparing collaboration between identified and anonymous-to-peers login modes. Educ. Inf. Technol. **1–52** (2025). https://doi.org/10.1007/s10639-025-13504-w
3. Zheng, L., Niu, J., Long, M., Fan, Y.: An automatic knowledge graph construction approach to promoting collaborative knowledge building, group performance, social interaction and socially shared regulation in CSCL. Br. J. Edu. Technol. **54**(3), 686–711 (2023). https://doi.org/10.1111/bjet.13283
4. Järvelä, S., Rosé, C.: Forms of collaboration matters: CSCL across the contexts. Int. J. Comput.-Support. Collab. Learn. **16**(2), 145–149 (2021). https://doi.org/10.1007/s11412-021-09348-4
5. Aderibigbe, S., Alotaibi, E., Alzouebi, K.: Exploring the impact of peer mentoring on computer-supported collaborative learning among undergraduate students. Int. J. Emerg. Technol. Learn. (IJET) **18**(13), 4–20 (2023). https://doi.org/10.3991/ijet.v18i13.39819
6. Barlow, A., Brown, S.: Correlations between modes of student cognitive engagement and instructional practices in undergraduate stem courses. Int. J. Stem Educ. **7**(1) (2020). https://doi.org/10.1186/s40594-020-00214-7

7. Lee, J., Song, H., Hong, A.: Exploring factors, and indicators for measuring students' sustainable engagement in e-learning. Sustainability **11**(4), 985 (2019). https://doi.org/10.3390/su11040985
8. Chen, Y., Preston, J.C., Li, Y.: Enhancing collaboration and critical thinking in CSCL environments: the interplay between team dynamics and pedagogical innovation. Int. J. e-Collabor. (IJeC) **21**(1), 1–24 (2025)
9. Garrison, D.R., Anderson, T., Archer, W.: Critical thinking, cognitive presence, and computer conferencing in distance education. Distance Educ. **15**(1), 7–23. https://doi.org/10.1080/08923640109527071
10. Kim, Y., Glassman, M., Williams, M.S.: Connecting agents: engagement and motivation in online collaboration. Comput. Hum. Behav. **49**, 333–342 (2015). https://doi.org/10.1016/j.chb.2015.03.015
11. Tao, Y., Zhang, M., Su, Y., Li, Y.: Exploring college English language learners' social knowledge construction and socio-emotional interactions during computer-supported collaborative writing activities. Asia Pac. Educ. Res. **31**(5), 613–622 (2022)
12. Slof, B., Leeuwen, A.V., Janssen, J., Kirschner, P.A.: Mine, ours, and yours: whose engagement and prior knowledge affects individual achievement from online collaborative learning?. J. Comput. Assisted Learn. **37**(1), 39–50 (2020). https://doi.org/10.1111/jcal.12466
13. Iskandar, R.P.F., Pahlevi, M.R.: Students' emotional engagement in online collaborative writing through google document. ETERNAL (English Teaching Journal), **12**(2), 58–67 (2021). https://doi.org/10.26877/eternal.v12i2.9191
14. Redmond, P., Heffernan, A., Abawi, L., Brown, A., Henderson, R.: An online engagement framework for higher education. Online Learn. **22**(1) (2018). https://doi.org/10.24059/olj.v22i1.1175
15. Lobo-Quintero, R., Sánchez-Reina, R., Theophilou, E., Hernández-Leo, D.: Intrinsic motivation for social media literacy, a look into the narrative scripts. In: International Workshop on Higher Education Learning Methodologies and Technologies Online, pp. 419–432. Springer (2022). https://doi.org/10.1007/978-3-031-29800-4_32
16. Lobo-Quintero, R.A., Sánchez-Reina, R., Hernández-Leo, D.: Studying the flow experience in computer-supported collaborative learning: a study with PyramidApp. J. Learn. Analy. **11**(3), 106–122 (2024). https://doi.org/10.18608/jla.2024.8185
17. Fass-Holmes, B.: Survey fatigue-what is its role in undergraduates' survey participation and response rates? J. Interdisciplinary Stud. Educ. **11**(1), 56–73 (2022)
18. Jin, H., Kapteyn, A.: Relationship between past survey burden and response probability to a new survey in a probability-based online panel. J. Offic. Stat. **38**(4), 1051–1067 (2022). https://doi.org/10.2478/jos-2022-0045
19. Wongpakaran, N., et al.: Development and validation of a 6-item Revised UCLA loneliness scale (RULS-6) using Rasch analysis. Br. J. Health Psychol. **25**(2), 233–256 (2020). https://doi.org/10.1111/bjhp.12404
20. Manathunga, K., Hernández-Leo, D.: Authoring and enactment of mobile pyramid-based collaborative learning activities. Br. J. Edu. Technol. **49**(2), 262–275 (2018). https://doi.org/10.1111/bjet.12588
21. Gutiérrez-Ferré, A., Hernández-Leo, D., Sánchez-Reina, J.R.: Generative AI chatbot in pyramidapp: students' behaviors and design principles. In the International Conference on Collaboration Technologies and Social Computing, pp. 248–256. Cham: Springer Nature (2024). https://doi.org/10.1007/978-3-031-67998-8_19
22. Revilla, M.A., Saris, W.E., Krosnick, J.A.: Choosing the number of categories in agree–disagree scales. Sociol. Methods Res. **43**(1), 73–97 (2014). https://doi.org/10.1177/0049124113509605

23. Gress, C.L., Fior, M., Hadwin, A.F., Winne, P.H.: Measurement and assessment in computer-supported collaborative learning. Comput. Hum. Behav. **26**(5), 806–814 (2010). https://doi.org/10.1016/j.chb.2007.05.012
24. Shrestha, N.: Factor analysis as a tool for survey analysis. Am. J. Appl. Math. Stat. **9**(1), 4–11 (2021)
25. Taber, K.S.: The use of Cronbach's alpha when developing and reporting research instruments in science education. Res. Sci. Educ. **48**, 1273–1296 (2018). https://doi.org/10.1007/s11165-016-9602-2
26. Theophilou, E., Sanchez-Reina, R., Hernandez-Leo, D., Odakura, V., Amarasinghe, I., Lobo-Quintero, R.: The effect of a group awareness tool in synchronous online discussions: studying participation, quality and balance. Behav. Inf. Technol. **43**(6), 1149–1163 (2024). https://doi.org/10.1080/0144929X.2023.2200543

Estimating Discussion State from Head Movements in Collaborative Learning Environments

Hayato Kawashima, Ryosuke Nakamura, Ryunosuke Nishimura, and Hironori Egi(✉)

Department of Informatics, Graduate School of Informatics and Engineering,
The University of Electro-Communications, Chofu, Japan
k2530038@gl.cc.uec.ac.jp

Abstract. This study explored whether learners' head movement and interhead distance could serve as behavioral cues related to learners' internal states in small-group collaborative discussions: understanding, willingness to participate, and psychological safety. Eighteen science and engineering university students (in six groups of three) participated in discussions. A ceiling-mounted depth camera continuously measured their head movements during 20 min sessions. After their discussions, the participants watched the video recordings and rated their internal states per 1 min segment. Two groups were excluded due to head recognition errors caused by hand gestures, so the analysis focused on data from the four remaining groups. No consistent correlations were found across all learners or groups. However, some individuals and groups showed positive or negative correlations between internal states and behavioral indicators. Additionally, spikes in head movement often coincided with movements such as laughter, posture adjustments, and gesturing. These findings highlight the potential of bodily behavior as cues for understanding discussion dynamics. Future work will address measurement and environmental issues to elucidate these relationships better, promoting the reliable estimation of internal states from bodily behavior.

Keywords: Collaborative Learning · Head Movement · Multimodal Learning Analytics

1 Introduction

Collaborative discussion not only deepens one's understanding through exposure to others' opinions. It also influences learners' attitudes and motivation toward learning [1,2]. Simply organizing groups of learners to engage in collaborative discussion does not ensure the accomplishment of learning outcomes [3]. Some groups may hesitate to share their thoughts due to certain internal states, such as fear and criticism or lack of trust [4,5]. Therefore, learners' internal states should be understood, to establish appropriate support [6,7]. Promoting socially shared regulation of learning (SSRL) is a promising way to address these challenges [8]. In SSRL, group members coordinate their learning by building on their individual self-regulation skills. Through this coordination, they align their activities toward achieving shared goals. In particular, the shared regulation of internal states, such as emotions and motivation, is a key component of SSRL [8]. Supporting SSRL, requires developing quantifiable indicators that can visualize the learning process [9]. These internal states may manifest in observable behaviors, such as utterances and body movements [10,11]. Utterances in collaborative work provide cues for interpreting a learner's internal state [10]. However, utterances alone may not be sufficient to fully understand learner's internal states, especially because learners are not always speaking [12]. In such cases, an approach that leverages bodily behaviors, such as gazes, gestures, and head movements, is effective [12,13]. Specifically, head movements serve multiple functions [14] and can provide cues regarding the internal states of group members [11]. Head-related behaviors can be viewed from two perspectives: the movement of the head itself, or the relative distance between learners' heads [11,15]. In the context of computer-supported collaborative learning (CSCL), these perspectives are mostly analyzed separately, and few studies have addressed them in an integrated manner. Their joint analysis may capture aspects of learners' internal states that conventional approaches overlook.

This study investigates the effectiveness of integrating two bodily indicators, namely, the head movement amount and interhead distance, as cues for estimating learners' internal states during collaborative discussions. Through this approach, we explore the potential of these indicators as behavioral measures for quantitatively capturing SSRL.

2 Related Works

2.1 SSRL

In SSRL, regulation includes cognitive aspects and the coordination of internal states. These shared processes enhance mutual understanding and improve the quality of collaboration within groups [8]. Supporting SSRL encourages strategic interactions and emotional sharing between learners. This enhances collaborative engagement, deepens learning, and improves outcomes [8]. Such support also helps learners better understand their own and their peers' interests and goals, thus increasing the effectiveness of learning environments [16]. However, SSRL is based on learners' internal regulation and social interactions. Thus, these processes are difficult to observe and assess externally, indicating a need for indirect, quantifiable indicators that can capture these regulatory behaviors [9].

To address this issue, we conduct a quantitative analysis using behavioral data related to learner interactions to capture SSRL-related regulation objectively.

2.2 Utterances and Body Movements

Spoken Utterances in collaborative tasks provide important cues for interpreting learners" internal states [10]. Acoustic features, such as pitch, speech rate, and intonation, have been shown to reflect changes in learners" emotional and cognitive conditions [10,17]. However, when learners are not always speaking, so spoken information alone may be insufficient to fully capture their internal states fully [12]. In such cases, bodily behaviors - such as gaze, gestures, and head movements - can serve as effective alternatives [12,13]. Studies have demonstrated that bodily behaviors, such as nodding, gazes, and gestures, are useful for estimating learners" engagement and understanding [13,18]. In particular, head movements are known to have multiple communicative functions [14]. For instance, speakers may use head movements to emphasize their message, while whereas listeners may use them to signal understanding or empathy.

2.3 Head Movement

Head movements provide valuable information about communication and group dynamics. They indicate internal states, such as empathy, atmosphere, enjoyment, motivation, and concentration [11,19]. The amount of head movement reflects the speaker's emotions and engagement. It also functions as a visual cue that shapes the role of speech and the flow of interaction [20,21]. In addition, the interhead distance between learners may reflect learning behaviors, such as looking at materials or writing [15]. This spatial cue is also useful for estimating learning outcomes [22].

Head-related behaviors are studied from two perspectives. The first one focuses on the head movement itself, including metrics such as the head movement amount and tilt. The other focuses on the relative spatial relationships between learners' head positions. In CSCL research, these perspectives are mostly examined separately. Few studies have integrated them. Their combined analysis may capture subtle aspects of learners' internal states that conventional approaches often miss.

This study investigates whether integrating head movement amount and interhead distance can be an effective cue for estimating learners' internal states in collaborative discussions. We aim to explore the potential of these bodily indicators as behavioral measures for quantifying SSRL.

2.4 Research Questions

This study investigates whether two bodily indicators, namely, head movement amount and interhead distance, can be integrated as effective cues for estimating learners' internal states during collaborative discussions. These internal states are understanding, willingness to participate, and psychological safety. Specifically, the following research questions are addressed:

- **RQ1:** Can head movement amount and interhead distance serve as behavioral indicators related to learners' internal states?

- **RQ2:** What is the relationship between head movement amount and learners' understanding, willingness to participate, and psychological safety?
- **RQ3:** What is the relationship between interhead distance and learners' understanding, willingness to participate, and psychological safety?

3 Method

3.1 Proposed System

To measure learners' head movement and interhead distance continuously, we constructed a noncontact measurement system using a ceiling-mounted depth camera. Figure 1 illustrates the system configuration. This system supported

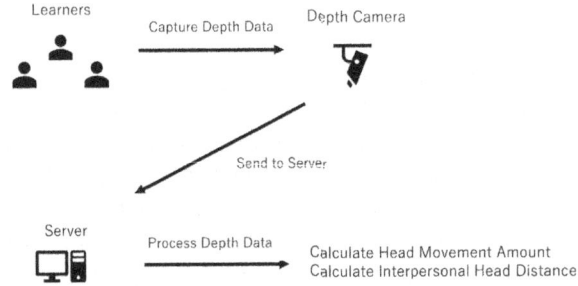

Fig. 1. Overall system configuration

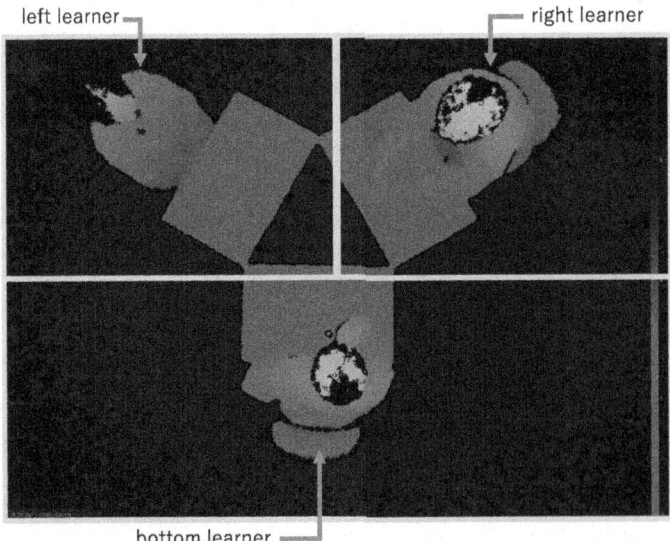

Fig. 2. Depth information segmentation method

a collaborative discussion involving three learners seated at separate desks for 20 min. By using a depth camera instead of visible-light imaging, we aimed to minimize the influence of clothing and hair color on the results. Moreover, the camera was mounted on the ceiling to reduce the participants' psychological burden. The depth camera was an Intel RealSense L515 [23].

The depth data obtained by the camera were sent to a server, where the head region was estimated and the interhead distance and head movement were calculated. The system continuously captured these metrics during the discussion. We analyzed the relationships between these bodily indicators and the learners' internal states across different groups.

Based on the method of Yamamoto et al. [15], the head region was defined as the area within a predefined range from the camera, with the top of the head being the lower bound and the shoulders being the upper bound. We distinguished between learners by dividing the depth data into three regions: the left and right halves of the upper area, and the lower half. Figure 2 shows an example of the divided regions and depth data. The learners in the left, right, and lower regions were called the left, right, and bottom learners, respectively. A binary mask image was generated per region, assigning 1 to coordinates within the head region and 0 elsewhere. The centroid of each mask was calculated per frame and averaged over 1 s intervals to determine each learner's head position. The Euclidean distance between centroids was deemed the interhead distance, resulting in three pairwise distances. The movement of each learner's centroid per second was defined as their head movement.

3.2 Internal State and Head Movement Amount/Interhead Distance

According to Järvelä et al., effective support for SSRL involves attention to the cognitive, motivational, and emotional aspects of learning [8]. In line with this perspective, we adopt three indicators to assess learners' internal states: understanding, willingness to participate, and psychological safety. These indicators capture key outcomes of collaborative discussion and the internal states needed to achieve them [8,24-26].

In this study, the learners' head movement and interhead distance were continuously collected, and their relationship with the learners' internal states (understanding, willingness to participate, and psychological safety) was analyzed.

To collect quantitative data on internal states, we conducted a reflection session after the discussion. In this session, the learners were shown a video recording of their discussion and asked to reflect on it. The entire discussion was divided into 1 min segments, and the learners rated on a five-point scale the extent to which each segment contributed to their understanding, willingness to participate, and psychological safety.

We aligned these subjective ratings with the corresponding head movement and interhead distance data per segment to investigate the relationships between the learners' bodily behavioral metrics and perceived internal states.

4 Experiment

The experiment consisted of two phases. In the first phase, three participants conducted a video recorded collaborative discussion, during which their head movements and interhead distances were measured. In the second phase, quantitative data on the learners' internal states were collected by showing them the video recorded in the first phase and asking them to reflect on the discussion.

Details are provided in Sect. 4.1 for the first phase and in Sect. 4.2 for the second phase.

4.1 Discussion Conditions

Each group participated in one 20 min discussion session. The discussion topic was "What is happiness?" Before the discussion, each participant was given 2 min to think about the topic individually. They were informed in advance that they would be asked to produce a written group conclusion after the discussion. This was intended to encourage the group to reach a conclusion during the discussion, so no scoring or evaluation was conducted.

Each participant was seated at a desk arranged to ensure equal distances between participants (Fig. 3). During the discussion, depth information was continuously collected using the ceiling-mounted depth camera (Fig. 4). In addition, the participants wore directional microphones to capture speech during the discussion, but the audio data were not analyzed in this study. The depth data were recorded at a resolution of 640 pixels (horizontal) by 480 pixels (vertical) at 30 frames per second.

Fig. 3. Discussion environment

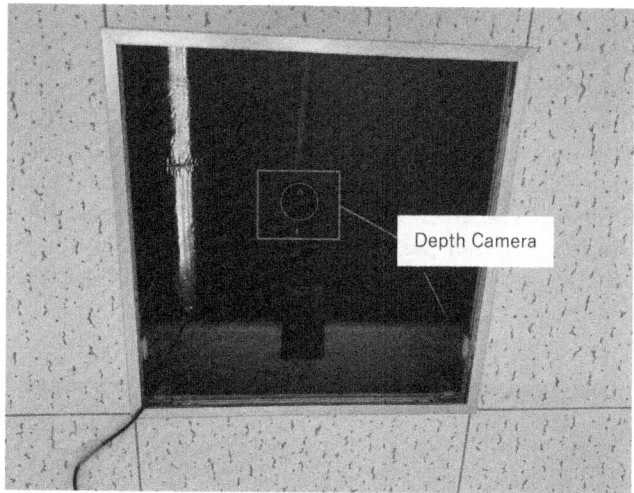

Fig. 4. Depth camera installation

4.2 Discussion Reflection

Data on the participants' internal states were gathered after the discussion by playing the video recording of the discussion at one point three times the normal speed and asking them to complete a subjective questionnaire. This playback speed was chosen because it allowed the learners to recall their internal states during each segment while supporting their intuitive responses.

The subjective questionnaire asked the participants about their understanding, willingness to participate, and psychological safety. The video was paused every 1 min from the start of the discussion, and the participants were asked to rate the extent to which each 1 min segment contributed to their understanding, willingness to participate, and psychological safety on a five-point scale: 5: strongly agree, 4: agree, 3: neutral, 2: disagree, and 1: strongly disagree. The questionnaire items for understanding, willingness to participate, and psychological safety are shown in Table 1.

Table 1. Question per internal state

Internal State	Question Content
Understanding	The discussion in this section contributed to my understanding of the agenda
Willingness To Participate	The discussion in this section helped increase my willingness to participate
Psychological Safety	The discussions in this section helped me speak with an open mind

5 Results

We conducted the experiment with 18 participants divided into six groups, hereinafter called Groups AF.

Figure 5 shows an image captured by the ceiling-mounted depth camera during a discussion. The green dot on each participant is the estimated centroid of their head region. The green lines connecting the dots visually represent the interhead distances between participants. In the figure, the top-left, top-right, and bottom participants are called the left, right, and bottom learners, respectively.

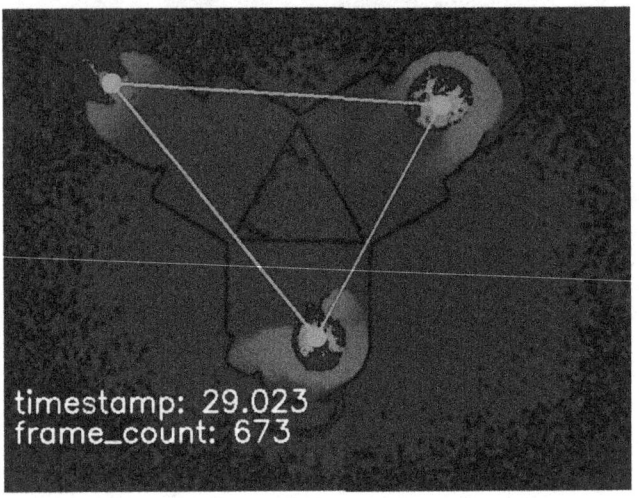

Fig. 5. Sample image captured by depth camera

5.1 Groups with Inaccurate Head Recognition

Head recognition was inaccurate for Groups E and F. Some group members raised their hands to head level and gestured during the discussion, which interfered with head recognition. Specifically, when a hand was positioned at the same height as the head but was spatially separate from it, the system calculated centroids between the two distinct objects (hand and head), causing recognition errors. Thus, we analyzed data from Groups AD, which had no recognition errors due to gestural interference.

5.2 Head Movement Amount and Spike Detection

The transitions of head movement amounts for all learners in the four groups were graphed. For example, Figure 6 shows the head movement amounts of the left learner in Group A, which included spikes, or sudden increases in head movement.

To detect spikes across all learners consistently, we defined a threshold based on each learner's average head movement and unbiased standard deviation. This threshold was the average head movement throughout the discussion plus five times the unbiased standard deviation. This threshold was determined in an exploratory manner to include clear spike candidates while minimizing ambiguous ones. The time points (s) during which the head movement exceeded this threshold were detected as spikes. If a spike was detected within 3 s of a previous one, then we reviewed the video recording to determine whether the second spike was a continuation of the first one. If so, then the second spike was excluded from the spike count. The areas enclosed by the red boxes in Fig. 6 are the detected spikes. A total of 78 spike seconds were identified across the 12 learners in the four groups.

All 78 spikes were then analyzed using the discussion video recordings. The verification revealed that these spikes corresponded to various behaviors, such as laughter due to excitement, posture or appearance adjustments, gestures, and placement of one's head in their hands.

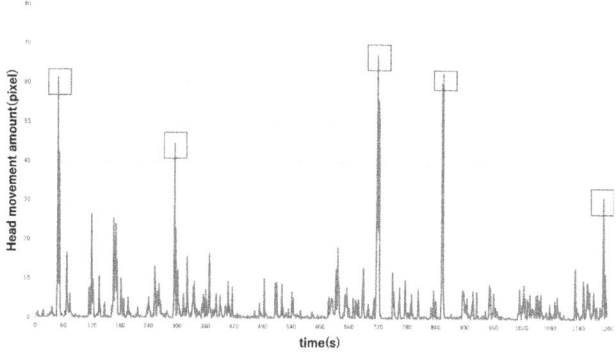

Fig. 6. Head movement amount (Group A left learner)

5.3 Head Movement Amount and Internal State

We explored the relationship between each learner's internal state and head movement amount by calculating Spearman's rank correlation coefficients between the collected ratings of internal states and the average head movement amount. Each discussion was divided into 1 min intervals, for a total of 20 segments. For each interval and learner, correlation coefficients were calculated between the average head movement amount and the ratings for understanding, willingness to participate, and psychological safety. The correlation coefficients between the internal state ratings and the average head movement amount are presented in Table 2.

The correlation coefficient for understanding exceeded 0.3 for the left learner in Group C but was less than −0.4 for the right learners in Groups C and D. Regarding the willingness to participate, the correlation coefficient was above 0.3 for the right and bottom learners in Group C and exceeded 0.4 for the bottom learner in Group B. As for psychological safety, the correlation coefficient exceeded 0.3 for the bottom learners in Groups A, B, and C.

Table 2. Correlation coefficient between internal state and average head movement amount

Group	Seating Position	Understanding	Willingness To Participate	Psychological Safety
GroupA	left	0.074	0.056	0.160
	right	−0.183	−0.272	−0.059
	bottom	0.2938	0.174	0.356
GroupB	left	−0.278	−0.065	0.150
	right	−0.162	0.123	−0.135
	bottom	0.112	0.499	0.311
GroupC	left	0.350	−0.316	0.017
	right	−0.489	0.352	0.194
	bottom	0.020	0.369	0.356
GroupD	left	−0.112	−0.095	0.262
	right	−0.482	−0.025	−0.108
	bottom	0.026	0.208	0.208

5.4 Interhead Distance and Internal State

To examine the relationship between the internal states and interhead distance within each group, we calculated Spearman's rank correlation coefficients between the collected ratings of the internal states and the average interhead distances of the learners.

The discussion was divided into 1 min intervals, for a total of 20 segments. For each interval, correlation was calculated between the group-level sum of the subjective ratings (understanding, willingness to participate, and psychological safety) and the average interhead distances. As the head distance was calculated between pairs, three distances were obtained per interval in a three-person discussion. The sum of these distances was used as the total interhead distance for that interval.

Table 3 presents the correlation coefficients between the total group ratings for understanding, willingness to participate, and psychological safety and the summed interhead distances per group.

The correlation coefficients related to understanding were 0.4 or higher in Groups A and D. For psychological safety, the coefficients were 0.3 or higher in Group A and 0.6 or higher in Group B.

Table 3. Correlation coefficients between internal states and average interhead distance per group

Group	Understanding	Willingness To Participate	Psychological Safety
GroupA	0.410	0.214	0.389
GroupB	0.119	0.142	0.666
GroupC	0.188	0.083	0.162
GroupD	0.404	0.240	0.142

6 Discussion

6.1 Head Recognition Errors

Gestures causing a hand to be at the same height as the head but at a distance from it, resulting in head recognition errors, were not observed by Yamamoto et al. [15], who also utilized the interhead distance. In their study, a tablet was placed between two learners and a worksheet was positioned in front of each learner, creating a constrained setup. These constraints likely limited learner movement, preventing gestures where a hand would have reached the height of the head. By contrast, the experiment in the present study imposed no such restrictions, allowing the learners to move freely. Consequently, they managed to perform gestures where a hand reached the height of the head, leading to recognition errors. This section discusses methods for improving head recognition accuracy in cases where gestures cause a hand to be at the height of, but at a distance from, the head. In this study, the head region was defined as the area where the depth from the camera fell within a prespecified range. The coordinates within this depth range were labeled 1 in the mask image, and the other coordinates were labeled 0. When a hand is at the height of the head but is spatially separated from it, two distinct masked regions can emerge: one for the head and one for the hand. These regions are likely to be separated by a certain spatial distance. Therefore, selecting only the masked region corresponding to the head (and ignoring the hand, which is at the same height but is spatially apart) may improve the accuracy of head recognition, even when such gestures occur.

6.2 Spikes in Head Movement Amount

Video observations of the detected head movement spikes revealed various physical behaviors, including laughter, posture adjustments, gestures, and head holding. First, behaviors accompanied by laughter appeared to result from moments of lively discussion, suggesting heightened interactions between learners. This may be associated with an increased willingness to participate and a sense of psychological safety. Next, actions such as posture adjustments and grooming may occur in a state of psychological safety or as attempts to feel such safety. However, because the intent behind these behaviors is difficult to determine, they must be interpreted with caution. Additionally, gestures and head holding, which may reflect speech support or cognitive load, could indicate that the learners were actively deepening their understanding. In summary, head movement spikes may suggest changes in or activation of the internal states. These findings can be considered partial affirmative evidence of RQ1. In future studies, multiple evaluators should independently classify behaviors during spike moments and verify inter-rater agreement. These measures will be crucial for assigning reliable meaning to spikes and developing a robust classification framework.

6.3 Relationship Between Head Movement Amount and Internal State

This section discusses the relationship between each learner's head movement amount and internal states. For understanding, some learners had correlation coefficients of 0.3 or higher, but some had values of -0.3 or lower. Therefore, some learners may have deepened their understanding during segments with high head movement amounts, whereas others may have done so during segments with small amounts. As for willingness to participate, some learners had correlation coefficients of 0.3 or higher, and some had values of -0.3 or lower, indicating a potential increase in the willingness to participate during segments with higher or lower amounts of head movement, respectively. As for psychological safety, the correlation coefficients of some learners were 0.3 or higher, implying that psychological safety may have increased during segments with larger amounts of head movement.

However, for all internal states, the number of learners with an absolute correlation coefficient of 0.3 or higher never exceeded half of the total number of participants (12).

In summary, although the presence and direction of correlations varied between learners, some learners showed correlations that may indicate potential relationships. Therefore, regarding RQ2, although partial indications were observed, the overall findings did not provide strong support. The possible reasons for this are discussed in Sect. 6.5.

6.4 Relationship Between Group-Level Interhead Distance and Internal State

This section explores the potential relationship between each group's internal state and interhead distance. About understanding, two out of the four groups showed correlation coefficients of 0.3 or higher. Similarly, for psychological safety, two groups also showed correlation coefficients of 0.3 or higher. Thus, in these groups, the internal states tended to improve during segments with larger interhead distances. However, for willingness to participate, no group showed a correlation coefficient of 0.3 or higher.

Absolute correlation coefficients of 0.3 or higher were found in two groups for understanding and two groups for psychological safety, neither of which comprised the majority of the total number of groups.

In summary, although some groups showed potential relationships between the interhead distance and internal states, no consistent patterns were observed across all groups. Therefore, although partial indications were observed regarding RQ3, the overall findings offered only limited support. The possible reasons for this are discussed in Sect. 6.5.

6.5 Head Movement Amount and Interhead Distance

Regarding the relationship between each learner's internal state and head movement, the number of learners with Spearman's correlation coefficients of 0.3 or higher did not exceed half of the total number of participants for any of the three internal states. Similarly, as for the relationship between each group's internal state and interhead distance, the number of groups with coefficients of 0.3 or higher did not exceed half of the total number of groups for any item. Therefore, neither head movement nor interhead distance was strongly related to the internal states.

One possible reason for this is the constraints imposed by the discussion environment. The participants were seated at separate empty desks. This reduced the likelihood of physical coordination behaviors, such as learners leaning toward each other or jointly manipulating worksheets or tablets. In this environment, head movement and interpersonal distance may have been strongly affected by actions unrelated to the internal states.

Additionally, the discussion topic—the meaning of happiness—involved deeply personal values and internal feelings. This may have caused the participants to avoid direct confrontations with the others. Such a topic can suppress physical reactions to others' remarks, resulting in reduced variabilities in head movement and interpersonal distance.

Therefore, although some correlations were observed in specific learners or groups for RQ1 (whether head movement and interhead distance can serve as behavioral indicators related to learners' internal states), a clear, consistent relationship was not found overall.

Future work should develop an experimental design that enables more accurate observation of the relationship between internal states and bodily behaviors by fostering environments that encourage physical coordination behaviors, such as environments with round tables, standing discussions, and sharing of tools (e.g., tablets and worksheets).

6.6 Overall Discussion of Findings

As described in Sect. 6.5, the relationships between each of the two indicators and the internal states were limited. However, correlations were observed in some learners and groups. In addition, spike-like changes in head movement seemed to be potential signs of subjective changes.

7 Conclusion

This study investigated whether integrating two bodily indicators (head movement amount and interhead distance) was effective for estimating the group state, particularly learners' internal states (understanding, willingness to participate, and psychological safety) during collaborative discussions.

Collaborative discussions were conducted with 18 science and engineering university students (six groups with three members each). A ceiling-mounted depth camera was used to measure head movements and interhead distances continuously throughout the discussion. After each discussion, the participants reviewed video recordings of their sessions to report their internal states quantitatively. Two groups were affected by head recognition errors due to depth camera limitations and were thus excluded; the subsequent analysis was performed on the four remaining groups.

No consistent relationships were found between the two indicators and the internal states across all learners or groups, and no clear trends were observed. This may be partly attributed to internal state-unrelated behaviors influencing the measurement results. However, in some learners and groups, positive or negative correlations were observed between one of the internal states (understanding, willingness to participate, or psychological safety) and either bodily indicator (head movement amount or interhead distance). Furthermore, spikes in head movement coincided with the occurrence of cognitive or emotional behaviors, such as laughter, posture adjustments, and gestures, suggesting the potential use of bodily behaviors for state estimation.

Future work will aim to estimate internal states while addressing measurement challenges and environmental factors.

Acknowledgments. This work has been partly supported by the Grants-in-Aid for Scientific Research (Nos. 21K02752 and 22K02951) by MEXT (Ministry of Education, Culture, Sports, Science and Technology) in Japan.

References

1. Chinn, C.A., Anderson, R.C., Waggoner, M.A.: Patterns of discourse in two kinds of literature discussion. Read. Res. Q. **36**(4), 378–411 (2001)
2. Li, X., Li, Y., Wang, W.: Long-lasting conceptual change in science education: the role of U-shaped pattern of argumentative dialogue in collaborative argumentation. Sci. Educ. **32**(1), 123–168 (2023)
3. Gillies, R.M.: Cooperative learning: review of research and practice. Aust. J. Teach. Educ. (Online) **41**(3), 39–54 (2016)
4. Conlin, L.D., Scherr, R.E.: Making space to sensemake: epistemic distancing in small group physics discussions. Cogn. Instr. **36**(4), 396–423 (2018)
5. Van De Bogart, K.L., Dounas-Frazer, D.R., Lewandowski, H., Stetzer, M.R.: Investigating the role of socially mediated metacognition during collaborative troubleshooting of electric circuits. Phys. Rev. Phys. Educ. Res. **13**(2), 020116 (2017)

6. Theophilou, E., Sánchez-Reina, J.R., Odakura, V., Hernández-Leo, D.: An exploratory study on empathy and online discussions in computer supported collaborative learning. In: International Conference on Collaboration Technologies and Social Computing, pp. 129–143. Springer (2024)
7. Järvenoja, H., Järvelä, S.: Emotion control in collaborative learning situations: do students regulate emotions evoked by social challenges. Br. J. Educ. Psychol. **79**(3), 463–481 (2009)
8. Järvelä, S., et al.: Enhancing socially shared regulation in collaborative learning groups: designing for CSCL regulation tools. Educ. Tech. Res. Dev. **63**, 125–142 (2015)
9. Nguyen, A., Järvelä, S.: Learning analytics framework for analysing regulation in collaborative learning (FARCL). In: Theory Informing and Arising from Learning Analytics, pp. 71–85. Springer (2024)
10. Dehbozorgi, N., Maher, M.L., Dorodchi, M.: Emotion mining from speech in collaborative learning. Adv. Sci. Technol. Eng. Syst. J **6**, 90–100 (2021)
11. Otsuchi, S., Ishii, Y., Nakatani, M., Otsuka, K.: Prediction of interlocutors' subjective impressions based on functional head-movement features in group meetings. In: Proceedings of the 2021 International Conference on Multimodal Interaction, pp. 352–360 (2021)
12. D'mello, S.K., Kory, J.: A review and meta-analysis of multimodal affect detection systems. ACM Comput. Surv. (CSUR) **47**(3), 1–36 (2015)
13. Zhou, Q., Suraworachet, W., Cukurova, M.: Detecting non-verbal speech and gaze behaviours with multimodal data and computer vision to interpret effective collaborative learning interactions. Educ. Inf. Technol. **29**(1), 1071–1098 (2024)
14. Otsuka, K., Tsumori, T.: Analyzing multifunctionality of head movements in face-to-face conversations using deep convolutional neural networks. IEEE Access **8**, 217169–217195 (2020)
15. Yamamoto, S., Funabashi, R., Noda, T., Kaneko, M., Egi, H.: An approach of multimodal learning analytics based on the distance between learners' heads during collaborative learning. In: 14th International Conference on Learning Analytics and Knowledge (LAK24) Companion Proceedings, pp. 94–96 (2024)
16. Khuder, B., Negretti, R.: Collaborative writing regulation: a comparative case study of co-regulation and socially shared regulation in higher education. High. Educ. 1–23 (2025)
17. Lubold, N., Pon-Barry, H.: Acoustic-prosodic entrainment and rapport in collaborative learning dialogues. In: Proceedings of the 2014 ACM Workshop on Multimodal Learning Analytics Workshop and Grand Challenge, pp. 5–12 (2014)
18. Paneth, L., Jeitziner, L.T., Rack, O., Opwis, K., Zahn, C.: Zooming in: the role of nonverbal behavior in sensing the quality of collaborative group engagement. Int. J. Comput.-Support. Collab. Learn. **19**(2), 187–229 (2024)
19. Yokozuka, T., Ono, E., Inoue, Y., Ogawa, K.I., Miyake, Y.: The relationship between head motion synchronization and empathy in unidirectional face-to-face communication. Front. Psychol. **9**, 1622 (2018)
20. Jeitziner, L.T., Paneth, L., Rack, O., Zahn, C.: Beyond words: investigating non-verbal indicators of collaborative engagement in a virtual synchronous CSCL environment. Front. Psychol. **15**, 1347073 (2024)
21. Danner, S.G., Krivokapić, J., Byrd, D.: Co-speech movement in conversational turn-taking. Front. Commun. **6**, 779814 (2021)
22. Spikol, D., Ruffaldi, E., Dabisias, G., Cukurova, M.: Supervised machine learning in multimodal learning analytics for estimating success in project-based learning. J. Comput. Assist. Learn. **34**(4), 366–377 (2018)

23. Intel realsense lidar camera l515. https://www.intelrealsense.com/lidar-camera-l515/. Accessed 22 Jan 2025
24. Weinberger, A., Fischer, F.: A framework to analyze argumentative knowledge construction in computer-supported collaborative learning. Comput. Educ. **46**(1), 71–95 (2006)
25. Loes, C.N.: The effect of collaborative learning on academic motivation. Teach. Learn. Inquiry **10** (2022)
26. Edmondson, A.C.: Managing the risk of learning: psychological safety in work teams. Division of Research, Harvard Business School, Cambridge, MA (2002)

Self-selected Groups vs. Random Groups: An Analysis of Student Engagement, Achievement, and Preferences in Collaborative Learning

Ati Suci Dian Martha[1](✉) , Sri Widowati[2] , Arinza Aurelvia[1] ,
Soraya Haidar Salma[1] , and Muhammad Dias Adani[1]

[1] Software Engineering Study Program, School of Computing, Telkom University, Bandung, Indonesia
aciantha@telkomuniversity.ac.id, {arinzaurelv,sorayaaahs,
diasdigital}@student.telkomuniversity.ac.id
[2] Informatics Study Program, School of Computing, Telkom University, Bandung, Indonesia
sriwidowati@telkomuniversity.ac.id

Abstract. This study examines how two group formation methods—self-selected and random—affect students' collaborative engagement, course learning outcomes (CLOs), and group formation preferences in a Software Engineering Professionalism course. A total of 247 students from a private university in Indonesia, across the Bandung and Purwokerto branch campuses, participated in the study. Data were gathered using the Collaborative Learning Engagement Scale (CLES) questionnaire, CLO scores based on project assessment rubrics, and preference questionnaires regarding group formation methods. The results indicated that the self-selected groups demonstrated significantly higher levels of behavioral and emotional engagement and performed better in achieving CLO 1 (professionalism). In contrast, the random groups had better scores on CLO 3 (professional communication) and maintained relatively stable cognitive engagement. Students showed a strong preference for the self-selected method, citing psychological comfort and work efficiency. However, the random grouping was beneficial in promoting adaptation and formal communication skills. These findings demonstrate that each method has distinct advantages: self-selected groups enhance comfort and collaboration, while random groups promote social resilience and professional skills. The study recommends adopting an adaptive or hybrid approach to group formation, aligned with specific learning objectives.

Keywords: Collaborative Learning · Group Formation · Self-Selected Groups · Random Groups · Group-based Learning · Student Preferences

1 Introduction

The digital transformation in Indonesian higher education, especially after the COVID-19 pandemic, has accelerated the implementation of online learning systems across universities [1]. This online environment encourages active student participation through flexible and interactive platforms [2]. In many university courses, group-based assignments are commonly used, requiring students to collaborate and share responsibilities to complete joint tasks [2]. Collaborative learning occurs as students co-construct knowledge through mutual interaction to achieve shared goals [3], often within small groups where each member contributes to specific aspects of a larger project [4].

The effectiveness of this learning approach heavily relies on how groups are formed, as well-structured group composition enables productive interaction and enhances learning outcomes [5]. Nevertheless, challenges such as unequal task distribution, poor communication, and low engagement can hinder group success [6]. To address these issues equitably, implementing appropriate group formation strategies is key to ensuring successful collaborative learning experiences for all students.

There are two main approaches to group formation in educational settings: instructor-assigned groups and student self-selected groups [7–9]. Instructors may assign groups randomly, either manually or using digital tools [10]. Random grouping is considered the most practical and time-efficient method, as it allows students to be mixed to achieve group heterogeneity [11]. Alternatively, when groups are formed deliberately, instructors often take into account students' cognitive abilities [7]. In addition, instructor-assigned groups also utilize algorithmic methods that incorporate pedagogical design objectives, such as controlling homogeneity/heterogeneity related to various attributes [12], including pre-existing knowledge or personality traits, or learning logs/learning analytics [13]. This is possible due to the support of data-driven platforms with rich data and learning analytics applications [13]. Some techniques used in algorithmic methods include ant colony, fuzzy c-means, multi-agent, genetic algorithms, clustering, regression [12], and the GroupAL algorithm [14]. However, this method requires substantial data collection and analysis, which can be burdensome for instructors already managing heavy teaching responsibilities, research demands, and administrative duties [15]. Moreover, such approaches may be inaccessible to educators who lack expertise in advanced quantitative techniques. These challenges are further amplified in online learning environments, where it becomes tough for instructors to assess students' characteristics and behaviors—especially in large classes with limited contact time.

Nafziger et al. [16] found that group formation methods can increase learning motivation and strengthen the sense of community among students. However, there was no significant difference in academic achievement between randomly formed groups and those selected by students [16–18]. Meanwhile, research by Hsiao & Rajagopal [19] showed that students choose group members based on comfort, previous interaction experiences, and personal compatibility. Although these factors can increase satisfaction in working together, they are not always directly proportional to objective academic effectiveness. Other studies have also noted that self-selected groups show higher collaborative behavior due to the familiarity between members and the use of social media to encourage the participation of less active members through explicit advice and support [4, 8]. Thus, self-selected groups often provide a stronger sense of comfort and team cohesion, increasing satisfaction in completing tasks together [9].

While giving students the freedom to choose their group mates can increase their sense of comfort, this approach also has the potential to create social exclusivity—that is, groups are formed based on pre-existing personal relationships [9], which can lead to social and cultural inequalities between groups [20]. Several studies have shown that self-selected grouping can negatively affect students' academic achievement and learning attitudes [7, 20]. Donovan et al. [21] noted that some students experience anxiety when they fail to find their group and end up asking for help from the instructor. Therefore, group formation by the instructor is seen as more inclusive and effective in reducing social pressure in the grouping process [20].

In collaborative learning, student engagement—both cognitive, affective, and behavioral—is an essential indicator of the success of the learning process. This engagement is greatly influenced by how learning groups are formed and managed. Research shows that effective group formation strategies can increase interaction, shared responsibility, and a sense of belonging within the group [7, 8, 15–19, 22]. Garshasbi et al. [23] showed that adaptive group formation based on engagement, motivation, and communication skills significantly increased collaborative engagement. Backer et al. [24] also emphasized that deliberate group formation and collaborative training strengthened student participation in the three domains of learning engagement. Meanwhile, technology such as automatic log systems [25] and consideration of personality traits [5] also influenced the success of group work in a collaborative context.

In the context of Indonesia, there is a lack of empirical research regarding how different methods of group formation influence engagement in collaborative learning. This issue is especially significant in online learning environments, which are characterized by varying levels of access to digital infrastructure, diverse group work cultures, and students' autonomy in selecting their collaboration partners. A systematic review by Wang et al. [26] did indicate the potential benefits of intelligent grouping strategies; however, these practices have been scarcely applied in complex local contexts like Indonesia. Given the critical role of collaborative learning engagement as a key factor in the success of group-based learning, there is an urgent need for an in-depth study of group formation strategies in online settings within Indonesia.

This study addresses the gap by exploring how group formation strategies affect student engagement in online learning. The findings aim to contribute both theoretically and practically to instructional design, particularly in Indonesia and other developing countries facing similar challenges in digital readiness and the shift toward active, collaborative learning. This study will focus solely on random and self-selected group formation to avoid placing any additional burden on instructors or technology. Consequently, the following research questions guide our study:

1. How do students' collaborative learning engagement levels in randomly formed groups differ compared to self-selected groups in the context of online learning?
2. How does the method of group formation affect student learning outcomes?
3. What are students' perceptions of group work based on the formation method?

By understanding how group formation methods impact student engagement, the findings of this study can be used as a basis for policy-making or instructional design in various regions facing comparable pedagogical and infrastructural challenges.

2 Materials and Methods

2.1 Participants

This study applied a quasi-experimental method with a mixed-methods approach. The design involved four classes that had been formed based on the course selection, consisting of two classes at the Bandung campus and two at the Purwokerto campus. Each location had one class randomly assigned as the experimental group and one as the control group, with treatments consisting of variations in the group formation method. The randomization process was conducted using a computer-generated sequence to ensure a balanced distribution of participants and enhance the study's internal validity.

A total of 247 s-year (semester 3) students from the Software Engineering undergraduate program at a private university in Indonesia participated in this study. The participants were divided into two groups: self-selected (n = 118) and random (n = 129). The sample consisted of 81% males (n = 201) and 19% females (n = 46), aged 18–20. Although the courses studied were compulsory, participation in this study was voluntary. Students were informed that participating would not affect their academic grades. Only data from students who provided informed consent to participate were included in the analysis.

2.2 Procedures and Materials

This six-week study was conducted in a Software Engineering Professionalism course using a blend of synchronous sessions via Microsoft Teams and asynchronous activities on Moodle (see Table 1). The course was chosen because it emphasizes professional attitudes, teamwork, and communication, aligning closely with the study's focus on collaborative engagement and related learning outcomes (CLOs).

The course employed a structured, collaborative project model, combining weekly individual tasks with group activities to enhance professionalism, group dynamics, and communication skills. Both experimental and control groups received duplicate instructional content and tasks. In the first week, students in the experimental group formed groups voluntarily, while those in the control group were randomly assigned. Throughout the process, instructors facilitated learning and provided ongoing support.

At the end of the 6th week, participants were asked to independently complete a collaborative engagement and reflection questionnaire without guidance or consultation, with an average completion time of approximately 15 min. They were informed beforehand that the data collected would only be used for research purposes. This procedure was designed to integrate technical, ethical, and communication aspects within a single project-based learning flow, combining individual and collaborative activities that represent real-world professional work dynamics.

2.3 Data Collection

This study employed the Collaborative Learning Engagement Scale (CLES), developed by Xu, Stephens, and Lee [27], to gain a comprehensive understanding of students' collaborative engagement in group-based learning. This instrument is specifically designed

Table 1. Asynchronous Activities via Moodle.

Week	Activity
1	*Creating an E-Portfolio (Individual)* Students create an e-portfolio on a provided wiki page to reflect on their experiences, understanding, and readiness for collaborative projects. This serves as a baseline to assess their engagement and professionalism development.
2	*Project Ethics Discussion (Collaborative)* Each student proposes a real-life example of a software project failure found online. In groups, students select one incident to discuss and identify the violated ethical principle based on the professional code of ethics. Each member shares their thoughts on professional actions that could have prevented the issue. The discussion concludes with a summary of the findings, which are documented in the discussion forum.
3	*Quiz (Individual)* Students complete an individual quiz to assess their basic understanding of professional ethics and related case studies in software projects.
4	*Complex Case Study (Collaborative)* Students receive a complex case study related to the development of a medical app. In groups, they analyze key issues, including unclear responsibilities, a lack of validation, and internal conflicts. They identify violated ethical principles and develop professional actions to prevent similar issues. Discussions are conducted asynchronously through a forum.
5	*Source Code Activity (Individual)* Each student searches for and analyzes four source code classes from open-source software projects available online. They provide explanatory comments on the code and create a summary that covers the main functions, structure, dependencies, and technical notes. The results are compiled into a wiki page for group presentations.
6	*Presentation (Collaborative)* In groups, students create a video presentation explaining each member's source code analysis from week 5. The video simulates professional communication, with structured delivery and peer feedback. It is uploaded to YouTube and shared via a wiki page for assessment and peer viewing.

to measure engagement in the context of collaborative learning in higher education, with a development basis that combines qualitative and quantitative approaches. CLES evaluates student engagement in three main dimensions, namely: (1) *Behavioral Engagement*, reflecting active participation and contributions in group activities; (2) *Cognitive Engagement*, assessing the level of mental effort, learning strategies, and focus during collaboration; and (3) *Emotional Engagement*, describing students' affective responses such as sense of belonging, satisfaction, and task value. The scale employs a 5-point Likert format for behavioral and cognitive engagement items and a 7-point Likert format for emotional engagement items, consistent with the original instrument design [27]. This distinction ensures adequate sensitivity in capturing both behavioral-cognitive effort and emotional variation in collaborative settings.

Data collection comprised three components: (1) the Collaborative Learning Engagement Scale (CLES) to measure behavioral, cognitive, and emotional engagement, (2) a rubric-based assessment of project assignments by four lecturers to evaluate Course Learning Outcomes (CLO), and (3) a questionnaire on students' group formation preferences. Together, these instruments provided a mixed-methods approach that quantified engagement and learning outcomes while capturing students' subjective views on group formation in software engineering projects.

2.4 Data Analysis

Quantitative data were analyzed using IBM SPSS version 31. Descriptive analysis was used to describe the mean score and standard deviation for each engagement dimension. An Independent Samples t-test was used to test for significant differences between the Random and Self-Selected groups on the three engagement dimensions and the three CLOs. Levene's test was conducted first to check the homogeneity of variance (see Table 2).

Table 2. Levene's Test for Equality of Variances.

Dimensions	F	Sig.	Note
Behavior engagement	0.72	0.99	Levene's test $p > 0.05$ equal variances assumed
Cognitive engagement	0.06	0.80	
Emotional engagement	0.05	0.81	
CLO 1	18.09	<0.001	Levene's test $p < 0.05$ equal variances not assumed
CLO 2	4.97	0.03	
CLO 3	9.21	0.003	

Student preferences and reasons were analyzed thematically, with frequencies and percentages calculated to identify dominant arguments. Quantitative results were then integrated with qualitative data and prior studies to provide a holistic understanding of how group formation methods affect engagement and learning outcomes.

3 Findings

3.1 RQ1: Differences in Levels of Collaborative Learning Engagement

The Collaborative Learning Engagement Scale (CLES) demonstrated strong reliability across three dimensions (see Table 3), with Cronbach's alpha values ranging from 0.71 to 0.94, person reliability from 0.72 to 0.87, and item reliability from 0.98 to 0.99. This indicates that CLES is a valid and reliable tool for measuring students' collaborative engagement. Additionally, Table 4 summarizes the statistical significance of group comparisons, supporting the interpretation of the results.

Table 3. Reliability of the Collaborative Learning Engagement Scale (CLES) Instrument.

Dimensions	Person reliability	Item reliability	Cronbach's alpha
Behavior engagement	0.72	0.99	0.71
Cognitive engagement	0.87	0.98	0.91
Emotional engagement	0.86	0.98	0.94

Based on the results presented in Table 4, the Self-Selected group demonstrated higher behavioral engagement than the Random group, indicating that students are more active and involved when they choose their own group members. However, there were no significant differences in cognitive engagement between the two groups, suggesting that they possessed similar thinking skills and conceptual understanding. The Self-Selected group also exhibited greater emotional engagement, feeling more comfortable and enthusiastic, which can promote a positive collaborative environment.

Table 4. Independent Samples t-test results between the Self-Selected and the Random Group.

Dimensions	$t(df)$	p-value	Mean Diff.	95% CI (lower-upper)	Cohen's d
Behavior engagement	-3.09 (245)	0.002*	-0.19	-0.32—-0.07	-0.39
Cognitive engagement	-1.46 (245)	0.146 (ns)	-0.10	-0.24—-0.04	-0.19
Emotional engagement	-3.96 (245)	< 0.001*	-0.64	-0.96—-0.32	-0.51

Note: * = significant ($p < 0.05$); ns = not significant; Power analysis result: $\beta = 0.97$ (high statistical power)

Overall, these results support the idea that allowing students the freedom to select their groups can enhance both behavioral and emotional engagement, although it does not necessarily affect cognitive engagement. To provide a more comprehensive understanding, this analysis was further developed by interpreting each item within each dimension, allowing for a more detailed examination of student involvement across all measured aspects.

Behavioral Engagement. Figure 1 illustrates that the Self-Selected group generally exhibited higher levels of behavioral engagement compared to the Random group, particularly in terms of active interaction, openness in sharing information, and willingness to help fellow group members. This indicates that the comfort and emotional closeness derived from voluntary member selection can enhance the quality of cooperation. However, the Random group has its own strengths. For several measures, the score differences between the Self-Selected group and the Random group were relatively small, such as in adherence to rules and attentive listening. This suggests that randomly formed groups can still uphold discipline, compliance, and practical listening skills, even in the absence of personal preferences for member selection. In summary, while self-selected groups excel in fostering close social interactions, random groups still possess the potential to promote formal, fair, and structured cooperative behavior.

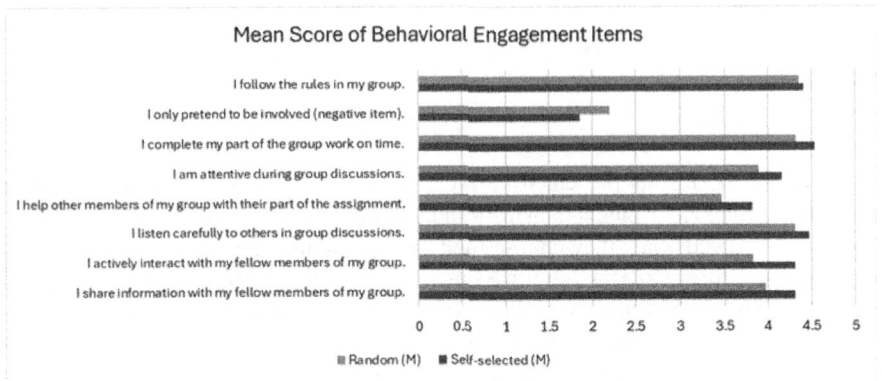

Fig. 1. Comparison of Behavioral Engagement Items between Self-Selected and Random Groups.

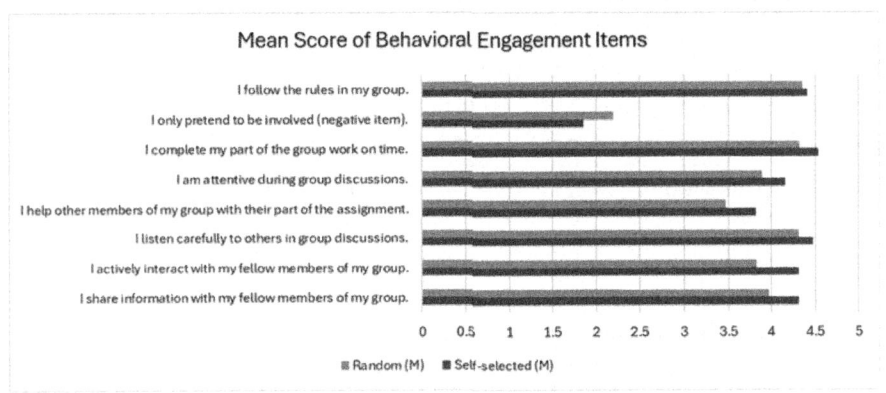

Fig. 2. Comparison of Cognitive Engagement Items between Self-Selected and Random Groups.

Cognitive Engagement. Based on the mean scores of cognitive engagement items (see Fig. 2), the self-selected group exhibited notable strengths in dedication, exploration, and cognitive reflection. They dedicated more time and effort to complete tasks and actively sought additional materials relevant to their work. Members of this group were also more proactive in facing challenges, either by independently seeking information or asking for assistance. They were more likely to double-check their work to ensure its quality. Furthermore, the self-selected group frequently integrated new knowledge to address problems, sought feedback, and engaged in collaborative reflection to improve their teamwork. As a result, they demonstrated strengths in self-management, learning initiative, and a long-term commitment to the quality of their group work.

On the other hand, the random group was more stimulated by the intellectual challenges presented in the group discussions. They enjoyed facing challenging problems, although they showed less consistency in their reflection and exploratory efforts beyond the task's demands. Their discussions were equal to those of the self-selected group in terms of sharing ideas and processing others' ideas. Still, they tended to be less active in seeking feedback or developing structured group planning. Thus, the self-selected group excelled in aspects of exploration, reflection, and cognitive initiative. In contrast, the random group excelled in enjoying intellectual challenges but had not yet fully maximized the potential for reflection and strategic planning in group work.

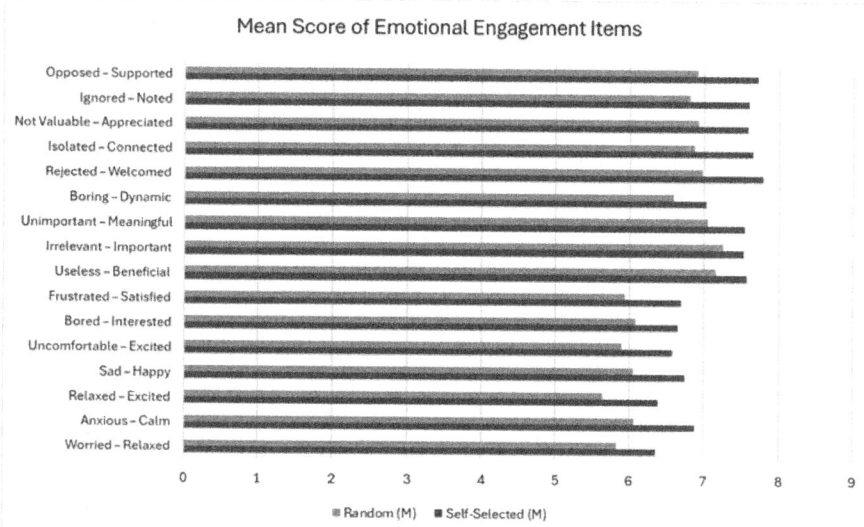

Fig. 3. Comparison of Emotional Engagement Items between Self-Selected and Random Groups.

Emotional Engagement. The emotional engagement measurements showed key differences between self-selected and random groups (Fig. 3). The self-selected group reported a more positive experience, feeling calmer, more motivated, and satisfied with group work. They also experienced greater social support and connection among members, enhancing their emotional well-being and relationship quality. In contrast, members of random groups felt involved and found the tasks meaningful, but their emotional comfort, motivation, and social support were lower. They had limited social connections, leading to weaker interactions compared to self-selected groups. While self-selected groups benefit from positive emotional experiences, they may also risk in-group bias and be less exposed to new ideas. Thus, both group types have unique advantages and disadvantages that impact emotional experiences and interactions.

Findings. Based on the analysis of student engagement, allowing students to choose their group members offers significant benefits, particularly in terms of behavioral and emotional aspects of engagement. Self-selected groups demonstrated more active participation, higher contributions, and more positive emotional engagement, including feelings of comfort, enthusiasm, intrinsic motivation, and better quality of relationships among members. These groups also excelled in learning initiative, reflection, and cognitive exploration, although there was no significant difference in overall cognitive engagement compared to random groups.

On the other hand, random groups maintained discipline, adhered to rules, developed listening skills, and engaged in more formal and structured collaboration. They enjoyed the intellectual challenge of discussions, but were less consistent in reflection, further exploration, and strategic planning. The disadvantages of random groups included limited emotional engagement and weaker social connections. In contrast, self-selected groups faced the risk of group bias or the development of a "comfort zone," which can limit exposure to new perspectives. Overall, voluntary group selection tends to enhance behavioral and emotional engagement, as well as the quality of social interactions. In contrast, random groups can promote more formal, equitable, and structured collaboration while stimulating intellectual challenges. Both group types have distinct advantages and disadvantages, so strategies for group formation should be tailored to the specific learning objectives to be achieved.

3.2 RQ2: The Effect of Group Formation Methods on Learning Outcomes

This study was conducted on the Software Professionalism course, which has three-course learning outcomes (CLOs), namely: the ability to demonstrate professionalism in the field of Software Engineering (CLO 1), the ability of students to understand group dynamics and psychological aspects in software projects (CLO 2), and the ability of students to practice professional communication techniques (CLO 3). Table 5 compares the distribution of CLO scores between the random and self-selected groups.

Table 5. CLO Score Distribution between Random and Self-Selected Groups.

CLO	Random (Mean ± SD)	Self-Selected (Mean ± SD)	Mean Dif.	p-value	Interpretation
1	74.74 ± 14.19	89.69 ± 10.47	+14.95	<0.001*	Self-Selected significantly higher
2	77.95 ± 18.12	78.16 ± 19.07	+0.21	0.93 (ns)	No significant difference
3	89.01 ± 11.13	78.08 ± 16.29	−10.93	<0.001*	Random significantly higher

Note: * = significant ($p < 0.05$); ns = not significant; Power analysis result: $\beta = 0.97$ (high statistical power)

The analysis shows that students in self-selected groups scored significantly higher in CLO 1 (professionalism), suggesting that familiarity and trust within the group foster collaboration, accountability, and effective communication. However, CLO 2 (understanding group dynamics) showed no significant difference, indicating that team interaction is shaped more by experience than group type. Notably, random groups outperformed in CLO 3 (professional communication), as working with unfamiliar peers encouraged more formal and structured communication, aligning with professional standards. While self-selected groups benefit from smoother coordination, their informal style may lack the communication rigor required in workplace settings. Conversely, random groups offer exposure to diverse working styles but may face initial challenges in trust and coordination.

In summary, self-selected groups offer a supportive and cohesive environment that enhances professionalism and group efficiency but may lack diversity and limit exposure to new perspectives. Meanwhile, random groups promote adaptability, diverse interactions, and professional communication skills, although they may face initial barriers in terms of trust and coordination. Each method presents unique strengths that can be leveraged depending on the intended learning outcomes.

3.3 RQ3: Students' Perceptions of Group Work Based on Formation Method

The third research question explored students' preferences for group formation in collaborative learning—random vs. self-selected. Data from both group types revealed that most students preferred the formation method they experienced. Figure 4 presents the distribution of these preferences.

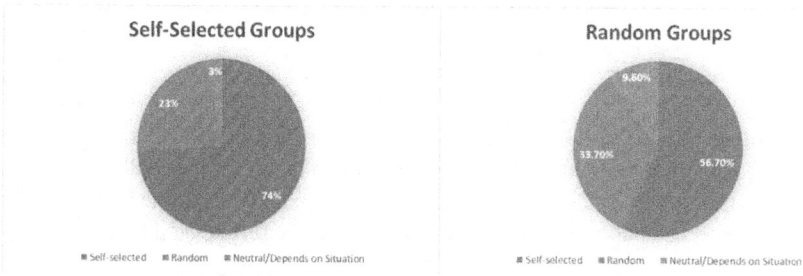

Fig. 4. Group preference distribution.

Figure 4 illustrates that most students in both groups preferred self-selected group formation, with a higher preference among those in self-selected groups. Specifically, 74.0% of students in self-selected groups favored this method, compared to only 56.7% of students in random groups. Conversely, students with direct experience using the random grouping system showed a greater preference for random formation, with 33.7% supporting it, while this preference dropped to 23.0% among students who chose their own group members. Each group offered different justifications for their preferences, reflecting their individual learning experiences. Table 6 presents the results of mapping the reasons for group formation based on student experiences.

These findings indicate that preference for self-selected groups tends to be higher, especially among those already in the system. This suggests that positive experiences in self-selected group work reinforce the perception that this model is more effective

Table 6. Motivation behind students' choice of group formation method.

Category	Random Group	Self-Selected Group
Reasons for Choosing Self-Selected Groups	• Communication is smoother because you already know the members • Team chemistry is stronger • Avoiding members who do not contribute • Coordination and division of tasks are more efficient • No need to re-adapt for each task	• Chemistry and comfort greatly support work efficiency • Communication is more structured and without obstacles • already know each other's strengths and weaknesses • Facilitates document organization and communication (WA, GDrive, etc.) • Relevant for ongoing tasks that require consistency
Reasons for Choosing Random Groups	• Train adaptation and cooperation with various types of people • Increase relationships and expand networks • Improve social skills and tolerance • So that you don't always group with the same people	• Train adaptation and get to know more colleagues • Provide equal and fair opportunities • Avoid the formation of exclusive groups

and comfortable. Students in self-selected groups feel they benefit from the ease of coordination, smooth communication, and cohesiveness formed, especially in ongoing tasks. In contrast, although students in random groups can understand the learning value of diversity and social adaptation, most still tend towards the self-selected model, mainly because of the obstacles in communication and coordination they often experience.

Thus, in the context of collaborative learning that demands intensive communication, continuity of ideas, and long-term collective responsibility, the self-selected group formation system is preferred by students because it builds trust, team stability, and work efficiency. However, random groups remain relevant and suitable for specific situations, such as short-term learning activities, exploratory tasks, or training sessions to train adaptation skills, expand relationships, and improve the ability to work in heterogeneous teams. This model can be a proper pedagogical strategy to avoid group exclusivity, encourage inclusivity, and develop social competence across individuals in diverse classrooms.

4 Discussion

The findings of this study highlight how group formation methods influence student engagement, achievement of learning outcomes (CLOs), and personal preferences in collaborative learning settings. Students in self-selected groups demonstrated significantly stronger behavioral and emotional engagement, marked by higher levels of participation, adherence to group norms, and a greater sense of psychological comfort. These outcomes align with prior research [20, 28], suggesting that familiarity and voluntary collaboration foster satisfaction, trust, and active involvement in group tasks. Although cognitive engagement was slightly higher in self-selected groups, the difference was not statistically significant, indicating that elements like task design and internal motivation may play a more pivotal role than group structure. Interestingly, randomly assigned groups maintained consistent cognitive engagement despite lower emotional and behavioral scores. This aligns with findings by Samudra et al. [29], who argue that random groupings may promote more balanced performance due to varied skill distributions.

In terms of learning outcomes, students in self-selected groups achieved significantly higher scores in CLO 1, which assesses professionalism in collaborative software projects. This suggests that a comfortable and trusting environment supports behaviors like accountability, loyalty, and constructive cooperation—reinforcing the notion that positive team dynamics enhance professional development [5]. In contrast, students in random groups excelled in CLO 3, which focuses on professional communication. Because students in these groups worked with unfamiliar peers, they were more likely to adopt formal, clear, and well-documented communication styles—practices that mirror real-world professional settings. This supports Jong et al. [30] and Wu et al. [31] who found that heterogeneous teams often experience improved communication due to the need for clarity. Meanwhile, no significant differences emerged in CLO 2 (understanding group dynamics), indicating that such understanding is shaped more by team interactions during the project than by group formation method.

Regarding student preferences, most participants—regardless of group assignment—favored the self-selected method. This preference grew from 56.7% in the random group to 74.0% in the self-selected group. Students cited efficient communication, easier coordination, and psychological comfort as reasons for this choice. These findings align with Chapman et al. [20], who noted that self-selected groups often lead to stronger social stability and long-term productivity. However, random grouping still offered benefits, particularly in fostering adaptability, expanding social networks, and encouraging tolerance for diversity. Wu et al. [31] emphasized that random grouping can reduce exclusivity and promote a more equitable classroom environment, although logistical issues—such as conflicting schedules and lower interpersonal chemistry—were noted as common challenges [32].

In summary, the study reveals a consistent pattern: self-selected groups are more effective in nurturing both the affective and behavioral aspects of learning, thereby contributing to a sense of team cohesion and professionalism. In contrast, random groups promote essential real-world skills such as formal communication, adaptability, and inclusive collaboration. Each approach offers distinct pedagogical benefits and limitations. Self-selected groups may risk homogeneity and exclusivity, while random groups, although less efficient initially, foster broader social learning and communication standards that are more reflective of professional environments. These insights provide valuable guidance for educators seeking to strike a balance between emotional safety and professional preparedness in collaborative learning contexts.

Furthermore, these findings are relevant for the development of data-driven group formation methods. By leveraging data on student behavior, preferences, and interactions, intelligent systems or LMSs can recommend more adaptive group formations. This implication opens up opportunities for the application of machine learning algorithms or educational analytics to balance collaborative comfort with the development of social and professional skills, resulting in more objective, personalized, and sustainable group formation strategies.

5 Conclusion

This study examines the effects of group formation methods—self-selected vs. random—on students' engagement, Course Learning Outcomes (CLO) achievement, and teamwork preferences in software projects. Engagement was analyzed across behavioral, cognitive, and emotional dimensions to capture the impact of both natural and conditioned interpersonal dynamics.

Findings show that self-selected groups foster stronger behavioral and emotional engagement, leading to better professionalism achievement (CLO 1) and a preference for this model due to efficiency and psychological comfort. In contrast, random groups promote professional communication (CLO 3), maintain stable cognitive engagement, and strengthen adaptability and social tolerance.

Limitations include the focus on a single project type and field, reliance on self-report measures, uncontrolled mediating factors (e.g., motivation, informal roles), and relatively short project duration, which may not capture long-term dynamics. Implications highlight that educators can align group models with learning goals: self-selected groups are suitable for long-term, cohesion-driven projects, while random groups are better suited for exploratory or short-term tasks that emphasize adaptation and communication. A hybrid model may balance comfort with skill development. For LMS developers, dashboards tracking behavioral, cognitive, and emotional engagement, alongside AI-based pedagogical agents, can enhance coordination and motivation. For researchers, future work should explore varied contexts, apply multidimensional and longitudinal measures, and design data-driven group formation methods informed by student behavior and preferences to achieve adaptive, goal-oriented collaborative learning.

Acknowledgments. This research was funded by the Skema Penelitian Non Kerjasama 2025 from the Directorate of Research and Community Service (PPM) at Telkom University, with grant number 010/LIT06/PPM-LIT/2025. The study is titled "Examining Online Collaborative Engagement and Learning Experiences in Group-Based Learning".

Disclosure of Interests. The authors have no competing interests to declare that are relevant to the content of this article

References

1. Budiyanto, C.W., Latifah, R., Saputro, H., Prananto, A.: The barriers and readiness to deal with digital transformation in higher education. TEM J. **13**(1), 334–348 (2024)

2. Wang, S., Zhang, R., Wang, X., Xu, D., Tian, F.: How do mobile social apps matter for college students satisfaction in group-based learning? The mediation of collaborative learning. Front. Psychol. **13**(795660), 1–14 (2022)
3. Lyons, K.M., Lobczowski, N.G., Greene, J.A., Whitley, J., McLaughlin, J.E.: Using a design-based research approach to develop and study a web-based tool to support collaborative learning. Comput. Educ. **161**(104064) (2021)
4. So, H.-J., Brush, T.A.: Student perceptions of collaborative learning, social presence and satisfaction in a blended learning environment: relationships and critical factors. Comput. Educ. **51**(1), 318–336 (2008)
5. Müller, A.M., Ropke, R., Konert, J., Bellhauser, H.: Investigating group formation: an experiment on the distribution of extraversion in educational settings. Acta Psyhologica **242**, 1–12 (2024)
6. Hall, D., Buzwell, S.: The problem of free-riding in group projects: looking beyond social loafing as reason for non-contribution. Act. Learn. High. Educ. **14**(1), 37–49 (2012)
7. Putzeys, K., van Keer, H., de Wever, B.: Unknown is not chosen: university student voices on group formation for collaborative writing. Educ. Sci. **14**(1), 1–18 (2023)
8. Su, F., Zou, D., Xie, H.: Integrating different group paterns into collaborative argumentative writing in the shimo platform. Technol. Knowl. Learn. **29**, 309–330 (2024)
9. Navlekar, A.S., Theobald, E.J., Griffith, K., Limeri, L.B.: Strategically creating maximally heterogeneous lab groups did not improve group performance in an introductory biology lab class. PLoS ONE **20**(5), 1–15 (2025)
10. Nalli, G., Amendola, D., Perali, A., Mostarda, L.: Comparative analysis of clustering algorithms and moodle plugin for creation of student heterogeneous groups in online university courses. Appl. Sci. **11**(13), 1–21 (2021)
11. Bacon, D.R., Stewart, K.A., Anderson, E.S.: Methods of assigning players to teams: a review and novel approach. Simul. Gaming **32**(1), 6–17 (2001)
12. Maqtary, N., Mohsen, A., Bechkoum, K.: Group formation techniques in computer-supported collaborative learning: a systematic literature review. Technol. Knowl. Learn. **24**(2), 169–190 (2017)
13. Liang, C., Horikoshi, I., Majumdar, R., Flanagan, B., Ogata, H.: Towards predictable process and consequence attributes of data-driven group work: Primary analysis for assisting teachers with automatic group formation. Educ. Technol. Soc. **26**(4), 90–103 (2023)
14. Konert, J., Burlak, D., Steinmetz, R.: The group formation problem: an algorithmic approach to learning group formation. In: Rensing, C., de Freitas, S., Ley, T., Muñoz-Merino, P.J. (eds.) Open Learning and Teaching in Educational Communities, Lecture Notes in Computer Science, vol. 8719. Springer, Cham (2014). https://doi.org/10.1007/978-3-319-11200-8_17
15. Bergtold, J.S., Shanoyan, A.: Assessment of group formation methods on performance in group-based learning activities. Front. Educ. **9**(1362211), 1–9 (2024) → 12
16. Nafziger, R., Meseke, J.K., Meseke, C.A.: Collaborative learning: the effect of group formation process on overall student performance. J. Chiropr. Educ. **25**(1), 11–15 (2011)
17. Gunderson, D.E., Moore, J.D.: Group learning pedagogy and group selection. Int. J. Constr. Educ. Res. **4**, 34–45 (2008)
18. Müller, A., Bellhäuser, H., Konert, J., Röpke, R.: Effects of group formation on student satisfaction and performance: a field experiment. Small Group Res. **53**(2), 244–273 (2022)
19. Hsio, Y.P., Rajagopal, K.: Students' perceptions of self-selected peer learning in a collaborative Chinese speaking assessment. Innovative Pract. High. Educ. **2**(1), 1–10 (2014)
20. Chapman, K., Meuter, M., Toy, D., Wright, L.: Can't we pick our own groups? the influence of group selection method on group dynamics and outcomes. J. Manag. Educ. **30**(4), 557–569 (2006)

21. Donovan, D.A., Connell, G.L., Grunspan, D.Z.: Student learning outcomes and attitudes using three methods of group formation in a nonmajors biology class. CBE-Life Sci. Educ. **17**(4), 1–14 (2018)
22. Sarode, N., Bakal, W.: Toward effectual group formation method for collaborative learning environment. In: Karuppusamy, P., Perikos, I., Shi, F., Nguyen, T.N. (eds.) Sustainable Communication Networks and Application 2021, LNDECT, vol. 55, pp. 351–361. Springer, Singapore (2021)
23. Garshasbi, S., Graf, S., Asgari, M., Shen, J., Howard, S.: An optimal grouping and regrouping method for effective collaborative learning: Leveraging the group dynamics. In: 2023 IEEE International Conference on Teaching. Assessment and Learning for Engineering (TALE), pp. 1–7. IEEE, Auckland, New Zealand (2023)
24. Backer, J.M., Miller, J.L., Timmer, S.M.: The effects of collaborative grouping on student engagement in middle school students. The St. Catherine University Repository Website. https://sophia.stkate.edu/maed/280. Accessed 22 June 2025
25. Liang, C., Majumdar, R., Ogata, H.: Learning log-based automatic group formation: system design and classroom implementation study. Res. Pract. Technol. Enhanc. Learn. **16**(14), 1–22 (2021)
26. Wang, Z., Yang, X., Li, K.: A systematic review of intelligent grouping in collaborative learning. Interactive Learn. Environ. 1–16 (2024)
27. Xu, B., Stephens, J.M., Lee, K.: Assessing student engagement in collaborative learning: development and validation of new measure in China. Asia Pac. Educ. Res. **33**, 395–405 (2024)
28. Myers, S.A.: Students' perceptions of classroom group work as a function of group member selection. Commun. Teach. **26**(1), 50–64 (2011)
29. Samudra, S., Walters, C., Williams-Dobosz, D., Shah, A., Brickman, P.: Try before you buy: are there benefits to a random trial period before students choose their collaborative teams? CBE-Life Sci. Educ. **23**(1), 1–19 (2023)
30. Jong, B., Wu, Y., Chan, T.: Dynamic grouping strategies based on a conceptual graph for cooperative learning. IEEE Trans. Knowl. Data Eng. **18**(6), 738–747 (2006)
31. Wu, T., Tang, X., Wong, S., Chen, X., Shaffer, C.A., Chen, Y.: The impact of group discussion and formation on student performance: an experience report in a large cs1 course. In: Proceedings of the 56th ACM Technical Symposium on Computer Science Education V. 1 (SIGCSETS 2025), pp. 1260–1266. IEEE, Pittsburgh, USA (2025)
32. Chang, Y., Brickman, P.: When group work doesn't work: insights from students. CBE—Life Sci. Educ. **17**, 1–17 (2018)

Technology-Mediated Communication and Online Environments

What Makes Turn-Taking Smooth? Analysis of Gaze Behavior During a Multitasking Videoconference

Taketo Imagawa[1](✉), Atsuto Kurokochi[1], Koki Yanagii[1], Kazuyuki Iso[2], Masayuki Ihara[3], and Minoru Kobayashi[1]

[1] Meiji University, 4-21-1, Nakano, Nakano-Ku, Tokyo, Japan
{taketo.imagawa,atsuto.kurokochi,koki.yanagii}@koblab.org,
minoru@acm.org
[2] Tokyo Information Design Professional University, 2-7-1, Komatsugawa, Edogawa-Ku, Tokyo, Japan
iso@tid.ac.jp
[3] RIKEN, 1-7-22, Suehiro-Cho, Tsurumi-Ku, Yokohama, Japan
ihara@acm.org

Abstract. The widespread use of remote meetings enabled collaborative work without being co-located. However, remote meetings require participants to engage in multiple tasks simultaneously, such as browsing the document, texting in chat, and taking notes. These multitasking environments make it difficult to recognize who is about to speak or when to speak, which can lead to speech contention or awkward silence. To address this issue, we analyzed gaze behavior during three meeting conditions, in-person, audio, and video meetings, and two multitasking tasks, document browsing and chat replying, to find out the cues for smooth turn-taking. We analyzed the next speaker's gaze direction just before taking a turn after speech contention or silence occurred. The result suggested that just before taking a turn after speech contention, the next speaker tends to gaze at the document or chat rather than at other participants, and after silence, the gaze direction is distributed. Based on these findings, we discuss the implications for facilitating smooth turn-taking in a multitasking videoconference.

Keywords: Gaze Analysis · Turn-Taking · Multitasking · Videoconference

1 Introduction

Remote meeting tools such as Zoom [1] and Microsoft Teams [2] enable participants to work from remote [3] and engage in multiple activities simultaneously, including sharing and browsing the document, taking notes, and replying to chat messages. However, such multitasking makes it difficult to perceive nonverbal cues, such as facial expressions, gestures, and gaze, causing challenges in recognizing who is about to speak or when to speak. As a result, speech contention or awkward silence may occur, hindering smooth turn-taking (Fig. 1).

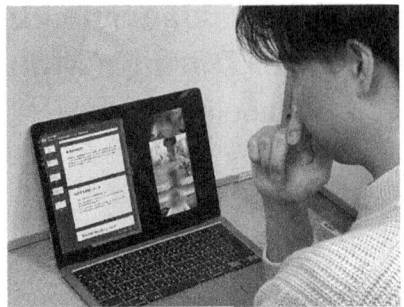

Fig. 1. Image of a multitasking videoconference

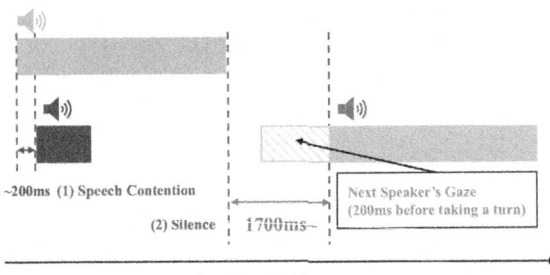

Fig. 2. Image of turn-taking after speech contention or silence occurred

This study aims to explore cues for supporting smooth turn-taking in a multitasking videoconference by analyzing participants' gaze behavior. We believe clarifying the next speaker's gaze direction just before taking a turn after speech contention or silence reveals the key to smooth turn-taking.

In this study, we conducted three types of meetings (in-person, audio, and video), where participants needed to pay attention to not only other participants but also a document and chat, to determine the role and effect of gaze behavior during the turn-taking in multitasking meetings. We found that shared attention on the document or chat and a proper gaze distribution to other participants are the factors that make turn-taking smooth.

2 Related Work

2.1 Definitions

We defined participants, types of speeches, and thresholds referring to related [4] and our previous study [5]. The detailed definitions of the terms used in this study are provided in the Appendix. In this study, we focus on turn-taking after speech contention or silence occurred (see Fig. 2 and Table.5). We believe that there is a key to smooth turn-taking by analyzing the next speaker's gaze direction just before taking a turn after non-smooth turn-taking, such as speech contention or silence. The reason is that the next speaker should be confident that the turn will be taken smoothly when taking a turn after a non-smooth turn-taking, based on the signals received from gaze behavior or other circumstances.

2.2 Role of Gaze Behavior in Turn-Taking

Several studies suggest that eye gaze plays a key role in turn-taking. Kendon [6] reported that eye gaze and turn-taking are closely connected. For example, a previous speaker may look at a non-speaker when they want to give them a turn to speak. Additionally, a non-speaker tends to avert their eyes while organizing the content of their utterance and ideas. Jokinen et al. [7] clarified that gaze direction helps identify who is preparing to speak or wants to continue speaking. Richardson et al. [8] found that in one-on-one in-person conversations, if both the speaker and listener are gazing at the same object, sharing attention increases comprehension of the utterance. Richardson et al. [9] also found that even when participants are speaking from remote locations, joint attention is likely to occur. Besides joint attention, many studies discuss mutual gaze (i.e., simultaneous eye contact) and suggest that it helps foster smooth conversations [6, 10–12].

Some studies focused on the effects of blocking the nonverbal information or comparing audio and video meetings. Jackson [13] et al. reported that the use of face coverings significantly reduced comprehension of the content of conversation, increased cognitive effort, and reduced ease of listening during videoconference compared to the non-face cover condition. Rutter et al. [14] investigated the effects of visual information during four types of meetings: face-to-face, audio, face-to-face with curtain (cue-less), and video meetings, and suggested that the combination of gaze cues and physical presence generates conversation full of humor and emotional expression. On the other hand, the fewer nonverbal cues there are, the more the conversation becomes indifferent to the feelings of the other participant and is carried out indifferently.

While these studies suggest that gaze has a significant impact on turn-taking, it has also been reported that conveying and perceiving the gaze cue in a remote meeting remains difficult.

2.3 Challenges of Remote Meetings and a Multitasking Environment

In remote meetings, we often experience difficulties related to video feeds, eye gaze, and multitasking. Chen et al. [15] reported that even if he or she is gazing at another person's face, the eye gaze is not conveyed and perceived by the other person correctly due to the position of the camera. The eye gaze is often delivered as looking down. What is worse, Bekkering et al. [16] noted that this misalignment in eye contact in the video meeting can reduce reliability on others. Although both speakers may look at each other's video feed, mutual gaze cannot be recognized due to the lack of shared gaze direction, which may hinder smooth conversation [17]. Conveying nonverbal cues such as gestures and facial expressions requires greater cognitive effort [18], and the limited size of the video window restricts the transmission of such cues, leading participants to exaggerate their actions and resulting in unnatural movements [19]. Moreover, many studies reported that multitasking during a remote meeting, such as texting chats, switching windows, or answering the phone, increases the cognitive load [20–24].

Table 1. Limitations of our previous study and solutions

Limitations of our previous study	Solution
1. The condition in the meeting was to only browse a supplemental material.	Add non-supplemental material condition to identify what will a speaker gaze when there is no shared document.
2. The cognitive load on the participants was few.	Add chat replying as an extra multitasking task to increase cognitive load.
3. The meeting formats were only in-person and video.	Add an audio meeting to investigate the effect of nonverbal cues on turn-taking.
4. Severe head movement and laugh lowered the accuracy of gaze data.	Attach a headband to the eye tracker to stabilize the precise data collection.
5. Participants had never met before which caused hesitation to make an eye contact	Recruit participants who are familiar with each other.

As mentioned above, it is difficult to make a smooth turn-taking during a multitasking remote meeting. However, there is little research about turn-taking and gaze behavior during a multitasking videoconference. In this study, we focused on this issue and conducted several experiments to analyze and solve it.

2.4 Our Previous Study

To determine the role of gaze in turn-taking during a multitasking videoconference, we conducted in-person and video meetings with supplemental materials and analyzed the gaze direction just before turn-taking [5]. The results showed that participants tend to look at the shared materials just before taking turns rather than at other participants in both in-person and video meetings.

However, our previous study had five limitations, therefore, we need to solve these and conduct improved experiments (see Table 1). We designed the new experiment to overcome these limitations and elucidate the gaze role in turn-taking during a multitasking videoconference.

3 Experiment

In this study, we designed in-person, audio, and video meetings with multitasking conditions, browsing the document and replying to the chat message (see Fig. 3). The experiment aims to find out what the next speaker looks at after speech contention and silence occurred, and determine the role of gaze cues for smooth turn-taking in a multitasking meeting.

3.1 Meeting Design

Participants. 12 students (8 graduate and 4 undergraduate, 4 males and 8 females) from the same Japanese university and the same laboratory participated in our experiment.

Fig. 3. Image of the experimental in-person (left), audio (middle), and video meeting (right)

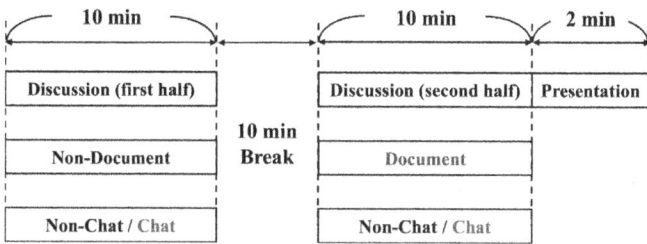

Fig. 4. Flow of the experimental meeting

We selected participants who were familiar with each other and experienced in using Zoom for remote meetings. Participants were separated into 3 groups of 4 members and conducted one of the three meeting formats (in-person, audio, or video meeting).

Apparatus. We provided 13-inch laptops to each participant for operating Zoom, browsing documents, and replying to chat messages. We informed participants that their gaze, utterance, and video are recorded via eye tracker (Tobii Pro Glasses 2, 3 [25, 26]), Zoom, and camera, and we obtained their consent.

Procedure. Before each meeting starts, participants attach the Tobii Glasses with a headband to stabilize the accuracy of gaze data. Also, participants were told to use chat freely to take notes. The layout of the laptop screen was fixed, with the left half displaying the document (or remaining blank), while the right half was divided between the meeting tool and the chat window. After each meeting ended, we conducted a questionnaire and interview with each participant and gained the opinions and comments about the discussion and conditions of the experiment.

Discussion. Each meeting is divided into two 10-min discussions with different conditions (see Fig. 4). All the meetings followed the same theme to discuss. The first half of the meeting was conducted with a non-document condition, in other words, without browsing the document, and the second half was a document condition. In these halves, two sub-conditions were arranged (non-chat and chat conditions). After the second half of the discussion, one participant made a presentation to summarize the results of the discussion. The presenter was freely chosen by the participants.

Discussion Topic. All meetings shared the same theme for discussion. "Decide on three ideal conditions for a laboratory". This topic was selected for two reasons. First, it can

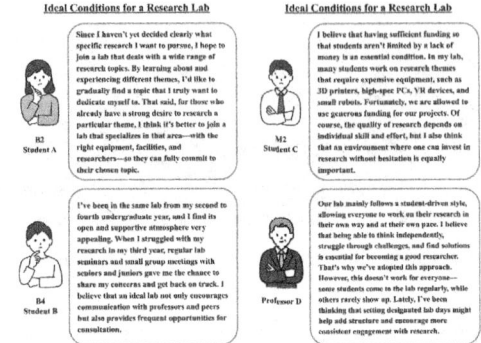

Fig. 5. Example of the shared document in the experimental meeting

Table 2. Example of questionnaire-like chat message

Please keep the content of this chat strictly confidential. Please respond to the following questions using 7-point Likert scale (1: Not at all, 7: Extremely). Here is the example of response, Q1: 3, Q2: 3, Q3: 3.
Q1, I feel anxious about interrupting others when I try to speak.
Q2, I feel anxious about uncomfortable silences occurring.
Q3, I feel stressed about replying to this chat.

be discussed without and with a document. Second, it allows all participants to reflect on their own experiences and can actively engage in the discussion.

3.2 Multitasking Conditions in the Meetings

In each meeting, we tasked participants to browse the document and/or to reply to chat messages as multitasking conditions. In the first half of the discussion, there were two conditions (non-document with non-chat & non-document with chat). In the second half, there were also two conditions (document with non-chat & document with chat).

Document Browsing. In the audio and video meeting, a PDF document (see Fig. 5) was shared using Zoom chat. In the in-person meeting, the same document was shared via Slack [27]. The document summarizes the responses from interviews with other students who are not involved in each meeting. Participants referred to it as needed during the second half of the discussion. We set the document browsing as a multitasking condition because it distracts participants' gaze, which leads to difficulty in checking other participants' nonverbal information.

Chat Replying. In the audio and video meeting, a direct chat message was sent by the experimenter via Zoom chat. In the in-person meeting, the same message was sent via Slack. The chat message consisted of a short introduction, an example of replying, and three questions (see Table. 2). The experimenter sent this in both halves of the discussion

Fig. 6. Example of gaze data preparation using Tobii Pro Lab. Manually mapping of in-person meeting (top-left), assisted mapping of video meeting (top-right), AOI setting in in-person and video meeting (bottom-left and bottom-right).

at one-minute intervals to the participants in random order. We set the chat replying as a multitasking condition because thinking about what to respond and texting increases the cognitive load of the responder. Also, while one participant is replying to a chat message, the other three participants need to circulate the discussion, which increases their workload as well. So, if no one was replying to a chat message, we considered it a non-chat condition, and if one or more of the participants were replying, we considered it a chat condition. We allowed participants to take notes on chat, and we consider taking notes as a non-chat condition because taking notes helps comprehension of the current discussion.

3.3 Setup and Method for Dataset Analysis

Data Preparation. Figure 6 shows the preparation process for gaze data analysis. First, we defined six Area of Interests (AOI i.e., where participants could be looking at) in each dataset using Tobii Pro Lab [28], and labeled them on first-person photographs of each participant. The six AOIs included: previous speaker, non-speaker, self (audio and video only), chat, document, and others. If gaze data were missing, it was labeled as "others". We then manually constructed the utterance timeline from the perspective of one participant, identifying when the speaker started and ended each turn, and synchronized this timeline with those of the other participants. To obtain accurate gaze data throughout the discussion, we combined assisted (automatic) mapping with manual mapping at 10 ms intervals. The resulting complete dataset was exported to Excel, and Python was used to align and process the gaze data.

Data Formatting. We extracted the timeline of turn-taking just after speech collision or silence occurred and manually identified the next speaker's most frequently viewed AOI during 200 ms before turn-taking. To consider network delay [29], 100 ms buffer was applied, in other words, we analyzed gaze direction during 300ms (100 ms extra) before turn-taking in the audio and video meeting. In addition, to address possible shifts

Table 3. The next speaker's gaze direction before taking the turn after speech contention (in-person: left, audio: middle, video: right).

Gaze Direction (In-Person)	Non-Document		Document	
	Non-Chat (N=1)	Chat (N=2)	Non-Chat (N=5)	Chat (N=0)
Previous Speaker	0	1	0	0
Non-Speaker	0	0	0	0
Self	-	-	-	-
Chat	1	0	3	0
Document	-	-	1	0
Others	0	1	1	0

Gaze Direction (Audio)	Non-Document		Document	
	Non-Chat (N=4)	Chat (N=1)	Non-Chat (N=2)	Chat (N=3)
Previous Speaker	1	0	0	0
Non-Speaker	0	0	0	0
Self	0	0	0	0
Chat	3	1	0	1
Document	-	-	2	2
Others	0	0	0	0

Gaze Direction (Video)	Non-Document		Document	
	Non-Chat (N=2)	Chat (N=1)	Non-Chat (N=1)	Chat (N=3)
Previous Speaker	0	0	0	0
Non-Speaker	0	0	0	1
Self	0	0	0	0
Chat	0	1	0	0
Document	-	-	1	1
Others	2	0	0	1

in utterance order due to latency, we determined the sequence of utterances manually by reviewing Zoom recordings from the perspective of non-speakers.

4 Gaze Analysis

The purpose of the analysis is to clarify the role of eye-gaze in turn-taking during multitasking videoconferences. We analyzed the next speaker's most frequently viewed AOI just before 200 ms of turn-taking after speech contention or silence occurred. We believe that this analysis determines the cues for smooth turn-taking since the next speaker should be confident that the turn will be taken smoothly when taking a turn after a non-smooth conversation. To facilitate interpretation of the results, supplementary heat maps are included in the Appendix (see Fig. 7, 8, 9). These figures provide additional context and should be consulted together with the tables in this section.

4.1 Turn-Taking After Speech Contention

Result. Table. 3 shows the result of the next speaker's AOI just before taking a turn after speech contention occurred in each meeting. We gained a total of 8 gaze data from in-person, 10 from audio, and 7 from video meetings, which means there were 8 speech contentions in in-person, 10 in audio, and 7 in video meetings, combining all multitasking conditions. Although the number of data is quite small, it is remarkable that gaze direction to the other participants, such as previous and non-speaker, is less than or equal to that of chat, document, and others in each condition.

Discussion. This result suggests that even after speech contention occurred, the next speaker does not pay much attention to other participants before taking their turn. We expected that the next speaker would start speaking while paying more attention to other participants. However, this result indicates the opposite, the next speaker tends to gaze at chat, document, or others rather than other participants when taking a turn after speech contention occurred. Additionally, the difference in the conditions, in other.

words, the difference in cognitive load did not make significant changes in gaze direction.

Possible reasons for these results are that there was a memo about the discussion using the chat tool in all conditions, so that participants were talking about it and kept their gaze on the chat. From the recording of each meeting, we found that participants were

Table 4. The next speaker's gaze direction before taking turn after silence (in-person: left, audio: middle, video: right).

Gaze Direction (In-Person)	Non-Document Non-Chat (N=24)	Non-Document Chat (N=13)	Document Non-Chat (N=23)	Document Chat (N=12)
Previous Speaker	0	0	0	0
Non-Speaker	1	0	1	2
Self	-	-	-	-
Chat	22	11	16	7
Document	-	-	4	0
Others	2	2	2	3

Gaze Direction (Audio)	Non-Document Non-Chat (N=29)	Non-Document Chat (N=6)	Document Non-Chat (N=23)	Document Chat (N=14)
Previous Speaker	2	0	1	0
Non-Speaker	1	0	1	0
Self	1	0	0	0
Chat	6	3	3	2
Document	-	-	17	12
Others	19	3	1	2

Gaze Direction (Video)	Non-Document Non-Chat (N=16)	Non-Document Chat (N=16)	Document Non-Chat (N=10)	Document Chat (N=15)
Previous Speaker	2	0	0	3
Non-Speaker	4	1	2	2
Self	0	1	0	0
Chat	1	1	2	1
Document	-	-	4	3
Others	9	13	2	6

frequently taking notes on chat, and their discussion was based on its content. Moreover, from the questionnaire, some participants in the video meeting noted that the existence of the shared document fosters conversation but might lead to speech contention. Although this is about speech contention itself and the document, the same thing can be said about the reason why the next speaker was gazing at the chat and document before taking a turn. It is likely that shared memo and document, in other words, shared attention, will be the key to smooth turn-taking.

However, whether the next speaker gazes at other participants may depend on conversation flow and situations. For example, if the previous speaker finished his or her speech completely by mentioning others or making a statement that gives the turn, the next speaker would feel free to take the turn without gazing at other participants. In addition, since we could not analyze the coincidence ratio of shared attention among the next speaker and the other participants, further analysis and discussion are needed to determine whether shared attention contributes to smooth turn-taking. Regardless, given the limited gaze data, these findings may not be generalizable and require further investigation.

4.2 Turn-Taking After Silence

Result. Table. 4 shows the result of the next speaker's AOI just before taking the turn after more than 1700 ms of silence occurred in each meeting. We gained a total of 72 gaze data from in-person, 72 from audio, and 57 from video meetings, which means there were 72 silences in in-person, 72 in audio, and 57 in video meetings combined across all multitasking conditions. Remarkably, gaze direction to the other participants, such as previous and non-speaker, is less than that of chat, document, and others in in-person and audio meetings in each condition, video meeting in non-document & chat condition. However, in video meetings, it is implied that gaze directions are distributed to not only chat, document, and others but also to previous and non-speakers in three conditions (non-document & non-chat, document & non-chat, document & chat).

Discussion. Although most of the results were consistent with that of turn-taking after speech contention, the next speaker tended to gaze at not only chat and document but also other participants, such as previous and non-speakers in a video meeting, except in the non-document & chat condition. This is what we expected, yet the times of gaze direction toward the other participants were relatively fewer than or equal to those of chat, document, and others.

Possible reasons for these results are that during the silence, participants were thinking of ideas while looking up. Tang et al. [30] indicated that even when silence occurred, participants could interpret its cause by observing others' behavior, such as looking upward in thought. Besides, owing to the difficulty of making eye contact in the video meeting, the next speaker can gaze at other participants without hesitation during silence, unlike in an in-person meeting. It is assumed that these factors led to these results. It is likely that not only shared attention on a document or chat but also distributed eye gaze during silence and before taking a turn, in other words, figuring out the cause of the silence by gazing at other participants, is the key to breaking the silence and starting the next turn smoothly.

However, we must be careful that every silence over 1700 ms does not necessarily mean that it is awkward, in other words, a non-smooth conversation. Silence in conversation can stem from various intentions, such as hesitation, cognitive processing, lack of motivation, or shared engagement with materials. Thus, it is important to distinguish between different types of silence into positive and negative silence for a discussion or participants. In addition, the number of each meeting is small, so further analysis is needed.

5 Limitation

5.1 Accuracy of the Collected Dataset

Although we considered network latency in audio and video meetings by applying 100 ms buffers and determining the sequence of utterance from the perspective of non-speakers manually, it is possible that our results may not fully reflect the actual phenomena. There may be discrepancies in the recorded timeline due to a latency, and the same utterance event could be recorded with slight differences in timestamp depending on the participant's perspective. To overcome this limitation, it is necessary to construct individual utterance timelines for each participant while considering precise latency.

5.2 Conditions of the Experiment

We set two multitasking conditions, document browsing and chat replying, but these conditions may not always cause cognitive load to the participants. From the questionnaire and interview, we gained comments related to document browsing: "I think that browsing the document helped us foster smooth conversation", "Information on the document gave me the idea to talk" (in every meeting). Furthermore, we also received opinions on chat replying, "I noticed that other participants were also replying to chat as me, so I could understand that he or she cannot speak right now" (audio and video meeting), "It was easy to find out who was replying to chat because a person was not speaking that much and his eye gaze was looked away" (video meeting). What is worse, although we tasked participants to reply to chat messages, some participants forgot or failed to reply to them. Consequently, there is a possibility that these conditions were not always regarded as multitasking by some participants and did not affect the gaze behavior. Thus, we should consider a new style of document, such as listing the graphs and tables that are related to the discussion topic instead of just listing the ideas for the topic. In addition, we should inform participants that they must reply to the chat message immediately, and the chat condition should be applied only to the participant who is replying to the chat message instead of applying to everyone.

5.3 Insufficient Number of Gaze Data and Detailed Analysis

Although we conducted the experiment that overcomes most of the previous study's limitations, the number of gaze data and the frequency of speech contention were quite low, so our findings may not reflect general trends. In addition, we could not conduct a detailed examination for each multitasking condition and between-group comparison. Such an analysis would allow us to clarify how differently viewing shared documents and responding to chat messages affects cognitive load and gaze patterns. Therefore, further analysis on each multitasking condition and between-group comparison is needed to provide robust insights.

5.4 Future Work

We plan to improve the conditions and conduct further experiments. Furthermore, we will analyze the correlation between the next speaker's gaze direction before turn-taking and the occurrence of non-smooth conversations, using a larger sample size. In addition, we aim to determine whether joint attention to a shared document or chat contributes to fostering smooth turn-taking by analyzing not only the next speaker's gaze direction but also that of other participants and comparing the rate of joint attention. Based on the findings, we intend to develop a system to support smooth turn-taking in a multitasking videoconference from the perspective of joint attention.

6 Conclusion

The purpose of this study was to clarify cues for smooth turn-taking in a multitasking videoconference by analyzing gaze behavior. We conducted the experimental meeting under three conditions (in-person, audio, and video) with two multitasking tasks (document browsing and chat replying) and obtained gaze data from each participant. We investigated the next speaker's gaze direction before turn-taking after non-smooth conversation, such as speech contention or silence. Our findings suggested that joint attention on the same document or memo, as well as inferring the cause of silence by observing other participants before initiating a turn, serve as cues for smooth turn-taking.

As discussed in the Limitation section, we will conduct further experiments to ensure more robust and accurate data analysis. Additionally, we will examine other aspects of turn-taking, gaze behavior of participants beyond the next speaker's gaze. These will lead to generalizing our findings, joint attention, and understanding the motivation behind silence, which can foster smooth conversation. Ultimately, we aim to propose a method to support smooth turn-taking in a multitasking videoconference (Tables 7 and 8).

Acknowledgments. We thank several members of the Kobayashi Laboratory at Meiji University for their cooperation as operators in the experiments. This work was supported by JSPS KAKENHI Grant Number JP22H03635 and 23K24891.

Appendix

Fig. 7. Heatmap visualizations of a participant's gaze during the in-person meeting. Non-document condition (left), and document condition (right).

Fig. 8. Heatmap visualizations of a participant's gaze during the audio meeting. Non-document condition (left), and document condition (right).

Fig. 9. Heatmap visualizations of a participant's gaze during the video meeting. Non-document condition (left), and document condition (right).

Table 5. Definitions of the terms used in our study

Previous speaker	A speaker who was previously speaking
Current speaker	A speaker who has a floor of a speech and currently speaking
Next speaker	A speaker who takes a floor of a speech from previous speaker and speaks next
Non-speaker	A participant who is neither speaking nor involving in a speech
Speech contention	When a person starts speaking within 200 ms after a current speaker starts and an overlap occurred
Silence	When there is a duration over 1700 ms between the end of the previous speaker's speech and the start of the next speaker's speech, and no one is currently holding the floor of a speech
Turn-Taking	When a next speaker takes a floor from a previous speaker and starts speaking

Table 6. The example of descriptive responses from the questionnaire during each type of meeting with a non-document condition. In-person participants were labeled as I-1, I-2, I-3, I-4, audio as A-1, A-2, A-3, A-4, and video as V-1, V-2, V-3, V-4.

Q1: Describe your thoughts on whether the turn-taking was smooth during the first half of the discussion.

"There were many moments of silence, during which everyone seemed to wait for someone else to speak. (I-1)"

"Frequent eye contact made it easier to follow the conversation. It also gave me the sense that others were listening, which encouraged me to share my thoughts. (I-2)"

"Since turn transitions were often preceded by silence rather than occurring instantaneously, I wasn't sure whether they were smooth. However, the fact that speech overlaps were rare could be seen as a sign of smoothness. (I-4)"

"There were brief silences and moments of hesitation as participants seemed to wait for others to speak, which made it slightly difficult to talk. (A-2)"

"There were several instances of overlapping speech. In addition, extended silences occurred when it was unclear who would speak next, which made turn-taking feel less smooth. (A-3)"

"There were moments when I felt some overlap occurred, but since my voice was not picked up well by Zoom, others likely did not notice the overlap. Therefore, it did not seem like a major issue. (A-4)"

"It felt like participants were hesitating out of politeness over who should speak next, which made the pauses feel longer. (V-1)"

"Turn-taking was sometimes facilitated by directly addressing others, and the conversation proceeded smoothly without any speech overlap (V-2)"

"There were few instances of speech overlap, and it felt that everyone was able to contribute to the conversation in a balanced and smooth manner. (V-3)"

Table 7. The example of descriptive responses from the questionnaire during each type of meeting with document condition. Participants were labeled as in the same category as the Table. 6.

Q1: Describe your thoughts on whether the turn-taking was smooth during the first half of the discussion.
"Compared to the first half, participants seemed to become more comfortable with the meeting, and the discussion became more active overall. (I-1)"
"Compared to the first half, I spent more time looking at the document, which made eye contact less frequent and turn-taking more difficult. (I-2)"
"Having the document allowed for more concrete and focused discussion. (I-3)"
"Compared to the first half, the pauses between speakers during turn transitions felt shorter. (I-4)"
"The conversation flowed without many interruptions, and the discussion goals were clear. (A-2)"
"Since the discussion in the first half had already reached some degree of consensus, there were fewer opportunities for open exchange of opinions. As a result, turn-taking felt smoother than in the earlier phase. (A-3)"
"Compared to earlier, there seemed to be fewer pauses, possibly because participants had become more comfortable with the environment or had more to say. At the same time, speech overlaps appeared to occur more frequently. (V-1)"
"The presence of materials and the limited time before the presentation made the discussion more active, which occasionally led to speech overlaps. (V-2)"
"I felt some instances of speech overlap this time. Since I found myself hesitating to find the right timing to speak, I felt that turn-taking was not entirely smooth. (V-3)"

Table 8. The example of descriptive responses from the questionnaire during each meeting with all conditions. Participants were labeled as in the same category as the Table. 6.

Q2: Please tell us your awareness of speech contention during the entire discussions.
"When speech overlaps occurred, both parties tended to hold back, which made harder to express opinions in the subsequent discussion. (I-1)"   "By looking at others' facial expressions and listening to their breathing, I could sense subtle cues that they were about to speak. (I-2)"   "It seemed that all four participants often began speaking during brief moments of silence, when no one else was talking. (I-4)"
"In the first half, I wasn't particularly aware of speech overlaps, but after completing the questionnaire, I became more conscious of them and began waiting for others to finish before speaking. (A-1)"   "I had to pay attention to giving backchannel responses and carefully consider when to start speaking. (A-2)"   "When speech overlaps occur on Zoom, one speaker's voice often gets cut off, creating an awkward situation. Therefore, I tried to be careful during the discussion. (A-3)"   "While I was somewhat conscious of speech contention, I did not strongly sense that others were equally aware. (A-4)"
"I tried to wait until the other person had finished speaking before taking my turn. However, I sometimes thought of things to say just as they were about to finish, which may have led to speech overlaps. (V-1)"   "In the first half, there was sufficient time for discussion, and turn-taking was smooth, often facilitated by directly addressing others during the idea generation phase. In contrast, the second half felt more active due to time pressure and the presence of the document, which seemed to reduce awareness of speech overlaps. (V-2)"   "I try to speak only when it seems that no one else intends to, to avoid speech overlaps. (V-3)"   "I felt that speech overlaps were detrimental to the quality of the meeting. (V-4)"
Q3: Please tell us the effect of the shared document during the entire discussions.
"Having the document allowed the discussion to build on existing ideas rather than starting from scratch, enabling deeper and more expansive conversations. (I-1)"   "Since time was spent looking at the document, it was harder to perceive cues indicating that someone was about to finish speaking. (I-2)"   "The document served as a resource for deepening the conversation in specific discussions. It also enabled continued engagement in the dialogue even while responding to chat messages. (I-3)"   "More ideas emerged when we discussed our own thoughts. In contrast, the document covered topics like those discussed in the first half, so the conversation in the second half felt less developed. (I-4)"
"The discussion about the document stimulated more active participation. (A-1)"   "We were able to talk about the document and exchange opinions on it, which facilitated the conversation. (A-2)"   "Since the content had been largely settled in the first half and everyone was looking at the same document, it was easier to anticipate what others wanted to say, which made turn-taking feel smoother. (A-3)"   "Having access to information made it easier to talk, and I felt that sharing a document with others helped convey nuances more effectively. (A-4)"
"I get accustomed to the multitasking environment and we were discussing more. (V-1)"   "Since the topics became clearer, there were fewer moments of hesitation before speaking. (V-4)"

References

1. Zoom. https://www.zoom.com. Accessed 23 June 2025
2. Microsoft Teams. https://www.microsoft.com/en/microsoft-teams/group-chat-software. Accessed 23 June 2025
3. Choudhury, P., Foroughi, C., Larson, B.: Work-from-anywhere: the productivity effects of geographic flexibility. Strateg. Manag. J. **42**, 655–683 (2020)
4. Tamaki, H., Higashino, S., Kobayashi, M., Ihara, M.: reducing speech contention in web conferences. In: 2011 IEEE/IPSJ International Symposium on Applications and the Internet, pp. 75–81 (2011)
5. Ohnaka, K., Imagawa, T., Iso, K., Ihara, M., Kobayashi, M.: Quantitative Observation to Explore the Turn-Changing Mechanisms of Conversations in Remote Meetings Accompanying Supplemental Materials. CollabTech 2025, vol. 14890, pp. 161–176 (2024)
6. Kendon, A.: Some functions of gaze-direction in social interaction. Acta Psycho logica **26**, 22–63 (1967)
7. Jokinen, K., Nishida, M., and Yamamoto, S.: On eye-gaze and turn-taking. In: Eye Gaze in Intelligent Human Machine Interaction (EGIHMI'10), pp. 118–123 (2010)
8. Richardson, D.C., Dale, R.: Looking to understand: the coupling between speakers' and listeners' eye movements and its relationship to discourse comprehension. Cogn. Sci. **29**, 1045–1060 (2005)
9. Richardson, D.C., Dale, R., Kirkham, N.Z.: The art of conversation is coordination. Psychol. Sci. **18**(5), 407–413 (2007)
10. Rossano, F.: Gaze in Conversation, pp. 308–329. The handbook of conversation analysis, Wiley-Blackwell (2012)
11. Jokinen, K., Furukawa, H., Nishida, M., and Yamamoto, S.: Gaze and turn-taking behavior in casual conversational interactions. ACM Trans. Interact. Intell. Syst. (TiiS) **3**(2), 12, 1–30 (2013)
12. Kendrick, K.H., Holler, J., Levinson, S.C.: Turn-taking in human face-to-face interaction is multimodal: gaze direction and manual gestures aid the coordination of turn transitions. Philos. Trans. R. Soc. B. **378** (2023)
13. Jackson, I.R., Perugia, E., Stone, M.A., Saunders, G.H.: The impact of face coverings on audio-visual contributions to communication with conversational speech. Cogn. Res. Principles Implications **9**(1), 25 (2024)
14. Rutter, D.R., Stephenson, G.M., Dewey, M.E.: Visual communication and the content and style of conversation. Br. J. Soc. Psychol. **20**(1), 41–52 (1981)
15. Chen, M.: Leveraging the asymmetric sensitivity of eye contact for videoconference. In: Proceedings of SIGCHI Conference on Human Factors in Computing Systems, pp. 49–56 (2002)
16. Bekkering, E., Shim, J.P.: Trust in videoconferencing. Commun. ACM **49**(7), 103–107 (2006)
17. Grayson, D.M., Monk, A.F.: Are you looking at me? eye contact and desktop video conferencing. ACM Trans. Comput. Hum. Interact. (TOCHI) **10**(3), 221–243 (2003)
18. Fauville, G., Luo, M., Muller Queiroz, A.C., Bailenson, J.N., Hancock, J.: Nonverbal mechanisms predict zoom fatigue and explain why women experience higher levels than men. Available at SSRN 3820035 (2021)
19. Bullock, A., Colvin, A. D., and Jackson, M. S.: Zoom fatigue in the age of COVID-19. J. Soc. Work Glob. Commun. **6**(1) (2022)
20. Riedl, R.: On the stress potential of videoconferencing: definition and root causes of Zoom fatigue. Electron. Mark. **32**(1), 153–177 (2022)
21. Ansah, A.A., et al.: "I need to respond to this" – contributions to group creativity in remote meetings with distractions. In: Proceedings of the 1st Annual Meeting of the Symposium on Human-Computer Interaction for Work (CHIWORK'22), pp. 1–12 (2022)

22. Cao, H., et al.: Large scale analysis of multitasking behavior during remote meetings. In: Proceedings of the 2021 CHI Conference on Human Factors in Computing Systems, pp. 1–13 (2021)
23. Lee, M., Park, W., Lee, S., Lee, S.: Distracting moments in videoconferencing: a look back at the pandemic period. In: Proceedings of the 2022 CHI Conference on Human Factors in Computing Systems, pp.1–21 (2022)
24. Reinecke, L., et al.: Digital stress over the life span: the effects of communication load and internet multitasking on perceived stress and psychological health impairments in a German probability sample. Media Psychol. **20**(1), 90–115 (2017)
25. Tobii Pro Glasses 2. https://www.tobii.com/en/products/discontinued/tobii-pro-glasses-2. Accessed 23 June 2025
26. Tobii Pro Glasses 3. https://www.tobii.com/en/products/eye-trackers/wearables/tobii-pro-glasses-3. Accessed 23 June 2025
27. Slack. https://slack.com/intl/en-gb. Accessed 23 June 2025
28. Tobii Pro Lab. https://www.tobii.com/products/software/behavior-research-software/tobii-pro-lab. Accessed 23 June 2025
29. Chang, H., Varvello, H., Hao, F., Mukherjee, S.: Can you see me now? a measurement study of Zoom, Webex, and Meet. In: Proceedings of the 21st ACM Internet Measurement Conference, pp. 216–228 (2021)
30. Tang, J.C., Isaacs, E.: Why do users like video? studies of multimedia-supported collaboration. Comput. Support. Cooper. Work (CSCW) **1**, 163–196 (1992)

A Proposal and Evaluation for Externalizing Thoughts of Passive Speakers in Three-Party Video Conferences with Gaze Tracking Functionality

Hiroya Miura[1(✉)], Kimitaka Yamamoto[2], Yoshinari Takegawa[2], and Keiji Hirata[2]

[1] RIKEN, Tokyo, Japan
hiroya.miura@riken.jp
[2] Future University Hakodate, Hokkaido, Japan

Abstract. The proliferation of online video conferencing systems has given people the freedom to choose between online or face-to-face meetings. However, one of the challenges of online video conferences is that when participants (*passive speakers*) lack enthusiasm or initiative in discussions, it often becomes difficult to reach a consensus. To address this, we analyzed the nonverbal characteristics and processes that lead to consensus formation, focusing on the gaze information of passive speakers in three-party video conferences. Furthermore, based on the insights obtained from these survey results, we propose a method to externalize the thoughts of passive speakers in three-party video conferences equipped with gaze tracking functionality. The experimental results demonstrate that the proposed method could externalize the thoughts of passive speakers and facilitate consensus building.

Keywords: Online Communication Support · Passive Speakers · Gaze Tracking

1 Introduction

With the advancement of digital technology, the nature of communication has undergone significant changes [1]. In particular, online meetings have become widely adopted, overcoming geographical constraints through the proliferation of various tools [2]. However, in multi-party video conferences, it is often difficult to interpret nonverbal cues, leading to frequent conversational overlaps and prolonged silences. Additionally, discussions can be dominated by a few participants, making it challenging for all members to express their opinions equally. Therefore, to facilitate smooth consensus building, each participant must clearly convey their intentions [3].

One of the challenges unique to online video conferences is the disparity in participation levels among attendees [4]. In particular, the presence of participants who speak extremely infrequently (hereafter referred to as "passive speakers") can lower the quality of discussions and hinder consensus building [5,6]. Passive speakers often struggle to articulate their opinions clearly, and their nonverbal cues are also difficult to interpret, preventing their intentions from being reflected in the discussion. While direct questioning can encourage their participation, it may disrupt the natural flow of conversation and impose an additional burden on other participants.

The objective of this study is to propose a support method for externalizing the thoughts of passive speakers in three-party video conferences. We aim to capture and share gaze information from all participants, including passive speakers, to infer their interests and concerns, thereby facilitating smoother consensus building. In general, gaze direction is not easily perceivable in multi-party video conferences, but recognizing where participants are focusing is crucial for improving discussion quality [7]. We hypothesize that gaze information remains a valuable indicator of attention even in online environments and seek to promote smoother turn-taking and consensus building through gaze sharing.

To achieve this, we first analyze the gaze behavior of passive speakers in three-party video conferences designed for decision-making and investigate the process leading to consensus formation. Based on the insights obtained, we propose a three-party video conferencing system and user interface (UI) utilizing gaze information and evaluate its effectiveness.

2 Related Studies

In face-to-face conversations, gaze plays a crucial role [8–10], particularly in speaker transitions, where gaze shifts at the end of utterances are significant [11,12]. Furthermore, nonverbal cues are essential for communication in online meetings as well [13]. Previous studies have proposed systems that facilitate smooth speaker transitions by estimating and sharing gaze direction [1,7,14,15], as well as methods that enhance interaction through eye contact or gaze heatmaps [16,17]. While these studies primarily focus on improving communication through gaze visualization, our research leverages gaze as a nonverbal communication tool to enhance discussion quality and facilitate consensus building.

Research on supporting passive speakers has primarily aimed at ensuring psychological safety and encouraging participation, proposing various methods such as nonverbal expressions of intent and personalized feedback [5,18]. These studies have demonstrated that improving the communication environment can increase speaking rates. In contrast, our study introduces a novel approach that utilizes gaze sharing in three-party video conferences to naturally externalize the thoughts and intentions of passive speakers. The novelty of this research lies in its focus on gaze information to support effective communication without relying on direct questioning.

Building on these insights, our research approaches video conferencing systems from a technical perspective, adopting a reductionist approach by focusing on the smallest unit of multi-party conversation: a three-party decision-making meeting. In particular, we focus on passive speakers in online meetings and emphasize gaze information as a key nonverbal cue. Specifically, we aim to validate the following two hypotheses:

- Hypothesis 1: Sharing gaze information facilitates speaker transitions.
- Hypothesis 2: Gaze information enables the externalization of passive speakers' thoughts.

Based on these hypotheses, we develop a system to support the externalization of passive speakers' thoughts, ultimately aiming to facilitate smooth consensus building in three-party video conferences.

3 Recording and Analysis of Three-Party Video Conferences

Based on previous research, we hypothesize that using gaze information as an indicator of discussion and incorporating it into the UI of video conferencing systems can facilitate smoother discussions. Specifically, we assume that participants' thoughts are reflected in their agreement with certain opinions and that they tend to gaze longer at subjects of greater interest or concern. Therefore, this section focuses on analyzing the gaze behavior of passive speakers in video conferences, examining the characteristics and processes of nonverbal communication leading to consensus formation.

3.1 Experimental Setup

We recorded three-party video conferences using a video conferencing system (Zoom)[1] and an online whiteboard tool (Miro)[2] The topic of discussion was planning a summer vacation. One of Miro's core functions is its sticky note feature, which allows participants to write their opinions on sticky notes and display them on a shared online board. This feature is designed to facilitate collaborative idea generation. In our study, participants were instructed to present their thoughts and opinions using sticky notes during the conference. Additionally, one of the three participants was equipped with an eye-tracking device (Tobii Eye Tracker 4C)[3] and a video recording tool (Open Broadcaster Software: OBS)[4] allowing us to capture speech, screen activity, and gaze data (Fig. 1). In this recording, the gaze information of the passive speaker was shared with the other participants.

---

[1] Zoom: https://explore.zoom.us/en/products/meetings.
[2] Miro: https://miro.com/online-whiteboard.
[3] Tobii: https://www.tobii.com/products/eye-trackers.
[4] OBS: https://obsproject.com.

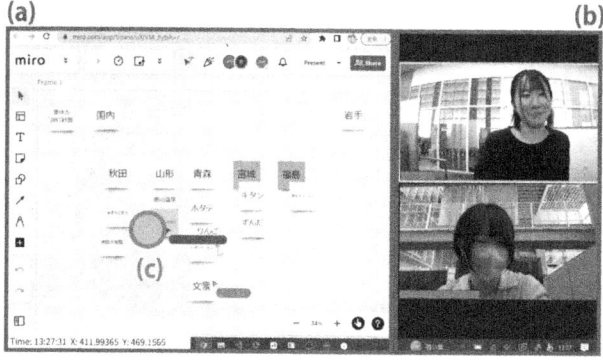

Fig. 1. Recorded screens: (a) Miro, (b) Zoom, (c) gaze information

The experiment participants were 15 university students (10 male, 5 female) divided into five groups, and we recorded each group's video conference (about 20 min each, totaling about 100 min). In this experiment, to assign passive speakers, we instructed one participant, who had their eye-gaze information recorded, to refrain from speaking during the discussion except in response to questions. Additionally, even when the microphone was muted during the discussion, participants were instructed to continuously express their thoughts. After the discussion, we asked the participants to respond to a survey by marking their agreement, disagreement, or neutrality towards the opinions written on sticky notes posted in Miro. Additionally, passive speakers were asked to rank their preferences for proposals raised during the meeting in a survey form.

To process the recorded data, we tagged the position of the passive speaker's gaze in all five video conference recordings using ELAN[5] (Fig. 2). Tags included each sticky note, UI displayed on the screen, cursor, speaker, and listener. To avoid bias in data processing due to tagging by only one person, two authors conducted the tagging, and the inter-annotator agreement was 64.8%.

3.2 Relationship Between Favorable and Unfavorable Opinion Sticky Notes and Gaze Retention Times

An analysis of gaze fixation durations on sticky notes revealed that a total of 133 sticky notes were posted across the five recorded discussions. Table 1 presents the top five sticky notes with the longest gaze fixation durations for Group 5's agreement and disagreement statements. The results indicate that participants tended to gaze longer at agreement-related sticky notes than at disagreement-related ones, a trend observed across all groups.

Table 2 shows the number of agreement/disagreement sticky notes and their average gaze fixation durations for each group. In Groups 1 to 3, agreement-related sticky notes had longer average gaze durations, whereas in Groups 4 and

---

[5] ELAN: https://archive.mpi.nl/tla/elan.

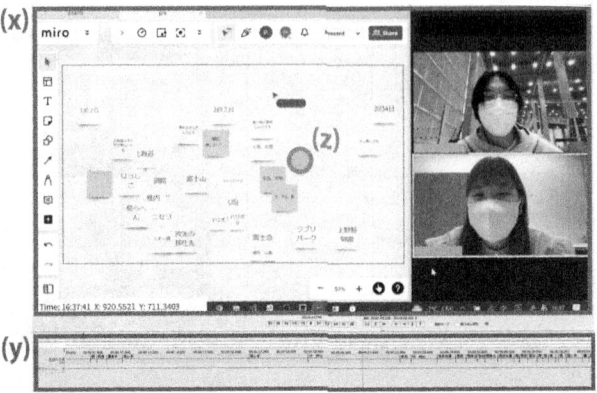

Fig. 2. Gaze position tagged using ELAN: (x) recorded video, (y) gaze information, (z) recording and tagging of gaze retention

Table 1. Overall gaze retention time for favorable/unfavorable sticky notes in Group 5 (top 5)

Opinion	Sticky	Gaze dwell time (sec.)
Favorable	2 nights and 3 days	48.7
	USJ	30.2
	Nara, Kyoto	22.7
	Osaka, Kansai	18.5
	FUJIKYU	17.9
Unfavorable	Fukuoka	22.5
	Food	18.1
	3 nights and 4 days	11.0
	Tokyo	3.8
	Okinawa	3.8

5, disagreement-related sticky notes had longer durations. Since disagreement-related sticky notes were generally fewer in number, gaze fixations were more concentrated on these notes in Groups 4 and 5.

A comparison of gaze fixation durations and participants' rankings of preferred proposals revealed that the sticky notes with the longest fixation durations aligned with the overall group consensus. Specifically, the top four sticky notes listed in Table 1 corresponded with the collective agreement of all participants, suggesting that longer gaze fixation durations may indicate shared interests and influence final consensus formation.

3.3 Correlation Between Gaze Fixation Duration and Passive Speaker Preferences

To examine the relationship between gaze fixation duration and preference rankings for sticky notes, we calculated Pearson's correlation coefficient for each group (Table 3). The results showed a statistically significant trend in Groups 1 and 3, whereas no significant trend was observed in Groups 2, 4, and 5 (at a 10% significance level).

Table 2. Number of favorable/unfavorable sticky notes and average gaze retention time in each group

Group	Opinion	Number of Sticky Notes	Average Gaze Retention Time (sec.)
1	Favorable	19	13.5
	Unfavorable	2	11.2
2	Favorable	21	20.5
	Unfavorable	3	17.4
3	Favorable	24	42.0
	Unfavorable	2	15.1
4	Favorable	18	24.8
	Unfavorable	3	25.7
5	Favorable	15	13.1
	Unfavorable	6	16.0

Table 3. Correlation coefficient between gaze retention time and preference ranking of passive speakers in each group

Group	Correlation Coefficient
1	0.46 ($t = 2.07$, $p = 0.055$, ad.p = 0.055)
2	0.30 ($p = 0.19$)
3	0.41 ($t = 1.99$, $p = 0.060$, ad.p = 0.060)
4	0.11 ($p = 0.66$)
5	0.34 ($p = 0.22$)

For groups where a significant trend was observed, passive speakers tended to gaze longer at agreement-related sticky notes that they ranked higher in preference. This suggests that gaze fixation duration could reveal implicit preferences not directly expressed through speech.

In contrast, the weaker correlations in Groups 2, 4, and 5 may be attributed to participant characteristics and discussion styles. For instance, the correlation between gaze fixation duration and the passive speaker's preference ranking was likely reduced when a facilitator ensured equal discussion time for each sticky note. In Group 4, where the correlation was particularly low, one participant took a leading role in structuring the discussion, allocating equal attention to all sticky notes. Conversely, when discussions were dominated by a specific participant, gazes tended to be concentrated on the notes emphasized by that individual, potentially increasing correlation.

4 Proposal and Implementation of Externalization Methods

4.1 Externalization Method for Passive Speakers

Based on the findings from the previous chapter, we hypothesize that the thoughts of passive speakers manifest as gaze fixation durations. Furthermore, sharing their prolonged gaze on agreement-related opinions or highly interesting topics may facilitate speaker transitions. Therefore, in this study, we propose a method for externalizing the thoughts of passive speakers by capturing and sharing their gaze information with other participants. This approach aims to provide a system that visualizes their thoughts through gaze fixation durations, thereby promoting smooth consensus formation when verbal participation is difficult.

4.2 Presentation Method for Gaze Dwell Time and Its Implementation

Gaze fixation durations for each sticky note are presented using background color intensity. In this method, the longer the gaze fixation duration, the darker the background color of the sticky note, and conversely, the shorter the duration, the lighter the color. The background color intensity S_n is calculated using the gaze fixation duration for each sticky note T_n and the average gaze fixation duration across all sticky notes A, as defined by the following equation:

$$S_n = \frac{T_n}{A} \times 100$$

Since heatmap-based visualization may interfere with online discussions, we adopted the background color intensity approach. Additionally, the proposed method is designed to present gaze fixation durations not only for sticky notes but also for other UI elements, such as camera feeds and additional interface components.

4.3 System Configuration

The system was implemented as a web application using JavaScript, HTML, and CSS (Fig. 3). For communication functions and the transmission of gaze

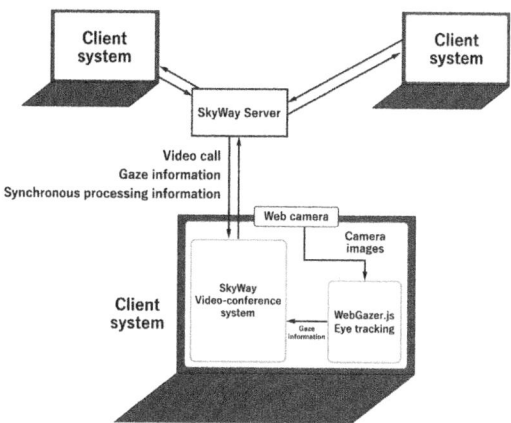

Fig. 3. System configuration

information and sticky note position data, we utilized SkyWay[6] a WebRTC platform. Gaze information was captured using WebGazer.js [19], a JavaScript library for detecting gaze points on a display. The obtained gaze data was used to calculate gaze fixation durations for each sticky note, which were then visualized through background color intensity. These gaze-related data were shared with participants via SkyWay.

Figure 4 shows the system interface displaying users' gaze fixation durations. Users can right-click anywhere on the screen to create sticky notes and move them freely using drag-and-drop operations. Additionally, by toggling the "Display My Gaze Fixation Duration" button at the top center of the screen, users can check their own gaze fixation durations through background color intensity. The system can also individually display other participants' gaze fixation durations.

5 Experimental Settings

5.1 Experiment Content

The objective of this experiment is to verify whether other participants can accurately understand the thoughts of passive speakers by referencing their gaze fixation durations. In the experiment, three participants engaged in a discussion using an online meeting system, aiming to reach a consensus on a given topic. For the task, we adopted Guilford's Alternative Uses Task (AUT) [20], which is commonly used for creativity assessment. The AUT requires participants to discuss and propose novel uses for a given object beyond its conventional function.

For example, if the object presented is a pot, participants would brainstorm alternative uses beyond its typical role as a cooking utensil. In this experiment,

---

[6] SkyWay: https://skyway.ntt.com/en/.

participants were given 15 min to come up with three alternative uses for a prespecified object. They then worked together to reach a consensus on a single best alternative use from a total of nine proposed ideas. The objects used in this experiment were a pot, a hanger, and a sock, selected based on the following three criteria:

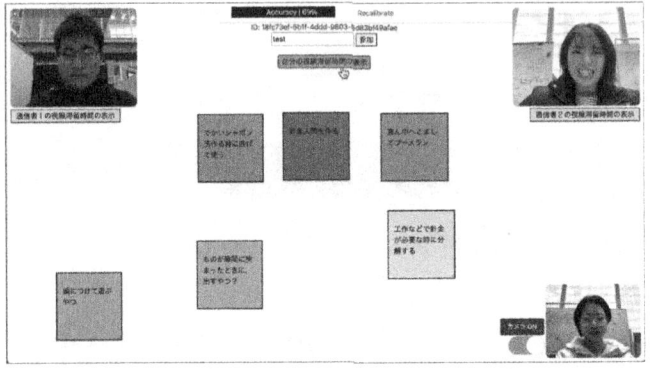

Fig. 4. System usage screen

- Topics that are moderately understandable and not too detailed
- Topics that have not been used for brainstorming new uses before
- Topics where devising new uses is not overly difficult

The effectiveness of the proposed method was evaluated through two experimental tasks, one where gaze information is shared (proposed method) and one where it is not shared (comparative method).

5.2 Experiment Participants and Setting of Passive Speakers

This experiment was conducted as a within-subjects study, where each participant experienced both the proposed and baseline methods. A total of 12 university students (7 male, 5 female) participated in the study, divided into four groups of three participants each. To minimize psychological stress from unfamiliar interactions, participants were grouped with people they already knew.

In each group, one participant was designated as the passive speaker and instructed to refrain from speaking unless directly responding to a question. All participants joined the online meeting using their own computers and headsets. During the experimental task using the proposed method, participants were instructed to refer to the gaze fixation durations displayed by the system when conducting their discussion.

5.3 Experiment Procedure

The experimental procedure is illustrated in Fig. 5. Before starting the main experiment, participants completed a questionnaire in which they brainstormed three alternative uses for each of the assigned objects as part of the AUT process. Next, participants were given explanations about the task and system operation. To account for potential learning effects, a practice task using a pot as the object was conducted before the main experiment.

For the main experimental tasks, the gaze calibration process was completed before starting the discussions. Participants then engaged in discussions using the system, focusing on a hanger and a sock' as the objects. The order of presentation for the experimental conditions and objects was randomized.

After each discussion, the passive speaker was asked to rank the proposed alternative uses based on their preference. The two other participants were asked to rank their own preferences and to predict the passive speaker's preference rankings. Finally, participants completed a questionnaire evaluating their impressions of the gaze fixation duration visualization method.

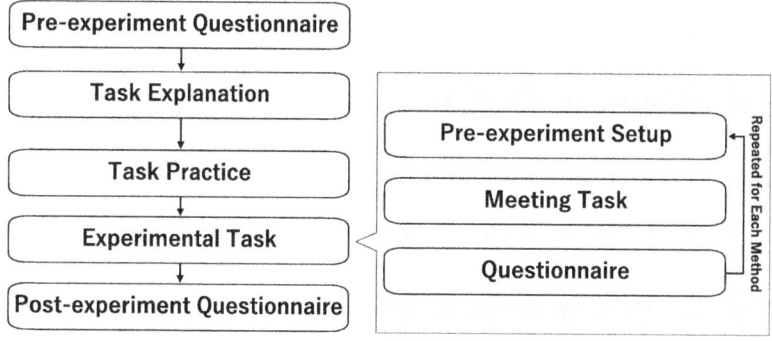

Fig. 5. Experimental Procedure

6 Experimental Results

6.1 Conversational Dynamics and Impression Evaluation of the Visualization Method

Figure 6 shows the average number of utterances per participant and the proportion of total discussion time occupied by speaking in each method. The Shapiro-Wilk test [22] for normality on utterance counts indicated non-normality; thus, we conducted a sign test using an exact binomial test. Although no significant difference was observed, more participants tended to speak more frequently in the baseline method than in the proposed method ($p = 0.062$, two-tailed test).

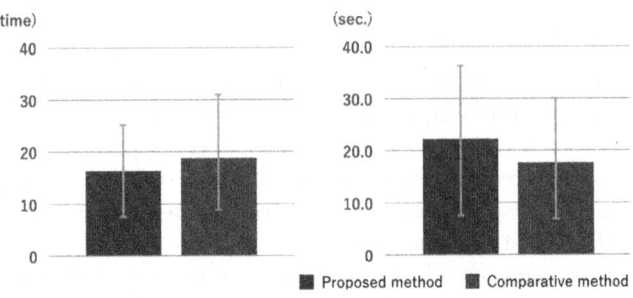

Fig. 6. Average number of utterances (left) and average percentage of speaking time (right) in each method

Table 4. Average value of answer items regarding presentation method (7-point Likert scale)

ID	Question Item	Average Value
1	Was the color gradation easy to recognize?	6.00
2	Did you feel like displaying it for a long time?	4.50
3	Did you feel like using it frequently?	6.17
4	Were you able to express your opinion to the other person?	5.67
5	Did you show interest in the other person?	6.34
6	Did you perceive it as the other person's opinion?	5.33
7	Did you perceive it as the other person's interest or concern?	6.00

For the proportion of speaking time, normality was confirmed, and a paired t-test was performed, but no significant difference was found ($p = 0.292$, two-tailed test).

Table 4 presents the results of the impression evaluation (7-point Likert scale) regarding the method for visualizing gaze fixation durations. The passive speakers responded to questions 1–5, while the other participants answered questions 1–3, 6, and 7.

6.2 Agreement Rate of Preference Ranking

We calculated the agreement rate between the preference rankings of passive speakers and the predicted rankings by the other participants (A & B) for each group (Table 5). The degree of agreement was assessed using Kendall's coefficient of concordance [21]. The average agreement rate was 68.1% ($SD = 0.168$) for the proposed method and 56.3% ($SD = 0.269$) for the baseline method. To examine the influence of similarity in preference rankings, we computed the rank correlation coefficients between passive speakers and other participants in each group. The results showed a high correlation ($r > 0.6$) in Groups 1 and 2 and a low correlation ($r < 0.3$) in Groups 3 and 4.

Table 5. Concordance rate of predicted preference rankings for passive speakers

Group	Subjects	Proposed Method (p-value)	Comparative Method (p-value)
1	A	0.72 (0.005)	0.71 (0.010)
	B	0.78 (0.002)	0.53 (0.055)
2	A	0.29 (0.358)	0.31 (0.272)
	B	0.61 (0.024)	0.81 (0.004)
3	A	0.66 (0.015)	0.76 (0.006)
	B	0.89 (0.001)	0.82 (0.003)
4	A	0.72 (0.005)	0.00 (1.000)
	B	0.78 (0.002)	0.56 (0.044)

For the proposed method, a significant difference in agreement rates was observed for Participant A & B in Group 1, Participant B in Group 2, Participant A & B in Group 3, and Participant A & B in Group 4 ($p < 0.05$). In the baseline method, significant differences were found for Participant A in Group 1, Participant B in Group 2, Participant A & B in Group 3, and Participant B in Group 4 ($p < 0.05$). A sign test using an exact binomial test was conducted for each participant's agreement rate, but no significant difference was found ($p = 0.726$, two-tailed test). The Cliff's delta effect size was $\Delta = 0.219$, indicating a small effect.

6.3 Differences Between Top, Middle, and Bottom Tiers of Preference Rankings

To evaluate the effects of the proposed method in more detail, we calculated the differences (hereafter referred to as "ranking differences") between the preference rankings of the passive speakers and the rankings predicted by other participants for the top (1st–3rd), middle (4th–6th), and bottom (7th–9th) tiers. The results are shown in Table 6, and their average is presented in Fig. 7.

The Shapiro-Wilk test for ranking differences among participants in the top tier indicated non-normality. No significant difference was observed between the

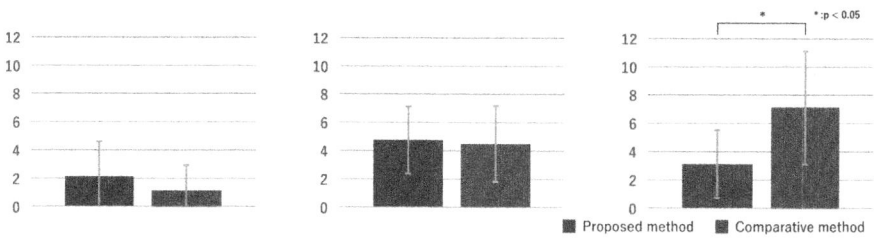

Fig. 7. Average rank difference between top (left)/middle (center)/bottom (right) predicted preference rankings for passive speakers

Table 6. Difference in top/middle/bottom rankings for predicted preference rankings of passive speakers

-	Group	Subjects	Proposed Method	Comparative Method
Top	1	A	7	2
		B	4	0
	2	A	1	0
		B	0	2
	3	A	2	5
		B	3	0
	4	A	0	0
		B	0	0
Middle	1	A	8	6
		B	5	1
	2	A	5	2
		B	5	6
	3	A	2	9
		B	3	6
	4	A	8	3
		B	2	3
Bottom	1	A	5	12
		B	1	5
	2	A	2	6
		B	1	8
	3	A	4	14
		B	2	6
	4	A	8	3
		B	2	3

two methods using the exact binomial test for the sign test (p = 0.687, two-tailed test). The effect size $\Delta = 0.266$ according to Cliff's delta, indicating that the proposed method had a small effect. The Shapiro-Wilk test for the middle tier ranking differences indicated normality. The paired t-test results showed no significant difference between the two methods (p = 0.865, two-tailed test). The effect size d = 0.0989 according to Cohen's d, indicating that the effect of the proposed method was not significant. The Shapiro-Wilk test for the bottom tier ranking differences indicated non-normality. A significant trend was observed in the results of the Wilcoxon signed-rank test for the two methods (p = 0.07, two-tailed test). The effect size $\Delta = 0.688$ according to Cliff's delta, indicating that the proposed method had a large effect.

7 Discussion

7.1 Can the Proposed Method Accurately Externalize the Thoughts of Passive Speakers?

The presentation method based on the proposed approach effectively functioned as a cue for appropriate speaker transitions. As shown in the results of Sect. 6.1, there was no significant difference between the two methods in terms of the average number of utterances and the ratio of average speaking time. However, while the number of utterances decreased, the proportion of speaking time increased. This suggests that the proposed system facilitated smooth speaker transitions without dispersing the discussion, thereby enabling more efficient conversation. This may be attributed to the proposed method's use of the density of gaze fixation time as an indicator of individual opinions and as a cue to initiate new discussions. In the actual experiment, in 64.7% of cases following utterances by reluctant speakers, after they had checked the information on gaze fixation, their statements were immediately followed by related discussion.

In contrast, in the comparative method, 74.5% of utterances by reluctant speakers were followed by a transition to a different topic. This may be due to the difficulty in visually interpreting cues for the next discussion. Moreover, during the consensus-building phase at the end of the discussions, three out of four groups ultimately relied on the density-based gaze representation as a final indicator. This suggests that visual confirmation of this representation contributed to appropriate speaker transitions and enabled the groups to reach a consensus based on a comprehensive understanding of each participant's opinions. Furthermore, since the final consensus aligned with the gaze density patterns, it can be inferred that smooth speaker transitions were achieved, leading to effective consensus formation. Taken together, these findings suggest that the density-based representation of gaze fixation time provided by the proposed method serves as a useful indicator for understanding opinions, facilitating appropriate speaker transitions, and supporting consensus building.

7.2 Can Gaze Externalize the Thoughts of Passive Speakers?

The proposed method, which utilizes gaze information, was found to be an effective means of externalizing the thoughts of passive speakers. According to the impression evaluation results in Sect. 6.1 (Table 4), participants found the intensity-based visualization of gaze fixation durations to be intuitive and appropriately displayed when needed. Passive speakers themselves reported that the method made it easier to express their opinions and interests, while other participants actively used gaze fixation durations as an indicator of engagement during discussions. However, visibility issues arose in the later stages of discussions, suggesting a need for improvements in color brightness adjustments and other display methods.

As noted in Sect. 6.2, no significant difference was observed in preference ranking agreement rates. This may be because active participation and the clustering of sticky notes in discussions allowed participants to infer general opinions without relying solely on gaze information. Meanwhile, Sect. 6.3 revealed that the proposed method had a smaller ranking discrepancy in lower-ranked preferences, with a large effect size. This suggests that participants were able to accurately recognize the passive speaker's lower-ranked preferences. In the baseline method, discussions related to disagreement by passive speakers were limited, making it difficult to grasp their rankings. However, in the proposed method, sticky notes with lighter background colors were more easily recognized as lower preferences.

Additionally, gaze fixation durations tended to be interpreted as reflecting group consensus, and the proposed method was particularly effective in cases where preference ranking discrepancies were small (Groups 1 and 2). Even in groups with larger discrepancies (Groups 3 and 4), the method still proved effective, indicating that the proposed approach is particularly useful for capturing lower-ranked preferences.

8 Conclusion

In this study, we focused on the gaze behavior of passive speakers in three-party video conferences and analyzed the characteristics and processes of nonverbal communication leading to consensus formation. Based on the insights gained from our investigation, we proposed a method to support the externalization of passive speakers' thoughts through gaze sharing and designed a corresponding system. Specifically, we developed a mechanism that visualizes passive speakers' thoughts by representing gaze fixation durations on sticky notes through variations in background color intensity. The experimental results demonstrated that the proposed method effectively facilitates speaker transitions, supports appropriate externalization of passive speakers' thoughts, and contributes to smoother consensus formation.

Future work includes UI improvements to enhance visibility, detailed conversational analysis using the proposed system, and extending the approach to multimodal dialogues with four or more participants. Additionally, incorporating features to actively encourage passive speakers to speak could lead to a more effective video conferencing system for thought externalization.

References

1. Tamaki, H., Higashino, S., et al.: Reducing speech contention in web conferences. In: Proceedings of the IEEE/IPSJ International Symposium on Applications and the Internet (SAINT 2011), pp. 75–81 (2011)
2. Osler, L., Zahavi, D.: Sociality and embodiment: online communication during and after Covid-19. Found. Sci. **28**(4), 1125–1142 (2023)
3. Hamada, Y., Shoji, H.: A study on the feature analysis of the success pattern of consensus building processes. Trans. Japan Soc. Kansei Eng. **16**(1), 43–50 (2017)

4. Hamada, Y., Takahashi, N., Shoji, H.: A comparison of online and face-to-face consensus-building processes. Trans. Japan Soc. Kansei Eng. **21**(1), 41–48 (2022)
5. Nabetani, K., Muraoka, T., et al.: Introducing a discussion support system using individual audio instruction to activate passive members. In: Proceedings of the IEEE International Conference on Engineering, Technology and Education (TALE 2021), pp. 550–557 (2021)
6. Nishida, T.: Designing social interaction support system with shyness in mind. In: Proceedings of the 2018 ACM International Conference on Supporting Group Work (Group 2018), pp. 140–144 (2018)
7. Iitsuka, R., Kawaguchi, I., Shizuki, B., Takahashi, S.: Multi-party video conferencing system with gaze cues representation for turn-taking. In: Hernández-Leo, D., Hishiyama, R., Zurita, G., Weyers, B., Nolte, A., Ogata, H. (eds.) CollabTech 2021. LNCS, vol. 12856, pp. 101–108. Springer, Cham (2021). https://doi.org/10.1007/978-3-030-85071-5_8
8. Argyle, M., Dean, J.: Eye-contact, distance and affiliation. Sociometry **28**(3), 289–304 (1965)
9. Ishii, R., Otsuka, K., et al.: In predicting next speaker and timing from gaze transition patterns in multiparty meetings. In: Proceedings of the ACM International Conference On Multimodal Interaction (ICMI 2013), pp. 79–86 (2013)
10. Vertegaal, R., Slagter, R., et al.: Eye gaze patterns in conversations: there is more to conversational agents than meets the eyes. In: Proceedings of the CHI Conference on Human Factors in Computing Systems (CHI 2001), pp. 301–308 (2001)
11. Kendon, A.: Some functions of gaze-direction in social interaction. Acta Physiol. **26**, 22–63 (1967)
12. Jokinen, K., Nishida, M., Yamamoto, S.: Eye-gaze experiments for conversation monitoring. In: Proceedings of the International Universal Communication Symposium (IUCS 2009), pp. 303–308 (2009)
13. Vargas, M.F.: Louder than words: an introduction to nonverbal communication. Iowa State University Press (1986)
14. Mukawa, N., Oka, T., et al.: What is connected by mutual Gaze? User's behavior in video-mediated communication. In: Proceedings of the CHI Conference Extended Abstracts on Human Factors in Computing Systems (CHI EA 2005), pp. 1677–1680 (2005)
15. Kobayashi, K., Komuro, T., et al.: A gaze-preserving group video conference system using screen-embedded cameras. In: Proceedings of the ACM Symposium on Virtual Reality Software and Technology (VRST 2017), pp. 1–2 (2017)
16. Maeda, K., Arakawa, R., Rekimoto, J.: CalmResponses: displaying collective audience reactions in remote communication. In: Proceedings of the International Conference on Interactive Media Experience (IMX 2022), pp. 193–208 (2022)
17. Burch, M.: Gaze-based monitoring in the classroom. In: Proceedings of the Symposium on Eye Tracking Research and Applications (ETRA 2023), no. 81, pp. 1–3 (2023)
18. Nishimoto, K., Wang, H.: CosplayChat: an online discussion system to elicit diverse viewpoints within individuals. In: Proceedings of the International Conference on Knowledge, Information and Creativity Support Systems (KICSS 2009), pp. 89–96 (2009)
19. Papoutsaki, A., Sangkloy, P., et al.: Webgazer: scalable webcam eye tracking using user interactions. In: Proceedings of the 25th International Joint Conference on Artificial Intelligence (IJCAI 2016), pp. 3839–3845 (2016)
20. Guilford, J.P.: Creative abilities in the arts. Psychol. Rev. **64**(2), 110–118 (1957)

21. Kendall, M., Smith, B.B.: The problem of m rankings. Ann. Math. Stat. **10**(3), 275–287 (1939)
22. Shapiro, S.S., Wilk, M.B.: An analysis of variance test for normality (complete samples). Biometrika **52**(3), 591–611 (1965)

Temporal Analysis of User Engagement, Technology Trends and Emotional Dynamics on Stack Overflow

Linda Okpanachi[✉][iD], Gema Rodríguez-Pérez[iD], and Ifeoma Adaji[iD]

Department of Computer Science, University of British Columbia, Okanagan, Canada
lindaa15@student.ubc.ca, gerope@mail.ubc.ca, ifeoma.adaji@ubc.ca

Abstract. This study presents a temporal analysis of user engagement, technology trends, and emotional dynamics on Stack Overflow across the pre-COVID, during-COVID, and post-COVID periods. Understanding these changes is crucial to identifying long-term shifts and enhancing digital engagement strategies in online developer communities. This is especially important during global disruptions like COVID-19, which reshape work patterns, collaboration, and community interactions. In this study, users were categorized by reputation and badges based on Stack Overflow's reward system. For example, regular users were regarded as newer contributors, intermediate users are moderately active participants, and expert users are those who are highly trusted and recognized for their significant contributions and expertise. Our analysis revealed that engagement declined post-COVID, with regular users experiencing the steepest drop. Intermediate users showed signs of disengagement, strengthening the phenomenon of 'leaky pipeline', while expert users recovered the fastest in terms of engagement post-COVID. Technology trends shifted toward full-stack development and AI, and emotional analysis indicated high confusion and frustration during COVID, followed by increased admiration and approval after the pandemic, reflecting improved knowledge exchange. These findings provide actionable insights for fostering sustained participation and inclusivity in technical communities.

Keywords: Stack Overflow · Post Quality · User Engagement · Emotional Expression · User Categories · User Modeling · Temporal Analysis

1 Introduction

The COVID-19 pandemic caused by the coronavirus SARS-CoV-2 [33] resulted in multiple dynamic changes to different aspects of society [12]. One area that saw such change was the technology sector. As interactions shifted online and with the rapid adoption of digitalized platforms for remote education and work, developers relied even more heavily on virtual platforms for support and collaboration [12].

The Stack Overflow platform, created in 2008, has since grown to become one of the largest and most active online communities for developers. The platform hosts millions of questions and answers on a wide range of programming topics, making it an invaluable resource for both new and experienced developers [7]. During the pandemic, this platform became even more critical [14], providing a unique vantage point to observe long-term changes in user behavior, technology trends, and overall community dynamics [25].

Understanding these shifts is essential for developing user models that are accurate and reflective of the changing behavior of different user categories. However, user behavior does not change uniformly, as it is also affected by external disruptions, new technologies, and changing learning paradigms. Thus, by studying user behavior across different user groups and temporal periods, we can separate short-term fluctuations from long-term behavioral shifts on Stack Overflow. These insights are important for knowledge sharing, user retention, and personalized support in technical communities [36]. We focus on engagement, technology, and emotion as complementary dimensions that together capture participation, topical evolution, and affective climate.

Previous studies like those of Oliveira et al. [24] and Odiete et al. [23] analyzed varying trends on Stack Overflow but were either carried out before the pandemic began or focused on the immediate effects of the COVID-19 pandemic. Limited attention has been given to the long-term shifts in developer behavior across distinct user categories and temporal phases, especially in the evolving post-pandemic period.

Therefore, this study addresses this gap by analyzing user engagement, technology trends, and emotional expressions across three distinct phases: pre-COVID (January 1, 2018 – December 31, 2019), during-COVID (January 1, 2020 – December 31, 2020), and post-COVID (January 1, 2021 – December 31, 2023). The pre-COVID period represents a stable baseline, the during-COVID period represents major changes mainly due to the global work-from-home trend and increased use of digital collaboration tools, and the post-COVID period represents a transitional phase where developer engagement stabilized after the disruptions of 2020 [10,20].

To provide a detailed analysis across the three phases, we categorized users into three groups: regular, intermediate, and expert users. We based this division on engagement metrics such as badges, reputation scores, and privileges [30], which represent quantifiable indicators of contribution quality and expertise.

We address the following research questions:

RQ1: How do user engagement patterns and post quality on Stack Overflow vary across different user categories (Regular, Intermediate, Expert)?

RQ2: How have user interactions with technological topics evolved on Stack Overflow across pre-, during-, and post-COVID periods?

RQ3: How did emotional expressions among different user categories on Stack Overflow evolve pre-, during-, and post-COVID periods?

Through this analysis, the study provides a data-driven foundation for understanding the evolution of developer interactions on Stack Overflow. The findings have implications for online learning platforms, developer forums, and AI-driven moderation, particularly in sustaining engagement and improving adaptive support in technical knowledge-sharing ecosystems.

2 Related Works

2.1 User Engagement and Post Quality

Prior work explored how the pandemic influenced developer activity on platforms like Stack Overflow and GitHub. Oliveira et al. [24] and Klotzman et al. [17] observed increased engagement during early COVID months, especially in questions related to Python and data visualization. Wang et al. [32] similarly noted higher contributions on GitHub. However, these studies offered limited insight into how engagement patterns varied across distinct user categories or how these patterns evolved post-COVID. Our work extends prior efforts like Adaji and Vassileva [1] by focusing on segmented users (regular, intermediate, expert) across temporal phases.

2.2 Technology Trends

Moutidis et al. [22] tracked the evolution of technologies on Stack Overflow from 20082020, noting growth in Python and R. Georgiou et al. [12] added that web development and ML tools saw increased mentions during COVID. Yet, there is limited exploration of how different user types engaged with these technologies across time. Our study addresses this gap by examining topic usage trends by user category.

2.3 Emotional Dynamics

Emotions in developer discussions reveal user satisfaction and learning challenges. Hosseinzadeh [14] used LIWC to detect sentiment shifts but didn't analyze trends by user type or time period. Newer studies like Batra et al. [8] and Bleyl and Buxton [9] applied BERT-based models for emotion detection but lacked longitudinal analysis. We build on these by segmenting user emotion trends across three phases.

2.4 Research Contributions

Past studies mostly focused on pandemic-era trends or general activity. Our work uniquely analyzes user engagement, post quality, technology trends, and emotional dynamics across user types and time phases—contributing a more comprehensive view of Stack Overflow's evolving ecosystem.

3 Methodology

3.1 Categorizing Users on Stack Overflow

To better understand contributions on Stack Overflow, we categorized users into three distinct groups based on reputation scores and badges: regular, intermediate, and expert users. This classification is consistent with previous research like the studies by Adaji and Vassileva [1,23] who classified users based on in-degree, reputation, privileges, and badges.

Reputation Scores: Stack Overflow employs a reputation system where reputation scores reflect a user's contributions and community trust[1]. According to Stack Overflow, a member is considered to be an established user if they have at least 1,000 reputation points, and a trusted expert user has between 20,000+ reputation points [26].

Badges are awards that are given for various activities like getting certain reputation thresholds, participating in community events, posting helpful answers, and demonstrating expertise in certain topics[2]. Bronze badges are given to recognize entry level achievements and participation. Silver badges are given to users with intermediate level of participation and expertise. Gold badges are given to users with high level of participation and expertise, and are given for very rare and high quality actions.

Building on this foundation, we defined three user categories which are: expert users (trusted users), intermediate users (established users) and the remaining active users as regular users (new or novice users).

Therefore, each user type is fully defined as follows:

- **Regular users:** Regular users are those with a reputation score less than 1000 and hold bronze badges. These users are relatively new contributors but are present on the platform.
- **Intermediate users:** Intermediate users are those with a reputation score between 1000 and 19,999 and have silver badges. These users are moderately active and participative in the platform.
- **Expert users:** Expert users are those with a reputation score of 20,000 or higher and hold gold badges. These users are trusted and recognized for their high level of participation and expertise.

Defining User Engagement and Post Quality. User engagement was measured by the total number of posts made by each user, including questions and answers, upvotes and downvotes. This metric gives an overall picture of user participation. To determine the quality of the posts, the proportion of unanswered questions to the total number of questions for all the users was calculated.

$$\text{Unanswered Question Ratio} = \frac{\text{Unanswered Questions}}{\text{Total Questions}}$$

---

[1] https://stackoverflow.com/help/whats-reputation.
[2] https://stackoverflow.com/help/badges.

This metric captures problems in formulating questions, relevancy of the questions asked or even the level of engagement within the community. High levels of unanswered questions may be an indication of low quality questions or topics where users need to concentrate more on asking better questions that are easier to comprehend [4].

3.2 Statistical Analysis

Given that our study examines three distinct time periods, a one-way ANOVA test was used to compare differences in engagement across these phases. To verify the assumptions of normality and homogeneity of variances, we applied the Shapiro-Wilk test and Levene's test, respectively. These tests confirmed that the data distributions were suitable for parametric analysis. ANOVA allows us to determine whether the variations in user activity are statistically significant across the three periods [21]. Additionally, we applied Tukey's HSD post-hoc test to identify which specific periods differed significantly from each other, ensuring a more granular understanding of engagement trends [3].

3.3 Data Collection for User Engagement and Post Quality

Data was collected from Stack Overflow via the Stack Exchange Data Explorer[3] using SQL queries structured to filter posts and comments by user category based on reputation and badges, time frame, and tags across the three periods.

- pre-COVID (January 1, 2018 - December 31, 2019): This period serves as a baseline to understand user behavior and engagement on Stack Overflow before the pandemic began. It provides a reference point for comparing subsequent changes.
- during-COVID (January 1, 2020 - December 31, 2020): The during-COVID phase accounts for the gradual onset of the pandemic. This takes into account when precautionary measures began to take effect up until when the pandemic was at its peak and lockdown, social distancing measures, and remote work became the norm [34].
- post-COVID (January 1, 2021 - December 31, 2023): The post-COVID phase represents the period of recovery and adjustment as societies and economies began to reopen after the pandemic. This phase (20212023) represents a transitional period marked by hybrid work adoption, online learning, and shifts in digital collaboration tools.

To maintain consistency and ensure comparability across the three phases, the average values were computed for each phase enabling a balanced analysis.

---

[3] https://data.stackexchange.com/.

3.4 Technology Trend Analysis

To examine how technological trends evolved on Stack Overflow, we collected posts spanning the three time frames. Our dataset included user posts categorized by the predefined user groups. Each post contained metadata such as post titles, body content, associated tags, user ID, and reputation score. The tags indicate the programming languages, frameworks, and technologies discussed on the platform. Given the large number of unique tags, we focused on the fifteen (15) most frequently occurring tags for each user category within each period. This selection was based on frequency to ensure that only the most widely discussed and relevant technologies were included in the analysis.

We computed tag frequencies for each user category and time frame, ensuring a segmented perspective of how each user group engaged with various technologies. We then visualized the trends using a line graph to illustrate changes in the popularity of programming languages, frameworks, and tools over time.

3.5 Emotion Dynamics Analysis

In our study, we employed EmoRoBERTa, a domain-adapted transformer model for emotion detection. Unlike sentiment analysis, this model categorizes posts into specific emotional states, allowing for a deeper understanding of developer emotions. The model was used to determine the emotional content of user posts and classify them into different categories such as anger, confusion, anxiety, and fear [16].

Furthermore, the detected emotions were linked to the respective posts and their associated tags to determine emotional expression patterns as a function of developer discussions. The choice of EmoRoBERTa is supported by its effectiveness in previous research, such as Lopez-Lopez et al. [19], who applied it to studentteacher conversations and validated its predictions using generative models like ChatGPT and Bard.

The dataset used was extracted from the Stack Exchange Data Explorer and included `PostTitle` and `PostBody`, which served as input for emotion classification. `PostTags` were used to associate detected emotions with relevant programming technologies. The preprocessed text was then passed to EmoRoBERTa, which categorized each post into one of several emotional states, such as anger, frustration, joy, or fear. To explore how different technologies correlated with emotions, we linked each detected emotion to the associated tags and aggregated the distributions across all three periods. For posts associated with multiple emotions, we selected the most dominant emotion within each category.

4 Results

This section presents the findings from the analysis of user engagement and post quality, technological trends, and emotional expressions on Stack Overflow. For ease of analysis, we split RQ1 into two parts: RQ1a: *How do user engagement patterns on Stack Overflow vary across different user categories*, and RQ1b: *How does post quality on Stack Overflow vary across different user categories?*

4.1 RQ1a: User Engagement Analysis

The overall trend in user engagement showed a decline from 2018 to 2023 (via upvotes/downvotes), with peak periods during-COVID as shown in Fig. 1. However, the most significant decline was experienced post-COVID.

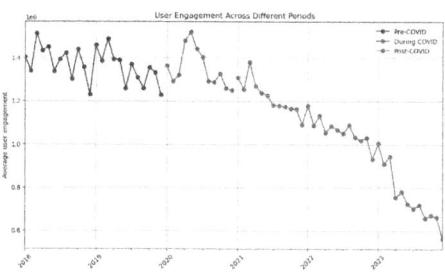

Fig. 1. User engagement for all user categories across all periods

To better understand engagement, we delved into user segmentation based on the three user categories.

Regular Users: Regular users experienced a decline in both questions and answers, with a 27.88% drop in questions and a 14.36% decline in answers during COVID, followed by further declines post-COVID. They were also found to ask more questions than they provided answers. Visual summary is available at image1.

Intermediate Users: Intermediate users provided more answers than they asked questions. Specifically, there was a 64.49% decrease in the average questions asked per user during-COVID period compared to the pre-COVID period and 10.82% increase in questions asked post-COVID compared to the during-COVID period. However, answer activity steadily declined over the three periods. Visual summary is available at image2.

Expert Users: Expert users saw the largest engagement decline during COVID (−65.43% for questions, −53.13% for answers) but also the highest post-pandemic recovery as question engagement rose by 21.06%, and answers increased by 39.41%. Visual summary is available at image3.

4.2 Statistical Analysis of User Engagement

The result from the ANOVA is shown in Table 1.

The results of the ANOVA showed significant variations in user engagement across time periods ($p < 0.0001$ for all user categories). Additionally, the Tukey

Table 1. ANOVA Results for User Engagement

User Category	Metric	F-Statistic	P-Value
Regular Users	Questions	585.76	<0.0001
Regular Users	Answers	111.11	<0.0001
Intermediate Users	Questions	298.45	<0.0001
Intermediate Users	Answers	259.91	<0.0001
Expert Users	Questions	183.54	<0.0001
Expert Users	Answers	102.63	<0.0001

HSD tests revealed statistically significant engagement differences, particularly between pre-COVID and during-COVID periods. Results from the Tukey HSD test are available in the OSF repository: User Analysis.

4.3 RQ1b: Post Quality Analysis

We assessed post quality using the unanswered question ratio, which indicates the percentage of questions without an accepted answer.

Table 2. Unanswered Questions Across Time Periods

User Category	Pre-COVID	During COVID	Post-COVID
Regular Users	15%	10%	23%
Intermediate Users	5%	6%	9%
Expert Users	1%	2%	3%

Key Observations from Table 2 indicate that regular users saw a decrease in unanswered questions during COVID (10%), but post-COVID, the rate increased significantly to 23%. Also, intermediate users experienced a steady increase in unanswered questions, rising from 5% pre-COVID to 9% post-COVID. Expert users remained the most reliable responders, but their unanswered question ratio moved from 1% to 3% post-COVID.

Additionally, the tags associated with unanswered questions revealed recurring topics across all user categories and periods. The prevalent tags include `Python`, `JavaScript`, `C#`, `Java`, and `C++`. Expert users however, also encountered questions tagged with `Type Script` and `C++` more frequently, highlighting unique challenges within advanced topics.

4.4 RQ2: Technology Trends on Stack Overflow

Regular Users: Before COVID-19, discussions focused on programming languages like `C#`, `Java`, `Python`, and `C`, along with database technologies such as

SQL and SQL Server. Web technologies (JavaScript, HTML, and jQuery) and platform-specific topics (Windows and iPhone) had steady engagement. During COVID-19, interest in JavaScript, C#, and Ruby on Rails grew, suggesting a shift toward web and full-stack development, while database and platform discussions remained stable. Post-COVID, C# saw a sharp rise, followed by Java, Python, and JavaScript, while frameworks like ASP.NET and Ruby on Rails, as well as technologies like PHP, SQL, and Windows, retained relevance.

Intermediate Users: Key insights show that the pre-COVID period showed a strong focus on Git, SQL Server, Apache Spark, and ASP.NET Core. However, during the pandemic Java and C# became more prominent, while discussions on software design patterns and cloud computing increased. Post-COVID, there was a preference for front end development and cloud based technologies indicated by the increase in usage of JavaScript, TypeScript, and Azure DevOps. Additionally, JavaScript and SQL remained consistently present across all periods.

Expert Users: Expert users predominantly engaged in discussions on C#, Node.js, Docker, and AWS-related technologies. The COVID-19 period saw an increase in Python, C++, and security-focused technologies, including OAuth 2.0 and cryptography. Post-COVID, programming languages like Python, Java, and C# remained dominant, while frameworks like Next.js and React.js and technologies such as Azure DevOps and cloud-based deployment tools gained traction.

See visual summaries for regular, intermediate, and expert users respectively, available at: Regular, Intermediate, and Expert.

4.5 RQ3: Emotional Dynamics in Developer Discussions

Regular Users: Our findings show that for regular users, the most common emotional expressions were: *neutral* (45.15%), *confusion* (24.03%), *curiosity* (23.54%), *gratitude* (3.64%), and *admiration* (3.64%). We also noticed an increase in the confusion emotion during the pandemic, especially for C#, however, this significantly decreased post-COVID. Also, curiosity remained high for Java and Python, indicating consistent engagement with these technologies across all periods. Additionally, positive emotions such as admiration and approval appeared more prominently post-COVID, particularly for C++ and C#.

Intermediate Users: The results for intermediate users show that the prominent emotional expressions on Stack Overflow across pre-COVID, during, and post-COVID were: *neutral*(51.89%), *confusion*(24.36%), *curiosity*(17.48%), *realization*(4.40%), and *admiration*(1.88%). We observed an increase in the *confusion* emotion during the pandemic, especially for JavaScript(26.59%), and Java(24.84%), suggesting that intermediate users faced increased challenges during this period. However, while confusion remained relatively high for JavaScript(25.00%) and Java(24.49%) post-COVID. We noticed a slight rise in positive emotions such as *admiration* and *approval* for Python, indicating a more satisfying experience with the language after the pandemic.

Expert Users: For expert users, the prominent emotional expressions on Stack Overflow across pre-COVID, during, and post-COVID were: *neutral* (51.06%), *confusion* (26.01%), *curiosity* (17.20%), *realization* (3.68%), and *disapproval* (2.05%). The results shows consistent *confusion* emotion, particularly for Python(31.58% pre-COVID, 24.13% during and post-COVID), highlighting ongoing challenges even with popular languages. Java, while showing high *curiosity* (29.17% pre-COVID), exhibited lower levels of positive emotions, indicating its continued complexity for expert users. However, there was a slight increase in *approval* and *admiration* for Python post-COVID, suggesting increased satisfaction after overcoming difficulties during the pandemic.

See emotional analysis visualizations for each user group at: Regular users, Intermediate users, and Expert users.

The dataset, analysis for each trend, statistical analysis, and images are available via the link: Files.

5 Discussion

5.1 Segmented User Analysis: Engagement and Post Quality Across Experience Levels

While the overall decline in engagement is evident, examining user categories offers deeper insight. Although the total number of unanswered questions decreased, the ratio of unanswered questions to total posts increased post-COVID. This paradox suggests fewer questions were asked, but those remaining were harder to answer.

Engagement among regular users dropped most significantly post-COVID, possibly reflecting a shift in how this group interacts with the platform. Though the reasons are beyond our scope, this aligns with Stack Overflow's own reports of declining traffic [28]. The drop could be due to changing work environments, shifting user priorities, and increased reliance on AI tools. Stack Overflow has long served as a knowledge base for beginners. The reduced activity among this group suggests possible barriers in framing clear questions, which is essential to participation [11,31,35]. This challenge worsened post-COVID, with the unanswered question ratio rising from 10% to 23% possibly reflecting a struggle to meet Stack Overflow's clarity standards [5].

Intermediate users also declined during COVID, particularly in asking and answering questions. While question rates improved post-COVID, unanswered ratios still rose. This reflects the "leaky pipeline" problem in technical communities, where users struggle to remain active contributors [6]. Though specific causes are not analyzed here, possible factors include changing responsibilities, motivation, or platform norms. Structured mentorship from expert users could help retention [27].

Expert users experienced the steepest engagement drop during COVID (−65.43% in questions, −53.13% in answers), but also the strongest recovery afterward. This supports findings that high-reputation users are essential to platform sustainability [2]. Their temporary disengagement may have been due to pandemic-related stress [15]. Still, they consistently had the lowest rate of unanswered questions and demonstrated robust post-COVID recovery.

5.2 Technology Trends on Stack Overflow

The analysis reveals both consistent and evolving trends in technology interaction across the pre-COVID, during-COVID, and post-COVID periods. Certain technologies, including `Python`, `JavaScript`, and `C#`, maintained consistent engagement across all user levels, emphasising their foundational role in software development. Similarly, frameworks like `React.js`, `Node.js`, and `TypeScript` remained relevant, reflecting their importance in scalable and robust application development. The presence of these technologies across user categories suggests that regardless of expertise, developers prioritize mastering tools central to modern programming.

However, distinct patterns still emerged across user categories. Regular users mostly interacted with foundational technologies like `Java`, `C`, and `HTML`, commonly taught in formal education and tutorials. During COVID-19, engagement with `JavaScript` and `C#` increased, suggesting a shift toward more accessible web frameworks—possibly due to the rise of online learning platforms and bootcamps [13]. Intermediate users engaged with backend and scalable systems like `PHP`, `Node.js`, and `TypeScript`, indicating a shift to maintaining more complex systems. Expert users showed increased use of `AWS`, `Git`, and `SQL`, pointing to deeper focus on cloud-native architecture and system optimization. Unlike other groups, expert users prioritized infrastructure reliability, aligning with trends in scalable and cloud-integrated solutions [29].

Technology adoption trends during the post-COVID phase (20212023) may also reflect broader industry shifts (e.g., AI assistants, full-stack frameworks) independent of the pandemic; future work should examine year-by-year variation to capture these dynamics more clearly.

5.3 Emotional Dynamics in Developer Discussions

Across all user categories, a common trend during the pandemic was a decline in engagement, increased confusion, and emotional strain. The stress of remote work, job loss, and rapid technological changes made learning harder and increased frustration—especially with complex languages like `C#`. Post-COVID, all groups expressed more positive emotions as they engaged with `Python`, `JavaScript`, and `C++`. This aligns with the accessibility of online courses, YouTube tutorials, and AI-powered coding assistants, which may have helped users regain confidence and learn new technologies [18]. Despite challenges, the post-COVID motivation boost shows developers at all levels were emotionally driven to enhance their skills.

What set each category apart was how they responded to challenges. Regular users struggled most with confusion, especially with C#, while maintaining curiosity for Python and Java, indicating a desire to learn. Intermediate users faced frustration with JavaScript and Java, likely due to shifts in web frameworks and remote work, but later developed appreciation for Python as they pursued growth. Expert users showed consistent confusion, particularly with Python, suggesting even seasoned developers faced adaptation challenges. Java remained a frequent topic among experts, yet fewer positive emotions reinforced its complexity.

Taken together, declining engagement, the pivot to AI/full-stack topics, and shifting emotional tone suggest interconnected dynamics, where novel, complex technologies may drive both disengagement and heightened user uncertainty.

6 Implications and Threats to Validity

Stack Overflow has a general approach to user engagement, offering the same set of features to all users regardless of their expertise or learning goals. While this facilitates ease of access, it does not fully address the specific difficulties encountered by various user groups. To enhance engagement and knowledge retention for all learners, strategies should be put in place to encourage participation and ensure long-term community sustainability.

Enhancing Personalized Support for Regular Users: Implementing systems such as real-time query assistants or recommendation systems can guide users in formulating effective questions and finding relevant solutions. Also, individual steering such as directing new users to well-documented solutions or learning pathways could reduce similar questions and enhance interaction. Previous research has shown that structured scaffolding techniques can improve the quality and engagement of questions [11,31].

Collaborative Features for Intermediate Users: Intermediate users transitioning between foundational and advanced knowledge would benefit from peer collaboration tools that connect users of similar skills to work together on solutions and share knowledge. Structured contributions such as allowing them to gain visibility by answering beginner questions or participating in Q&A challenges can also motivate engagement.

Retaining Expert Users: Expert users are responsible for high-quality contributions and knowledge preservation. While their engagement remained relatively stable, ensuring continued participation is critical. This could include advanced filtering options to help them find complex questions where their expertise is most needed. Additionally, providing visibility into trending topics and advanced technologies can keep them at the forefront of discussions [2].

Supporting Long-Term Retention and Community Growth: There is also a need for systems that offer progressive learning tracks tailored to each user's progress. These would include personalized pathways guiding users from foundational skills to advanced content. Beyond user-specific strategies, improving Stack Overflow's engagement model overall could support long-term knowledge retention and community growth.

Our findings offer meaningful insights into user behavior across experience levels, but certain limitations must be considered when interpreting results.

Selection and Survivorship Bias: The dataset may not fully represent the Stack Overflow user base, as it focuses on users with sustained activity. This excludes those who joined or dropped out during the study periods, potentially limiting generalizability. Focusing on sustained users introduces survivorship bias; analyzing users who disengaged could provide complementary insights into community dynamics.

Temporal and Measurement Bias: The chosen time frames (pre-, during-, and post-COVID) may not fully capture all behavioral transitions. Additionally, metrics like unanswered question ratios and engagement counts do not reflect all dimensions of user interactions. Our use of the unanswered question ratio as a proxy for post quality is limited, as high values may also reflect niche or complex problems; future work should integrate additional indicators such as edits or comment sentiment.

External Validity and Confounding Factors: Given Stack Overflow's unique structure, the results may not extend to other developer communities. Broader influences such as industry shifts, evolving technologies, and platform-specific changes may also affect user behavior independently of the pandemic.

While our results describe what changed, qualitative follow-ups (e.g., surveys or interviews) could clarify why developers' behaviors shifted.

7 Conclusion

This paper explored user engagement, technology trends, and emotional dynamics on Stack Overflow during the pre-COVID, COVID, and post-COVID eras. The results of the study revealed that while there was an overall trend in platform engagement across all user categories, regular users experienced the sharpest decline. A look at post quality for these users further indicated that this drop could be attributed to problems in formulating questions and receiving answers. For intermediate-level users, engagement levels dropped for both questions and answers, with the answer rate showing continued decline post-COVID. This we ascribed to their shifting engagement from the role of learners to that of contributors. Experts' participation was steady, which suggests that they act as knowledge supporters.

The emotional analysis revealed that all user categories were most likely to feel confused and curious during the COVID period, but after the pandemic, admiration and approval started to emerge as the most prevailing emotions. This may indicate that experts' contributions were better appreciated and the knowledge exchange process became more effective. These findings suggest that personalized support is required to enhance engagement, assist new users, encourage participation of intermediate users, and retain experts. Therefore, to ensure sustained participation, it is crucial for platforms like Stack Overflow to implement features such as structured mentorship, AI-assisted question refinement, and tailored engagement incentives to ensure knowledge retention and overall community health.

These findings contribute to a deeper understanding of long-term user engagement on Stack Overflow and provide actionable strategies to enhance knowledge retention in online technical communities. This can also inform the design of collaboration platforms by aligning moderation and support tools with user expertise and emotional needs. By jointly analyzing engagement, technology, and emotion, this study offers a unique multi-perspective view of Stack Overflow's evolution across pandemic phases.

References

1. Adaji, I., Vassileva, J.: Predicting churn of expert respondents in social networks using data mining techniques: a case study of stack overflow. In: Proceedings of the 2015 IEEE 14th International Conference on Machine Learning and Applications (ICMLA), Miami, FL, USA, pp. 102–107. IEEE (2015). https://doi.org/10.1109/ICMLA.2015.22
2. Anderson, A., Huttenlocher, D., Kleinberg, J., Leskovec, J.: Discovering value from community activity on focused question answering sites: a case study of stack overflow. In: Proceedings of the 18th ACM SIGKDD International Conference on Knowledge Discovery and Data Mining (KDD 2012), pp. 850–858. Association for Computing Machinery, New York (2012). https://doi.org/10.1145/2339530.2339661
3. Argyrous, G.: Statistics for Research: With a Guide to SPSS, 3rd edn. SAGE Publications, Los Angeles (2011). Accessed 30 Jan 2023
4. Asaduzzaman, M., Mashiyat, A.S., Roy, C.K., Schneider, K.A.: Answering questions about unanswered questions of stack overflow. Department of Computer Science, University of Saskatchewan, Canada, and University of Toronto, Canada (2013)
5. Atwood, J.: Asking better questions (2010). https://stackoverflow.blog/2010/10/04/asking-better-questions/. Accessed 26 Jan 2025
6. Bachschi, N., Contributors, S.: Exploring the leaky pipeline phenomenon on stack overflow. In: Proceedings of the International Conference on Online Community Engagement, pp. 56–67. Association for Computing Machinery (ACM), New York (2020)
7. Barua, A., Thomas, S.W., Hassan, A.E.: What are developers talking about? An analysis of topics and trends in stack overflow. Empir. Softw. Eng. **19**(3), 619–654 (2014). https://doi.org/10.1007/s10664-012-9231-y
8. Batra, H., Punn, N.S., Sonbhadra, S.K., Agarwal, S.: Bert-based sentiment analysis: a software engineering perspective. arXiv preprint arXiv:2106.02581 (2021). https://doi.org/10.48550/arXiv.2106.02581
9. Bleyl, D., Buxton, E.K.: Emotion recognition on stackoverflow posts using bert. In: Proceedings of the 2022 IEEE International Conference on Big Data (Big Data 2022), Los Angeles, CA, USA, pp. 5881–5885. IEEE (2022). https://doi.org/10.1109/BigData55660.2022.10020161. https://ieeexplore.ieee.org/document/10020161/

10. Company, M..: The state of organizations 2023: Ten shifts transforming organizations (2023). https://www.mckinsey.com/capabilities/people-and-organizational-performance/our-insights/the-state-of-organizations-2023
11. Gao, Z., Xia, X., Lo, D., Grundy, J.: Technical Q&A site answer recommendation via question boosting. arXiv preprint arXiv:2210.15753 (2022). https://arxiv.org/abs/2210.15753
12. Georgiou, K., Mittas, N., Chatzigeorgiou, A., Angelis, L.: An empirical study of covid-19 related posts on stack overflow: topics and technologies. J. Syst. Softw. **182**, 111089 (2021). https://doi.org/10.1016/j.jss.2021.111089
13. GitHub Octoverse: The state of open source and rise of AI in 2023. GitHub Blog (2023). https://github.blog/news-insights/research/the-state-of-open-source-and-ai/
14. Hosseinzadeh, P., Zareipour, M., Baljani, E., Moradali, M.R.: Social consequences of the covid-19 pandemic: a systematic review. Investigación y Educación en Enfermería **40**(1), e10 (2022). https://doi.org/10.17533/udea.iee.v40n1e10
15. Hsiao, J.H., Peng, S.W., Lin, Y.T.: Stressors, burnout, and coping mechanisms: implications for online knowledge-sharing communities. J. Knowl. Manag. **16**(3), 441–453 (2012). https://doi.org/10.1108/13673271211246179
16. Kamath, R., Ghoshal, A., Eswaran, S., Honnavalli, P.B.: An enhanced context-based emotion detection model using roberta. In: Proceedings of the 2022 IEEE International Conference on Electronics, Computing and Communication Technologies (CONECCT), Bangalore, India, pp. 1–6. IEEE (2022). https://doi.org/10.1109/CONECCT55679.2022.9865796. https://ieeexplore.ieee.org/document/9865796
17. Klotzman, V., Farmahinifarahani, F., Lopes, C.: Public software development activity during the pandemic. In: Proceedings of the 15th ACM/IEEE International Symposium on Empirical Software Engineering and Measurement (ESEM 2021), pp. 1–12. ACM, New York (2021). https://doi.org/10.1145/3475716.3475778
18. Li, X., Odhiambo, F.A., Ocansey, D.K.W.: The effect of students' online learning experience on their satisfaction during the covid-19 pandemic: the mediating role of preference. Front. Psychol. **14** (2023). https://doi.org/10.3389/fpsyg.2023.1095073. https://www.frontiersin.org/articles/10.3389/fpsyg.2023.1095073/full
19. López-López, A., García-Gorrostieta, J.M., González-López, S.: Emotion detection in educational dialogues by transfer learning. J. Intell. Fuzzy Syst. 1–11 (2024). https://doi.org/10.3233/JIFS-219340
20. Microsoft: The 2022 work trend index: Annual report (2022). https://www.microsoft.com/en-us/worklab/work-trend-index
21. Montgomery, D.C.: Design and Analysis of Experiments, 9th edn. Wiley, Hoboken (2017). Accessed 30 Jan 2023 edn. (2017), accessed: 2023-01-30
22. Moutidis, I., Williams, H.: Community evolution on stack overflow. PLOS ONE **16**, e0253010 (2021). https://doi.org/10.1371/journal.pone.0253010
23. Odiete, O., Jain, T., Adaji, I., Vassileva, J., Deters, R.: Recommending programming languages by identifying skill gaps using analysis of experts: a study of stack overflow. In: Adjunct Publication of the 25th Conference on User Modeling, Adaptation and Personalization (UMAP 2017), pp. 159–164. ACM, New York (2017). https://doi.org/10.1145/3099023.3099040
24. de Oliveira, P.A.M., de Alcântara dos Santos Neto, P., Silva, G., Ibiapina, I., Lira, W., de Castro Andrade, R.M.: Software development during covid-19 pandemic: an analysis of stack overflow and github. arXiv preprint arXiv:2103.05494 (2021). https://arxiv.org/abs/2103.05494. Presented at the 3rd ICSE Workshop on Software Engineering for Healthcare

25. Peruma, A., Simmons, S., AlOmar, E.A., Newman, C.D., Mkaouer, M.W., Ouni, A.: How do i refactor this? An empirical study on refactoring trends and topics in stack overflow. Empir. Softw. Eng. **27**(1), 1–35 (2022). https://doi.org/10.1007/s10664-021-10045-x
26. Robinson, D.: Does anyone actually visit stack overflow's home page? Stack Overflow Blog (2017). https://stackoverflow.blog/2017/03/09/does-anyone-actually-visit-stack-overflows-home-page/. Accessed 02 July 2024
27. Smailes, J., Gannon-Leary, P.: Peer mentoring - is a virtual form of support a viable alternative? Res. Learn. Technol. **19** (2011)
28. Stack Overflow: Insights into stack overflow's traffic: We're setting the record straight (2023). https://stackoverflow.blog/2023/08/08/insights-into-stack-overflows-traffic/. Accessed 08 Jan 2025
29. Stack Overflow: Stack Overflow Developer Survey 2023 (2023). https://survey.stackoverflow.co/2023. Accessed 11 Mar 2025
30. Stack Overflow: Stack overflow badges: Understanding reputation and achievements (2024). https://stackoverflow.com/help/badges. Accessed 30 Jan 2024
31. Ulfa, S., Surahman, E., Fatawi, I., Hirashima, T.: Development of adaptive instructional scaffolding on online forum discussion to improve personalization in MOOCS learning environments. In: Proceedings of the International Conference on Learning Technologies. State University of Malang and Universitas Terbuka, Indonesia (2021). https://eric.ed.gov/?id=ED615548
32. Wang, L., Li, R., Zhu, J., Bai, G., Su, W., Wang, H.: Understanding the impact of covid-19 on github developers: a preliminary study. In: Proceedings of the 33rd International Conference on Software Engineering and Knowledge Engineering (SEKE 2021), pp. 249–254. Knowledge Systems Institute Graduate School, Pittsburgh, PA, USA (2021). https://doi.org/10.18293/SEKE2021-132
33. World Health Organization: Coronavirus disease (covid-19) pandemic. World Health Organization (2020). https://www.who.int/europe/emergencies/situations/covid-19. Accessed 02 July 2024
34. World Health Organization (WHO) Regional Office for Europe: Coronavirus disease (covid-19) pandemic (2023). https://www.who.int/europe/emergencies/situations/covid-19. Accessed 20 Dec 2024
35. Yang, L., Ma, Y., Cheng, J.: Question quality in community Q&A sites: a case study of stack overflow. arXiv preprint arXiv:1710.04692 (2017). https://arxiv.org/abs/1710.04692
36. Zhou, J., Bhat, S.: Modeling consistency using engagement patterns in online courses. In: Proceedings of the 11th International Learning Analytics and Knowledge Conference (LAK 2021), pp. 226–236. ACM, New York (2021). https://doi.org/10.1145/3448139.3448161

Do You See What I See? Vocal Cues to Visual Acuity Discrepancies in VR-Based Stargazing

Sora Iida(✉) and Satoshi Nakamura

Meiji University, 4-21-1 Nakano, Nakano-ku, Tokyo, Japan
sorabun.iida@gmail.com

Abstract. Stargazing often involves conversation about celestial objects, but perceptual differences such as visual acuity can cause misalignments in what participants see, making communication difficult. As a preliminary investigation, this study examined how visual acuity differences influence conversational behavior during collaborative stargazing. In a VR-based constellation search task, we compared pairs with matched and unmatched acuity. Although results were not statistically significant, consistent trends emerged: more clarification requests, higher question frequency, and longer response latency under acuity differences. These findings suggest that perceptual asymmetry may affect mutual understanding and point to the potential of conversation-based support systems.

Keywords: Stargazing · Conversation · Visual acuity difference · VR

1 Introduction

In collaborative tasks, perceptual differences in what participants see can create communication challenges. To our knowledge, this study is among the first to investigate, through vocal cues, how discrepancies in visual acuity affect conversation during the specific activity of stargazing. While stargazing is a shared activity, communication can be difficult because stars are distant and hard to distinguish. Such perceptual misalignments can disrupt conversation and shared recognition.

Existing tools attempt to reduce these misalignments. Mobile applications such as Star Walk2 [16] and Sky Guide [5] align perceptions by displaying the same screen. In addition, prior research has developed stargazing support systems [10–12]. Among them, AR-based systems overlay constellation information or support recognition tasks [14,17]. Furthermore, physical means such as laser pointers are also used to point at stars. However, both digital and physical aids are often impractical in natural stargazing: screen brightness impairs dark adaptation, and laser pointers are unsuitable for outdoor use.

To address this gap, we adopt a conversation analysis perspective. Research shows that clarification questions, repair initiators such as "Eh?" [7] or

"Huh?" [4], and turn-taking patterns [3,13,15] are key to maintaining mutual understanding. Yet, prior work has largely focused on linguistic or cognitive asymmetries, with little attention to the *perceptual asymmetries* arising from vision differences. Although vision research has used VR/AR to study the impact of impairments such as low vision or color deficiencies [1,2,6], these investigations emphasized individual performance rather than collaborative dialogue [8,9].

Against this background, we investigate how visual acuity differences influence conversation during collaborative stargazing. Using a VR-based constellation search task, we analyze conversational features such as clarification requests, occurrences of "Eh?", and response latency. Our study serves as an initial step toward conversational support systems that can detect and mediate perceptual asymmetries in real time. We are guided by the following research question:

How do visual acuity differences between partners influence conversational behavior during a shared stargazing task?

The contributions of this study are summarized as follows:

1. We introduced a novel perspective by focusing on conversation content during collaborative stargazing. This area had been overlooked in previous research, which primarily addressed visual aids or learning outcomes.
2. We proposed and implemented a VR-based simulation environment in which visual acuity could be systematically varied between two participants while preserving a shared visual field. This enabled controlled experiments on perceptual asymmetry in naturalistic dialogue.
3. We conducted an empirical study with manipulated visual acuity differences and suggested that such differences tended to bring about measurable changes in conversational behavior. Specifically, we observed tendencies toward increased clarification requests such as "Eh?", higher question frequency, and longer response latency.
4. We provided initial evidence that perceptual asymmetry affects mutual understanding in visually grounded dialogue. This finding lays the groundwork for future conversational support systems, for example, voice assistants that intervene when misalignments are detected.

2 Experiment

To examine how visual acuity differences influence conversational behavior, we designed a VR-based constellation search task. Participants collaborated under conditions where their visual acuity was either matched (Equal) or different (Unequal). We analyzed conversational indicators such as clarification questions, "Eh?" utterances, and response latency.

We tested the following hypotheses:

H1. Clarification questions will occur more frequently in the Unequal condition than in the Equal condition.
H2. "Eh?" utterances will occur more frequently in the Unequal condition than in the Equal condition.

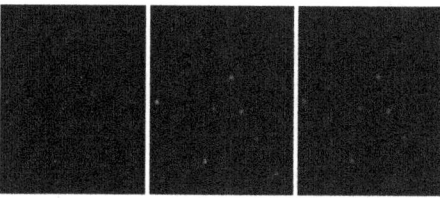

Fig. 1. Simulated views of the star field under each visual acuity condition, from left to right: Good, Normal, Poor.

Fig. 2. Examples of synthetic constellations used in the experiment, from left to right: Cat, Butterfly, Moai.

H3. Response latency between speaker turns will be longer in the Unequal condition than in the Equal condition.
H4. Subjective ratings of conversational smoothness will be lower in the Unequal condition than in the Equal condition.

System. The system was implemented in Unity and presented using Meta Quest 3. A star field of several hundred stars, created for this study, was arranged on a hemispherical dome, with varied sizes to approximate natural appearance. Three visual acuity levels (Good, Normal, Poor) were simulated using different levels of blur (Fig. 1). To provide common reference points, simple landmarks such as mountains and planets were included. Avatars were omitted, so participants could not directly see each other's gaze or pointing gestures.

Task and Design. Each pair was assigned fixed roles: a *Describer*, who explained the target constellation verbally, and an *Identifier*, who attempted to locate it. Four star field patterns containing 14 synthetic constellations were used (Fig. 2). To support explanations, the Describer was given supplementary information about constellation shapes. In the experiment, we compared two conditions: the Equal condition, in which both participants had the same level of visual acuity, and the Unequal condition, in which their visual acuity levels differed. Combinations of Good and Poor visual acuity levels were excluded.

Participants and Procedure. Before the experiment, participants completed a questionnaire and received instructions on roles and procedures. In each trial, the Describer studied the target constellation and explained it, while the Identifier attempted to locate it. Each trial lasted up to 10 min, followed by a brief questionnaire on conversational smoothness and recognition alignment. This sequence was repeated across conditions. Eight participants (5 male and 3 female), all members of the same laboratory, took part in the experiment. They were undergraduate and graduate students aged 20 to 23. All had a visual acuity of 0.7 or higher (with or without corrective lenses) and no astigmatism that affected daily activities. Each participant was paired with others two or three times and participated in three or four conversation trials per pairing. To prevent overfamiliarization with all three visual acuity conditions within a single star field, only two acuity levels were assigned per star pattern.

3 Results

3.1 Analysis

To analyze question frequency, we followed previous research on utterance classification and divided both Describer and Identifier utterances into individual Idea Units (IUs). One IU was defined as a single simple sentence. In cases involving compound or multiple sentences, we counted them as two IUs. We then classified all IUs into the following nine categories:

- **Explanation**: Describes what the speaker sees or explains the shape and position of a constellation.
- **Confirmation**: Checks whether the listener shares the same perception.
- **Question**: Seeks clarification or repetition.
- **Response**: Provides answers to questions, confirmations, or requests.
- **Request**: Affects conversation flow, such as "Please wait" or "Can you repeat that?".
- **Backchannel**: Listener feedback like nods or utterances such as "uh" or "Eh?".
- **Incomplete**: Utterances that stop mid-sentence without continuation.
- **Gaze instruction**: Specifies directions for finding a constellation.
- **Other**: Unrelated talk or self-directed speech.

Response latency was measured as the interval between speaker turns, using the *pyannote.audio* speaker diarization model and excluding within-speaker pauses.

In addition, we focused on the Japanese token "Eh?", which functions as a repair initiator indicating recognition misalignment. Following prior work, we treated the frequency of "Eh?" utterances as an objective measure of recognition misalignment.

3.2 Subjective Evaluations of Conversation

Table 1 summarizes participants' questionnaire ratings. Overall, conversational smoothness and comprehension were consistently rated higher in the Equal condition than in the Unequal condition. This suggests that matched visual acuity facilitated smoother interaction and better mutual understanding. Participants also reported less conversational fatigue when visual acuity was matched.

Regarding strategies, Describers tended to begin with the constellation's name and shape, often referring to bright landmarks such as Mercury or Mars. Identifiers reported repeatedly checking information and attempting to visualize the constellation shape. These findings suggest that participants actively adapted their explanation and listening strategies depending on their partner's condition.

3.3 Objective Measures of Recognition Misalignment

Time to Constellation Recognition Alignment. We analyzed thirty conversations, equally divided between the Equal and Unequal conditions. For each conversation, we measured the time required for both participants to reach recognition alignment of the constellation. As shown in Fig. 3, the mean alignment time was 345 s in the Equal condition and 465 s in the Unequal condition. A paired-samples t-test revealed no significant difference, but there was a marginal trend toward longer alignment times in the Unequal condition ($t(14) = -1.94, p = 0.073$). Furthermore, the number of trials that exceeded the 600-second time limit and were thus considered unsuccessful was higher in the Unequal condition (7 trials) compared to the Equal condition (4 trials). When trials exceeding the 600-s limit were excluded, the mean times were 252 s (Equal) and 347 s (Unequal). These results suggest that transmitting constellation information tended to take longer when visual acuity differed.

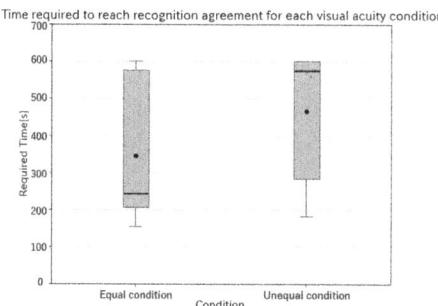

Fig. 3. Time to recognition alignment under Equal and Unequal conditions.

Table 1. Evaluation Results by Vision Level (Good, Normal, Poor) under visual acuity conditions

Item	Good		Normal		Poor	
	Unequal	Equal	Unequal	Equal	Unequal	Equal
Smoothness of conversation	2.75	2.50	2.63	3.00	2.33	2.90
Difficulty understanding partner's utterances	2.63	3.00	2.00	1.20	1.83	1.20
Agreement on constellation recognition	0.75	0.70	0.69	1.00	0.67	1.00
Conversation fatigue	2.13	2.50	2.31	2.60	3.17	2.22

Response Latency. We also examined turn-taking and response latency. The Equal condition yielded an average response latency of 0.87 s, whereas the Unequal condition yielded 0.98 s. Although not statistically significant, participants tended to respond more quickly when their visual acuity was matched.

Number of "Eh?" Utterances. We counted "Eh?" utterances in 30 trials (15 Equal, 15 Unequal), excluding self-directed tokens. A total of 40 occurred in the Equal condition and 61 in the Unequal condition. Although a paired-samples t-test showed no significant difference ($t(14) = -0.94, p = 0.362$), the tendency indicates that clarification requests were more frequent when visual acuity differed.

Comprehension Test Results. After each conversation, the Identifier completed a brief test by identifying stars and drawing the constellation shape (max = 2 points). The Equal condition yielded an average score of 1.60, compared to 1.33 in the Unequal condition. Although the difference was not statistically significant ($t(14) = 0.89, p = 0.389$), the trend suggests that matched visual acuity supported better comprehension (as shown in Fig. 4 for an example).

Utterance Protocol. We coded all conversational data into utterance protocol, with the full breakdown shown in Table 2. The proportion of question-category utterances was 9.2% in the Equal condition and 10.8% in the Unequal condition. This difference was not statistically significant ($t(14) = 0.99, p = .337$), but the pattern suggests that participants in the Unequal condition initiated slightly more clarification questions.

Table 2. Proportion of utterance protocol by Visual Acuity Condition

	Unequal (%)	Equal (%)
Explanation	25.1	27.7
Backchannel	21.0	26.2
Response	17.1	15.1
Question	10.8	9.2
Confirmation	11.1	10.1
Gaze instruction	1.2	1.7
Request	0.4	0.2
Incomplete utterance	0.2	0.3

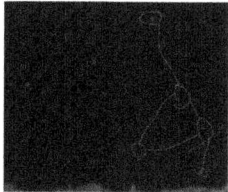

Fig. 4. An example of participant annotation from the comprehension test.

4 Discussion

Summary of Findings. This study investigated how visual acuity differences affect conversational behavior during collaborative stargazing. Although most differences did not reach statistical significance, consistent tendencies were observed. Unequal visual acuity pairs required longer time to align constellation recognition, produced more clarification questions and "Eh?" utterances, and reported lower smoothness and comprehension in post-trial questionnaires. These findings suggest that perceptual asymmetry can complicate mutual understanding, even in a shared visual environment.

Interpretation of Key Metrics. Among the indicators we examined, question-category utterances and "Eh?" utterances provide useful signals of recognition misalignment. Even though the differences were not significant, their higher frequency in the Unequal condition suggests that perceptual asymmetry increased the need for repair. These conversational cues may serve as real-time markers for detecting when partners are looking at different stars.

Furthermore, subjective ratings revealed a gap in perceived alignment. The difference between Describer and Identifier responses to the question "Did your recognition match?" was larger in the Unequal condition. This suggests that Describers may have overestimated how well their explanations were understood, a form of overconfidence that can hinder timely clarification and exacerbate recognition mismatches. This highlights that not only visual access but also a mutual awareness of each other's understanding plays a critical role in collaboration.

Interestingly, another finding emerged regarding visual complexity. Participants with Good visual acuity in the Equal condition reported more difficulty understanding their partner compared to those in the Normal or Poor conditions. One possible explanation is that an abundance of visible stars introduced ambiguity when selecting or referring to specific constellations. This suggests that higher visual clarity does not always benefit communication, especially when the visual scene becomes overly complex, and implies that support systems must manage visual density, not just enhance clarity. In addition, constellation complexity may interact with perceptual asymmetry, underscoring the need to balance visual scene design in future experiments.

Implications for Support Systems. The observed tendencies suggest that conversational cues such as question-category utterances and "Eh?" can be leveraged to estimate recognition misalignment in real time. Rather than relying on intrusive visual aids, a support system could monitor these cues during stargazing conversations and infer when partners are likely to be looking at different stars. Such a system could then provide minimal interventions, for example by suggesting relevant landmarks or prompting clarification, without disrupting the natural flow of dialogue. This approach highlights the potential of conversation-based monitoring for designing lightweight and context-sensitive support tools in collaborative astronomy tasks.

Limitations. This study has several limitations. The small, homogeneous sample of participants from the same laboratory limits the generalizability of our findings. Furthermore, the analysis of conversational features, such as "Eh?" utterances and question-category utterances, by a single coder raises concerns about reliability. The presence of prominent landmarks in the experimental environment may also have influenced conversation strategies and distorted the nature of the task. Future work must address these issues by recruiting a more diverse participant pool, ensuring robust annotation through multiple coders, and refining the experimental environment to better simulate real-world conditions. By overcoming these challenges, we aim to develop a real-time system that detects conversational cues to mediate recognition misalignments.

5 Conclusion

This study investigated how visual acuity differences influence conversational behavior during collaborative stargazing in VR. Across multiple measures, pairs with unequal acuity tended to show conversational friction: they appeared to require more time to achieve recognition alignment, produced more clarification questions, and reported lower smoothness and comprehension. These tendencies suggest perceptual asymmetry is reflected in measurable vocal cues, the central finding of this work.

Future work should validate these findings with larger and more diverse participant samples, improve annotation reliability, and control for factors such as constellation difficulty, which may amplify the effects of acuity differences. Ultimately, these findings may inform the design of lightweight, context-sensitive conversational agents that leverage vocal cues to mediate perceptual asymmetries without disrupting the natural flow of collaborative stargazing.

References

1. Aoki, T., Fujiwara, Y., Nakamura, S.: Validation of game advantage disadvantage control considering color vision characteristics: a basic study on "Among Us" with different color settings. Procedia Comput. Sci. **225**, 2982–2991 (2023)
2. Chen, C.F., Huang, K.C.: Effects of background lighting color and movement distance on reaching times among participants with low vision, myopia, and normal vision. Percept. Mot. Skills **122**(2), 518–532 (2016)
3. Clark, H.H., Schaefer, E.F.: Contributing to discourse. Cogn. Sci. **13**(2), 259–294 (1989)
4. Dingemanse, M., Torreira, F., Enfield, N.J.: Is "huh?" a universal word? conversational infrastructure and the convergent evolution of linguistic items. PLoS ONE **8**(11), e78273 (2013)
5. Fifth Star Labs: Sky Guide. https://www.fifthstarlabs.com/. Accessed 31 May 2024
6. Fujiwara, Y., Nakamura, S.: Fundamental study of color combinations by using deuteranope-simulation filter for controlling the handicap of color vision diversity in video games. In: Baalsrud Hauge, J., C. S. Cardoso, J., Roque, L., Gonzalez-Calero, P.A. (eds.) ICEC 2021. LNCS, vol. 13056, pp. 127–138. Springer, Cham (2021). https://doi.org/10.1007/978-3-030-89394-1_10
7. Hayashi, M.: Marking a 'noticing of departure' in talk: Eh-prefaced turns in Japanese conversation. J. Pragmat. **41**(10), 2100–2129 (2009)
8. Jones, P.R., Somoskeöy, T., Chow-Wing-Bom, H., Crabb, D.P.: Seeing other perspectives: evaluating the use of virtual and augmented reality to simulate visual impairments (OpenVisSim). NPJ Dig. Med. **3**(1), 32 (2020)
9. Neugebauer, A., Castner, N., Severitt, B., Stingl, K., Ivanov, I., Wahl, S.: Simulating vision impairment in virtual reality: a comparison of visual task performance with real and simulated tunnel vision. Virtual Real. **28**(2), 97 (2024)
10. Ohama, M., Soga, M.: Collaborative constellation learning environment with sharing learners' gazing points in the real night sky. In: 2012 IEEE Fourth International Conference On Digital Game And Intelligent Toy Enhanced Learning, pp. 123–125. IEEE (2012)
11. Soga, M., Matsui, K., Takaseki, K., Tokoi, K.: Interactive learning environment for astronomy with finger pointing and augmented reality. In: 2008 Eighth IEEE International Conference on Advanced Learning Technologies, pp. 542–543. IEEE (2008)
12. Soga, M., Ohama, M., Ehara, Y., Miwa, M.: Real-world oriented mobile constellation learning environment using gaze pointing. IEICE Trans. Inf. Syst. **94**(4), 763–771 (2011)
13. Stolcke, A., et al.: Dialogue act modeling for automatic tagging and recognition of conversational speech. Comput. Linguist. **26**(3), 339–373 (2000)
14. Tian, K., Urata, M., Endo, M., Mouri, K., Yasuda, T., Kato, J.: Real-world oriented smartphone AR supported learning system based on planetarium contents for seasonal constellation observation. Appl. Sci. **9**(17), 3508 (2019)
15. Varonis, E.M., Gass, S.: Non-native/non-native conversations: a model for negotiation of meaning. Appl. Linguis. **6**(1), 71–90 (1985)
16. Vito Technology: Star Walk 2. https://starwalk.space/ja. Accessed 31 May 2024
17. Zhang, J., Sung, Y.T., Hou, H.T., Chang, K.E.: The development and evaluation of an augmented reality-based armillary sphere for astronomical observation instruction. Comput. Educ. **73**, 178–188 (2014)

AI in Education: LLMs and Content Generation

Simulating Collaborative Learning with Data-Driven LLM-Agents

Yu Yan(✉), Changhao Liang, and Hiroaki Ogata

Kyoto University, Kyoto 606-8501, Japan
yan.yu.83x@st.kyoto-u.ac.jp

Abstract. Simulating collaborative learning is a critical yet challenging goal in educational technology. While recent Large Language Model (LLM) advancements show promise, existing approaches often rely on static error models and rigid dialogue control and are primarily designed as student-facing training tools. To address these limitations, we present an autonomous 'zero-player' multi-agent simulation platform, powered by GPT-4o, designed as a computational testbed for research. Our key contributions are a data-driven, probabilistic engine for modeling a realistic spectrum of student capabilities, and a fine-grained, consensus-driven dialogue protocol that fosters emergent, bottom-up collaboration. Qualitative evaluations demonstrate that our system generates sound, expert-aligned problem solutions and, critically, produces plausible collaborative dynamics, including peer-to-peer error identification and correction. Our work establishes a high-fidelity platform for studying the mechanisms of collaborative learning and lays the groundwork for future predictive tools to help educators optimize student grouping.

Keywords: Collaborative Learning · Multi-Agent Simulation · Data-Driven Agent Modeling · Large Language Models in Education

1 Introduction

The foundational vision for using simulated students in education, with applications from teacher training to formative evaluation, was articulated nearly three decades ago [6]. Within this framework, however, the simulation of collaborative learning, a cornerstone of modern pedagogy rooted in socio-constructivist theories [8], remains a formidable challenge. Historically, this has stemmed from the twin difficulties of modeling the fluid, unpredictable dynamics of group interaction and capturing the nuances of individual student reasoning through natural language, limitations that early computational models could not overcome [4]. The recent advent of Large Language Models (LLMs) now offers a transformative opportunity to address this gap, enabling the creation of robust tools to model these complex dynamics [1].

Existing technological interventions have only partially addressed this gap. Intelligent Tutoring Systems (ITS), while proficient at personalizing instruction for individual learners, are fundamentally designed for a one-to-one paradigm and thus possess a socio-cognitive blind spot [7]. Conversely, Computer-Supported Collaborative Learning (CSCL) platforms provide the essential digital environments for human collaboration but typically act as passive facilitators; they provide the "stage" but not the autonomous "actors" [3]. This leaves a critical need for a high-fidelity, autonomous platform capable of not only hosting but actively simulating these complex group dynamics.

The simulation of student collaboration has been explored using Multi-Agent Systems (MAS), but these agents were often constrained by scripted or simplified rule-based models, failing to capture the linguistic nuance of human reasoning [2]. The recent advent of LLMs offers a solution, and the potential of using LLMs to create such autonomous actors has been demonstrated in pioneering work like MATHVC [9], which introduced a virtual classroom populated by LLM-simulated students. Their work validated the feasibility of this approach, using a meta-planner to guide conversation through predefined pedagogical stages and symbolic schemas to model student knowledge. Despite these contributions, their approach also presents critical challenges for achieving authentic, flexible collaboration. A core issue stems from its design as a "human-in-the-loop" system, where the goal is to facilitate learning for a human student. This pedagogical objective inherently shapes the simulation's components to be more artificial. For instance, the simulated student agents themselves are not grounded in authentic student data, but are instead synthesized to enact specific, controlled behaviors for the user's benefit. Similarly, the dialogue management tends to follow a top-down, fixed-stage progression to guide the pedagogical experience, rather than emulating the more fluid, bottom-up process of genuine peer consensus-building.

In response, our work establishes a new paradigm by developing a fully autonomous, 'zero-player' computational testbed designed specifically for research. Free from the constraints of serving a human user, our focus shifts entirely to maximizing simulation fidelity. Therefore, our agents are endowed with profiles derived from data-driven models of real student performance, and the dialogue is orchestrated by a manager that enforces a granular, bottom-up consensus, allowing genuine understanding to be co-constructed. The significance of this high-fidelity, autonomous architecture is its potential as a predictive, decision-support tool for educators.

The primary contributions of this work are threefold:

- **A Data-Driven Probabilistic Student Modeling Engine:** We introduce a novel engine that moves beyond static error lists. Informed by real-world student data, our system probabilistically models a spectrum of initial student responses, ranging from fully correct solutions to plausible, personalized misconceptions. This creates a high-fidelity simulation of a truly heterogeneous student group, providing a more authentic foundation for studying collaborative dynamics.
- **A Fine-Grained, Consensus-Driven Dialogue Protocol:** In contrast to rigid, stage-based frameworks, our Dialogue Manager implements a dynamic, consensus-driven protocol. It monitors the group's understanding at the level of individual concepts and sub-problems, allowing the discussion to advance only after shared understanding is verified. This bottom-up approach actively scaffolds the co-construction of knowledge and provides a more realistic model of emergent collaboration.

- **A Novel Multi-Agent Cognitive Architecture for Research:** We design and implement a cognitive architecture where each agent's behavior is driven by an LLM-powered model that synthesizes a persistent, data-grounded knowledge profile with real-time conversational context. This architecture, framed as a "zero-player" computational testbed, is explicitly designed to enable researchers to conduct controlled, replicable experiments on the mechanisms of collaborative learning, distinct from the goal of direct human-student interaction.

2 Methodology

To create high-fidelity simulations grounded in authentic student behaviors, our platform utilizes the Open Knowledge and Learner Model (OKLM) [5], a framework that allows for a holistic understanding of a student's knowledge state. The nuanced profiles for our autonomous agents are constructed from two distinct categories of data derived from this model, sourced from an authentic dataset of a second-year middle school class in Japan:

- **Per-unit Performance Metrics:** This category provides a granular measure of a student's proficiency by assessing their mastery of individual knowledge concepts within each learning unit. A student's mastery level for a unit is determined by their correctness rate on all questions tied to the knowledge points within that unit. We derive this fine-grained data from two primary sources: (1) **Unit Tests**, which are assessments dedicated to evaluating the knowledge points within a single learning unit, and (2) **Disaggregated Midterm/Final Exams**, which consist of performance data extracted from questions related to specific knowledge points within broader midterm and final examinations.
- **Overall Academic Profiles:** This category provides a summative, holistic label of a student's academic standing relative to their cohort. It is a derived indicator based on the student's overall class rank and is used to categorize agents into general performance tiers (e.g., high-proficiency, average-proficiency, or low-proficiency).

This combination of granular, per-unit metrics and a holistic performance profile enables the construction of rich agent archetypes, ensuring each simulation is initialized with a realistic and diverse range of cognitive states.

The simulation process is initiated through a streamlined web-based interface (see Fig. 1). The user, typically a researcher conducting an experiment, configures the simulation parameters by inputting the mathematical problem to be solved, the desired length of the conversation (e.g., number of messages), and optional pedagogical guidance. Upon initiation, the system populates a virtual discussion environment with the generative agents, which then begin to autonomously collaborate on the given task. The resulting dialogue, emulating a natural, multi-person student discussion, is rendered in a clear, turn-by-turn conversational format for observation and analysis.

The system's architecture, depicted in Fig. 2, is conceptually divided into three core components: (1) an **Individual Solution Generation Module** responsible for creating initial agent states, (2) an **Agent Brain** that models the cognitive cycle of each simulated student, and (3) a central **Dialogue Manager** that orchestrates the entire learning process.

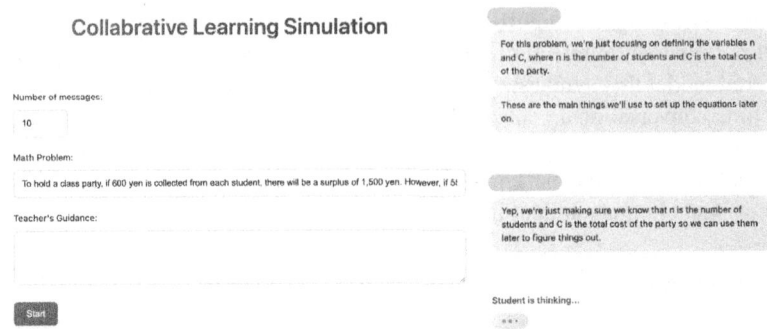

Fig. 1. The Simulation Setup Interface

The behavior of each processing unit within this architecture is not defined by rigid, hard-coded logic, but is instead realized by OpenAI's GPT-4o model executing tasks guided by a set of carefully engineered prompts.

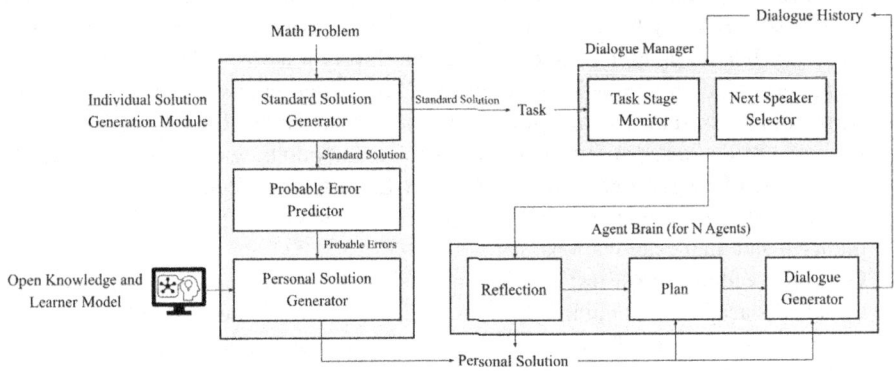

Fig. 2. System Architecture

2.1 Initial Cognitive State Generation

The simulation begins in the **Individual Solution Generation Module**, which pre-pares a unique cognitive starting point for each agent. This automated process, as depicted in Fig. 2, unfolds in three distinct steps, each handled by a specialized component:

- **Standard Solution Generation:** The **Standard Solution Generator** first creates a canonical, step-by-step solution by prompting GPT-4o to act as a mathematical expert. The output is a structured JSON object that segments the problem into sub-tasks, defining the ground truth and agenda for the collaborative discussion.
- **Probable Error Prediction:** Next, the Probable Error Predictor leverages the OKLM to generate a dynamic error profile for each agent. Specifically, it embeds the agent's proficiency data directly into a prompt for GPT-4o, instructing the model to act as an expert and infer a set of potential misconceptions based on that data.

- **Personal Solution Generation:** Finally, the **Personal Solution Generator** synthesizes a personalized cognitive artifact for each agent. It instructs GPT-4o to integrate the standard solution with the agent's profile and its unique error profile. The resulting solution JSON reflects a plausible initial cognitive state, ranging from fully correct to containing specific, data-informed flaws, that is then passed to the agent's "brain."

2.2 Dialogue Orchestration and Consensus-Driven Progression

The **Dialogue Manager** is the central nervous system of the simulation, performing two critical functions to guide the collaborative process:

- **Next Speaker Selection:** This function, handled by the **Next Speaker Selector** component, utilizes GPT-4o to manage the conversation's turn-taking. The selection is not random; it is based on a holistic analysis of the dialogue history and natural conversational flow to emulate realistic group dynamics and ensure a smooth interaction.
- **Consensus-Driven Progression:** More critically, this function is implemented by the **Task Stage Monitor** to intelligently guide the group's progress. Before each turn, it prompts GPT-4o to analyze the entire dialogue transcript to determine if the agents have collectively reached a consensus on the variables and calculations required by the current task. The simulation is permitted to advance to the next stage only when this consensus is confirmed, serving as an automated scaffolding that prevents premature conclusions and ensures the discussion is deeply grounded.

2.3 The Agent Cognitive Cycle

Each of the N agents operates using its own **Agent Brain**, which executes a recurring cognitive cycle of reflection, planning, and utterance generation.

- **Metacognitive Reflection and Self-Correction:** When an agent is selected to speak, it first enters a metacognitive reflection phase. It is prompted to analyze the ongoing dialogue history in the context of its own personal solution JSON, with its focus constrained by the task guidance from the Dialogue Manager. The prompt requires the agent to perform a comparative analysis, identifying any discrepancies between the values discussed by the group and the values within its own cognitive artifact. This process may lead to the agent identifying a flaw in its own reasoning. A key feature of our design is that the output of this reflection can trigger a self-correction process, where the agent prompts itself to generate a revised version of its personal solution, effectively modeling a moment of conceptual change and learning from the discussion.
- **Strategic Planning and Dialogue Generation:** Following reflection, the agent formulates a strategic Plan for its conversational turn. This plan, informed by its (potentially updated) understanding, outlines the communicative goal. This abstract plan is then passed to a final Dialogue Generator prompt. This prompt synthesizes the agent's personal solution, its strategic plan, and strict conversational constraints (e.g., maintaining the persona of a middle school student, adhering to the current task) to produce the final, natural-language utterance. This utterance is then appended to the dialogue history, and the cycle repeats.

3 Pilot Evaluation

Our evaluation is designed to assess the fidelity and plausibility of our simulation across two key dimensions: (1) the logical soundness of the system's standard solution generation process, and (2) the qualitative realism of the emergent, multi-agent collaborative dialogues.

3.1 Fidelity of Automated Solution Scaffolding

The first phase of our evaluation assesses the quality of the system's Standard Solution Generation. This automated process, which deconstructs a given problem into a normative, step-by-step solution to serve as the ground truth for the simulation's agenda, was validated through a comparative analysis with the assistance of an expert mathematics educator. For this, we compared the system-generated solution steps against a human-authored solution for a high-school-level algebra problem: "Given a quadratic equation $x^2 + (a+2)x + 2a = 0$ with two distinct roots α and β satisfying. $\alpha(\alpha - 1) + \beta(\beta - 1) = 12$, find the value of a." The analysis revealed a high degree of congruence between the system's output and the human expert's approach in both the logical progression and the conceptual decomposition of the problem.

Table 1. Comparison of Human-Authored and System-Generated Solution Steps.

	Human-Authored Solution	System Generated Solution
Step 1	Express $\alpha + \beta$ and $\alpha\beta$ in terms of a using the relationship between roots and coefficients.	Apply Vieta's formulas to obtain the sum $\alpha + \beta$ and product $\alpha\beta$ of the roots in terms of a.
Step 2	Use the condition $\alpha(\alpha - 1) + \beta(\beta - 1) = 12$ to derive a quadratic equation in a.	Rewrite the given condition by expanding and grouping terms into $(\alpha^2 + \beta^2) - (\alpha + \beta) = 12$.
Step 3	Solve the equation to obtain possible values for a.	Substitute the sum and product of the roots into the rewritten condition to derive a quadratic equation in a.
Step 4	Examine whether each value of a satisfies the condition for two distinct roots (i.e., Discriminant > 0).	Obtain two solutions by factoring, yielding two potential solutions for a.
Step 5	Conclude the final value of a.	Check the discriminant of the original equation for each potential value of a to ensure two distinct roots exist, concluding the valid solution.

Table 1 provides a detailed example of this alignment, illustrating how our system autonomously generates a correct and logically sound solution path that provides a solid foundation for the subsequent agent-based simulation.

3.2 Qualitative Analysis of Emergent Collaborative Dialogue

Beyond component-level fidelity, we analyzed the end-to-end simulation output to assess whether the system could generate plausible, emergent collaborative dynamics. Through qualitative analysis of numerous simulation transcripts, we identified several key phenomena:

- **Successful Peer-to-Peer Scaffolding:** We observed that agents, driven by their individual cognitive models and the consensus-driven protocol, cooperate to solve problems. Crucially, the simulation authentically models peer-to-peer error identification and correction, a cornerstone of effective collaborative learning.
- **Plausible Group Failure and Success Modes:** The simulation realistically models outcomes based on group composition. When a group was populated exclusively with low-proficiency agents, they often collaboratively reached an incorrect consensus. Conversely, groups of high-proficiency agents typically resolved problems efficiently with minimal debate.

To illustrate these phenomena concretely, we present a case study of a simulation run. This case features a mixed-proficiency group of three anonymized agents, consisting of two high-proficiency agents, 'Student 1' and 'Student 3', and one low-proficiency agent, 'Student 2'. All agent profiles were instantiated as archetypes derived from our OKLM datastore. The complete profile for each agent is available in our public repository (see chapter 5). Table 2 presents the resulting dialogue from this group.

Table 2. An Excerpt of Simulated Dialogue Demonstrating a Peer-Correction Loop.

Speaker	Dialogue
Student 1	Hey guys, I figured out the least common denominator (LCD) for the fractions with denominators 7 and 2, and it's 14! Does anyone have questions about how I got that?
Student 2	Hey 'Student 1', I converted 5/7 to the equivalent fraction 10/14 using the LCD of 14, just making sure we're on the same page!
Student 3	Hey 'Student 2', yeah, 5/7 turns into 10/14 with the LCD of 14, so we're totally on the same page!
Student 1	So, I converted 1/2 into 7/14 using the LCD of 14. Does anyone have questions about how I got that?
Student 2	To add the two equivalent fractions, we take 12/14 and 7/14, add the numerators to get 19, and keep the denominator as 14. So, the sum is 19/14. Does anyone have questions about this calculation?
Student 3	Hey 'Student 2', I think we should be adding 10/14 and 7/14, not 12/14 and 7/14, so the sum should be 17/14 instead.
Student 1	Hey 'Student 2', I think we should focus on adding 10/14 and 7/14, which gives us 17/14 as the correct sum. Does that make sense?
Student 2	Thanks for catching that, 'Student 3' and 'Student 1'! You're right, we should be adding 10/14 and 7/14, which makes the sum 17/14. My bad for the earlier mix-up!

In this dialogue, the agent 'Student 2' makes a calculation error ("12/14" instead of "10/14"). This error is promptly identified and corrected by 'Student 3' and reinforced by 'Student 1'. The group then realigns around the correct calculation, and 'Student 2' acknowledges the correction and updates its understanding. This sequence demonstrates the system's ability to model not just dialogue, but also the crucial learning processes of cognitive conflict, peer scaffolding, and conceptual repair.

4 Implications and Future Work

In this paper, we presented a novel multi-agent platform for simulating collaborative learning, distinguished by its data-driven student modeling, a fine-grained consensus-driven dialogue protocol, and its architecture as a "zero-player" computational testbed for research. While our work establishes a strong theoretical foundation, it also opens several exciting avenues for future investigation that can bridge the gap from a research-focused prototype to a transformative tool for educational practice.

The primary significance of our platform lies in its potential to reshape how we understand, design, and facilitate collaborative learning. For educators, it offers a paradigm shift from intuitive classroom management to proactive, evidence-based pedagogy. By enabling 'in-silico' experiments, our platform allows teachers to forecast the dynamics of different student group compositions, helping them to design optimal groupings that can maximize peer scaffolding and ensure equitable participation. For researchers and curriculum designers, the platform serves as a computational microscope to unpack the "black box" of collaboration, allowing for controlled studies on how factors like task design or student profiles influence the emergence of learning processes like cognitive conflict and conceptual change.

Realizing this vision requires a clear path forward. A critical next step is to rigorously establish the simulation's external validity by comparing its outputs against a corpus of real-world student dialogues. With its fidelity confirmed, our long-term vision is to evolve this research testbed into a user-friendly, predictive decision-support tool for educators, fulfilling the potential discussed above and truly optimizing collaborative learning in the classroom.

5 Availability of Prompts and Agent Profiles

The complete set of prompts and the anonymized agent profiles used in this study are publicly available on GitHub at: https://github.com/Kuminia/Prompts-for-MAS.

References

1. Denny, P., et al.: Generative AI for education (GAIED): Advances, opportunities, and challenges. arXiv preprint arXiv:2402.01580 (2024)
2. Mannekote, A.: Towards a neural era in dialogue management for collaboration: A literature survey. arXiv preprint arXiv:2307.09021 (2023)
3. Stahl, G., Koschmann, T., Suthers, D.: Computer-supported collaborative learning: an historical perspective. In: Cambridge Handbook of the Learning Sciences, pp. 409–421 (2006)
4. Stahl, G.: Group Cognition: Computer Support for Building Collaborative Knowledge (Acting with Technology). The MIT Press (2006)
5. Takii, K., Liang, C., Ogata, H.: Open knowledge and learner model: mathematical representation and applications as learning support foundation in EFL. In: International Conference on Computers in Education, vol. 1, pp. 595–604 (2024)
6. VanLehn, K., Ohlsson, S., Nason, R.: Applications of simulated students: an exploration. J. Artif. Intell. Educ. 5(2), 135–175 (1994)

7. VanLehn, K.: The relative effectiveness of human tutoring, intelligent tutoring systems, and other tutoring systems. Educ. Psychol. **46**(4), 197–221 (2011)
8. Vygotsky, L.S.: Mind in Society: The Development of Higher Psychological Processes. Harvard University Press (1978)
9. Yue, M., Lyu, W., Mifdal, W., Suh, J., Zhang, Y., Yao, Z.: Mathvc: An llm-simulated multi-character virtual classroom for mathematics education. arXiv preprint arXiv:2404.06711 (2024)

Evaluation of LLM-Based Feedback Generation for Distance Project-Based Learning

Kosuke Sasaki[1,2](✉) and Tomoo Inoue[3](✉)

[1] Graduate School of Library, Information and Media Studies, University of Tsukuba, Ibaraki, Japan
ksasaki@slis.tsukuba.ac.jp
[2] Faculty of Global Management, Chuo University, Tokyo, Japan
[3] Institute of Library, Information and Media Science, University of Tsukuba, Ibaraki, Japan
inoue@slis.tsukuba.ac.jp

Abstract. In distance project-based learning (PBL), reduced communication between teachers and learners makes it difficult to provide appropriate feedback, especially for inexperienced teaching assistants (coaches). This study proposes an LLM-based feedback generation method using learners' activity reports and evaluates its effectiveness against coach-created feedback. An analysis of 216 informatics PBL activity reports showed that LLM-generated feedback outperformed coach-created feedback across feedback requirements, principles, and learning impact conditions. The findings suggest that LLM-based feedback generation can effectively support distance PBL.

Keywords: Project-based Learning · Large Language Models · Feedback Generation

1 Introduction

Project-based learning (PBL) is a learner-centered approach in higher education that integrates knowledge acquisition with real-world problem-solving [9]. In PBL, learners receive regular feedback from teachers while progressing independently. Various studies have examined appropriate feedback for learners [10, 16, 26]. Appropriate feedback facilitates PBL execution and promotes learning advancement [1].

PBL in distance environments faces challenges with reduced teacher-learner communication, making it difficult to understand learners' situations and provide appropriate feedback [12, 18]. Distance PBL uses activity reports to help teachers understand learners' situations and provide feedback. Learners can use these reports to reflect on their learning [6].

In distance PBL, the provision of feedback through activity reports imposes a burden on teachers, as they are required to review reports for all learners and create individualized feedback for each learner. Consequently, in practical educational contexts, instructional assistants, such as teaching assistants (referred to as "coaches" in this study), may provide feedback to learners instead of the teacher [15]. The primary objective of feedback is to guide learners toward achieving their goals rather than supplying direct answers [10,28]. Nonetheless, coaches, who often possess less experience providing feedback than teachers, frequently encounter difficulties in offering appropriate feedback to learners [5].

This study introduces a feedback generation method that utilizes a large language model (LLM) based on learners' activity reports as a feedback mechanism for distance PBL. A prior design proposed the use of an LLM to automatically generate feedback from learner activity reports. However, the quality of this feedback and learners' perceptions of it have not been thoroughly investigated. This study sought to compare the quality of feedback produced by coaches with limited instructional experience in distance PBL with that generated by an LLM, specifically in the field of informatics. This study aimed to clarify the usefulness of and challenges associated with LLM-generated feedback.

The contributions of this study are as follows:

- The comparative evaluation results show that LLM-generated feedback outperforms coach-created feedback in nearly all aspects of feedback requirements for distance PBL, principles of good feedback, and conditions for positively impacting learning.
- It is shown that preferred characteristics of feedback include clarity of next actions, specific evaluations, and detailed information provision, while conciseness and positive expressions are also desired.
- The potential of LLM-based feedback generation as an effective educational support tool in distance PBL is presented.

2 Related Work

2.1 Feedback in Education

Feedback in education is defined as information that bridges the gap between current and target performance (e.g., [3,21]).

We adopted Hattie and Timperley's framework [10] as our foundation. This framework defines feedback as information addressing three questions: feedup ("Where am I going?"; goals), feedback ("How am I going?"; current performance), and feedforward ("Where to next?"; strategies to improve).

This framework aligns with the consensus that feedback reduces the gap between current and desired performance. We define feedback as information that (1) addresses the three questions above, (2) focuses on performance rather than the person, and (3) provides actionable guidance.

Feedback can affect learning positively or negatively, with excessive feedback potentially overwhelming learners or decreasing motivation [10,24,27]. Sasaki and Inoue proposed five feedback requirements for distance PBL [22]:

1. Feedback should show the learner's goal.
2. Feedback should show the learner's current stage.
3. Feedback should include the assessment of the learner's activity.
4. Feedback should include information about the next step.
5. Feedback should NOT include evaluating the learners themselves.

The Assessment Experience Questionnaire (AEQ V3.3) evaluates teacher feedback's impact on student learning through six questions about feedback understanding and expectations [7,8].

Previous studies have demonstrated feedback's usefulness in education and proposed evaluation methods.

2.2 Large Language Models in Higher Education

AI technologies, such as LLM, have made it easier to provide personalized learning content. Studies have emphasized the importance of learner-centered environments [2,13]. Research has focused on generating formative feedback for specific tasks [25], evaluating programming assignments [19,29], and automating feedback in blended learning [14].

PBL requires individualized formative assessments for each learner's progress [4], increasing the burden on teachers compared to traditional settings. LLMs that can handle diverse learning activities can effectively support PBL feedback. However, research on the use of LLMs in PBL remains limited.

Sasaki and Inoue proposed a prompt for generating feedback using an LLM following PBL requirements [22,23], but the quality of the generated feedback remains to be evaluated.

3 Objectives

This study proposes a feedback generation method using a large language model (LLM) based on activity reports from PBL learners for distance PBL, aiming to clarify its usefulness and challenges in this context. By comparing feedback from coaches with limited experience to LLM-generated feedback, we examined its applicability in educational settings to verify research question RQ_1.

RQ_1: Does LLM-generated feedback produce higher quality feedback compared to coach-created feedback?

To examine RQ_1, we established research hypotheses H_1 to H_3:

H_1: LLM-generated feedback better satisfies the feedback requirements for distance PBL compared to coach-created feedback [22].
H_2: LLM-generated feedback better satisfies the principles of good feedback from the learner's perspective compared to coach-created feedback [17].
H_3: LLM-generated feedback better satisfies the conditions for positively impacting learners' learning compared to coach-created feedback [8].

To clarify the feedback characteristics that learners prefer, we examined research question RQ_2:

RQ_2: What are the characteristics of feedback that learners find preferable?

Table 1. Number of activity reports, learning stage, and learning goal for each learner.

Learner	# of activity reports	Learning stage	Learning goal
L1	56	middle	prototype system development
L2	23	middle	prototype system development
L3	33	middle	conducting experiments and analysis
L4	33	middle	analysis of existing data
L5	37	early	determining a research theme
L6	16	early	determining a research theme
L7	18	middle	conducting experiments and analysis

4 Experiment

This study focuses on PBL in informatics, where research activities are the primary learning content. During PBL, learners report their daily activities and progress through the activity reports. We assumed that teaching assistants review these reports instead of teachers and provide feedback. As these assistants have less instructional experience than teachers, their feedback quality may be insufficient. We conducted an experiment in which participants acting as "raters" compared LLM-generated feedback with feedback created by participants with limited teaching experience ("coaches").

This chapter outlines the experiments conducted in this study. We explain the activity reports used, describe the LLM feedback generation experiment, detail how coaches created the feedback, and explain how the evaluators assessed both types of feedback. The experiments were approved by the Ethics Committee on Library, Information and Media Studies at University of Tsukuba (Approval No. 25–39).

4.1 Activity Reports Used for Feedback Generation/Creation

In this study, we analyzed 216 activity video reports from seven learners (L1–L7) during informatics PBL in 2020, which was conducted online due to COVID-19 [11]. The videos were 30-second bust-shots of learners reporting their daily learning. All videos were transcribed using OpenAI's Whisper [20], and the experimenter corrected any recognition errors. Proper nouns and personal names were replaced with common nouns and pseudonyms, respectively. Table 1 shows each learner's learning stage, goals, and number of recorded videos.

4.2 Feedback Generation Using LLM

This study used the prompt for feedback generation in distance PBL proposed by Sasaki and Inoue [23]. The LLM was provided with learners' text-based activity reports, learning stages (early/middle/late), learning goals, and previous activity reports to generate feedback in Japanese. Claude (claude-sonnet-4-20250514) was used as the LLM. The prompt included teacher role setting ("You are a university teacher who instructs project-based learning. You are familiar with informatics.") and feedback requirements with XML tags. The input prompt is shown in Fig. 1. The maximum number of tokens was set to 8192, and the temperature was set to 0 to minimize generation randomness.

An example of the generated feedback for learner L4's 17th activity report is shown in Table 2, which considers the previous activity report content.

```
You receive a short activity report (approximately 100 characters) from the learner under
your guidance. Your task is to read this activity report and consider the feedback that
should be provided.
Please follow the procedures below to consider the feedback:

<procedure>
The procedure you will follow is as follows:

1. You receive the following input:
- Previous activity report
- Current activity report
- Learner's current learning goals
- Learner's current learning stage (early/middle/late)

2. Create feedback for the learner based on the current activity report. As you are a
teacher, polite language is necessary but avoid excessive honorifics. The following rules
must be followed when creating feedback:
- Feedback should show the learner's goal.
- Feedback should show the learner's current stage.
- Feedback should include an assessment of the learner's activity.
- Feedback should include information about the next steps.
- Feedback should not include evaluating the learners themselves.
</procedure>
```

Fig. 1. Prompt excerpt provided to the LLM for generating feedback

4.3 Feedback Creation by Coaches

Participants as Coaches. Four undergraduate students or persons holding master's degrees (C1–C4, one female) with insufficient teaching experience participated as coaches. Their teaching experience and fields are listed in Table 3. All coaches had experience providing feedback on learners' activities weekly for over six months.

Procedure for Feedback Creation. Each coach created feedback in Japanese for learners L1–L7's activity reports using the same reference information as the LLM: learning stage, learning goal, and previous and current activity reports. C1 was assigned L1, C2 was assigned L2 and L3, C3 was assigned L4 and L7, and C4 was assigned L5 and L6, respectively.

We presented the instructions to the coaches, as shown in Fig. 2. The instruction text was modified from the LLM prompt described in Sect. 4.2 for better readability. Coaches used reference information, including learning stages, objectives, and activity reports, to create feedback in Japanese. Activity reports were presented chronologically for each learner.

Table 2. Example of feedback generation by the LLM and by the coach for the 17th activity report of learner L4 (learning stage: middle, learning goal: analysis of existing data)

Activity report

Monday, September 7, 2020. Today, I created a slide report on the challenges of utilizing data in mental health care. I consulted my professor regarding the possibility of continuing to work on this project in the future.

Generated feedback by the LLM

Following the previous paper survey on statistical testing using SPSS, you have now progressed to creating slides on data utilization issues in the field of mental health care. I appreciate that you have set specific application areas and are working toward the learning objective of analyzing existing data.

Your approach to applying theoretical knowledge to actual issues is appropriate for the middle stage. The field of mental health care is highly socially significant, and I believe it is a good subject for practical learning in data analysis.

In the next step, please consider the analysis methods using actual datasets based on the content of the slides you have created. We recommend that you also investigate statistical issues specific to mental health care data, including the sample size issues discussed in the previous lesson. Based on the results of the consultation on sustainability, please develop a concrete analytical plan.

Created feedback by the coach C3

Thank you for your report. In the middle stage of learning, it is also necessary to consider whether you can continue with the tasks. In addition to analyzing existing data, new data can be gathered. Please inform me of the results of your consultation with your teacher.

You are an expert coach (university faculty member) who instructs project-based learning. You receive a short activity report (approximately 100 characters) from a learner under your guidance. Read the activity report and write feedback for learners.

Please refer to the following information when creating feedback.
- Learner's current learning goals
- Learner's current learning stage (early / middle / late)
- Previous activity report (Not presented in the first activity report)
- Current activity report

When creating feedback, please follow these rules:
- Feedback must include the learner's current learning goals
- Feedback must include the learner's current learning stage
- Feedback must include an evaluation of the learner's activities
- Feedback must include content about what the learner should do next
- Feedback must not include self-evaluation by the learner

As you are a coach, polite language is necessary, but avoid excessive honorifics.

Fig. 2. Instructions provided to the coach for creating feedback

Table 3. Profiles of the coaches

Coach No.	Field of study	Teaching license	Teaching experience
C1	Educational technology	Junior high schools/High schools (mathematics)	Teaching assistant for university classes/Proofreading papers written by other students
C2	Learning sciences	None	Teaching assistant for undergraduate students
C3	Informatics	None	Discussions with other students regarding research activities
C4	Informatics	None	Discussions with other students regarding research activities

Results of Feedback Creation. For each activity report by learners L1–L7, one feedback was obtained from a coach. An example of feedback by coach C3 for learner L4's 17th activity report is shown in Table 2. We examined the differences in Japanese character counts between coach feedback and LLM-generated feedback. Table 4 shows the character counts for coach and LLM feedback for the same learner, with paired t-test results. The feedback from all the coaches had significantly fewer characters than the LLM feedback for the same reports.

Table 4. Number of characters (in Japanese) in LLM-generated and coach-created feedback.

Coach No.	LLM-generated feedback		Coach-created feedback		Result of paired t-test
	Mean	SD	Mean	SD	
C1	366.0	35.9	156.5	27.5	$t(55) = 39.4$, $p < .01$
C2	335.8	45.2	69.3	15.4	$t(55) = 48.9$, $p < .01$
C3	352.6	37.4	126.5	35.5	$t(51) = 39.9$, $p < .01$
C4	366.8	40.3	91.1	15.6	$t(52) = 50.0$, $p < .01$

4.4 Feedback Evaluation by Raters

Participants as Raters. Eight undergraduate or graduate students (R1–R8, four females) participated as raters in the experiment, separate from the coaches. Their teaching experience and fields are presented in Table 5. All raters had experience providing feedback on learners' activities weekly for over five months.

Table 5. Profiles of the raters

Rater No.	Field of study	Teaching license	Teaching experience
R1	Educational technology	Junior high schools/ High schools (mathematics)	Teaching assistant for university classes/Feedback on research activities
R2	Philosophy of education	Elementary schools	Teaching assistant for undergraduate students
R3	Educational technology	None	Teaching assistant for university classes/Proofreading papers written by other students
R4	Educational technology	None	Teaching assistant for university classes
R5	Informatics	None	Teaching assistant for university classes/Feedback on research activities
R6	Informatics	None	Feedback on research activities
R7	Informatics	None	Teaching Chinese to university students/Feedback on research activities
R8	Informatics	None	Feedback on research activities

Procedure for Feedback Evaluation. Each rater evaluated the feedback from the LLM and coaches on a webpage created for this experiment, as shown in Fig. 3. Two pieces of feedback were displayed randomly on the left and right sides, with raters evaluating them without knowing which one was LLM-generated. R1 and R2 were assigned feedback for learner L1; R3 and R4 for L2 and L3; R5 and R6 for L4 and L7; and R7 and R8 for L5 and L6, respectively.

Questionnaire for Feedback Evaluation. The evaluation included 19 questions (Table 6) corresponding to the research hypotheses and questions. Questions Q1–5 addressed H_1 (LLM-generated feedback better satisfies the feedback requirements for distance PBL compared to coach-created feedback [22].), Q6–11 for H_2 (LLM-generated feedback better satisfies the principles of good feedback from the learner's perspective compared to coach-created feedback [17].), Q12–17 from AEQ V3.3 [7] for H_3 (LLM-generated feedback better satisfies the conditions for positively impacting learners' learning compared to coach-created feedback [8].), and Q18–19 for RQ_2 (What are the characteristics of feedback that learners find preferable?). Q1–17 used a 7-point Likert scale, Q18 assessed the preference for feedback (displayed on the left vs. right), and Q19 collected free-text responses explaining Q18 answers.

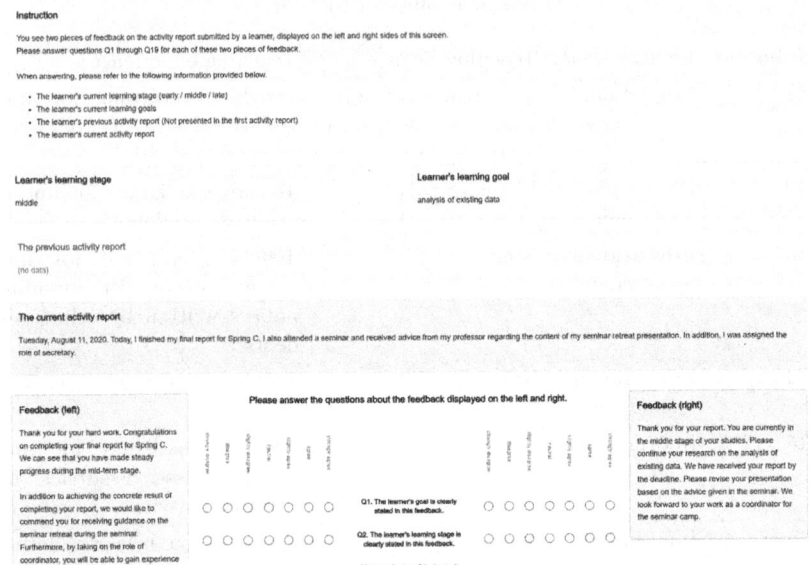

Fig. 3. A screenshot of the webpage for feedback evaluation

Results of Feedback Evaluation. For each learner's activity report, two raters evaluated all feedback. Figure 4 shows the results for Q1–Q17, comparing LLM-generated and coach-created feedback. Wilcoxon signed-rank tests revealed significant differences between the scores. For Q5, coach-created feedback scored higher. For Q12 and Q17, coach-created feedback also scored higher, but because higher scores indicated negative evaluations, the LLM-generated feedback was more positively evaluated. For the other questions, the LLM-generated feedback scored higher.

We summarize the results R_1 to R_3 for hypotheses H_1 to H_3:

R_1: LLM-generated feedback better meets distance PBL feedback requirements [22], except for not including learner evaluation, where coach feedback may excel.

R_2: LLM-generated feedback better satisfies good feedback principles from learners' perspective [17].

R_3: LLM-generated feedback better supports positive learning impacts [7].

Thus, for research question RQ_1 (Does LLM-generated feedback produce higher quality feedback compared to coach-created feedback?), LLM-generated feedback may have a more positive impact on learners than coach-created feedback does.

The distribution of responses to Q18 is shown in Fig. 5. Raters answered from "strongly prefer left" to "strongly prefer right" for feedback displayed on both sides. The results were converted to a 7-point scale from "strongly prefer coach-created feedback (-3)" to "strongly prefer LLM-generated feedback (3)." A

Table 6. Questions for feedback evaluation. Questions Q1 to Q17 were rated on a 7-point Likert scale (strongly disagree to strongly agree). A seven-point scale (strongly prefer left to strongly prefer right) was used for Q18. Q19 was open-ended.

No.	Question
1	The learner's goal is clearly stated in this feedback
2	The learner's learning stage is clearly stated in this feedback
3	An evaluation of the learner's activity is clearly stated in this feedback
4	Information about what the learner should do next is clearly stated in this feedback
5	The learner's self-evaluation is not included in this feedback
6	The feedback helps clarify what good performance is (goals, criteria, expected standards)
7	The feedback facilitates the development of self-assessment (reflection) in learning
8	The feedback delivers high-quality information to students about their learning
9	The feedback encourages teacher and peer dialogue about learning
10	The feedback encourages positive motivational beliefs and self-esteem
11	The feedback provides opportunities to close the gap between current and desired performance
12	I did not understand some of the feedback on my work
13	I used the feedback I received to go back over what I had done in my work
14	The feedback I received prompted me to review the material covered in my learning
15	I paid careful attention to the feedback on my work and tried to understand what it was saying
16	It was always easy to know the standard of work that was expected
17	It was often difficult to discover what was expected of me in this PBL
18	Which feedback do you prefer?
19	Explain the reason for your answer to Q18

one-sample Wilcoxon signed-rank test showed that the LLM-generated feedback was more preferable than the coach-created feedback ($W = 9191.5, p < .01$, 95% CI [1.5, 1.5]).

The coach-created feedback was significantly shorter than the LLM-generated feedback, as shown in Sect. 4.3. We calculated Spearman's rank correlation coefficients to determine relationships between feedback length and Q18 evaluation scores (scatter plots in Fig. 6). The results showed significant differences between the LLM-generated feedback length and Q18 score ($\rho = .13$, $p = .007$, 95% CI [0.04, 0.22]) and between the coach-created feedback length and Q18 score ($\rho = .11$, $p = .02$, 95% CI [0.02, 0.20]). However, no significant difference emerged between the length difference of the two feedback types and Q18 score

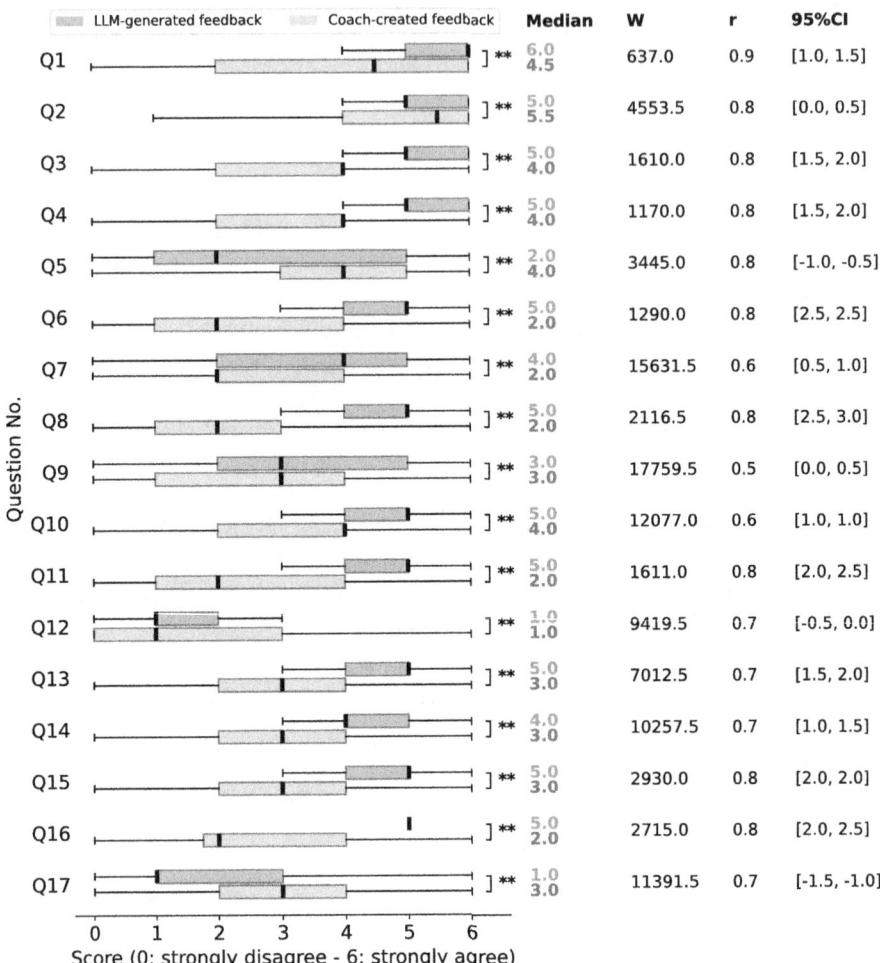

Fig. 4. The distribution of answers to questions Q1–17. **Bold lines** indicate the median, and the boxes indicate the interquartile range. ** indicate significant differences between the LLM-generated feedback and the coach-created feedback ($p < .01$) according to the Wilcoxon signed-rank test. Confidence intervals show the differences between the score of both feedback.

($\rho = .04$, $p = .39$, 95% CI [-0.05, 0.14]). Both feedback types required a certain character count, and the length difference did not influence feedback preferences.

For Q19 responses, Table 7 presents examples of the reasons why respondents preferred LLM-generated feedback (scores 1–3) or coach-created feedback (scores -3 to -1). LLM-generated feedback was preferred for clear next actions, detailed information, learner activity evaluation, and step-by-step instructions. Coach-created feedback was favored for its conciseness, positive expressions, and appropriate amount of information provided.

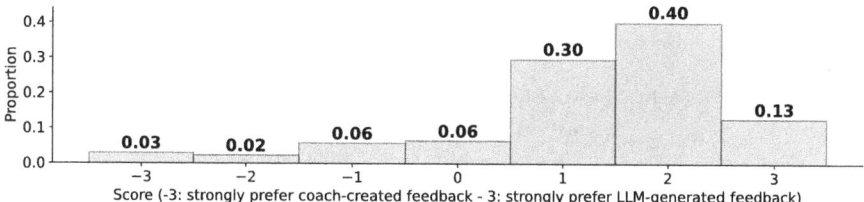

Fig. 5. The distribution of answers to question Q18.

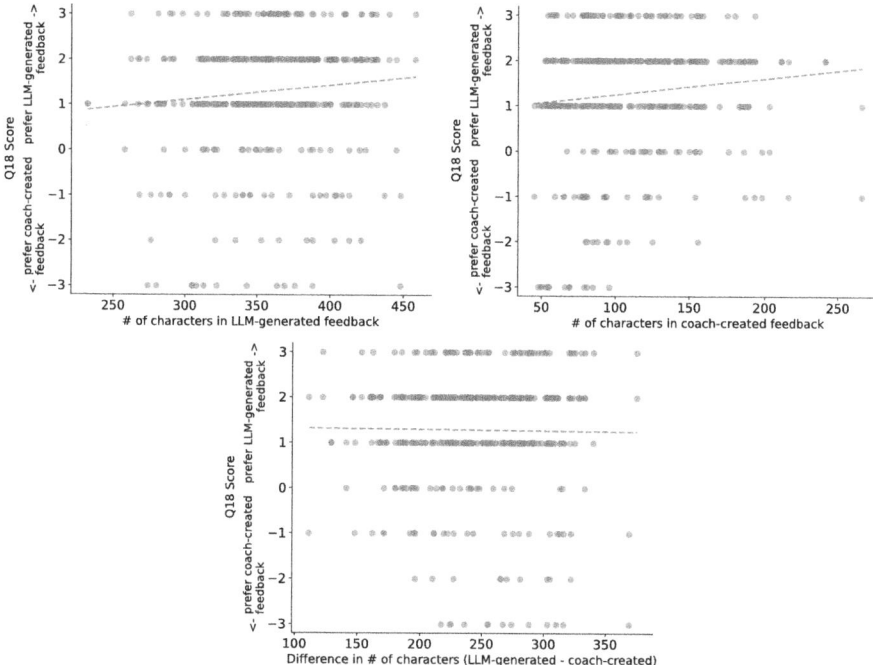

Fig. 6. Scatter plots of question Q18 scores against feedback character count. Top left shows LLM-generated feedback character count vs. Q18 score, top right shows coach-created feedback character count vs. Q18 score, bottom shows the difference in character count between the two feedback types vs. Q18 score. Red dashed lines indicate regression lines fitted by least squares method. (Color figure online)

For research question RQ_2 (What are the characteristics of feedback that learners find preferable?), the results suggest that learners prefer feedback with the following characteristics: (1) clarity of next actions, (2) specific evaluation, (3) detailed information, (4) consideration and encouragement, (5) stepwise guidance, (6) conciseness, (7) positive expressions, and (8) appropriate information amount.

Table 7. Reasons for preferring LLM-generated feedback or coach-created feedback according to response to Q19.

Reasons for preferring LLM-generated feedback ($N = 356$)

Topics	Responses (excerpt)
Clarity of next actions	"Because it clearly showed guidelines for filling the gap based on desired performance." (R1) "It shows what is lacking and how to approach them." (R4) "Because it clearly states how the learner should proceed." (R6) "The learner can get specific instructions on what to work on next." (R7)
Concrete evaluation and feedback	"Because there was an evaluation of their activity." (R3) "They specifically evaluated the learner's actions and made it clear what the learner should do next." (R5)
Detailed information provided	"Because current issues and future directions are clearly stated." (R2) "I felt that in the early stages of experiments, until getting into the swing of things, thorough advice would be easier to proceed with." (R6) "Long feedback provides more information." (R8)
Consideration/encouragement for learners	"Because the learner's efforts were appreciated and I felt they could work hard on future activities." (R3) "I personally prefer it because it recognizes the learner's efforts, specifically shows the next direction to proceed, and is structured to draw out growth motivation." (R5) "It's a sentence that conveys consideration for the learner's situation while gently suggesting that research progress should be slightly accelerated." (R6)
Stepwise guidance	"Next steps are shown step by step, so the learner can work with peace of mind." (R5) "The feedback states 'first' and 'second' step by step, which is very clear." (R8)

Reasons for preferring coach-created feedback ($N = 48$)

Topics	Responses (excerpt)
Conciseness	"Concise and easy to understand, the learner can understand what to do next." (R3) "Since the content is similar, concise is better." (R4) "Because it was short and easy to understand the key points, and the learner can quickly understand what to do next." (R5)
Positive wording	"Because feedback that considers the learner's mental and physical aspects is provided." (R2) "There are many positive words that enhance learning motivation." (R5)
Appropriate amount of information (not overly detailed)	"Because I felt that at the current stage, the learner wouldn't be able to understand if too much content was provided as feedback." (R3) "I think these are very similar, but for experiments, 'continue to conduct' is sufficient." (R8)

5 Discussion

5.1 Evaluation of LLM-Generated Feedback

This study compared the feedback from inexperienced instructional assistants (coaches) in a PBL setting with that generated by an LLM. The results showed that LLM-generated feedback outperformed coach-created feedback on most evaluation criteria. This demonstrates that LLMs, using structured prompts [23] designed to satisfy feedback requirements [22], can generate feedback that meets the principles of Nicol and Macfarlane-Dick [17] and the conditions of Gibbs et al. [8]. For Q5, regarding "should not include evaluating learners themselves," coach-created feedback received a better evaluation, indicating an area for LLM prompt improvement.

Q19 responses showed that learners preferred feedback with clear next actions, specific activity evaluations, and detailed information, aligning with previous research. However, concise feedback using positive language is also preferred. The balance between specificity and conciseness may vary according to learner preferences, learning stages, and goals, and remains a challenge for future studies. Positive language was not included in the LLM prompts or coach instructions, suggesting the potential addition of this as a requirement.

The feedback needed in PBL may differ from that in traditional, lecture-based education. PBL emphasizes learner autonomy and creativity, with tasks lacking clear correct answers, requiring feedback that supports learning processes and provides guidance rather than simple correctness assessment [9]. Q19 responses highlighted preferences for "clarity of next actions" and "stepwise guidance," reflecting PBL-specific needs. Traditional lecture-based education focuses on understanding verification and knowledge correction, for which direct feedback may be more appropriate. Future research should examine how educational formats influence the feedback needs of learners.

5.2 Potential as a Support Tool for Coaches

In the experiment to create feedback described in Sect. 4.3, coaches with limited learning instruction experience created shorter feedback than the LLM-generated feedback. The coaches were not instructed on the length of feedback to determine their natural feedback patterns. The coaches' feedback was short, possibly due to inexperience in writing feedback or because the length of the activity report influenced the length of the feedback. As indicated in the responses to Q18, learners require feedback that contains sufficient information. This suggests that LLM-generated feedback can serve as a reference for coaches and can be used both as an educational support tool and as a practice for creating effective feedback.

5.3 Limitations and Future Work

This study had some limitations. First, feedback was created and evaluated by learners in the fields of education or informatics. Evaluating LLM-generated feedback across different fields remains a subject for future research. This study used students with limited teaching experience as a comparison group for coaches to simulate coaches' feedback. However, it is unclear how this evaluation differs from that of experienced teachers in the same context. A study with more experienced coaches could enable diverse feedback evaluation.

Second, because coach-created feedback had significantly fewer characters than LLM-generated feedback, this difference may have influenced the evaluation, excluding preferences. For content-based evaluations, comparing feedback with similar character counts may be necessary.

Finally, we used Claude Sonnet 4 as the LLM in this study. Given the rapid progress of LLMs, it is uncertain whether other LLMs or different versions will yield similar results. However, this study demonstrated the potential of LLMs to generate preferred feedback, and advances in LLM technology are expected to produce higher quality feedback.

6 Conclusion

This study examined the effectiveness of LLM-based feedback generation in distance PBL. Using 216 activity reports, we showed that LLM-generated feedback better meets feedback requirements and educational principles than coach-created feedback and is preferred by learners. Feedback with clear next actions and specific evaluations is favored, and conciseness and positivity are important factors. These results suggest that LLM-based feedback generation can be a useful educational tool for distance PBL.

Acknowledgements. This research was partially supported by the JSPS KAKENHI Grant Number 25K15367.

The authors acknowledge the use of generative AI tools. Claude Sonnet 4 (Anthropic) and Gemini 2.5 Pro (Google) were utilized to construct the system for the experiments of this study, code tables in LaTeX format, shorten the manuscript, and enhance the readability of this paper. The authors confirm that we originated all ideas and concepts presented in this paper.

Disclosure of Interests. The authors have no competing interests to declare that are relevant to the content of this article.

References

1. Almulla, M.A.: The effectiveness of the project-based learning (pbl) approach as a way to engage students in learning. SAGE Open **10**(3), 2158244020938702 (2020). https://doi.org/10.1177/2158244020938702
2. Bernacki, M.L., Greene, M.J., Lobczowski, N.G.: A systematic review of research on personalized learning: personalized by whom, to what, how, and for what purpose(s)? Educ. Psychol. Rev. **33**(4), 1675–1715 (2021). https://doi.org/10.1007/s10648-021-09615-8
3. Black, P., Wiliam, D.: Assessment and classroom learning. Assess. Educ. Princip. Policy Pract. **5**(1), 7–74 (1998)
4. Chanpet, P., Chomsuwan, K., Murphy, E.: Online project-based learning and formative assessment. Technol. Knowl. Learn. **25**(3), 685–705 (2018). https://doi.org/10.1007/s10758-018-9363-2

5. Denny, P., MacNeil, S., Savelka, J., Porter, L., Luxton-Reilly, A.: Desirable characteristics for AI teaching assistants in programming education. In: Proceedings of the 2024 on Innovation and Technology in Computer Science Education, ITiCSE 2024, vol. 1. pp. 408–414. Association for Computing Machinery, New York (2024). https://doi.org/10.1145/3649217.3653574
6. Etkina, E., Harper, K.A.: Weekly reports: student reflections on learning. J. Coll. Sci. Teach. **31**(7), 476–480 (2002)
7. Gibbs, G., Dunbar-Goddet, H.: The effects of programme assessment environments on student learning. In: The Higher Education Academy, pp. 1–30 (2007)
8. Gibbs, G., Simpson, C.: Conditions under which assessment supports students' learning. Learn. Teach. High. Educ. **1**, 3–31 (2005)
9. Guo, P., Saab, N., Post, L.S., Admiraal, W.: A review of project-based learning in higher education: student outcomes and measures. Int. J. Educ. Res. **102**, 101586 (2020). https://doi.org/10.1016/j.ijer.2020.101586
10. Hattie, J., Timperley, H.: The power of feedback. Rev. Educ. Res. **77**(1), 81–112 (2007). https://doi.org/10.3102/003465430298487
11. He, Z., Sarcar, S., Inoue, T.: Exploring the feasibility of video activity reporting for students in distance learning. In: Data Science, Human-Centered Computing, and Intelligent Technologies, pp. 44–55 (2022)
12. Huumonen, J., Poranen, T., Zhang, Z.: Communication challenges in distributed student projects. In: SEFI 50th Annual Conference of The European Society for Engineering Education, Barcelona, pp. 334–343 (2022). https://doi.org/10.5821/conference-9788412322262.1225
13. Kumar, H., et al.: Guiding students in using LLMs in supported learning environments: effects on interaction dynamics, learner performance, confidence, and trust. Proc. ACM Hum.-Comput. Interact. **8**(CSCW2), 1–30 (2024). https://doi.org/10.1145/3687038
14. Lee, H.Y., Chen, P.H., Wang, W.S., Huang, Y.M., Wu, T.T.: Empowering ChatGPT with guidance mechanism in blended learning: effect of self-regulated learning, higher-order thinking skills, and knowledge construction. Int. J. Educ. Technol. High. Educ. **21**(1), 16 (2024). https://doi.org/10.1186/s41239-024-00447-4
15. Lim, R.S., Krause-Levy, S., Villegas Molina, I., Porter, L.: Student expectations of tutors in computing courses. In: Proceedings of the 54th ACM Technical Symposium on Computer Science Education, vol. 1, pp. 437–443 (2023)
16. Narciss, S.: Feedback strategies for interactive learning tasks. In: Handbook of Research on Educational Communications and Technology, pp. 125–143. Routledge (2008)
17. Nicol, D.J., Macfarlane-Dick, D.: Formative assessment and self-regulated learning: a model and seven principles of good feedback practice. Stud. High. Educ. **31**(2), 199–218 (2006)
18. Pocevičienė, R.: Changes of teacher-student/students communication in study process: context of remote teaching/learning. In: Education and New Developments, vol. 2, pp. 548–552. Science Press (2023). https://doi.org/10.36315/2023v2end121
19. Pwanedo Amos, J., et al.: A bibliometric exposition and review on leveraging llms for programming education. IEEE Access **13**, 58364–58393 (2025). https://doi.org/10.1109/ACCESS.2025.3554627
20. Radford, A., Kim, J.W., Xu, T., Brockman, G., McLeavey, C., Sutskever, I.: Robust speech recognition via large-scale weak supervision. In: International Conference on Machine Learning, pp. 28492–28518. PMLR (2023)
21. Sadler, D.R.: Formative assessment and the design of instructional systems. Inst. Sci. **18**(2), 119–144 (1989)

22. Sasaki, K., Inoue, T.: Design of feedback for a system to support distance project-based learning. In: Data Science and Reliable Machine Learning, pp. 61–76 (2024). https://doi.org/10.30819/5855
23. Sasaki, K., Inoue, T.: Prompt design for supporting feedback in distance project-based learning. In: The 25th IEEE International Conference on Advanced Learning Technologies (2025)
24. Shute, V.J.: Focus on formative feedback. Rev. Educ. Res. **78**(1), 153–189 (2008)
25. Steinert, S., Avila, K.E., Ruzika, S., Kuhn, J., Küchemann, S.: Harnessing large language models to develop research-based learning assistants for formative feedback. Smart Learn. Environ. **11**(1), 62 (2024). https://doi.org/10.1186/s40561-024-00354-1
26. Wiliam, D.: Assessment: the bridge between teaching and learning. Voices Middle **21**(2), 15 (2013)
27. Williams, A.: Delivering effective student feedback in higher education: an evaluation of the challenges and best practice. Int. J. Res. Educ. Sci. **10**(2), 473–501 (2024). https://doi.org/10.46328/ijres.3404
28. Wisniewski, B., Zierer, K., Hattie, J.: The power of feedback revisited: a meta-analysis of educational feedback research. Front. Psychol. **10**, 487662 (2020)
29. Yousef, M., Mohamed, K., Medhat, W., Mohamed, E.H., Khoriba, G., Arafa, T.: BeGrading: large language models for enhanced feedback in programming education. Neural Comput. Appl. **37**(2), 1027–1040 (2025). https://doi.org/10.1007/s00521-024-10449-y

Generating Vicarious Dialogue for Online Learning Using Knowledge Graph-Based Retrieval-Augmented Generation

Yaofei Ding[1] and Tomoo Inoue[2(✉)]

[1] Graduate School of Comprehensive Human Sciences, University of Tsukuba, Ibaraki, Japan
[2] Institute of Library, Information and Media Science, University of Tsukuba, Ibaraki, Japan
inoue@slis.tsukuba.ac.jp

Abstract. Dialogue-style learning materials are superior to lecture-style learning materials in many aspects. However, creating dialogue-style learning materials places a significant burden on teachers. In this paper, we propose a generative AI system that applies Knowledge Graph-based Retrieval-Augmented Generation (KG-RAG) for creating dialogue-style learning materials. The initial evaluation suggested that the KG-RAG approach has the potential to generate consistent and educationally appropriate dialogues, even when high-quality existing teaching materials are not available. These findings indicate that KG-RAG may offer a promising direction for producing dialogue-style materials in resource-scarce contexts, potentially reducing instructor workload while maintaining pedagogical value.

Keywords: Educational Technology · Learning Material Generation · Vicarious Learning · Teacher Support · Retrieval-Augmented Generation

1 Introduction

Introduced by Bandura, vicarious learning is widely recognised fundamental to education. It enables learners to internalise knowledge and skills through observation rather than direct experience. According to Bandura, people can acquire complex patterns of behaviour by observing others without having to construct them through repetitive trial and error [1]. Further empirical research has confirmed the benefits of vicarious learning [2]. Building on this theoretical foundation, a series of studies on vicarious learning were undertaken in the context of technology-enhanced learning [3]. Online learning, especially learning from educational video materials, often lacks the classroom environment that typically provides natural opportunities for vicarious learning. Recent research has shown that learners benefit more from dialogue-based video formats than from traditional monologic lecture-style videos [4–6]. These findings suggest that vicarious dialogues, which are scripted conversational materials designed to simulate peer or tutor-tutee interactions, can serve as an effective tool for supporting vicarious learning, leading to greater learning gains. However, creating such dialogues is time-consuming and laborious for instructors.

Recent research has explored the potential of large language models(LLMs) to alleviate instructors' workload by converting monologues or Q&A scripts into vicarious dialogue. For example, a system called VIVID has been developed to enable instructors to collaborate with LLMs to transform a monologue lecture script into pedagogically meaningful dialogue [7]. Another study used LLMs to convert Q&A texts into scripted vicarious dialogue [8]. However, these approaches rely on high-quality instructional materials. Even recent studies on using LLMs to generate other types of educational content typically rely on complete textbooks or other educational materials as input [9,10], leaving a gap for generating vicarious dialogues when such resources are not easily accessible.

The aim of this research is to support the creation of vicarious dialogues for online learning, a process that is labor-intensive for instructors. To achieve this aim, we developed a dialogue generation system based on Knowledge Graph-based Retrieval-Augmented Generation (KG-RAG) and conducted an initial evaluation of its pedagogical quality through expert assessment. While LLMs have been used to automate this process and generate various types of educational content through different methods, these approaches typically rely on high-quality instructional materials, which are not always available, limiting their applicability in resource-scarce contexts. Quantitative and qualitative analysis suggested that the system may generate pedagogically meaningful vicarious dialogues based solely on factual knowledge graph input, providing preliminary evidence of its potential even when high-quality instructional materials are unavailable.

2 Related Work

2.1 Vicarious Learning and Vicarious Diaologue

According to vicarious learning theories, students can learn by drawing on the experiences of others [11]. Empirical research has confirmed that the benefits of vicarious learning are both cognitive, resulting in increased knowledge and understanding of the subject area, and social [2].

Deep-level-reasoning questions have been found to enhance the effectiveness of vicarious learning as a feature of dialogue [12]. Such questions, categorized into six functional types–antecedent, consequence, goal-orientation, instrumental/procedural, enablement, and expectationalare highly correlated with the deeper levels of cognition in Bloom's Taxonomy of educational objectives in the cognitive domain [13].

Bloom's Taxonomy, originally proposed by Bloom et al. as cumulative hierarchical framework for classifying educational objectives [14], was later revised by Krathwohl into six levels: Remember, Understand, Apply, Analyze, Evaluate, and Create. This revised taxonomy is a valuable tool for examining the relative emphasis of instructional content and ensuring curriculum alignment [15].

Although vicarious learning has traditionally been studied in classroom environments, recent research has shown that it can also be effectively applied in digital contexts. Nugraha et al. found that converting monologue-based instructional videos into dialogue-like formats significantly improves learners' attention and their experience of watching and learning in digital settings [4-6].

Designing effective vicarious dialogue requires to meet pedagogical conditions such as integrating deep-level reasoning questions and applying Bloom's taxonomy. It makes the creation of high-quality dialogue both cognitively demanding and time-consuming.

2.2 Authoring Vicarious Dialogue via LLMs

Recent studies have explored the use of LLMs to support the automated creation of vicarious dialogues that facilitate vicarious learning, aiming to reduce the manual effort required to design such multi-turn instructional interactions.

Although this was not the main focus of their study, Tanprasert et al. conducted a brief experiment demonstrating that LLMs could be used to convert Q&A texts into scripted dialogues, suggesting its potential for future exploration [8]. Choi et al. developed a system called VIVID, which offers a more systematic approach, enabling instructors to collaborate with LLMs to transform a monologue lecture scripts into pedagogically meaningful dialogue [7].

However, these approaches rely on high-quality instructional materials, which are not always readily available. Moreover, as Liu et al. have noted, large language models struggle to robustly access and utilize information in long input contexts [16].

2.3 LLM-Generated Educational Materials

In order to reduce instructors' workload and improve the quality of teaching, large language models (LLMs) are increasingly used to generate a wide range of educational materials, including instructional questions, exercises, and domain-specific content [9,10,17].

Several strategies have been proposed to enhance the quality and pedagogical alignment of generated content, including prompt engineering, cognitive-level conditioning, and retrieval-augmented generation (RAG), which has been adopted to retrieve domain-specific content, improving factuality and contextual relevance in e-learning [18,19].

Despite the potential of these approaches, prior studies have highlighted that substantial human oversight remains necessary due to concerns regarding accuracy and quality [17]. While RAG has been shown to improve accuracy and relevance, it was suggested that it may fail to capture the structured relationships between concepts and lose key information due to its reliance on unstructured text and lengthy contexts [20,21].

2.4 Retrieval-Augmented Generation (RAG) with Knowledge Graph

As mentioned in Sect. 2.3, LLMs face challenges such as limited factual accuracy. RAG addresses this by combining retrieval and generation. However, RAG has its own limitations, including its reliance on unstructured text and lengthy contexts, which can lead to incoherent outputs and cause the model to lose focus, obscuring key information in the process.

Knowledge graphs (KGs) are structured representations of real-world entities and their relationships. They are typically implemented as graph databases, where nodes represent entities and edges represent the semantic relationships between them [22,23]. As structured abstractions of domain knowledge, KGs can supplement existing RAG approaches based on semantics by integrating factual and relational information [24].

Enhanced RAG by knowledge graphs has been shown to significantly improve factual accuracy and reduce hallucination. It also supports more sophisticated multi-hop reasoning, and enhances the explainability of LLM-generated outputs, particularly in knowledge-intensive domains such as question-answering systems and educational agents [20,25].

3 Research Methodology

The primary aim of this study is to support the generation of vicarious dialogue for online learning. Since it is laborious for instructors to create pedagogically meaningful vicarious dialogue, we aimed to develop a system to assist in the automatic generation of such dialogue using LLMs, particularly in a scenario where suitable high-quality instructional materials are unavailable.

We propose a novel system that uses KGs as the information source and integrates KG-RAG to generate pedagogically meaningful vicarious dialogue. As discussed in Sect. 2.4, although KG-RAG has been known to be effective in various fields, including educational agents, this research focuses on the under-investigated area of its potential for creating instructional materials, particularly on vicarious dialogue.

The overall study consists of the following steps: (1) We construct a domain-specific knowledge graph by extracting factual triples from scientific content. These triples are automatically generated using LLM-based extraction tools and stored in a Neo4j database with vector indices to support semantic retrieval. Additional triples can be incorporated from open resources such as Wikidata or extracted from publicly available scientific and educational content. (2) We develop a system that is leveraged by KG-RAG and pedagogical prompting to generate pedagogically meaningful vicarious dialogues. To demonstrate the effectiveness of the proposed approach, we present examples of generated dialogues. (3) These dialogues are evaluated through expert review based on pedagogical criteria and then compared with dialogues produced by baseline methods, which applied the same pedagogical design but without incorporating a knowledge graph or KG-RAG.

4 KG-RAGBased Vicarious Dialogue Generation System

4.1 Overview

The system takes scientific content, user-specified learning objectives, and pedagogical goals as input. The system then constructs a domain-specific knowledge graph from the content. After annotating each triple of the graph with Bloom's taxonomy levels, the system retrieves relevant information and combines it with instructional prompts to generate dialogues aligned with the provided goals.

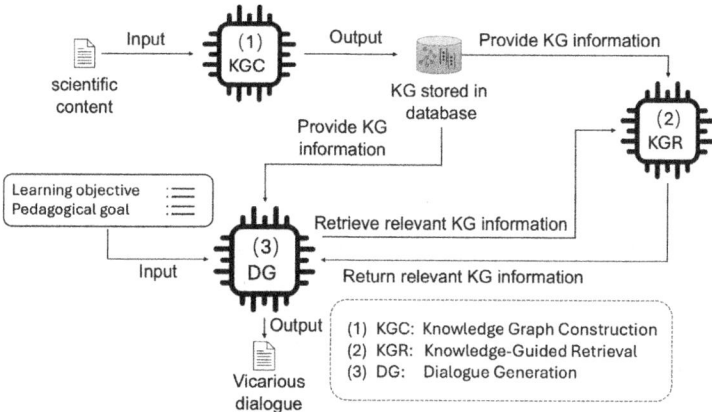

Fig. 1. The architecture of the proposed system including three core components

4.2 Design of the Vicarious Dialogue Generation System

Based on previous studies [14,26,27], we have identified three design goals(DGs) for the dialogues generated by our system:

1. DG1. Ensure factual accuracy: The dialogue must convey factually correct information, following textbook quality criteria from Ivić et al. [26].
2. DG2. Ensure conceptual coherence: Instructional content should reflect logical connections between concepts, also inspired by Ivić et al.'s emphasis on structured and clear content [26].
3. DG3. Support pedagogical alignment: The dialogue should align with learning objectives and provide cognitive scaffolding, drawing on Bloom's taxonomy [14] and Gagné's instructional principles [27].

As illustrated in Fig. 1, the system was designed with three core components, described below, to fulfill the three design goals introduced above.

(1) Knowledge Graph Construction(KGC). To achieve DG1 (Ensure factual accuracy), we construct a domain-specific knowledge graph to ground LLM-generated content in factual information.

(2) Knowledge-Guided Retrieval(KGR). To achieve DG2 (Ensure conceptual coherence), we designed a knowledge-guided retrieval component, inspired in part by the work of Barry et al. [21], which integrates semantic retrieval with graph-based reasoning. Their approach consists of: (1) converting textual data into a knowledge graph composed of entities and relations; (2) storing text chunks and their embeddings as nodes, and linking them to the entities they reference; and (3) using a user query to retrieve the most relevant chunks via embedding similarity, then exploring the graph from these chunks as seed nodes to collect related entities and relations in the form of triples.

(3) Dialogue Generation(DR). To achieve DG3 (Support pedagogical alignment), we designed a dialogue generation component that uses the prompts to guide the generation of instructionally meaningful utterances from the retrieved knowledge.

4.3 Process and Implementation of the Vicarious Dialogue Generation System

The system was implemented in Python, connecting to a Neo4j-based knowledge graph via the Neo4j API and to OpenAI's GPT-4o via API access, with a temperature setting of 0.7 to encourage responses that both coherent and moderately diverse. This section details the process and implementation of each system component.

(1) Knowledge Graph Construction. Figure 2 illustrates our knowledge graph construction process. We used the LLMGraphTransformer to extract KG triples from scientific content, annotated each triple with a Bloom's taxonomy level, and stored them in a Neo4j-based database. In parallel, we converted each triple into a natural language text chunk using GPT-4o, embedded them into a 1536-dimensional vectors using the `text-embedding-3-small` model, and linked to their entities. Finally, each chunk, its embedding, and entity links were stored as a unified data unit in the KG.

As shown in Fig. 3, by providing the system with content from the Japan Meteorological Agency (JMA) webpage explaining the causes of earthquakes [28], a domain-specific knowledge graph, was automatically generated.

The authors annotated each triple with a cognitive level corresponding to the revised Bloom's Taxonomy [15], following Japan's junior high school curriculum standards [29]. Higher-order levels (e.g., *Analyze*) are assigned to concepts involving causal or mechanistic reasoning (e.g., "understanding the causes of earthquakes in relation to internal geodynamic forces"), while lower-order levels (*Understand, Remember*) are used for basic facts based on the required cognitive process. For example, the triple `Lower Mantle--PART_OF--Mantle` was annotated with the level *Understand*, while the triple `Earthquake--CAUSE_BY--Bedrock` was annotated with the level *Analyze*.

(2) Knowledge-Guided Retrieval. Figure 4 illustrates our knowledge-guided retrieval process. Given a textual input, we converted it into an embedding and perform a vector similarity search over the knowledge graph database. We then retrieved the top-k vectors ($k = 3$) with a similarity threshold of 0.5

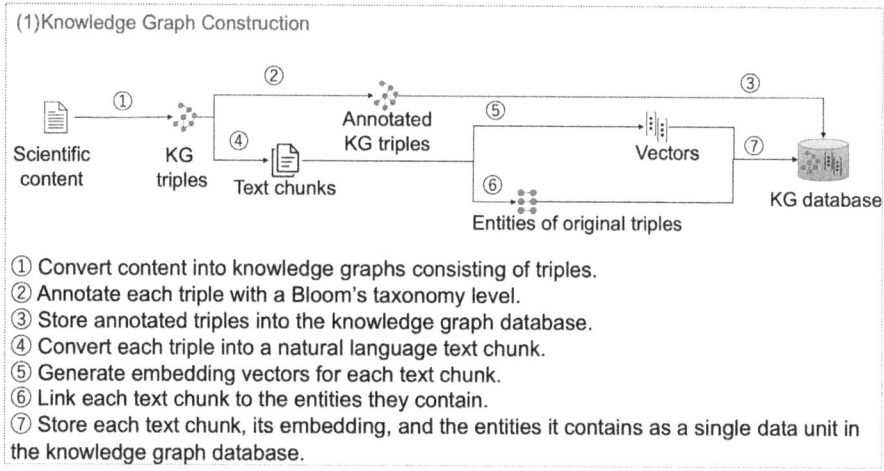

Fig. 2. Process of the knowledge graph construction component.

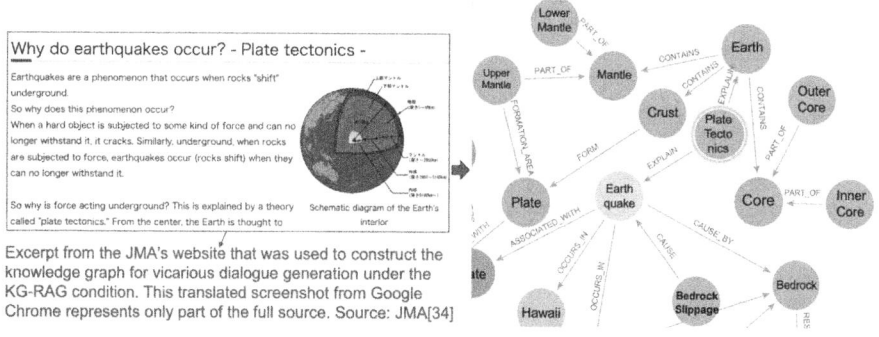

Fig. 3. Source material and resulting knowledge graph for KG-RAG dialogue generation. The left side shows an excerpt from the Japan Meteorological Agency's website, used to extract factual content. The right side displays a portion of the domain-specific knowledge graph constructed from this source, visualized in Neo4j.

to ensure relevance while reducing noise. These vectors were mapped to entities, from which a depth-2 subgraph is collected. The resulting subgraph, containing structural information, semantic relations, and Bloom's taxonomy annotations, was used as context for dialogue generation.

(3) Dialogue Generation. Figure 5 illustrates our dialogue generation process. We first gave the LLM the learning objective and pedagogical goal to guide generation, and then filled the prompt template with supporting content retrieved from the knowledge graph. Using the OpenAI API, we generated the tutee's initial question, retrieves a Bloom-annotated subgraph as context, and produced the tutor's answer. Question-answer pairs were combined into dialogues until a target length was reached. Figure 6 shows a prompt template

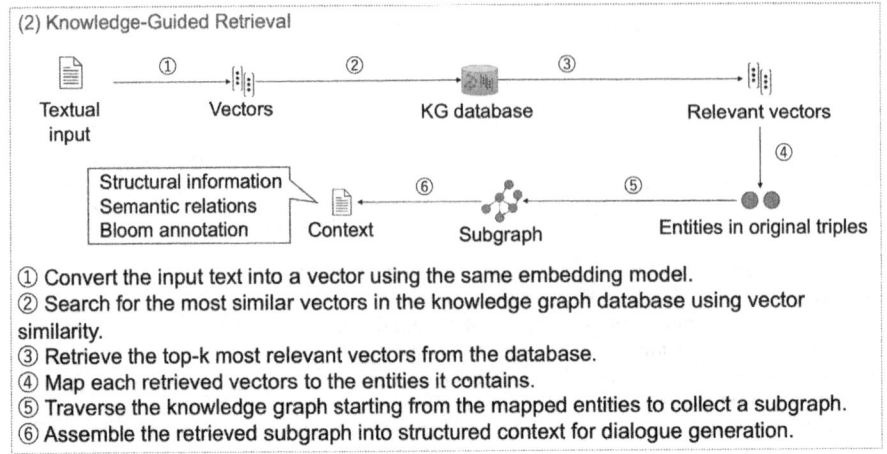

Fig. 4. Process of the knowledge-guided retrieval component.

excerpt, which consists of four main elements: (1) LLM Role, specifies the model's persona. (2) Pedagogical Instruction, controls the cognitive depth and discourse style based on Bloom's taxonomy or deep-reasoning question types. (3) Supporting Content, provides factual grounding by including relevant knowledge retrieved from the knowledge graph. (4) LLM Task, defines the model's output action. Finally, we revised the dialogues via zero-shot prompting, using the revision prompt shown in Fig. 7 to ensure logical flow and pedagogical alignment. The prompt incorporated Bloom's taxonomy, deep-level reasoning questions, and representative utterance patterns, which prior studies have shown to enhance vicarious learning outcomes [7,12,13].

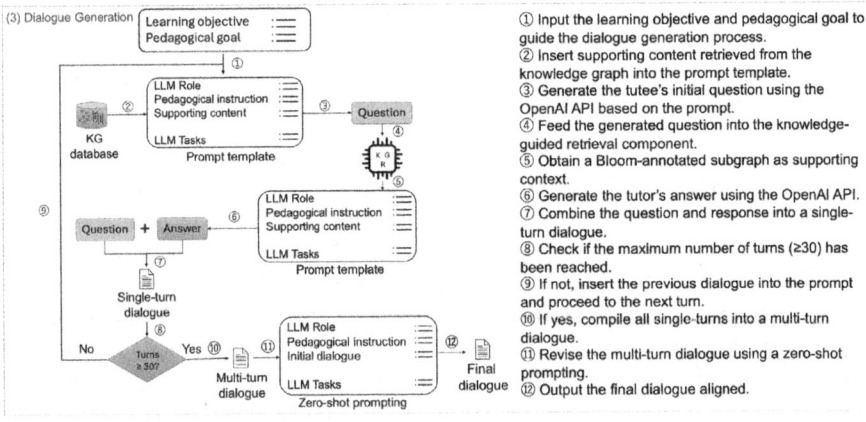

Fig. 5. Process of the dialogue generation component.

```
answer_prompt = ChatPromptTemplate.from_messages([
    ("system",
    "You are a pedagogically-aware instructional designer.\n"
    "Your job is to generate natural Japanese dialogue content between a teacher and a student. \n"   ①LLM Role
    "You do not directly answer student questions yourself, \n"                                        ④LLM Tasks
    "but create realistic teacher responses as part of the teaching material.\n"
    "Please answer in Japanese only, never use English in your responses.\n"
    "The response should be 2-3 sentences long and conversational in tone.\n"
    "Instruction: {prompt_style}"),   ②Pedagogical instruction
    ("human",
    "Student question: {question}\n"
    "Cypher query used: {query}\n"
    "Database result: {response}\n"   ③Supporting content
    "Please answer in Japanese:")
])

remember_style = "Provide a concise explanation of facts or definitions (e.g., names, terms, or numerical values)."
understand_style = (
    "Paraphrase the content using other words, illustrations, or examples. "
    "Use analogies, simple comparisons, or intuitive explanations to aid understanding. "
    "Avoid complex structure or causal reasoning."
)
apply_style = "Demonstrate how the concept can be applied in real-world or practical contexts."
analyze_style = (
    "Break the topic into components and describe how they relate to each other. "
    "Clarify logical flow and causality. "
    "Go beyond examples by detailing each part's role and connections."
)
evaluate_style = (
    "Make reasoned judgments based on criteria or standards. "
    "Compare different perspectives and explain which one is more appropriate and why."
)
create_style = (
    "Combine multiple ideas to generate original thoughts or proposals. "
    "Link related knowledge and provide unique synthesis or perspective."
)
```

Fig. 6. Excerpt of prompt used for the dialogue generation.

5 Initial Evaluation

5.1 Purpose

To evaluate the quality of the vicarious dialogue generated by our proposed system, we compared two conditions: 1) The KG-RAG condition, in which dialogues were generated by our KG-RAG-based system integrating a knowledge graph and pedagogical prompting; 2) The baseline condition, in which dialogues were generated by GPT-4o using a zero-shot prompting with pedagogical instructions, but without knowledge graph grounding.

5.2 Materials

To compare the performance of our KG-RAG-based system with that of a zero-shot prompting approach without knowledge graph grounding, we prepared two sets of vicarious dialogues from different domains: one in geoscience (earthquake mechanisms) and one in computer science (generative AI).

(1) Experimental Condition: KG-RAG Generated Dialogue. In the experimental condition, we used dialogue generated by our proposed system. For the geoscience domain, the dialogue was produced based on the knowledge graph

> You are a pedagogically-aware instructional designer and science teacher. Your task is to revise and enhance an existing multi-turn dialogue in natural Japanese between a teacher and a curious middle school student. The instructional objective is: To help students understand the causes and mechanisms of earthquakes. Your goal is to improve the dialogue so that it becomes:
> 1. Pedagogically rich and natural for middle school educational settings;
> 2. Structured based on Bloom's taxonomy (from Understanding to Creating);
> 3. Includes at least 20% Deep Reasoning questions. These should come from these categories: Antecedent (Why?), Consequence (What if?), Goal orientation (Why?), Enablement (Why/How?), Instrumental/Procedural (How?), Expectational (Why not?).
>
> At each turn: Internally choose one tutor utterance category from: Self-monitoring, Lecturing, Demonstrating, Questioning, Summarizing, Answering, Scaffolding, Diagnosing, Off-topic. Internally choose one student utterance category from: Questioning, Answering, Reflecting, Explanation, Off-topic.
>
> Apply Bloom's taxonomy styles as follows:
> Remember: Provide a concise explanation of facts or definitions.
> Understand: Paraphrase using analogies or illustrations. Avoid complex causal chains.
> Apply: Show how the concept is used in real-world examples.
> Analyze: Break the topic into parts and explain how they relate.
> Evaluate: Compare different perspectives and explain what makes one better.
> Create: Combine concepts to generate new insights or ideas.

Fig. 7. Excerpt of prompt used for revising the generated dialogues.

constructed in Sect. 4.3, which consisted of 29 triples extracted from Japan Meteorological Agency text on earthquake mechanisms [28]. For the computer science domain (Generative AI), the dialogue was generated from a knowledge graph consisting of 334 triples extracted from the 5,900-word Wikipedia article "Generative artificial intelligence." [31], which covers dispersed topics such as definitions, applications, and ethical or societal issues. Figure 8 shows the geoscience dialogue, while Fig. 9 shows the computer science dialogue.

> ... (dialogue omitted) ...
> 🧑 I see — so the Earth has different layers, and each one has its own role?
> 👨‍🏫 That's a very insightful question. For example, the heat from the inner core warms the outer core, and that heat drives the movement of the mantle. The convection of the mantle then moves the plates, which can trigger earthquakes. In this way, the layers of the Earth are all connected and work together.
> ... (dialogue omitted) ...

Fig. 8. Excerpt of Vicarious Dialogue Generated by KG-RAG Method(Geoscience).

(2) Baseline Condition: Zero-shot Prompting without KG or KG-RAG. For both domains, the baseline dialogues were generated using GPT-4o with zero-shot prompting and no knowledge graph grounding. For the geoscience domain, no external text was provided as input. The dialogue was generated solely from the pedagogical instructions in the prompt, simulating scenarios where instructional materials are unavailable. For the computer science domain (Generative AI), the same Wikipedia text used for knowledge graph construction was directly input into the LLM without constructing a knowledge graph. This served as an ablation condition to isolate the contribution of KG-RAG. As shown in Fig. 10,

> ... (dialogue omitted) ...
> 🧑 If a computer can create stories and drawings on its own, how does it do that?
> 👨‍🏫 A computer can create stories and drawings because it uses a technology called generative artificial intelligence. It's like giving the computer a magic book that lets it imagine and create new things based on what we say (which we call a prompt). Generative AI is like a clever student—it studies lots and lots of books and pictures, and then uses that knowledge to generate new content.
> ... (dialogue omitted) ...

Fig. 9. Excerpt of vicarious dialogue generated by the KG-RAG method (Computer Science).

the baseline prompt shared the same overall structure and key instructional elements as the prompt used for revising the initial vicarious dialogue in Fig. 7. The only difference was the task–it was used for direct generation rather than refinement. Figure 11 shows the geoscience dialogue, while Fig. 12 shows the computer science dialogue.

> You are a pedagogically-aware instructional designer and science teacher. Your task is to simulate a multi-turn vicarious dialogue in natural Japanese between a teacher and a curious middle school student. The instructional objective is: To help students understand the causes and mechanisms of earthquakes. Your goal is to generate a dialogue that is:
> (with the same conditions listed in Fig.7.)

Fig. 10. Excerpt of prompt used for the baseline (geoscience) condition.

> ... (dialogue omitted) ...
> 🧑 Why do tectonic plates move so slowly? What is making them move?
> 👨‍🏫 The movement of plates is caused by the mantle inside the Earth. The mantle is extremely hot and moves slowly like a fluid. This movement gradually pushes and pulls the plates.
> ... (dialogue omitted) ...

Fig. 11. Excerpt of Vicarious Dialogue Generated by Baseline Method(Geoscience).

5.3 Participants

Two expert teachers served as evaluators: one high school geography teacher (4 years' teaching experience, acquaintance of the first author) for the geoscience dialogues for the geoscience dialogues, and one elementary school information technology teacher (20 years' teaching experience, relative of the first author) for the generative AI dialogues. Both were invited for their professional expertise and conducted blind reviews without knowing which outputs were produced by the proposed method or the baseline.

> ... *(dialogue omitted)* ...
> 🧑 Then how does it(generative artificial intelligence) work?
> 🤖 Behind generative AI is a technology called a generative model. Simply put, these models learn patterns and structures from large amounts of data, and then use those patterns to create new content. It's like how you learn to write essays—you first read many articles, and then you try writing on your own.
> ... *(dialogue omitted)* ...

Fig. 12. Excerpt of vicarious dialogue generated by the baseline method (Computer Science).

5.4 Procedure

To ensure an unbiased assessment, we conducted a blind evaluation in which the evaluators compared the KG-RAG and baseline dialogues without knowing their origin. The geoscience dialogues were evaluated on four dimensions using a 5-point scale: (1) knowledge coverage and depth, (2) instructional structure, (3) dialogue coherence and naturalness, and (4) accuracy and factuality. These criteria were based on prior research in instructional design [14,26,27,30]. The computer science (Generative AI) dialogues were evaluated using four criteria adapted from Achieve's OER rubrics: (1) degree of alignment to standards, (2) quality of explanation of the subject matter, (3) utility of materials designed to support teaching, and (4) opportunities for deeper learning [32]. Different criteria were applied because geoscience is a well-established subject with mature textbooks, making textbook-quality frameworks appropriate, whereas Generative AI is an emerging and fast-evolving field where textbooks are still developing, so OER-based criteria were more suitable.

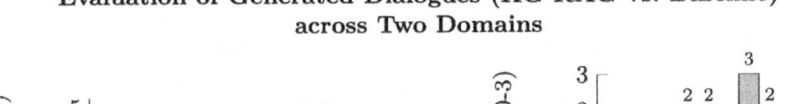

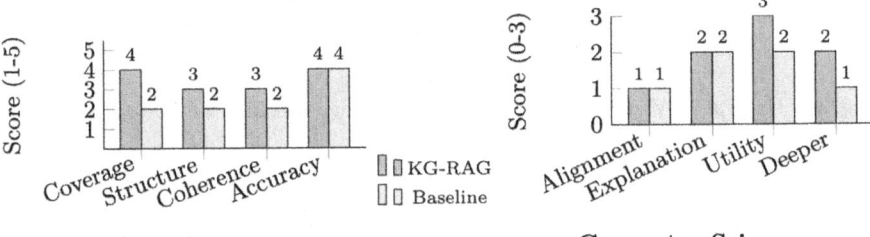

Fig. 13. Expert ratings of KG-RAG and baseline dialogues across two domains (single evaluator per domain). Left: 4-dimension rubric for Geoscience. Right: 4-item OER-adapted rubric for Generative AI.

6 Results

Figure 13 shows the results of the expert evaluation comparing the dialogues generated by KG-RAG with those produced by the baseline method. For the geoscience domain, the KG-RAG dialogue received higher scores in three of the four evaluation dimensions: (1) knowledge coverage and depth, (2) instructional structure, and (3) dialogue coherence and naturalness. Both dialogues received the same score in the fourth dimension, Accuracy and Factuality. For the computer science (Generative AI) domain, the KG-RAG dialogue scored 8 out of 12, while the baseline scored 6 out of 12, with KG-RAG achieving higher scores in (3) utility of materials designed to support teaching and (4) opportunities for deeper learning.

For the geoscience domain, the evaluator provided qualitative comments justifying their ratings. For the KG-RAG dialogue, the evaluator noted that the explanation of the underlying mechanism of earthquake was logically structured and reasonably in-depth. The dialogue first introduced the internal structure of the Earth and used it to explain the asthenosphere's role in generating seismic activity. This was followed by an explanation of the driving force behind mantle movement and a brief discussion of surface-level impacts, such as wave propagation and prevention strategies.

In contrast, the baseline dialogue was criticized for its shallow treatment of the earthquake mechanism. The evaluator noted that the student questions felt disjointed and did not follow a natural progression of inquiry.

7 Discussion

This study provides preliminary evidence that the proposed KG-RAG system, which grounds LLM outputs in knowledge graphs, may generate pedagogically coherent vicarious dialogues without relying on high-quality instructional materials.

However, several limitations should be acknowledged. The system currently relies on a single LLM (GPT-4o), and the performance of other language models has not yet been evaluated. Although the present study demonstrates a knowledge graph built from a single source document, future work will extend this to integrate multiple documents as inputs to construct a larger and more comprehensive graph. In addition, the human evaluation sample size is small and future work will involve a larger number of evaluators to enhance the statistical robustness of the results. Moreover, both evaluators were personally known to the first author. Although blind evaluation procedures were adopted to mitigate potential bias, this relationship remains a limitation. Future work will recruit independent evaluators through open calls to avoid such concerns.

8 Conclusion

This study focused on generating pedagogically meaningful vicarious dialogues in the absence of high-quality instructional materials.

To address this challenge, we proposed a system that is leveraged by Knowledge Graph-based Retrieval-Augmented Generation(KG-RAG) to guide and ground the dialogue generation process.

The initial expert evaluation suggested that the KG-RAG approach might produce better dialogue-style learning materials compared to the zero-shot prompt. This study provides preliminary but promising foundation for future expansion into broader educational domains.

Acknowledgement. This work was partially supported by JSPS KAKENHI Grant Number JP25K15367.

Competing interests. The authors have no competing interests to declare that are relevant to the content of this article.

References

1. Bandura, A., Walters, R.H.: Social Learning Theory, vol. 1, pp. 141–154. Prentice Hall, Englewood Cliffs (1977)
2. Stenning, K., McKendree, J., Lee, J., Cox, R., Dineen, F., Mayes, T.: Vicarious learning from educational dialogue. In: Proceedings of the 1999 Conference on Computer Support for Collaborative Learning (CSCL '99), Art. 43. International Society of the Learning Sciences (1999)
3. Mayes, J.T.: Still to learn from vicarious learning. E-Learn. Digital Media **12**(3–4), 361–371 (2015)
4. Nugraha, A., Harada, T., Wahono, I.A., Inoue, T.: A tool to add a tutee agent in a monologue lecture video improves students' watching experience. In: CHI EA '20, pp. 1–7. ACM, New York (2020)
5. Nugraha, A., Wahono, I.A., Zhanghe, J., Harada, T., Inoue, T.: Creating dialogue between a tutee agent and a tutor in a lecture video improves students' attention. In: CollabTech 2020, pp. 96–111. Springer, Cham (2020)
6. Nugraha, A., Inoue, T., Salim, T.A., Inamullah, M.H.: A dialogue-like video created from a monologue lecture video provides better learning experience. Int. J. Dist. Educ. Technol. **21**(1), 1–21 (2023)
7. Choi, S., Lee, H., Lee, Y., Kim, J.: VIVID: human-AI collaborative authoring of vicarious dialogues from lecture videos. In: CHI '24, pp. 1–26. ACM, New York (2024)
8. Tanprasert, T., Fels, S.S., Sinnamon, L., Yoon, D.: Scripted vicarious dialogues: educational video augmentation method for increasing isolated students' engagement. In: CHI '23, pp. 1–25. ACM, New York (2023)
9. Do, T.D., Shafqat, U.B., Ling, E., Sarda, N.: PAIGE: examining learning outcomes and experiences with personalized AI-generated educational podcasts. In: CHI '25, Art. 896, pp. 1–12. ACM, New York (2025)
10. Huang, C.-Y., Wei, J., Huang, T.-H.K.: Generating educational materials with different levels of readability using LLMs. In: In2Writing '24, pp. 16–22. ACM (2024)
11. Roberts, D.: Vicarious learning: a review of the literature. Nurse Educ. Pract. **10**(1), 13–16 (2010)

12. Craig, S.D., Chi, M.T., VanLehn, K.: Improving classroom learning by collaboratively observing human tutoring videos while problem solving. J. Educ. Psychol. **101**(4), 779–789 (2009)
13. Graesser, A.C., Person, N.K.: Question asking during tutoring. Am. Educ. Res. J. **31**(1), 104–137 (1994)
14. Bloom, B.S., Engelhart, M.D., Furst, E.J., Hill, W.H., Krathwohl, D.R.: Taxonomy of educational objectives: the classification of educational goals. In: Handbook 1: Cognitive domain. Longman, New York (1956)
15. Krathwohl, D.R.: A revision of bloom's taxonomy: an overview. Theory Pract. **41**(4), 212–218 (2002)
16. Liu, N.F., et al.: Lost in the middle: how LMs use long contexts. Trans. Assoc. Comput. Linguist. **12**, 157–173 (2024)
17. Shultz, B., DiDomenico, R.J., Goliak, K., Mucksavage, J.: Exploratory assessment of GPT-4's effectiveness in generating valid exam items in pharmacy education. Am. J. Pharm. Educ. **89**(5), 101405 (2025)
18. Alawwad, H.A., Alhothali, A., Naseem, U., Alkhathlan, A., Jamal, A.: Enhancing textbook QA with LLMs and RAG. Pattern Recogn. **162**, 111332 (2025)
19. Lewis, P., et al.: Retrieval-augmented generation for knowledge-intensive NLP tasks. In: NeurIPS '20, pp. 9459–9474 (2020)
20. Dong, C., Yuan, Y., Chen, K., Cheng, S., Wen, C.: How to build an adaptive AI tutor for any course using knowledge graph-enhanced retrieval-augmented generation (KG-RAG). In: ICEIT '25, pp. 152–157. IEEE (2025)
21. Barry, M., Caillaut, G., Halftermeyer, P., Qader, R., Mouayad, M., Gesnouin, J.: GraphRAG: leveraging graph-based efficiency to minimize hallucinations in LLM-driven RAG for finance data. In: COLING '25 Workshop on KG & GenAI (2025)
22. Hogan, A., Blomqvist, E., Cochez, M., D'Amato, C., De Melo, G., Gutierrez, C., Zimmermann, A.: Knowledge graphs. ACM Comput. Surv. **54**(4), 71 (2021)
23. Prahlad, D., Lee, C., Kim, D., Kim, H.: Personalizing large language models using retrieval augmented generation and knowledge graph. In: WWW '25 Companion, pp. 1259–1263. ACM (2025)
24. Zhu, X., Xie, Y., Liu, Y., Li, Y., Hu, W.: Knowledge graph-guided retrieval augmented generation. In: NAACL-HLT '25, pp. 8912–8924. ACL (2025)
25. Feng, Y., Zhou, L., Ma, C., Zheng, Y., He, R., Li, Y.: Knowledge graph–based thought: a knowledge graph–enhanced LLM framework for pan-cancer question answering. GigaScience **14**, giae082 (2025)
26. Ivić, I., Antic, S., Pešikan, A. (eds.): Textbook Quality: A Guide to Textbook Standards, vol. 2. V&R unipress GmbH, Göttingen (2013)
27. Gagné, R.M.: The Conditions of Learning and Theory of Instruction, 4th edn. Holt, Rinehart and Winston, New York (1985)
28. Japan Meteorological Agency: How earthquakes occur. https://www.jma.go.jp/jma/kishou/know/jishin/jishin/about_eq.html. Accessed 8 May 2025
29. Ministry of Education, Culture, Sports, Science and Technology, Japan: Junior High School Curriculum Standards. https://www.mext.go.jp/content/20230120-mxt_kyoiku02-100002604_02.pdf, last accessed 8 May 2025
30. Ji, Z., Lee, N., Frieske, R., Yu, T., Su, D., Xu, Y., Fung, P.: Survey of hallucination in natural language generation. ACM Comput. Surv. **55**(12), 1–38 (2023)
31. Wikipedia contributors: Generative artificial intelligence. http://wien.wikipedia.org/wiki/Generative_artificial_intelligence. Accessed 8 Sept 2025
32. Achieve, A.: Rubrics for evaluating open education resource (OER) objects. Achieve, Inc., Washington, D.C. (2011). http://www.achieve.org/achieve-oer-rubrics. Accessed 8 Sept 2025

Social Interaction, Community and Public Spaces

Dynamic Analysis of Social Capital in Commercial Areas Using Connection Networks

Yuya Ieiri[1](✉), Ryo Okutani[2], Hiroshige Dan[2], and Osamu Yoshie[1]

[1] Graduate School of Information, Production and Systems, Waseda University, Fukuoka, Japan
`yuya.ieiri@aoni.waseda.jp`
[2] Graduate School of Creative Science and Engineering, Waseda University, Tokyo, Japan

Abstract. Social capital (SC), defined as the network of relationships, trust, norms, and mutual support that facilitate cooperation within a community, plays a vital role in sustaining local economies, fostering community resilience, and preserving urban social cohesion. Despite its recognized importance, particularly within traditional commercial districts, quantitatively assessing SC remains a major challenge. This study introduces a dynamic analytical framework for evaluating SC in such districts by constructing interaction networks that capture relationships between individuals and retail establishments. A field experiment was conducted in a Tokyo shopping district by incorporating two interaction modalities: visitor-driven word-of-mouth (WOM) and store-driven communication. SC was measured using five questionnaire-based indicators encompassing necessity, attachment, trust, and social norms. Connection networks were constructed as weighted graphs based on interaction intensity. The results revealed that both WOM and store-driven communication significantly enhanced SC values, as confirmed through pre- and post-intervention statistical tests. A predictive model was developed to explore the SC and network structure relationships using eight network indicators. The model achieved reasonable accuracy and interpretability, with comparisons between complete and reduced feature sets providing insights into the trade-offs between generalization performance and explanatory power. This integrated approach of network analysis and machine learning offers a robust framework for understanding and quantifying SC dynamics. The proposed framework contributes methodologically and practically to the study of urban revitalization by capturing how specific interactions reshape network structures and community cohesion.

Keywords: Social capital dynamics · Network structure relationships · Human–computer interaction

1 Introduction

In many parts of the world, traditional commercial spaces, such as Japan's shopping streets and the United Kingdom's high streets, have recently faced increasing risk of decline. This decline goes beyond a simple reduction in the number of retail stores and includes the weakening of urban identity and the erosion of social connections. In Japan, this issue has become increasingly visible since the 1990s, with a declining population and the expansion of suburban shopping malls leading to the widespread closure of local stores in traditional shopping districts [1]. This phenomenon is considered to be a symbolic representation of regional economic decline; the resulting hollowing out of shopping streets has been shown to adversely affect the sustainability of local communities [2]. A similar trend has been observed in the United Kingdom, where traditional high streets are under severe pressure. In 2024 alone, an average of 37 stores closed each day, totaling over 13,000 closures across the country [3]. A survey conducted by Public First [4] revealed that over half the respondents believed that their local high streets had deteriorated, reflecting growing economic and social dissatisfaction.

Such a commercial decline is not temporary, but is increasingly recognized in academic literature as a structural and multifactorial challenge. Powe et al. [5] emphasized that maintaining the functionality of commercial centers in small towns requires not only economic policies but also an integrated perspective that considers the role of social capital (SC) within communities. Similarly, Robertson [6], drawing on urban redevelopment cases in the United States, has long argued for the necessity of community-led spatial strategies. Briefly, these insights suggest that the decline of shopping streets should not be understood merely as a "shrinking of retail" but instead as a comprehensive issue requiring redesigning social relationships, cultural practices, and the fabric of urban functionality.

A representative attempt to revitalize such traditional commercial areas is the use of consumer behavior data, which directly affect commercial revitalization [7,8]. In contrast, when traditional commercial areas are perceived not simply as places to shop, but as places that play an important role in local communities, revitalization is required from the perspective of SC. SC denotes the relational networks that underpin societal functionality, encompassing trust, shared norms, and collective values that facilitate cooperation and community cohesion [9,10]. Fostering SC is essential for improving commercial areas from a quality-of-life perspective. For instance, Seomun et al. [11] demonstrated that strong SC in commercial areas might mitigate the negative effects of commercial gentrification.

Although the importance of SC is well known, its quantitative measurement still poses several methodological challenges. Quantitative measurement methods include using county-level statistical information, such as voter turnout and volunteer rates, [12] and using the results of questionnaire surveys by Likert scales that enable measurement at the individual level [13]. However, these measurements are limited to deriving static indicators during the surveys. Owing to this limitation, discussions on the real world phenomena that foster SC are still in their infancy.

Thus, tracking dynamic changes in SC over time is necessary. Consequently, this study proposes a method to dynamically analyze the relationship between the interactions occurring in traditional commercial districts and SC using connection networks as a medium. The experiment focuses on two types of interactions that occur in commercial districts: word-of-mouth (WOM) among visitors and store-driven communication. The proposed method, tested experimentally with 16 participants, revealed that WOM and store-driven communication positively impact the SC of a community. In addition, the study confirmed the effectiveness of an SC prediction model that integrates network indicators with machine learning (ML) techniques. The main contributions of this study are as follows:

- Dynamic analysis of SC in commercial districts that enables quantitative evaluation of the dynamics of SC creation, strengthening, and transformation.
- Empirical verification of the causal effects of WOM and store-driven communication on SC that provides essential insights into community policies in commercial districts.
- Integration of network indicators and ML that enables an SC prediction model capable of capturing nonlinear relationships and accounting for the complexity of network structures.

2 Related Works

This section presents a review of prior research related to the measurement of SC and the roles of WOM and store-driven communication in shaping social structures.

2.1 Quantitative Measurement of SC

SC has garnered attention in various fields such as urban planning, education, and public policy as a concept that captures social relationships such as trust, mutual assistance, and participation in local communities. However, quantitative measurement of SC is both theoretically and technically complex, involving challenges such as the multidimensionality of its components, the abstract nature of the concept, and the need to account for regional and temporal variations. Three main approaches have been used to address these challenges.

The first approach involves questionnaire-based surveys. It considers the components of SC as subjective consciousness and attitudes, and generally measures trust, sense of belonging, and community participation using a Likert scale. Gentry et al. [13] reported that this approach is the most widely used for measuring SC in higher education. Huang et al. [14] examined structural, relational, and cognitive SC in urban regeneration projects in China using factor analysis and structural equation modeling, demonstrating the effectiveness of a multidimensional measurement framework.

The second approach measures SC on a regional basis using statistical information such as voter turnout, volunteer rate, religious participation rate, and marriage stability. Vâlsan et al. [12] derived several SC indices using Z-score average, principal component analysis, and partial least squares method based on county-level statistics, and examined their relationship with each social outcome. Kim et al. [15] used Google Street View and independently collected social statistical data to clarify the relationship between streetscape characteristics (green space, building density, and walking environment) and SC for 1,000 urban residents in South Korea.

The third approach measures social connections and mutual behavior using big data such as social networking service (SNS) and location-based apps. Chetty et al. [16] used Facebook friend network data to quantify indicators such as economic connectedness, clustering, and group participation rate on a regional basis, and analyzed their relationship with economic mobility. This innovative approach can estimate structural SC on a large scale; however, it is still limited to static evaluations based on data at a single time point and is unable to track changes.

Despite the diversity of components and statistical methods, conventional SC measurement research has often been limited to static measurements of "SC levels at a certain time." This renders capturing the dynamic aspects of changes over time, such as the creation, strengthening, and loss of SC, challenging. Consequently, this study aims to develop a method to dynamically analyze the relationship between interactions occurring in traditional commercial areas and SC using connection networks as a medium.

2.2 Word-of-Mouth and Store-Driven Communication

Recently, the impact of WOM among consumers and store-driven communication on the social network structure of local communities has garnered attention for the revitalization of commercial districts. These activities increase sales, create new connections within the community, and enhance social cohesion and brand value.

First, Choi et al. [17] discussed knowledge sharing behavior in electronic WOM on an SNS from the perspective of SC theory and demonstrated a correlation between trust and a sense of belonging to the community and knowledge sharing through SNS. Yuan et al. [18] adopted a new approach and revealed that SC positively influences electronic WOM engagement among passive SNS users. These studies reveal that WOM is not only an individual consumption behavior but also strongly related to social cohesion within local communities. Regarding store-driven communication, Chen [19] demonstrated the importance of considering the structural characteristics of community networks in effective electronic WOM marketing strategies in business.

Previous studies have demonstrated that WOM and store-driven communication are strongly related to the social network structure in commercial districts. Thus far, most studies have focused only on changes in social networks; none has achieved an understanding of the dynamics of SC through these social networks. Consequently, this study aims to analyze the mechanism through which information sharing via WOM and store-driven information changes the social network structure of commercial districts and contributes to the formation and strengthening of SC.

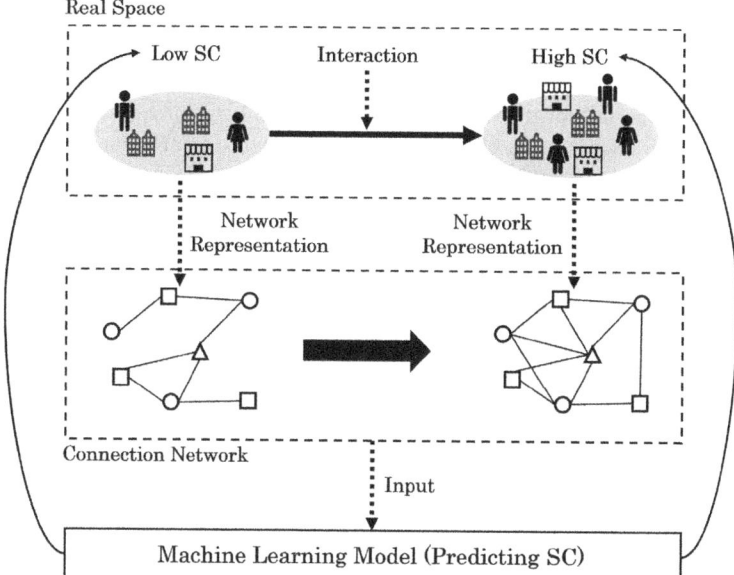

Fig. 1. Dynamic analysis framework for SC. Circles, squares, and triangles represent nodes, which are differentiated based on attributes. In particular, circles, squares, and triangles represent people, stores, and organizations, respectively.

3 Method

This section outlines the proposed approach for performing a dynamic SC analysis. First, we introduce an overview of the dynamic analysis framework for SC. Then, the SC analysis scenario in commercial districts, the focus of this study, is described.

3.1 Dynamic Analysis Framework for SC

Comprehending the effect of interactions between people and among people and stores in the real world on SC still remains a challenge. This study proposes a method to dynamically analyze the relationship between interactions and SC using a connection network that represents the connections between people and stores in the real world as a network structure. This method enables discussions on the effect of real-world interactions on the connection network and the resultant effect on the SC. Figure 1 shows an overview of the analysis method.

This study focused on commercial districts. SC can be significantly transformed through various interactions among people and stores in commercial districts. The SC value is a quantitative representation of SC. The relationships between people and between people and stores in commercial districts in the real world were represented by a network structure to discuss changes in the SC value. The nodes in the connection network represent people and stores, whereas the links represent connections between people and between people and stores. The nature of these connections depends on the type of SC being measured. These connections indicate the degree of need for a store, degree of trust in people, or frequency of visiting a store or meeting people.

The SC value of a commercial area was estimated using the connection network formed in this manner. Conventional static SC values were derived by measuring the SC index of each node through questionnaire surveys in the real world and by calculating a simple average. This method uses the network index of each node in the connection network as the input and the SC index of each node as the output, and constructs a model that predicts the SC value of a commercial area using ML.

Combining these components enables the analysis of the SC value of a commercial area. Changes in the connection network in the real world are dynamically reproduced in a multi-agent system, based on observed real-world interactions. For instance, agents are assumed to be either people or stores, and behavioral rules are connection-network variations that occur during real-world interactions. These variations are modeled as the creation of new links between nodes or the strengthening of links. If dynamically capturing observed interactions from the real world is possible, this multi-agent system will enable the automatic tracking of dynamic variations in the connection network. The SC value is then dynamically calculated from the dynamically reproduced connection network using a model that predicts the SC value. This framework enables a dynamic analysis of the SC value of commercial areas.

3.2 SC Analysis Scenario in Commercial Districts

This section outlines the study scenario based on the proposed framework. First, the target field of this study is a shopping street in Shinjuku Ward, Tokyo, Japan. Shinjuku Ward has several shopping streets and various efforts have been devoted toward revitalizing them [7,8]. The interactions on which this study focuses are WOM between consumers and store-driven communication, based on a case[1] in which WOM and store-driven communication about croquettes led to the revitalization of a shopping street in Japan.

People and stores are used as nodes in the connection network, representing real-world connections in the network structure. The links between people and

---

[1] https://www.togoshiginza.jp/en/about.

stores were weighted and assigned according to the degree of necessity for the store. In the questionnaire survey to confirm the presence or absence of such links, the "To what extent do you need the store?" item was designed to measure the perceived functional necessity or personal reliance on each store in daily life. Participants responded on a five-point Likert scale: "I can't live without it," "I need it very much," "I need it," "I need it occasionally," and "I don't need it." These items were converted to numerical values of 4, 3, 2, 1, and 0 and networked as weighted links.

This study constructed a five-item questionnaire based on local ties, mutual trust, and normative consciousness to measure the SC value in commercial areas. The first was "Degree of necessity for stores in the target area," which measures the degree to which local services and facilities are required. This is consistent with the fact that questions about satisfaction with and the necessity of local resources were used in the Community Life Survey [20] conducted by the UK government. The second was "How attached are you to the target area?" based on the measurement of place attachment, as highlighted by Lewicka [21], wherein emotional ties to the community promote social engagement. The third item, "Can you trust the people in the community?", corresponds to the measurement of trust, a central concept in Putnam's theory of SC [10] in which trust between residents is the foundation that supports community stability and cooperation. The fourth and fifth items, "Do you want to help the community more than yourself?" and "Do you feel you must help other people in the community?", evaluate social norms such as altruism and reciprocity, and correspond to the SC measurement index developed by Onyx et al. [22]. These questions were rated on a five-point Likert scale, and the SC scores of each individual were calculated as the average. The average of the individual scores was used to estimate the SC of the entire community. Adopting the simple average of the Likert scale is a classical approach to SC measurement and has been employed in other studies [23, 24].

This study aimed to quantitatively estimate the SC value by adopting several indices based on the structural position of a node in the network as features. First, weighted degree centrality [25], which measures the connection strength of a node, was used to evaluate the total degree of involvement in the network. Weighted closeness centrality [25, 26], which indicates the inverse of the average distance to other nodes, was introduced as an index of accessibility to information and resources. Furthermore, the weighted betweenness centrality [26], which indicates the extent to which a node functions as a relay point in the network, is effective in visualizing the intermediate position and bridging function. In addition, weighted eigenvector centrality [27] was incorporated to evaluate the indirect influence of connections on essential others. The weighted clustering coefficient [28] reflects the density and link strength of triangular ties around a node and is an index of the strength of trust and closeness of the network.

SC is determined not only by the number of connections but also by the presence or absence of diversity and structural flexibility. From this perspective, structural constraints [29] measure the degree to which a node is dependent on a limited number of partners; the lower the value, the more flexible the structural position. In contrast, participation coefficients [30] indicate the degree to which a node is connected across multiple clusters, and are a measure of cross-border network participation. The weighted average neighbor degree [28] indicates the average activity of adjacent nodes and suggests the quality of the surrounding social environment. These eight indices are theoretically valid to capture the structural components of SC, such as accessibility, spillover, and betweenness, from multiple angles and are meaningful for adoption as explanatory variables in the empirical analysis.

Further, this study adopts a method of extracting multiple network indices from a network structure in which individuals and stores are nodes and relationships are edges, and constructs an ML model using these as input features to quantitatively predict the SC value. Specifically, the eight aforementioned network indices were set as explanatory variables. In addition, the SC value based on the questionnaire survey is an objective variable for estimating the SC value based on structural features. To reduce model complexity and avoid overfitting, a feature selection step was introduced prior to training. Specifically, we computed Pearson correlation coefficients between each of the eight network indicators and the SC scores obtained from the questionnaire survey. Based on these correlation values, a subset of the indicators with relatively high statistical relevance was selected for use as explanatory variables. This threshold was set to include approximately the top half of the indicators, aiming to strike a balance between model interpretability and generalization performance. This correlation-based selection approach is widely adopted in prior studies integrating network features and regression modeling [31].

Support vector regression (SVR), which is suitable for modeling nonlinear relationships, was adopted as the learning algorithm, and a radial basis function (RBF) kernel was used to flexibly express the relationship between complex network structures and SC values. SVR has a stable performance even with small amounts of data and is considered effective in predicting continuous and latent social attributes, such as the SC value [32]. K-fold cross-validation (k = 8) with a fixed random seed was applied to ensure reproducibility, and standard regression performance indices, such as the coefficient of determination (R^2) and mean squared error (MSE), were used to evaluate the model [33]. Valente et al. [31] discussed the relationship between SC values and network indices, and suggested the validity of an approach that measures and predicts SC values using network indices. In addition, compared with conventional techniques, this method is unique in that it employs a nonlinear regression model instead of a multivariate regression model, and aims to predict SC values that reflect the structural diversity and dispersion of relationships, rather than being limited to conventional simple network indices.

4 Experiment

This study applied the use scenario of this framework to a shopping district in Shinjuku, Tokyo. The target store nodes included 20 stores in the target shopping district. First, an experiment focusing on WOM is described. This experiment was conducted with eight people (seven male and one female, the average age is 23.6), with four people in each group, for two days: November 26 and December 6, 2024. In the experiment, participants shared information about the target 20 stores within the group for 30 min. This experiment recorded conversations about stores; sharing information about these stores within the group was treated as WOM. Next, we describe an experiment focusing on store-driven communication. This experiment was conducted with eight people (eight male, the average age is 21.9): three on November 20, 2024, and five on November 25, 2024. In the experiment, participants read an original map listing the information for the 20 target stores in 5 min. The original map, created by the authors, summarized, in a specific format, the appeal of each store, as confirmed through interviews with the store owners. The original map included basic information such as the name, description, illustration, and opening hours of the store. This map was used in the target shopping district and positioned as one way of disseminating information from the stores.

The participants were surveyed on five indicators to measure their SC value before and after the experiment, as described in Sect. 3.2. To understand the connection network before and after the experiment, the survey also included questions regarding the degree of requirements for the target 20 stores, as described in Sect. 3.2. Based on this information, links were generated between people and stores in the connection network. Additionally, when conducting experiments with the same group, the links between people in the connection network were set to the weakest weight.

5 Results and Discussions

This section presents the empirical results obtained from the field experiments, including changes in SC scores and connection networks before and after the interventions. In addition, the effects of different interactions (WOM and store-driven communication) on SC values are described, followed by an exploration of the predictive model and its interpretability.

5.1 Changes in Connection Network and SC

Figure 2 shows the connection network before and after the WOM intervention, and Fig. 3 depicts the network changes resulting from the store-driven communication intervention. In both figures, nodes A to H represent participants in the WOM experiment, nodes I to P represent participants in the store-driven communication experiment and nodes 1 to 20 denotes stores involved in both experiments, indexed in order. In the post-intervention network, newly formed links or reinforced links are highlighted in red, and weakened links are highlighted in blue. Although one blue link indicating reduced weight appears in Fig. 3, as shown in Fig. 2 and Fig. 3, the connection network in the community had been strengthened by WOM and store-driven communication.

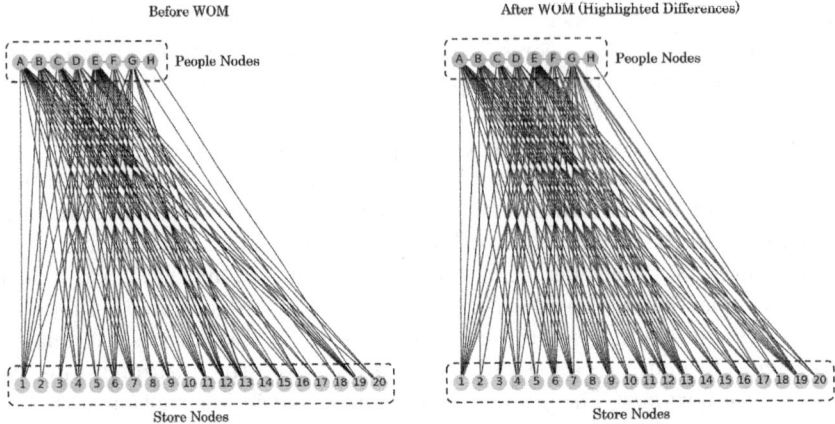

Fig. 2. Changes in the connection network before and after WOM intervention

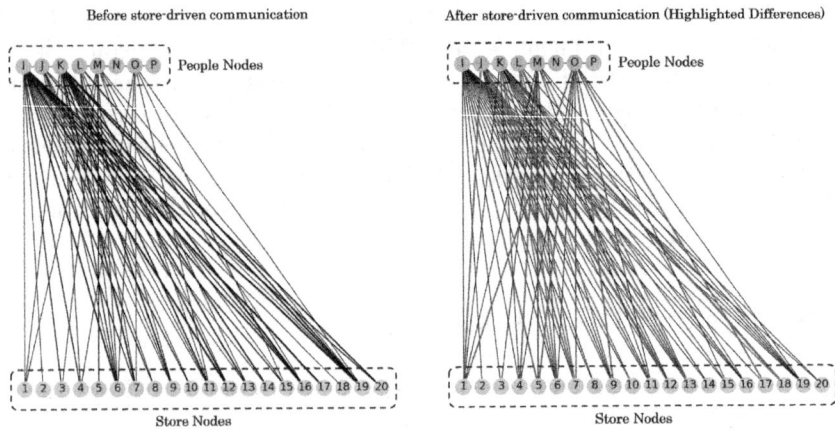

Fig. 3. Changes in the connection network before and after store-driven communication intervention

Table 1 summarizes the SC values of each participant (the average answers to five questions related to SC) before and after the WOM and store-driven communication interventions. A paired t-test was used to determine whether a change occurred in the SC values before and after the intervention. For WOM, the average value before the intervention was 2.625 ($V = 0.268$, V indicates variance), average value after the intervention was 3.075 ($V = 0.251$), and p-value was 0.017 (< 0.05). For store-driven communication, the average value before the intervention was 2.625 ($V = 0.519$), average value after the intervention was 2.775 ($V = 0.691$), and p-value was 0.020 (< 0.05). These results confirmed that WOM and store-driven communication interventions significantly improved

SC value in the community. This finding indicates that WOM and store-driven communication are effective interactions for improving SC.

Table 1. SC score of each participant before and after the intervention

WOM intervention			Store-driven communication intervention		
Participants	SC (before)	SC (after)	Participants	SC (before)	SC (after)
A	2.8	3.8	I	3.0	3.2
B	2.8	3.0	J	2.4	2.6
C	2.8	3.2	K	3.0	3.0
D	3.2	3.4	L	3.8	4.2
E	3.2	3.4	M	3.0	3.2
F	2.4	2.6	N	1.8	1.8
G	1.8	3.0	O	2.4	2.6
H	2.0	2.2	P	1.6	1.8

To illustrate the impact of WOM on changes in the connection network, we focused on the WOM generated within the group on November 26th and its subsequent effects. The conversation during the experiment was transcribed from video and audio recordings. WOM was defined as the act of sharing store-related information within a group, where the referenced store could be identified from the context. Table 2 presents the extracted WOM instances and their corresponding impact on network connectivity. The "Store" and "Participant" columns indicate the store mentioned and the individual who initiated WOM, respectively. The "WOM" column shows the content of the interaction, and the "Changes" column lists the participant ID where network modifications occurred. WOM entries 1, 2, and 3 are initiated by the same participant; however, only the store referenced in entry 2 is associated with the formation of new links or reinforcement of existing links. These findings indicate that the influence of WOM on changes in the connection network is strongly related to both the interpersonal relationship between the speaker and the listener and the semantic content of the WOM. Similar patterns are observed for entries 4–7, reinforcing the validity of this result. Notably, in entry 9, the store is described using terms that may initially convey negative connotations, such as "old" and "not clean." Nevertheless, this WOM instance leads to the creation of new links or the strengthening of existing links between the two participants. Although entry 5 references the same store and may have contributed similarly, the link strengthening for Participant A can be specifically attributed to entry 9. These results imply that even negatively framed descriptions can exert a positive influence on network connectivity under certain conditions. In this case, the store, a long-established Chinese restaurant, may have been perceived as more authentic or historically significant, outweighing aesthetic considerations.

5.2 SC Prediction Model

The aim of this study was to construct an ML model that predicts SC using eight network indices: weighted degree centrality, weighted closeness central-

Table 2. WOM generated during the experiment and its impact on connection-network changes

No.	Store	Participant	WOM	Changes
1	4	D	My general impression is that the staff are friendly. When my companion asked questions such as "What does this look like? How should I take care of it?", they were quite frank in explaining the answers	–
2	6	D	The staff are friendly. She even put stickers with different expiration dates on each item without showing any annoyance. It is a shop that felt like it belonged in a shopping street	A, C
3	7	D	The staff are generally lovely. They gave me a 100 yen coupon that I would receive after paying the bill and said I could use it. <Store specialty> is delicious	–
4	9	A	I've been to <Store name>, and it feels like an ordinary soba restaurant. It's a soba restaurant, but they also serve dishes such as katsu don	D
5	19	A	The store always sells something like a bento box at night. We can get it for about 1000 yen for lunch	C
6	1	A	I used to go to a Chinese restaurant near this store a lot until quite recently. When I was walking past this store, I thought they were practicing	–
7	12	A	I've been to <Store name> a few times to buy drinks, and the refrigerator is cold. When I purchased a bottled drink, it was covered in water droplets, and when I got it home, it was still cold	–
8	12	C	One of the features is that they give you cash back as part of a points system	A
9	19	B	The restaurant has a slightly old-fashioned ambiance. Their signature dishes are gyoza and ramen. It's not a particularly attractive place, but it's a classic Chinese restaurant	A, C
10	13	C	Looking at the storefront, it looked quite stylish, so it seemed a little pricey. However, for lunch, we can choose from pasta, meat, or fish, all for exactly 1,000 yen. And the quality of the food was excellent	A, B

ity, weighted betweenness centrality, weighted eigenvector centrality, weighted clustering coefficient, constraint, participation coefficient, and weighted average neighbor degree. The experiment generated four connection networks before and after intervention by WOM and store-driven communication. Eight network indices and SC values were collected for each node. This section presents data from 32 participants (eight participants, four times).

First, the Pearson correlation coefficient between the eight network indices and the SC value was calculated. This calculation selected four types of indices in the top half: weighted degree, weighted eigenvector, weighted closeness, and weighted betweenness. An SVR model with an RBF kernel was constructed using the selected features as explanatory variables.

A grid search of hyperparameters was performed in the range of regularization parameters $(0, 1, 10)$, epsilon widths $(0.01, 0.1, 0.5)$, and kernel coefficients (scale, auto, $0.01, 0.1, 1$) to optimize model performance. The parameter combinations that exhibited the highest prediction accuracy were $C = 10$, $epsilon = 0.1$, and $kernel coefficient = auto$. K-fold cross-validation (k = 8) was performed to evaluate the model on 32 samples, and R^2 and MSE were used as evaluation indices.

A comparison of the model performance with and without feature selection (four vs. eight items) revealed that the average R^2 score and MSE were 0.4996 and 0.1093 for the selected-feature model and 0.5419 and 0.1189 for the full-feature model, respectively. These results indicate that the average R^2 score was higher for the model using all features than for that with selected features. This finding indicates that the model using all features can explain more of the SC variance. In contrast, the model with selected features achieved slightly better results in the MSE. One possible reason for this is that the model using all features contained noise, such as outliers, owing to the large number of variables.

The generalization performance (fewer minor errors) tended to improve by limiting the features considered. This suggests that the simplicity of the model can suppress overfitting. However, regarding the comprehensiveness of the explanatory variables (R^2), the version that covered all features was advantageous, suggesting the value of incorporating more structural information. This result indicates that the number of features and good accuracy results are not always equal, and selecting a trade-off according to the purpose is essential, such as prediction accuracy or interpretability.

6 Conclusion and Future Directions

This study introduced a dynamic analytical framework for evaluating SC in traditional commercial areas, leveraging network-based representations and ML techniques. Interpersonal and store–consumer relationships were modeled as weighted networks, and SC was quantified via structured survey instruments. The framework captures the influence of distinct interaction modalities—namely, WOM and store-initiated communication—on community cohesion. Field Experiments revealed that both interaction types significantly improved participants'

SC metrics. Additionally, a SVR model exhibited that a combination of network features can reliably predict individual SC scores.

Despite these contributions, the study has several limitations. First, the relatively small sample size may constrain statistical robustness and generalizability. Second, although the concept of dynamic change was central to the proposed framework, real-time network evolution—such as agent-based simulation—was not fully implemented in this study.

Several research directions, building on the present findings, merit further exploration. First, applying the framework to larger participant cohorts and across diverse cultural and geographic contexts would enhance its external validity and generalizability to heterogeneous urban environments. Second, future work should aim to fully implement the dynamic simulation module via multiagent systems capable of modeling temporal evolution in connection networks. This would enable fine-grained analysis of how specific interactions trigger structural shifts in SC. Third, incorporating qualitative methodologies—such as semi-structured interviews or focus groups—could yield nuanced insights into how individuals perceive SC and interpret interaction experiences. These data would complement quantitative network metrics and improve the interpretability of predictive models. Finally, further investigation is needed into how communicative content and the social relationship between speaker and listener influence the formation and reinforcement of ties. This would refine models of communication-driven network evolution and advance the theoretical understanding on SC dynamics.

Overall, this study contributes both methodologically and empirically to urban informatics and SC research. By linking suitable interactions with quantifiable network structures and computational simulations, the proposed framework offers a robust foundation for data-driven strategies to sustain and regenerate traditional commercial communities.

Acknowledgement. This study was supported by the Grant-in-Aid for Young Scientists (22K14444) and the JST PRESTO (JPMJPR24I2).

References

1. Kurosaki, H.: Failing Japanese shopping area using nostalgia to reclaim past glory. Kyodo News https://english.kyodonews.net/news/2024/06/9205ceff0e18-feature-failing-japanese-shopping-area-using-nostalgia-to-reclaim-past-glory.html
2. Tatsuhiko, Y.: Symbolic phenomenon of a declining regional economy of Japan the issue of "shuttered shopping streets". Discuss Japan (2016). https://www.japanpolicyforum.jp/society/pt20160323212452526.html
3. Goodley, S.: UK lost 37 shops a day in 2024, data suggests. The Guardian https://www.theguardian.com/business/2025/jan/02/uk-lost-37-shops-a-day-in-2024-data-suggests
4. Corfe, S.: High streets have changed dramatically over the past 15 years and much of the public isn't happy about it. PUBLIC FIRST. https://www.publicfirst.co.uk/6593.html

5. Powe, N., Hart, T.: Market towns: understanding and maintaining functionality. Town Plan. Rev. **79**(4), 347–370 (2008)
6. Robertson, K.A.: Downtown redevelopment strategies in the United States: an end-of-the-century assessment. J. Am. Plann. Assoc. **61**(4), 429–437 (1995)
7. Ieiri, Y., Tengfei, S., Yoshie, O.: A consumer behavior analytics model for commercial district marketing using network-structured stamp rally data. Decis. Anal. J. **15**, 100567 (2025)
8. Ieiri, Y., Yamaki, K., Hishiyama, R.: Community-based management for low-digitalized communities using cross-cutting purchasing behavior. Human. Soc. Sci. Commun. **11**(1), 1–12 (2024)
9. Coleman, J.S.: Social capital in the creation of human capital. Am. J. Sociol. **94**, S95–S120 (1988)
10. Putnam, R.D.: Bowling Alone: The Collapse and Revival of American Community. Simon and Schuster (2000)
11. Seomun, G., Kim, H., Woosnam, K.M., Kim, H.: Commercial gentrification revisited: social capital and community governance in regenerated neighborhoods of south korea. Cities **149**, 104970 (2024)
12. Vâlsan, C., Goschin, Z., Druică, E.: The measurement of social capital in America: a reassessment. Soc. Indic. Res. **165**(1), 135–161 (2023)
13. Gentry, A.N., Martin, J.P., Douglas, K.A.: Social capital assessments in higher education: a systematic literature review. In: Frontiers in Education, vol. 9, p. 1498422. Frontiers Media SA (2025)
14. Huang, R., Xie, F., Fu, X., Liu, W.: Modeling residents' multidimensional social capital in china's neighborhood renewal projects: sem and mimic approaches. Front. Psychol. **14**, 1127510 (2023)
15. Kim, S., Jeon, J., Noh, Y., Woo, A.: Impacts of streetscape features on individual social capital: applying Korea's neighborhood data to street view images to improve lives of the socially vulnerable. Land **13**(5), 631 (2024)
16. Chetty, R., et al.: Social capital i: measurement and associations with economic mobility. Nature **608**(7921), 108–121 (2022)
17. Choi, J.H., Scott, J.E.: Electronic word of mouth and knowledge sharing on social network sites: a social capital perspective. J. Theor. Appl. Electron. Commer. Res. **8**(1), 69–82 (2013)
18. Yuan, L., Deng, X., Zhong, W.: Encouraging passive members of online brand communities to generate ewom based on tam and social capital theory. IEEE Access **9**, 12840–12851 (2021)
19. Wang, T., Yeh, R.K.J., Chen, C., Tsydypov, Z.: What drives electronic word-of-mouth on social networking sites? Perspectives of social capital and self-determination. Telematics Inform. **33**(4), 1034–1047 (2016)
20. Community life survey 2023/24 questionnaire (2024). https://www.gov.uk/government/statistics/community-life-survey-202324-annual-publication
21. Lewicka, M.: Place attachment: how far have we come in the last 40 years? J. Environ. Psychol. **31**(3), 207–230 (2011)
22. Onyx, J., Bullen, P.: Measuring social capital in five communities. J. Appl. Behav. Sci. **36**(1), 23–42 (2000)
23. Chen, X., Stanton, B., Gong, J., Fang, X., Li, X.: Personal social capital scale: an instrument for health and behavioral research. Health Educ. Res. **24**(2), 306–317 (2009)
24. Kouvonen, A., et al.: Psychometric evaluation of a short measure of social capital at work. BMC Public Health **6**, 1–10 (2006)

25. Opsahl, T., Agneessens, F., Skvoretz, J.: Node centrality in weighted networks: generalizing degree and shortest paths. Social Netw. **32**(3), 245–251 (2010)
26. Freeman, L.C.: A set of measures of centrality based on betweenness. In: Sociometry, pp. 35–41 (1977)
27. Bonacich, P.: Power and centrality: a family of measures. Am. J. Sociol. **92**(5), 1170–1182 (1987)
28. Barrat, A., Barthelemy, M., Pastor-Satorras, R., Vespignani, A.: The architecture of complex weighted networks. Proc. Natl. Acad. Sci. **101**(11), 3747–3752 (2004)
29. Burt, R.S.: The social structure of competition. Netw. Knowl. Econ. **13**(2), 57–91 (2003)
30. Guimera, R., Nunes Amaral, L.A.: Functional cartography of complex metabolic networks. Nature **433**(7028), 895–900 (2005)
31. Valente, T.W., Coronges, K., Lakon, C., Costenbader, E.: How correlated are network centrality measures? Connections (Toronto, Ont.) **28**(1), 16 (2008)
32. Smola, A.J., Schölkopf, B.: A tutorial on support vector regression. Stat. Comput. **14**, 199–222 (2004)
33. James, G., Witten, D., Hastie, T., Tibshirani, R., et al.: An Introduction to Statistical Learning, vol. 112. Springer, Heidelberg (2013)

Emotional Analysis of Excluded Person Using Review Texts

Megumi Yasuo[1(✉)], Kaito Shingu[2], Junjie Shan[2], Kazuho Yamaura[3], and Yoko Nishihara[2]

[1] Ritsumeikan Global Innovation Research Organization, Ritsumeikan University, 2-150 Iwakura-cho, Osaka, Ibaraki 567-8570, Japan
yasuo-ri@fc.ritsumei.ac.jp
[2] College of Information Science and Engineering, Ritsumeikan University, 2-150 Iwakura-cho, Osaka, Ibaraki 567-8570, Japan
is0619hx@ed.ritsumei.ac.jp, {shan,nisihara}@fc.ritsumei.ac.jp
[3] College of Sport and Health Science, Ritsumeikan University, 1-1-1 Noji-higashi, Shiga, Kusatsu 525-8577, Japan
kazuho@fc.ritsumei.ac.jp

Abstract. The aim of this study is to identify indicators of social exclusion in written texts expressing individuals' impressions of content. Previous research has demonstrated that loneliness stemming from reduced interpersonal interaction negatively affects individuals' health. Social exclusion is one of the reasons for causing loneliness. Nevertheless, many people find it difficult to openly disclose experiences of social exclusion. Accordingly, there is a need to develop methods that can find such exclusion without requiring explicit self-disclosure. In this study, we analyzed textual characteristics of reviews written by the experimental subjects. We divided the subjects into two groups by using cyber-ball task: a social excluded group and control group. Then, we asked the subjects in both group to read an assigned document and write a review of it. We analyzed these written review texts using natural language processing, such as sentiment and polarity analysis, to observe the emotional states of different experimental subjects. The findings indicate that texts produced by individuals experiencing social exclusion tend to exhibit heightened expressions of anger and a reduced use of neutral expressions.

Keywords: Social Exclusion · Cyberball Task · Sentiment Analysis

1 Introduction

Humans are social creatures that require interaction with others. When interaction with others decreases and connection to society is reduced, there will be negative effects on physical and mental health. Being ignored or rejected by others is referred to as "social exclusion." Previous research has shown that social exclusion has an impact on mental and physical health [1].

Social exclusion means not only mean being alone, but also being isolated from others. It is a concept implying that a negative psychological state could be caused by rejection from others or groups. It is challenging for a third party to identify situations related to an individual's psychological state, as they can only be revealed by the person involved through self-disclosure. However, people who experience social exclusion are often reluctant to self-disclose their situation. There is a need for a mechanism to identify situations of social exclusion without relying on self-disclosure.

The purpose of this study is to infer a social exclusion state by using texts that describe evaluations and impressions of content. Previous research has suggested that social exclusion affects the perceptions of group members [2]. A state of social exclusion could also be reflected in review texts that serve as evaluations of content. In this paper, we conducted an experiment in which subjects were presented with stimuli that induced a short-term state of social exclusion, after which they were given a document. We asked them to write about their impressions. We examined whether a state of social exclusion would be reflected in the characteristics of texts written by individuals.

2 Related Research

2.1 Previous Studies in Social Exclusion

Social exclusion has been widely studied, with evidence of its negative impact on mental and physical well-being. [1,3]. It reduces basic psychological needs, predicts further exclusion, and creates disadvantages in education, employment, housing, and health. Excluded individuals are also reported to have complex health needs and limited access to care [4].

Research has further shown that witnessing exclusion influences bystanders' social sensitivity and perception of psychological safety. [5,6]. While most studies focus on its physical and psychological consequences, this study instead examines exclusion through the written impressions of excluded individuals, clarifying differences from those not excluded.

2.2 Sentiment Analysis as a Tool

Sentiment analysis is a widely used method for examining emotions in text data [7]. In this study, it is employed to compare individuals who have experienced exclusion with those who have not. For example, Okada et al. analyzed emotional trends in social media posts during the COVID-19 pandemic [8].

By analyzing text data, it is possible to detect emotions that are difficult to capture objectively. This study uses the same approach to identify emotional differences associated with social exclusion.

3 Experimental Method

An experiment was conducted in which subjects were subjected to a state of social exclusion through a "Cyberball task" and then asked to write a review text. Subsequently, we observed differences in the review texts of individuals who had experienced short-term social exclusion and those who had not. The subjects were undergraduate or graduate students attending a university of information sciences. The total number of subjects in the excluded group was eight, comprising six men and two women, while the control group consisted of 10 subjects, with four men and six women.

The experimental procedures were as follows:

1. Subjects participate in a Cyberball task
2. Subjects read documents and write reviews
3. Reviews are analyzed using sentiment and emotional analysis
4. Results are compared between the excluded and control groups

3.1 Cyberball Task

This experiment utilized the Cyberball task [9] to induce a state of temporary social exclusion in the excluded group. The experimenter instructs a group of three to four participants, including the subject catchball. The Cyberball task consisted of two conditions: the first half was the acceptance condition, and the second half was the exclusion condition. In the acceptance condition, the ball is passed around equally to all subjects. In the exclusion condition, the ball is passed around to the target a few times at first, but then it is no longer passed around at all.

In this study, the Cyberball task was conducted with three players, including the subject. A total of 60 balls were thrown: the first 30 were randomly passed to the subject, while in the last 30, the subject received only two passes and the remaining 28 were exchanged between the other players. The task lasted about five minutes. Participants were told a cover story that the task was part of an experiment on imagination training, and that the two other players (actually computer-controlled) were in separate rooms (Table 1).

Then, participants were asked to answer two types of questionnaires: the Positive and Negative Affect Scale (PANAS) and the Need to Belong Scale [10]. We used the Japanese edition of the PANAS [11] for the Positive and Negative Affect Scale.

The PANAS is a 16-item scale, with eight items each for positive (PA) and negative affect (NA), applicable to high school students and older. Each item is rated on a 6-point Likert scale, and total scores for PA and NA indicate the level of positive or negative affect.

The Need to Belong Scale is an index that measures individual differences in the need to belong, consisting of 10 items, including three reversed items. Table 2 shows the questions of the Need To Belong Scale. Responses are collected for each of these 10 items based on a 5-point Likert scale. Scoring is performed

Table 1. The scale of PANAS (Japanese edition)

Negative Aspects (NA)	Positive Aspects (PA)
Guilty	Active
Scared	Proud
Upset	Strong
Attentive	Inspired
Distressed	Determined
Nervous	Excited
Ashamed	Alert
Irritable	Enthisiastic

Table 2. The 10 questions included in the Need To Belong Scale (based on the reference [10]). Questions marked with (R) are reversed items.

1	If other people don't seem to accept me, I don't let it bother me. (R)
2	I try hard not to do things that will make other people avoid or reject me.
3	I seldom worry about whether other people care about me. (R)
4	I need to feel that there are people I can turn to in times of need.
5	I want other people to accept me.
6	I do not like being alone.
7	Being apart from my friends for long periods of time does not bother me. (R)
8	I have a strong "need to belong."
9	It bothers me a great deal when I am not included in other people's plans.
10	My feelings are easily hurt when I feel that others do not accept me.

by calculating the total score for the 10 items, with a higher score indicating a stronger desire to belong among respondents.

After the experiment was completed, the subjects received a debriefing to explain that the two players were programs and the original purpose of the experiment.

3.2 Describing Reviews

Participants were required to complete two tasks. The first task involved reading two different documents and selecting five sentences that interested them. The second task involved writing a free-form review of at least 160 Japanese characters about each of the documents they had read. The reviews were subjected to sentiment analysis and emotional analysis. The types of documents selected for use in this experiment were "Novel" and "Product Introduction." The difference between these documents is whether or not there is a target with which the reader can empathize.

The "Novel" is a narrative text selected from the novel-posting site Syosetsuka ni Naro[1]. It features a protagonist with whom participants could easily identify, and consists of 3,697 Japanese characters (approx. 8 min reading time). The story depicts a shift in the protagonist's emotions from negative to positive, with both affective elements embedded in the text.

The "Product Introduction" is a hypothetical text introducing a fictitious massage machine, generated using ChatGPT (OpenAI). It consists of 2,553 Japanese characters (approx. 6 min reading time). Unlike the novel, it contains no character for emotional projection; instead, positive elements emphasize product benefits, while negative elements highlight low review ratings.

The text mining tool[2] is used for sentiment analysis. This tool performs two types of sentiment analysis: "positive/negative scale" and "emotional scale." The "positive/negative scale" outputs the ratio of positive, negative, and neutral emotions in the input documents. The "emotional scale" section outputs numerical values of the degree of five types of emotions: joy, liking, sadness, fear, and anger. The output value is the deviation score relative to the baseline, which is the average of all emotions.

Table 3. Average scores of PANAS. The top eight items belong to NA, and the bottom eight items belong to PA.

Scale	Excluded Group	Control Group
Guilty	2.00	1.90
Scared	1.75	1.80
Upset	2.87	2.20
Attentive	3.75	3.20
Distressed	3.00	2.00
Nervous	1.87	1.50
Ashamed	1.75	1.50
Irritable	3.37	1.30
Active	3.00	3.40
Proud	1.37	2.60
Strong	2.00	2.40
Inspired	2.37	3.60
Determined	1.75	2.70
Excited	3.25	4.20
Alert	2.87	2.10
Enthisiastic	2.00	1.90
Average_NA	20.62	16.10
Average_PA	19.25	22.20

[1] https://syosetu.com/ (confirmed 2025/02/26).
[2] https://textmining.userlocal.jp/ (confirmed on 2025/02/25).

Table 4. Average scores of Need To Belong Scale

Questions	Excluded Group	Control Group
1	3.40	3.10
2	3.90	4.10
3	3.60	3.60
4	4.40	4.00
5	4.10	4.00
6	3.00	2.10
7	2.90	3.20
8	2.80	2.60
9	2.50	2.30
10	3.60	3.50
Total Score	33.50	32.00

3.3 Results

The average scores achieved by the exclusion and control groups on the PANAS are shown in Table 3, and the results for the Need To Belong Scale of the exclusion and control groups are shown in Table 4. On the negative scale of the PANAS, the average score for the excluded group (20.62, standard deviation 6.67) was significantly higher than that for the control group (16.1, standard deviation 3.66) ($p = 0.0426$, $p < 0.05$). On the other hand, on the positive scale, the average score for the excluded group was 19.25 (standard deviation 1.58), and the average score for the control group was 22.2 (standard deviation 5.99), with no significant difference being observed. For each item in the PANAS, the mean values of the excluded group and the control group were compared using t-tests. The results showed that the positive items "Proud" ($p = 0.002$) and "Alert" ($p = 0.024$) were significantly lower in the excluded group ($p < 0.05$). The negative item "Irritable" was significantly higher ($p = 0.0002$, $p < 0.05$). The Need to Belong scale showed that the mean value for the excluded group was 33.5 (standard deviation 8.96), while the mean value for the control group was 32 (standard deviation 5.63), with no significant difference ($p < 0.05$).

Table 5 shows the results of the emotional analysis of the impressions on the Novel and Product Introduction documents.

The percentage of "positive" impressions in the review text on the Novel was 0.1 (standard deviation 1.48) on average for the excluded group and 7.09 (standard deviation 11.61) on average for the control group. The percentage of "negative" impressions was 41.6 (standard deviation 21.77) on average for the excluded group and 32.51 (standard deviation 21.98) on average for the control group, with no significant differences ($p < 0.05$). A comparison of the "emotional scale" in the review text on the Novel between the groups showed that

Table 5. The results of the emotional analysis of reviews. Items in bold indicate items that were significantly different in the t-test.

Emotion Metric	Task	Excluded Group (N = 8) Ave(S. D.)	Control Group (N = 10) Ave(S. D.)
Positive(%)	Novel	0.10(1.48)	7.09(11.61)
	Product Introduction	21.80(25.70)	8.83(15.30)
Negative(%)	Novel	41.60(21.77)	32.51(21.98)
	Product Introduction	33.70(32.30)	21.80(17.50)
Neutral(%)	Novel	58.28(21.70)	60.40(22.60)
	Product Introduction	**44.50(36.39)**	**69.29(21.27)**
Joy	Novel	47.70(11.90)	55.90(18.80)
	Product Introduction	73.90(16.00)	74.70(16.70)
Liking	Novel	33.00(11.90)	35.20(4.47)
	Product Introduction	38.80(16.50)	38.80(10.60)
Sadness	Novel	75.00(15.00)	70.20(17.50)
	Product Introduction	46.60(16.10)	50.9(14.10)
Fear	Novel	54.90(12.00)	56.90(18.00)
	Product Introduction	48.90(17.40)	53.10(20.90)
Anger	Novel	**39.26(11.27)**	**31.68(7.06)**
	Product Introduction	41.60(20.20)	32.30(3.21)

the emotion of "Anger" was significantly higher in the excluded group (39.26 (standard deviation 11.27) than that in the control group (31.68 (standard deviation 7.06)) ($p = 0.049$, $p < 0.05$). The results of the analysis of the review texts on the Product Introduction documents showed that the percentage of "neutral" was significantly lower ($p = 0.048$, $p < 0.05$) in the excluded group (average 44.5 (standard deviation 36.39)) than in the control group (average 69.29 (standard deviation 21.27)). It suggests that the percentage of neutral sentiments in the text of impressions from the excluded group decreased compared to the control group. In contrast, the percentage of positive and negative words increased. On the other hand, there was no significant difference between the two groups in the "emotion" category.

4 Discussion

4.1 Results of the PANAS and the Need to Belong Scale

The PANAS results showed lower scores for the positive indicators Proud and Alert in the excluded group. This may reflect a loss of confidence from temporary social exclusion in the Cyberball task (Proud) and a self-evaluation of impaired reaction speed under stress (Alert). The negative indicator Irritable was higher, consistent with prior findings that social exclusion induces anger [12], suggesting that the Cyberball task elicited similar effects.

In contrast, no group difference was observed in the need to belong. This may be due to many participants being new students with a weak organizational identity.

4.2 Results of Sentiment Analysis and Emotional Analysis of Review Text

The significantly higher "Anger" score in the excluded group's Novel reviews likely relates to the elevated 'Irritable' score reported in the PANAS analysis.

We theorize that when subjects experiencing exclusion read a story with a protagonist, they could project their own negative emotions onto the character. This self-projection was then reflected in their written impressions, a tendency supported by comments from subjects who noted strong empathy with the protagonist's feelings.

Analysis of the review text on the Novel revealed that some impressions indicated self-projection and empathy with the story, such as "I was able to strongly empathize with the protagonist's feelings of wanting to soak in lukewarm water for a while[3]" Thus, excluded participants may have expressed impressions that included anger. These results likely reflect the content of the review text, and depending on the text and exclusion context, emotions other than anger may also emerge. Analysis of the review text on the Product Introduction revealed no significant differences between the excluded group and the control group in terms of "positive," "negative," or any of the five emotional indicators. This result may stem from the absence of a self-projection target in the text, so emotions such as "Irritable", seen in the text for the Novel, were not reflected. When no projection object was present, excluded participants did not express impressions tied to their own emotions. However, their lower "neutral" scores suggest that socially excluded individuals may focus more on emotional words.

5 Conclusion

This study investigated social exclusion through participants' review texts. Participants experienced temporary exclusion via a Cyberball task and then wrote reviews of a presented text.

Emotion analysis revealed two main findings: (1) the excluded group's Novel reviews contained more anger than the control group, and (2) their Product Introduction reviews showed fewer neutral emotions, suggesting a more emotional state. These results indicate that writers' experiences of social exclusion can be inferred from their texts, which could help develop early intervention strategies in schools, workplaces, or online environments.

The study has two main limitations: the small, homogenous sample limits generalizability, and the Cyberball-induced exclusion was temporary, so effects may differ from long-term real-world exclusion. Future research should replicate these findings with larger, more diverse samples.

---

[3] The expression "soak in lukewarm water" is often used in Japanese to refer to the state of being dependent on a comfortable situation.

References

1. Williams, K.D.: Ostracism: the kiss of social death. Soc. Person. Psychol. Compass **1**(1), 236–247 (2007)
2. Reece, A., Carr, E.W., Baumeister, R.F., Kellerman, G.R.: Outcasts and saboteurs: intervention strategies to reduce the negative effects of social exclusion on team outcomes. PLoS ONE **16**(5), e0249851 (2021)
3. Siersbaek, R., O'Donnell, C., Parker, S., Ford, J., Burke, S., Cheallaigh, C.: Social exclusion and its impact on health over the life course: a realist review protocol. HRB Open Res. **6**, 34 (2023)
4. Zhang, S., et al.: The reciprocal relationship between social exclusion and basic psychological needs through cross-lagged analysis. Sci. Rep. **14**, 12 (2024)
5. Palmer, S., Filippou, A., Argyri, E.K., Rutland, A.: Minority- and majority-status bystander reactions to, and reasoning about, intergroup social exclusion. J. Exp. Child Psychol. **214**, 105290 (2021)
6. Dunn, K.R.: Neural and behavioral effects of being excluded by the targets of a witnessed social exclusion. In: Honors Projects, vol. 164 (2015)
7. Nandwani, P., Verma, R.: A review on sentiment analysis and emotion detection from text. Soc. Netw. Anal. Min. **11**(1), 1–19 (2021). https://doi.org/10.1007/s13278-021-00776-6
8. Okada, T., Toriumi, F., Sakamoto, M.: A study on emotional analysis focusing on onomatopoeia used on SNS for the COVID-19. In: IEEE/WIC/ACM International Conference on Web Intelligence and Intelligent Agent Technology. WI-IAT '21, pp. 109–116. Association for Computing Machinery, New York, NY, USA (2022)
9. Williams, K.D., Jarvis, B.: Cyberball: a program for use in research on interpersonal ostracism and acceptance. Behav. Res. Methods **38**(1), 174–180 (2006)
10. Leary, M.R.: Need to belong scale (NTBS) [database record]. apa psyctests (2013)
11. Sato, T., Yasuda, A.: Development of the Japanese version of positive and negative affect schedule (panas). Jpn. J. Person. **9**(2), 138–139 (2001). (in Japanese)
12. Chen, Z., Du, J., Xiang, M., Zhang, Y., Zhang, S.: Social exclusion leads to attentional bias to emotional social information: evidence from eye movement. PLOS ONE **12**(10), 1–19 (2017)

Public Quest: A Communication Game to Foster Understanding and Relationships in Public Space

Shinya Nishide[1,2](✉) and Takeshi Nishida[1]

[1] Graduate School of Intercultural Studies, Kobe University, Kobe, Japan
215c304c@stu.kobe-u.ac.jp
[2] Senri International School of Kwansei Gakuin, Osaka, Japan

Abstract. In public spaces, communication among people with diverse values not only causes friction but also makes it hard to build relationships that bridge those differences. Simply expressing opinions is not enough to overcome divisions. To address this, we designed and implemented "Public Quest," a communication game that frames a three-stage process within an RPG theme: (1) creative opinion expression through word games, (2) collaborative reconstruction of opinions via party formation, and (3) relationship building through face-to-face "Encounter" events. Through an exploration study, we observed that word games encouraged diverse expression. The "Name the Party" process led to the acceptance of a balanced range of opinions, while the "Encounter" event fosters positive dialogues and connections across differing views. This framing of communication as a shared quest supports not just creative expression, but also constructive engagement and relationship building in public spaces.

Keywords: Public Space · Word Games · Name the Party · Encounter

1 Introduction

Small tensions or conflicts can arise in public spaces because people with different values and expectations share the same environment [1]. For instance, in places like libraries, station waiting rooms, public parks, and even semi-public environments such as food courts, individual differences in perceptions—such as what constitutes an appropriate volume level or what behaviors are permissible—can easily lead to communication friction. While continuous communication is essential for fostering a common understanding in such environments, engaging in dialogue with strangers carries a significant psychological burden [2]. In particular, the fear of others' gazes and negative reactions can hinder the free expression of opinions, leading to silence or unwilling conformity [1].

Communication challenges in public spaces can be understood as involving two stages. The first stage concerns the expression of diverse opinions, which is often limited by fear of negative judgement and psychological barriers [3]. Combining diverse opinions and building relationship is often challenging in the second stage. Rushing to a conclusion risks overlooking minority views and deepening divisions within the community [4].

Previous work has focused on lowering communication barriers by utilizing tools such as emojis [5] and anonymity [6, 7], as well as promoting participation through visualizing contribution levels [8] and facilitating neutral discussions with chatbots [9]. However, these supports are not always effective for all participants, particularly those who are naturally sensitive to how they are perceived by others. For such individuals, the support may even create new psychological burdens, such as a sense of being excessively supported or an over-awareness of others' reactions. While previous work has also paid considerable attention on opinion aggregation, often based on methods such as the KJ method [10] and the Nominal Group Technique (NGT) [11], the broader user experience, including how these interactions contribute to long-term relationship building, remains underexplored.

We have explored an alternative approach using creative constraints, such as word games, to deliberately add difficulty to communication [12]. The rationale is that a shared, game-like challenge can foster psychological safety; participants can blame failures on the rules and thus express themselves more freely. While this approach effectively lowered the barrier for opinion expression, it leaves the challenge of meaningfully integrating diverse opinions and building community relationship.

Building on this work, we introduce Public Quest, a communication game designed to support the entire communication process from individual expression to community relationship building. Our approach uses creative constraints for opinion expression, embedded in a broader, three-stage process framed within a role-playing game (RPG) theme. (1) opinion expression through word games, (2) collaborative reconstruction of opinions in a process called "Name the Party," and (3) relationship building through face-to-face "Encounter" events.

The contributions of this research are twofold. First, we propose a novel, game-based methodology for communication in public spaces that provides consistent support from creative opinion expression using word games, through the collaborative reconstruction of opinions, to face-to-face relationship building. Second, through an initial real-world implementation in a public library, we provide empirical insights into its potential to facilitate creative opinion exchange and relationship building, while gaining important insights for future applications.

2 Design of Public Quest

Public Quest is a prototype system developed to address communication challenges in public spaces. It uses an RPG theme to frame three distinct phases: (1) opinion expression through word games, (2) opinion synthesis through party formation, and (3) relationship building through face-to-face encounter events.

The system was implemented as a web application that integrates with "LINE," a messaging app ubiquitous in Japan. This allows users to easily participate via a QR code through a familiar UI without needing to register for an account.

2.1 Word Games

The primary objective of the first phase is to encourage opinion expression by reducing psychological burden. Since the difficulty of speaking in public spaces often stems from evaluation apprehension, this phase leverages the "creative constraints" inherent in word games like acrostics. By framing opinion expression as a game, participants can attribute any failures to the rules of the game, which helps reduce the fear of being judged or criticized.

Figure 1 illustrates the overall process. First, the system prompts users to post their creations based on a theme, such as, "What are you thinking in the library right now, starting with the Japanese syllable し (shi)?" Users can then show their support to others' creations by voting with a heart icon.

Fig. 1. Phase 1: "Word Games" for opinion expression.

2.2 Name the Party

The second phase addresses the challenges identified in prior work regarding the synthesis of diverse opinions after initial expression. To avoid the pitfalls of rushed consensus, the system introduces a process inspired by RPG party formation. Participants group submitted creations, assign them "roles." For example, strong assertions like, "I want the space to be quiet," can be assigned the "Hero" role and harmony-valuing opinions like, "It would be nice if everyone could use this space comfortably," can be assigned the "Sage" role. They then give the group a unique party name (Fig. 2). This process provides an opportunity for participants to experience how diverse opinions can be reorganized. Participants can also vote for parties, providing input for the selection of a party in the next phase.

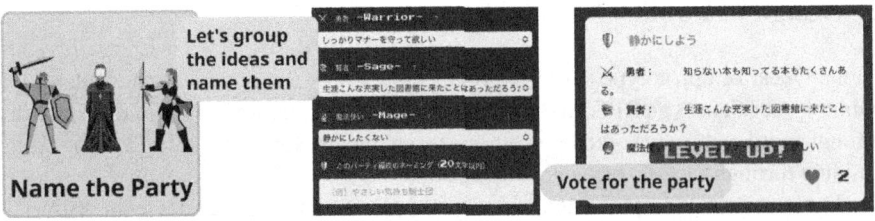

Fig. 2. Phase 2: "Name the Party" for opinion aggregation.

2.3 Encounter

The third phase is the "Encounter" event, designed to encourage participants to move beyond merely sharing the same space or just exchanging creations within the system, toward building relationships face-to-face. The term "Encounter" originates from gaming, where it describes a character meeting an enemy. In Japan, the term was adopted to describe a practice in which people who first met anonymously through SNS (mostly X) meet face-to-face for the first time. In this practice, it is common to take a commemorative photo by lining up their smartphones with their anonymous profiles visible, signaling that they have met in person while maintaining public anonymity.

A party will be selected with reference to the votes in the previous phase, and the system will provide a profile-like screen for each role showing the opinion assigned to the role in the selected party. Participants receive feedback prompts to consider which opinion they resonate with, followed by an invitation message to gather at a specific spot. The invitation message is entitled "Encounter" and includes an illustration depicting smartphones lined up in a circle, evoking the familiar "Encounter" scene.

By presenting participants with a party representing diverse opinions, we expect that the event will foster positive face-to-face encounters, not only among like-minded peers but also across differing viewpoints. The fun of embodying distinct roles, such as being the "Hero" or the "Sage" within the party is expected to create a sense of belonging and encourage engagement and interaction. We anticipate that these gatherings will lead to deeper mutual understanding and relationship building that cannot be fully achieved through communication within the system alone.

2.4 Usage Scenarios

The system is designed to be used in a public space like a library over a defined period, such as one week. During this time, the three phases: (1) opinion expression, (2) opinion synthesis, and (3) a face-to-face event—form a single, self-contained cycle called a "Quest." By changing the word game theme, these "Quests" can be repeated. This creates a mechanism for the community to continuously engage with timely issues.

The progression of a "Quest" is managed by facilitator who, like a Game Master in an RPG, intervenes based on participant activity. For example, if opinion posting stagnates, facilitators can trigger a scenario in which they distribute items to encourage participation. Another prepared intervention is the "Game Over" event, used when party formations become rigid and lack diversity. In this scenario, participants are notified of a narrative message: "All parties have been defeated by the Demon Lord!" This evokes the image of the final boss in an RPG. We expect the scenario to encourage participants to reconsider what makes a good balance and to reform their parties.

3 Design Exploration Study

We conducted an initial real-world implementation of the system in a school library to explore its potential to facilitate creative opinion exchange and relationship building, and to gain insights for future applications.

The study took place in a school library located on a campus housing two distinct schools: a Japanese combined junior and senior high school, and an international school with a broad range of students from kindergarten to high school. As a space where students from diverse cultural backgrounds regularly interact, the library offers an ideal environment for this study. Its lively and sometimes noisy atmosphere presents a real challenge that some users find problematic, making it a fitting site for investigating ways to facilitate opinion exchange and relationship building despite such difficulties.

Approximately 700 students who regularly use the library serve as the target population for this study. The study took place over five days (May 26–30, 2025). The primary method for joining was through QR codes on posters and tabletop signs placed within the library. Participants could also join the study through invitations from friends. To encourage opinion expression, we installed two components in the library: a noise meter to raise awareness of noise levels, and a public display showing a ranked list of widely supported opinions.

This experiment consists of three main phases: (1) opinion posting through word games, (2) opinion synthesis through party formation, and (3) an event where participants gather. The transition between phases was not strictly pre-scheduled but was flexibly determined based on participant activity and the overall flow of the Quest. This adaptive approach allowed the facilitator to respond organically to the dynamics of communication. We intentionally chose "words beginning with the syllable し(shi)" as the theme for the first phase. This choice was meant to guide participants by evoking words like しずかに(quietly), thereby directing their attention toward the library's noise environment.

As described in Sect. 2.4, we prepared several intervention scenarios for facilitators to flexibly respond to participant activity while maintaining the RPG worldview. These interventions were not merely for improving the efficiency of the experiment. We believe similar design features would be necessary when deploying the system more broadly. One aspect of our study was also to observe how participants would perceive and react to these interventions, as this would inform future system design.

4 Observations and Discussion

We structure our observations and discussion on the following research questions.

RQ1: Do "Word Games" reduce participants' psychological burden and promote the expression of diverse opinions?

RQ2: Does the "Name the Party" process encourage participants to recognize and accept a balance of diverse opinions?

RQ3: Does the "Encounter" event promote the exchange of diverse opinions and the building of relationships?

4.1 RQ1: Do "Word Games" Reduce Participants' Psychological Burden and Promote the Expression of Diverse Opinions?

We examined the ease of expression by analyzing the content and number of submitted posts. We also measured participation motivation based on the number of registered users and the dropouts. The high level of activity, opinions posted, and "hearts" of resonance collected, suggests that the system functioned effectively as a trigger for participation. Furthermore, participants expressed resonance with others' opinions indicates that the shared, creative experience of the word games nurtured a foundation for positive interaction, preventing opinion differences from being viewed as hostile. We believe this environment helped reduce the participants' psychological burden.

4.2 RQ2: Does the "Name the Party" Process Encourage Participants to Recognize and Accept a Balance of Diverse Opinions?

We first analyzed the balance of opinions of posts. Among opinion-focused categories, the "Pro-Quiet/Follow Manners" group had the most submissions, indicating many participants favored quietness and etiquette. However, the "Anti-Quiet/Don't care About Manners" category received more hearts, suggesting stronger resonance for opposing views. Other categories captured observations and requests related to the library environment and user behavior. These results demonstrate the diversity and complexity of opinions expressed during the first phase.

Based on the midway observation that the formed parties were far from balanced, we triggered the "Game Over" intervention to raise awareness of balance among the participants. We observed that more parties tended to include both pro-quiet and anti-quiet opinions after this intervention, suggesting that the process can effectively guide participants toward accepting diverse opinions.

The results revealed both the potential of the concept and challenges in its practical application. We cannot conclude that more detailed instructions about balance should have been provided from the start. Allowing participants to first form parties freely and then introducing the "Game Over" event may have been more effective in prompting deeper reflection and awareness of balance. Future design should carefully consider how to balance initial freedom with guidance in order to foster both participation and meaningful reflection.

4.3 RQ3: Does the "Encounter" Event Promote the Exchange of Diverse Opinions and the Building of Relationships?

Participants were invited to the "Encounter" event, which took place in a room designated by the facilitator next to the library. Following the "Game Over" event, the system notified participants that the Demon Lord had been defeated by one of the newly submitted parties, symbolizing the overcoming of imbalanced party formations. The victorious party was introduced as consisting of a "Hero" supporting "I cannot be quiet", a "Sage" supporting "Be quiet!" and a "Mage" supporting "There are many books I know and don't know".

During the face-to-face event, ceremonial practices aligned with the game's worldview were naturally accepted (Fig. 3). For example, participants who resonated with the same opinion type gathered and took commemorative photos while displaying a character badge reflecting their type on their smartphones. Furthermore, we observed participants, who had initially gathered with like-minded peers, spontaneously invite groups with different opinions to take photos together. In a dialogue between these groups, one participant from a "Be quiet!" type revealed their complex feelings in front of an opposing group, stating, "To be honest, I talk too. But when it's annoying, I really do think, 'Be quiet!'" In response, the other groups were not hostile and showed mutual understanding, saying, "We get what each other is saying."

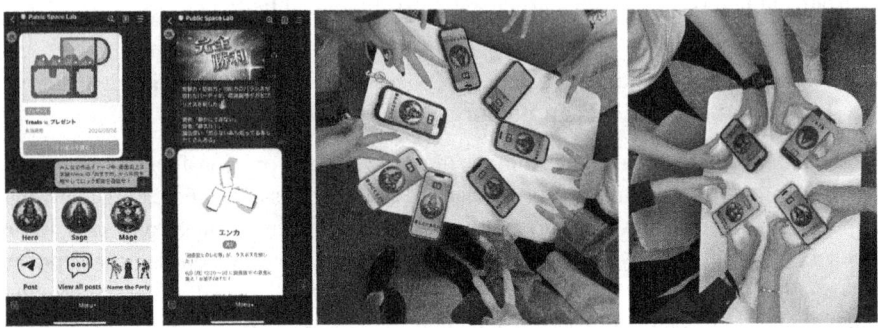

Fig. 3. "Encounter" event for relationship building.

Observations from the "Encounter" event aligned with our expectations. Initially, the event functioned as a space for identity formation, as participants with the same opinions gathered to reaffirm their supported type. When groups of differing opinions encountered, this did not result in conflict. Instead, dialogue emerged, featuring expressions of mutual understanding. As a result, the event was perceived not as a division based on opinion types, but as an "encounter" between individuals with different roles.

5 Conclusion and Future Work

To address the challenge of fostering the coexistence of diverse opinions and a flexible common understanding in public spaces, this research proposed a new communication game, "Public Quest." Our method wraps a three-stage process within a game-like narrative: (1) creative opinion expression through word games, (2) collaborative reconstruction of opinions, and (3) relationship building through face-to-face encounters.

We explored its potential and challenges through empirical study in a real-world public space. The study yielded several insights: that the creative constraints of a game can reduce the psychological burden of expression; that system interventions can promote the acceptance of a balanced range of opinions; and that connecting activities conducted within the system with face-to-face interaction can foster mutual understanding beyond conflict and help build relationships.

Future work includes verifying the reproducibility of the method, particularly addressing the reliance on extrinsic motivation and the practical interventions by facilitators, and assessing its generalizability and effectiveness in other public spaces with more transient and diverse users.

While conventional communication support research has focused on lowering barriers to expression or on efficient opinion consolidation, our work is novel in that it designs the entire journey, from expression to synthesis and subsequent relationship building, within a unified game-based narrative. This approach uniquely connects activities conducted within the system with face-to-face interactions, leveraging game mechanics to reframe conflicts as a shared mission. We believe this perspective offers a promising foundation for future research on fostering constructive dialogue in public spaces.

Acknowledgments. This work was supported by JSPS KAKENHI Grant Number JP23K28127.

References

1. Sandstrom, G.M., Boothby, E.J.: Why do people avoid talking to strangers? a mini meta-analysis of predicted fears and actual experiences talking to a stranger. Self Identity **20**(1), 47–71 (2021)
2. Sandstrom, G.M., Boothby, E.J., Cooney, G.: Talking to strangers: a week-long intervention reduces psychological barriers to social connection. J. Exp. Soc. Psychol. **102**, 104356 (2022)
3. McCroskey, J.C., Richmond, V.P.: Communication apprehension and shyness: conceptual and operational distinctions. Commun. Stud. **33**(3), 458–468 (1982)
4. Sistrunk, A., Self, N., Biswas, S., Luther, K., Verdezoto, N., Ramakrishnan, N.: Redistrict: online public deliberation support that connects and rebuilds inclusive communities. In: Proceedings ACM on Human-Computer Interaction, pp. 1–23 (2024)
5. Bai, Q., Dan, Q., Mu, Z., Yang, M.: A systematic review of emoji: current research and future perspectives. Front. Psychol. **10**, 2221 (2019)
6. Nishida, T., Igarashi, T.: Bringing round-robin signature to computer-mediated communication. In: Proc. ECSCW 2007, pp. 219–230 (2007)
7. Clark-Gordon, C.V., Bowman, N.D., Goodboy, A.K., Wright, A.: Anonymity and online self-disclosure: a meta-analysis. Commun. Rep. **32**(2), 98–111 (2019)
8. DiMicco, J.M., Hollenbach, K.J., Pandolfo, A., Bender, W.: The impact of increased awareness while face-to-face. Human-Comput. Interaction **22**(1–2), 47–96 (2007)
9. Kim, S., Eun, J., Oh, C., Suh, B., Lee, J.: Bot in the bunch: Facilitating group chat discussion by improving efficiency and participation with a chatbot. In: Proceedings CHI 2020, pp. 1–13 (2020)
10. Scupin, R.: The KJ method: a technique for analyzing data derived from Japanese ethnology. Hum. Organ. **56**(2), 233–237 (1997)
11. Van De, A., Delbecq, A.L.: Nominal versus interacting group processes for committee decision-making effectiveness. Acad. Manag. J. **14**(2), 203–212 (1971)
12. Nishide, S., Nishida, T.: Using word games as facilitator to awareness raising communication in public spaces. In: Proceedings CollabTech 2024, pp. 212–219 (2024)

How Do People Use Others' and Their Own Traces in Free Exploration?

Ayaka Negishi[1(✉)], Hiroki Echigo[1], Kazuyuki Iso[2], Masayuki Ihara[3], and Minoru Kobayashi[1]

[1] Meiji University, 4-21-1, Nakano, Nakano-Ku, Tokyo, Japan
ayaka.negishi@koblab.org, minoru@acm.org
[2] Tokyo Information Design Professional University, 2-7-1, Komatsugawa, Edogawa-Ku, Tokyo, Japan
iso@tid.ac.jp
[3] RIKEN, 1-7-22, Suehiro-Cho, Tsurumi-Ku, Yokohama, Japan
ihara@acm.org

Abstract. Traces left by people—such as footprints or signs of frequent passage—can serve as social cues that reveal the presence and activities of others in a space. This helps individuals decide where to look or what might be important, especially in unfamiliar environments or situations with many options. However, how such traces are interpreted and utilized during open-ended, unguided exploration remains poorly understood. Moreover, it is unclear how one's own traces in such contexts influence cognition and exploratory behavior. In this study, we investigated in detail how traces left by others and one's own past behavior are used during goal-free exploration and how they shape exploration patterns. Our results showed that traces left by others mainly functioned as cues for identifying exhibits with many or darker footprints as places worthy of attention, while the absence of traces sometimes stimulated curiosity. At the same time, however, they posed the risk of excessive expectations or overreliance. In contrast, seeing one's own traces not only helped participants recall past behavior but also encouraged them to intentionally explore previously unvisited areas or try different routes.

Keywords: Social cues · Trace · Social awareness · Interface · Public space · Social navigation · VR · Footprint

1 Introduction

Human traces can serve as *social cues* that make visible the presence and activities of others in a given space [1, 2]. For example, footprints or signs of heavy foot traffic can reveal how a space is socially used, providing hints that help people interpret its significance [3, 4]. This kind of social information is particularly useful in unfamiliar environments or situations with many options, as it can guide decisions about *where to look* or *what might be important*. Such traces of others have primarily been explored in the context of *social navigation* [1, 5]. However, most existing studies have focused on task-driven or constrained settings, and it remains largely unclear how people interpret and utilize traces in open-ended, unguided exploration. Moreover, these studies typically involve sharing traces left by others, but presenting people with traces of their *own* past behavior might lead to different patterns of use. In the field of HCI, there is growing interest in technology design that supports *reflection* [6–8], suggesting it is valuable to investigate how visualizing one's own behavioral traces could influence cognition and exploratory actions.

Against this backdrop, this study examined in detail how traces—both those left by others and by oneself—are utilized during free exploration without a specific goal, and how they impact exploratory behavior. As a result, traces left by others were found to primarily serve as cues for identifying exhibits with many or darker footprints as places deserving attention, while the absence of traces sometimes stimulated curiosity toward exhibits. At the same time, however, they also posed the risk of creating excessive expectations or overreliance. In contrast, participants who saw their own traces used them not only as reminders of past behavior but also actively explored areas they had not visited before and tried different routes, as revealed by subjective reports from the intervention group. The findings of this study may contribute not only to museum exploration but also to design principles for interfaces that present others' behavioral traces in broader contexts.

2 Related Work

2.1 Studies Presenting Others' Traces

Several studies have examined the effects of presenting traces of others' behavior within a space. For example, Monastero et al. [9] conducted a six-week field experiment in a university lobby where they visualized people's walking traces, demonstrating how such traces influenced social awareness in the space. They observed that walking trajectories were implicitly used as information reflecting how the space was utilized over time. Hirsch et al. [10, 11] explored trace visualization in virtual environments, reporting that such traces heightened social presence among asynchronous users. These studies indicate that traces of others help convey the sense that *"someone was here,"* enriching the social context of the space. Moreover, traces do not merely enhance social awareness; they have also been shown to affect people's exploratory behavior and choices. For instance, Albarrak et al. [12] investigated the impact of footprints presented at a fork in a path, finding that these social cues influenced route selection. Unlike studies focusing on route decisions, our research examines traces in the context of open-ended exploration, where we expect to uncover a wider range of interpretations and uses. Wong et al. [5] visualized others' exploration traces (as visual footprints) on a web-based map and tasked participants with finding as many hidden targets as possible. Their findings showed that participants who could see others' traces achieved significantly higher scores. Similarly, Shirai et al. [13] presented traces on bulletin boards—such as marks indicating where posts had been replaced or where others had lingered—and found that the average viewing time decreased. They interpreted this as evidence that traces functioned as important cues for information seeking.

Collectively, these studies suggest that traces like footprints effectively serve as cues for efficient information seeking in goal-oriented or search tasks. In contrast, we believe that in open-ended exploration without specific goals or correct answers, traces of others may lead to new discoveries or spark initial interest, thereby serving a different yet valuable role.

2.2 Reflection Supported by Viewing Personal Behavior

In the field of HCI, supporting *reflection*—the process by which individuals revisit and make sense of their own actions and experiences—has emerged as an important research theme [6–8]. Numerous studies have shown that presenting people with their own data or behavioral histories can produce various beneficial effects. For example, displaying blood glucose levels to patients with diabetes has been shown to improve their self-management [14], showing the use of shortcut keys has increased their adoption [15], and visualizing mouse accuracy has helped reduce excessive movements and enhance performance [16]. These findings suggest that prompting reflection through personal data can encourage behavioral adjustments and improvements.

In this study, we examine how visualizing participants' own traces of prior movements in large, open-ended exploration settings—such as museums—affects the way they reflect on and subsequently approach exploration.

2.3 Design of Trace Visualizations

Wong et al. [5] highlighted a design trade-off in visualizing exploration traces on the web: whether to minimize traces to avoid visual clutter or to faithfully present all available information. They pointed out that how traces are presented is a critical factor that greatly influences how they are interpreted and utilized.

In our study, we asked participants to compare two designs during their first and second explorations: one that visualized only footprints indicating long-duration stays and another that visualized all footprints, to evaluate which was easier to use.

3 Study

3.1 Reflection Supported by Viewing Personal Behavior

The aim of this study is to explore how traces of others and traces of one's own behavior are utilized during free exploration. Specifically, we investigate the following research questions:

RQ1. How are traces of others utilized in the context of free exploration?
RQ2. How are one's own traces utilized in the context of free exploration?

Additionally, we asked participants to compare two different trace designs—one visualizing only footprints indicating long-duration stays, and the other visualizing all footprints—during their first and second explorations, to evaluate which type of trace design they found easier to use.

3.2 Experimental Design

In this study, we investigated how traces left by others and by oneself are utilized by participants. To do this, we constructed a VR museum that simulated a real museum, enabling participants to freely explore a large-scale environment. Within this setting, we presented traces and collected both behavioral data and subjective evaluations from participants. The experiment consisted of the following two phases.

First Exploration (Presentation of Others' Traces). In the control condition, participants explored the VR museum freely with no traces displayed on the floor. Participants P1 through P6 were assigned to this condition. In the intervention condition, participants explored freely with traces left by another individual (P0) displayed on the floor. Participants P7 through P12 were assigned to this condition (see Fig. 2).

Second Exploration (Presentation of One's Own Traces). One to two weeks later, the same participants (P1 through P12) explored the same VR museum again. Participants who had been in the control condition during the first exploration (P1 through P6) were again assigned to the control condition and explored without any traces displayed. Participants who had been in the intervention condition during the first exploration (P7 through P12) were again assigned to the intervention condition, but this time explored with their own traces from the first session displayed on the floor (see Fig. 2).

This experimental design allowed us to analyze the differences in how participants utilized traces left by others versus their own traces. Additionally, by maintaining an equal number of participants in the control condition across both explorations, we were able to account for the potential effects of simply revisiting the same location on exploration behavior.

3.3 Trace Design

Based on the findings of Albarrak et al. [12], we chose to represent traces using footprints, as they are intuitively interpreted as such. However, if too many footprints are displayed, they can become visually cluttered and difficult to use as information, whereas removing too many can make them unreadable. To explore what level of information is most usable for people, we presented different footprint design patterns in the first and second explorations, and after the second exploration, asked participants in the intervention group to evaluate which design they found easier to use via a questionnaire (see Table 1). The following describes each design in detail.

Design of Others' Traces. In this study, we used the walking trajectory of P0 as the traces of another person. P0 first explored the VR museum without any footprints displayed on the floor, and we designed the traces of others based on this trajectory. To reduce visual clutter, we visualized only prominent footprints representing meaningful stays of at least two seconds. The color intensity of the footprints was adjusted to reflect the duration of stays, with darker colors indicating longer durations (see Fig. 4). The orientation of each footprint was manually adjusted based on video recordings, and in cases where the viewing angle varied during a single stay, the footprint direction was set to the median angle. To replicate realistic trace presentation conditions, the model of the other's traces (P0) was assigned randomly.

Design of One's Own Traces. For participants' own traces, we displayed all footprints, including the walking trajectory, so they could more fully interpret their past behavior. Similar to the design for others' traces, the color intensity reflected the duration of stays, and the orientation of footprints was adjusted in the same manner.

3.4 Participants

13 participants (6 female), aged between 20 and 31 years (M = 22.7 years old), were recruited from our laboratory. The participants included students at the undergraduate, master's, and doctoral levels, and all were unfamiliar with the study space.

3.5 Experimental Environment

In this study, we constructed a VR museum and had participants freely explore it to analyze how traces influence human behavioral changes. The experiment was conducted by having participants experience the VR museum through a desktop PC monitor (dimensions: 332.1 mm × 567.7 mm, resolution: 2560 × 1440) (see Fig. 1).

We chose a VR environment because it provides a large space that participants can explore freely, while also allowing the experiment to be conducted under controlled conditions without external factors such as other visitors influencing behavior. Additionally, the VR environment made it possible to present traces precisely and flexibly on the floor, allowing for easy switching of trace designs. Another major advantage was the ability to accurately record detailed behavioral data, such as participants' walking trajectories and dwell times.

VR Museum (Contents). The VR Museum was created using Blender and Unity, with the theme set to Buddhist art. This theme was chosen because relatively few participants are expected to have prior knowledge about Buddhist art, and Buddhist statues, with their symbolic hand gestures and ornaments, can be appreciated from all angles, leading to diverse viewing behaviors. Moreover, exhibits such as sutras and hanging scrolls require higher-level understanding of cultural backgrounds and meanings based on explanatory texts, making it possible to analyze not only superficial viewing but also more focused, in-depth observation. The features of each area are as follows (see Fig. 3):

Area 1: Hanging scrolls and Buddhist paintings are displayed along the walls with accompanying descriptions, and sutras are exhibited in the center.

Area 2: Buddhist statues (Tathagata), primarily statues of Tathagata.

Area 3: Buddhist statues (Bodhisattva), primarily statues of Bodhisattvas.

Area 4: A large mural located in a recessed space, requiring participants to walk deeper into the area to view it.

Operation. Participants could move forward, backward, left, and right using the keyboard arrow keys or WASD keys and adjust their viewpoint by moving the mouse.

Recording Movement Paths. When a key was pressed, a log of the participant's movements was saved as an image file. In these images, walking trajectories were depicted as green solid lines, and stopping points were plotted with colors representing dwell times: gray for 0–1 s, yellow for 1–10 s, orange for 10–20 s, and red for 20 s or more (see Fig. 5).

3.6 Procedure

The experimental procedure for participants in each condition across was as follows:

1. **Operation check:** Participants launched the application and were given instructions on how to operate it, followed by a practice session.
2. **Initial instructions (all participants):** Participants were instructed: *"Please explore the VR museum freely, just as you would when visiting a real museum. There is no time limit, so feel free to finish whenever you like. When you decide to finish, please give us a signal."*
3. **Additional instructions (intervention group only):** Participants in the intervention group (P7–P12) received the following explanations about the footprints displayed on the floor:

    Before the first exploration: *"The footprints on the floor represent the traces of a previous participant. Only footprints where the person stopped are shown, and the color intensity increases with the length of stay."*

    Before the second exploration: *"The footprints on the floor represent traces of where you previously walked. The color intensity increases with the length of stay."*
4. **Exploration:** Participants in the control condition (P1–P6) explored the VR museum *without any traces displayed* during both Phase 1 and Phase 2. Participants in the intervention condition (P7–P12) explored the museum *with others' traces (P0)* displayed during Phase 1 and *with their own traces* displayed during Phase 2. There was no time limit, and participants could finish whenever they chose.
5. **Informed consent:** Participants were informed that their movement data, video recordings, questionnaire responses, and interview content would be collected and analyzed anonymously, and that the results might be presented at conferences or published in papers. Consent was then obtained.
6. **Questionnaire:** Participants completed the questionnaire shown in Table 1.
4. **Interview:** In Phase 1, all participants were asked which exhibits interested them and why.

4 Result

4.1 First Exploration: Influence of Others' Traces

In Sect. 4.1, we analyze how traces left by others affected participants' exploration. Figures 6(1-a) and (1-b) show participants' exploration overlaid on a 20 × 20 grid representation of the exploration paths of P0 and the participants. In these figures, grids

Fig. 1. Scenes from the Experiment.

Fig. 2. Experimental environment.

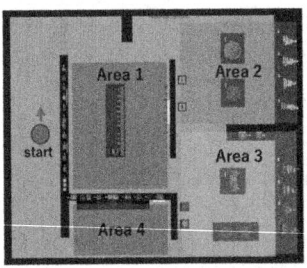

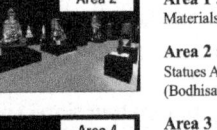
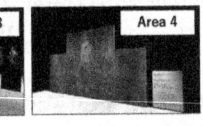

Fig. 3. Area map.

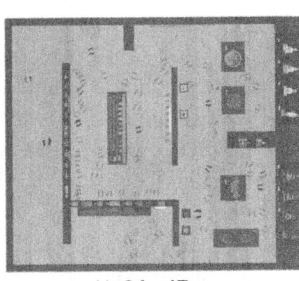
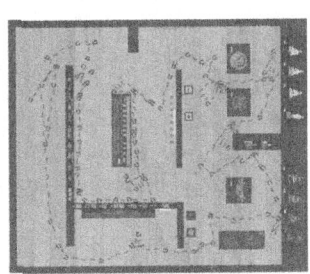

Fig. 4. Visualization of Traces: (a) Others' trace (long-duration stays only) (b) Own trace (all footprints)

visited by P0 are used as a baseline, with light orange indicating areas where participants' walking trajectories were present (*only visited*) and orange indicating areas where participants stopped (*stayed*). This visualization reveals the extent to which participants followed P0's exploration areas. Conversely, Figs. 6 (1-c) and (1-d) show how participants explored areas that P0 had not visited. Here, light blue indicates areas where participants walked (*only visited*) and blue indicates areas where participants stopped (*stayed*), highlighting how participants explored new areas outside of P0's path. By comparing these patterns between the control and intervention groups, we analyzed how traces of others (P0) influenced participants' exploration behavior.

Table 1. Post-Experiment Questionnaire.

Intervention group				
First Visit	others' traces	Q1.	Did the traces influence or change your behavior during the exploration? (1: Not at all – 5: Very frequently)
		Q2.	If the traces affected your behavior, please describe in as much detail as possible. (Open-ended)
Second Visit	your own traces	Q1.	Did the traces influence or change your behavior during the exploration? (1: Not at all – 5: Very frequently)
		Q2.	If the traces affected your behavior, please describe in as much detail as possible. (Open-ended)
		Q3.	Compared to the previous session (with others' traces), how did your own behavior differ? (Open-ended)
	the trace design	Q4.	(About the trace design) In the previous session, only "long-duration stays" were displayed, while this time "all footprints" were shown. Which type of trace did you find easier to use?
		Q5.	Please explain the reason for your answer to Q6.
Control group				
Second Visit	Revisiting behavior	Q1.	You revisited the same museum. Compared to your previous visit, how did the way you explored change? (Open-ended)

Average Exploration Time. Exploration time was defined as the duration from when participants began moving until they chose to stop. Across all participants in the first exploration phase, the average free exploration time was 560.33 s (SD = 239.36). In the control condition, the average was 516.67 s (SD = 304.1), whereas in the intervention condition (with traces of others), the average was 604.0 s (SD = 183.59). These results suggest that participants in the intervention condition tended to explore for a longer duration on average than those in the control condition. Additionally, the smaller standard deviation in the intervention condition indicates that participants exposed to others' footprints may have shown more consistent exploration durations, possibly using the footprints as a guide.

Visiting Patterns in Areas With Others' Footprints. Figures 6 (1-a) and (1-b) show, within the areas visited by P0 (i.e., areas with footprints in the intervention group), the proportions of grids that participants only visited (light orange) and grids where they stopped (orange). A Mann–Whitney U test revealed that for the orange areas (*stayed*), the intervention group had a significantly higher proportion compared to the control group (U = 5, p = 0.021). This indicates that participants in the intervention group, who were presented with P0's traces, stayed more frequently within areas previously visited by P0 than participants in the control group. In other words, even during free exploration, participants in the intervention group tended to follow and stay in areas indicated by others' traces.

Furthermore, analysis of individual exploration paths in Fig. 5 shows that during the first exploration, two participants in the control group failed to notice and did not visit Area 4—a location situated deeper within the space—and one of them still did not visit it during the second exploration. In contrast, all participants in the intervention group noticed and visited Area 4 from their first exploration. This suggests that P0's footprints may have served as cues that helped participants recognize the presence of Area 4.

Visits to New Areas Unvisited by P0. Figures 6 (1-c) and (1-d) show, within areas not visited by P0 (i.e., areas without footprints in the intervention condition), the proportions of grids that participants only visited (light blue) and grids where they stopped (blue). Mann–Whitney U tests revealed no significant differences between the control and intervention conditions for either the light blue or blue areas.

4.2 Participants' Subjective Evaluations of Others' Traces.

During free exploration with the presentation of others' traces, participants in the intervention group frequently described how footprints guided their attention. Illustrative comments include: *"I wanted to quickly see the places where the footprints were dense, and I intended to look at those areas carefully"* (P7); *"I tried to pass through places where there were many footprints"* (P10); *"When I saw exhibits with dense traces, I felt they might be important, so I went to look"* (P9); *"I carefully checked places with many footprints to see if something interesting was written there"* (P11, P12); and *"Since there were many faint footprints, I thought those must basically be the points to look at"* (P8). These responses indicate that all participants in the intervention group used dense or numerous footprints as cues for identifying exhibits of interest.

In contrast, interview results showed that 3 out of 6 participants (P7, P9, P11) expressed interest in exhibits without footprints, explaining that they visited them because they were curious why no traces had been left despite the presence of exhibits.

Furthermore, traces influenced not only which exhibits participants chose to view but also how they positioned themselves to read the exhibits and explanations. For example, one participant (P8) stated, *"When I stood where the footprints were, the explanations were easier to read, so I began to follow the footprints to view the exhibits more comfortably."* Another participant (P9) remarked, *"Since many footprints were near explanations, I later came to think that wherever there were traces, there would be explanations."*

Finally, some comments suggested that traces shaped exploration strategies even before participants examined details. For instance: *"It would be too much to look at everything carefully, so I adjusted my focus time based on how many and how dark the footprints were"* (P12), and *"The traces helped me decide routes at entrances or when there were multiple paths"* (P9).

However, participants also noted potential risks. For example, one remarked, *"I relied too much on the traces to decide whether to look at an exhibit"* (P12), while another stated, *"I expected more because there were so many traces but felt a letdown when it wasn't that interesting"* (P11). These comments highlight how traces can bias attention toward certain exhibits.

Regarding the trace design, one participant (P8) remarked, *"The impression changed a lot depending on the color intensity,"* suggesting that representing dwell time through color intensity may support trace use. The same participant also questioned the accuracy of traces in reflecting exhibit importance, indicating an area for further investigation.

4.3 Second Exploration: Influence of One's Own Traces

In Sect. 4.2, we analyze how participants' own traces influenced their exploration.

The analysis method was the same as in Sect. 4.1: we divided the exploration path data from participants' first and second explorations into a 20×20 grid and examined the status of visits during the second exploration within areas visited in the first exploration.

Figures 6 (2-a) and (2-b) show, for areas visited during the first exploration, the proportion of grids that were again visited during the second exploration (light orange) and where participants stopped (orange). This visualization reveals how much participants retraced the areas they had explored previously. Figures 6 (2-c) and (2-d) show the exploration status in areas *not* visited during the first exploration. Here, the proportion of newly visited grids in the second exploration is shown in light blue, and grids where participants stopped are shown in blue. This visualizes the extent to which participants explored new areas during the second exploration. By comparing these patterns between the control and intervention groups, we examined how viewing one's own traces influenced exploration behavior.

Average Exploration Time During The Second Exploration. Across all participants, the average time spent on free exploration during the second phase was 459.83 s (SD = 205.58). In the control group, the average was 424.0 s (SD = 77.89), whereas in the intervention group (with their own traces displayed), it was 495.67 s (SD = 289.54). Participants in the intervention group explored for a longer average time than those in the control group, with greater variability observed among individuals.

Visiting Patterns in Areas With One's Own Footprints. Figures 6 (2-a) and (2-b) show, for areas that each participant visited during the first exploration (i.e., areas with footprints in the intervention group), the proportion of grids that were not revisited in the second exploration (gray), only visited (light orange), and where participants stopped (orange). These results indicate how much participants in the intervention group revisited areas where they previously left footprints. From Fig. 6 (2-b), the proportions of light orange and orange areas were roughly the same as in the control condition, with no significant differences observed.

Visiting Patterns in Areas Without One's Own Footprints. Figures 6 (2-c) and (2-d) show, for areas *not* visited during the first exploration (i.e., areas without footprints in the intervention group), the number of grids that remained unvisited in the second exploration (gray), were newly visited (light blue), and where participants stopped (blue). This visualizes the extent to which participants in the intervention group explored new areas beyond where they had previously left footprints. From the results in Fig. 6 (2-d), the proportions of light blue and blue areas were found to be nearly identical to those in the control condition (with no significant differences). Thus, regarding the ratio of visit patterns, there was no observed influence of one's own traces.

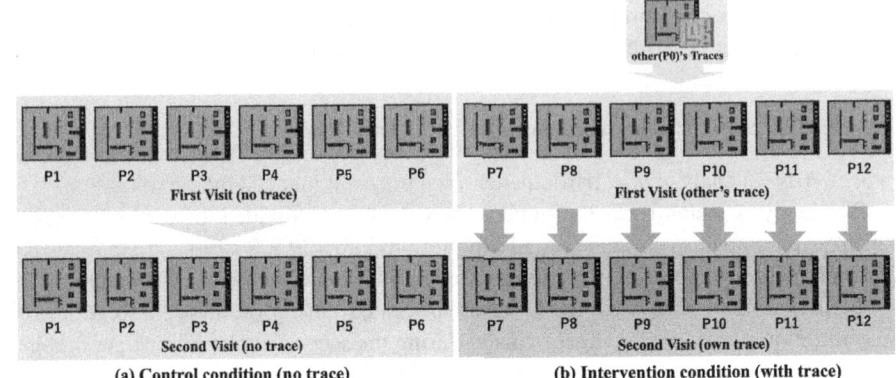

Fig. 5. Exploration Paths of Participants.

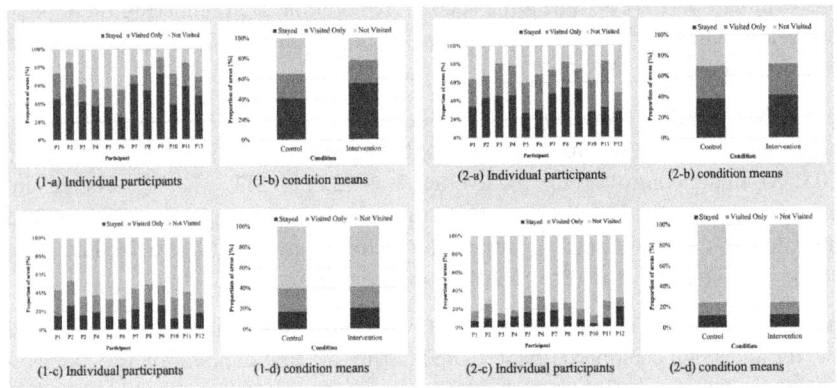

Fig. 6. (1-a) (1-b) Visits/stays in regions visited by P0; (1-c) (1-d) Visits/stays in regions not visited by P0. (2-a) (2-b) Revisits/stays in regions from the first exploration; (2-c) (2-d) New visits/stays in regions not visited in the first exploration.

4.4 Participants' Subjective Evaluations of Their Own Traces.

Subjective Impressions From The Control Group (Behavior During Revisitation): Participants P1, P3, P4, and P6 reported that they explored in the same way as before, revisited the places they had seen previously, or looked more closely at them. Meanwhile, P1 and P5 mentioned that they tried to explore areas they had not visited in the first session. Additionally, P2 noticed that their exploration route was the reverse of the previous time and intentionally changed their path.

Subjective Impressions From The Intervention Group (Influence of One's Own Traces): When participants were presented with their own traces, there was a general tendency to adjust their exploration behavior to confirm areas they had missed previously or to seek new discoveries. This tendency was observed across all participants in the intervention group. Notably, P9 and P12 stated that "there's no point in looking at the same place again," and proactively explored areas without their own footprints. Meanwhile, P7, P8, P10, and P11 also revisited areas with their own footprints, using them as cues to recall what they had viewed or how they had explored previously. Participants such as P8, P9, and P10 leveraged their traces as reference points to "reflect on the previous exploration and choose a different route," thereby using them to revise their exploration strategies. Additionally, P11 remarked that since they did not have a strong interest in the exhibits themselves, they mostly explored by following their own footprints, showing a case where the traces themselves became a motivation to continue exploring.

These results suggest that, compared to traces left by others, participants used their own traces in more varied ways: intentionally exploring areas without footprints, developing new exploration strategies, or employing them as cues to recall previous experiences.

4.5 Evaluation of Footprint Design

In this study, we used two different footprint designs: others' traces were shown only for long-duration stays, whereas participants' own traces displayed all footprints. When asked which design they found easier to use, three of the six participants in the intervention group preferred seeing all footprints, two preferred only long-duration stays, and one reported that both were equally easy to use. Participants who preferred seeing all footprints explained: *"There were few footprints last time, so I wondered whether areas without any had been ignored, which made me curious."* and *"With all traces visible, it was easier to understand the order in which things were viewed."* In contrast, participants who preferred only long-duration footprints noted: *"Too many footprints created visual clutter that distracted from the exhibits."* Others expressed more balanced views, such as: *"With all traces, it's harder to see detailed movements, but easier to grasp the overall flow—so it has both pros and cons."* and *"Showing only long-duration footprints seemed to prioritize certain pieces, highlighting which might be most worth viewing."*

5 Discussion

5.1 How Are Others' Traces Utilized During Free Exploration?

In this study, we investigated how participants utilize traces of others during free exploration. The results showed that others' traces were primarily used as cues to judge which exhibits were interesting or deserved closer attention. Specifically, participants directed their attention to areas with many or darker footprints, using them as indicators to decide where to focus and how much time to spend on each exhibit. Instead, there were also reports that participants became curious about why no traces were present despite the existence of exhibits, which prompted them to visit those areas. Furthermore, before examining the details of exhibits, some participants formed their exploration strategies based on the distribution of traces—for example, determining their routes or deciding which exhibits to spend more time on. This suggests that traces functioned as cues that provided an immediate understanding of how the space was socially utilized, serving as valuable reference points for planning exploration. Especially in unfamiliar spaces or situations where participants lacked prior knowledge, others' traces appeared to play a navigational role that could be relied on instantly, helping to streamline exploration and providing a sense of assurance. However, there was a risk that participants might rely too heavily on the traces or hold excessive expectations toward exhibits with traces, which could lead to biased exploration or disappointment when the actual exhibits did not meet those expectations. Regarding the way footprints were represented, using color intensity to indicate dwell time appeared to be an effective means of providing information during exploration. Yet there were also comments noting that showing only long-duration footprints sometimes led to misunderstandings, such as assuming areas were unvisited despite being briefly explored, or questioning whether the traces truly reflected the importance of exhibits. This points to the need for careful consideration of how much information to present and the level of detail required—such as whose traces are being shown and to what granularity.

5.2 How Are One's Own Traces Utilized During Free Exploration?

We also examined how participants utilized their own traces during free exploration. The results revealed that participants did not merely revisit areas with footprints to recall their previous exploration but also consciously chose to explore areas they had missed before or to take different routes. Some participants used their own traces to reflect on and refine their exploration strategies, intentionally avoiding previously traced paths in search of new discoveries. In this way, their own traces did not simply guide them to retrace past actions but also motivated them to restructure their exploration strategies and venture into unknown areas. Interestingly, even some participants in the control group—who did not see any traces—showed a tendency to focus on areas they had not explored during their previous visit. This suggests that the mere context of revisiting might naturally encourage people to explore differently from before. However, it is possible that participants' own traces served as an additional means to support this desire for new discoveries during a revisit. Quantitative analysis did not show a significant difference between the control and intervention groups in how traces influenced exploration patterns, likely because the ways in which participants utilized their own traces varied widely, resulting in no strong average trend. Additionally, we found that one's own traces might help sustain exploration. For instance, even a participant (P11) who showed relatively little intrinsic interest in the exhibits continued to explore by following their own footprints. Considering that participants in the intervention group spent more time exploring on average than those in the control group in both the first and second explorations, it is plausible that one's own traces also help maintain the interest of users who might otherwise lack motivation.

5.3 Footprint Design and the Level of Information Presented

This study used different visualization approaches: others' traces were shown as only long-duration footprints, while one's own traces displayed all footprints. We collected subjective feedback on which design was easier to use. The results suggested several conflicting issues inherent in trace design:

Noise vs. Lack of Information: Showing all footprints allows detailed behavioral histories to be understood, but excessive information may increase visual noise and reduce readability. In contrast, limiting traces to only long-duration stays risks insufficient information, potentially leading to misunderstandings such as assuming an area had not been visited at all.

Overall vs. Fine-Grained Movement: Displaying all footprints makes it easier to grasp the overall route of exploration, but small-scale movements become cluttered and harder to read. On the other hand, showing only salient footprints makes localized behavior easier to interpret, while losing information about the overall flow.

Risk of Evaluative Interpretation: Especially with filtered footprints, such as showing only salient traces, the information can appear curated, giving an impression of what is "worth seeing" or "highly evaluated," similar to how likes or reviews rank content on social media.

These points indicate that the amount of information presented can affect not just visual clarity but also fundamentally change the role traces play. Therefore, determining an appropriate level of information is an important challenge for future work, requiring careful adjustment depending on how the traces are intended to be used.

5.4 Limitations of This Study

This study has several limitations. First, our analyses were limited to the presence or absence of stays; we did not capture gaze or eye-tracking data. Staying in a location does not necessarily indicate attention, and indeed, one participant (P10) noted that although they thought they had spent a long time looking at an exhibit, the records showed otherwise, suggesting that memorable experiences do not always correlate with long observation times. This highlights the need for future studies to include gaze or eye-tracking to enable more detailed analyses. Furthermore, while participants' subjective evaluations revealed various ways they used their own traces, the behavioral analysis did not show clear differences compared to the control group. This suggests that simple measures such as visit rates or revisitation rates may not fully capture the influence of traces. Additionally, the footprint designs used in this study were manually created, limiting their accuracy. While we attempted to reconstruct footprint orientation from video data, how to visualize dynamic behaviors such as looking around or changing direction remains a challenge. Even though we adjusted color intensity according to dwell time, long stays might include moments of indecision or checking surroundings, which do not necessarily indicate strong visual attention. Moreover, this study did not independently manipulate the type of trace (one's own vs. others') and the design expression (all footprints vs. only long-duration footprints), so it is unclear how each factor individually influenced exploration behavior. Finally, given the small sample size, the generalizability of these findings requires cautious interpretation.

5.5 Applications

The findings of this study extend beyond museum exploration and can contribute to the broader design of interfaces that present traces of others' behavior. For example, in our ongoing research on turn-taking and attention distribution in remote meetings, participants often engage in multiple simultaneous activities—such as following the discussion, viewing shared materials, and responding to chat messages. In such multitasking environments, attention can become fragmented, increasing the risk of missing important cues such as others' intention to speak. Our results suggest, however, that participants were able to attend to footprints while still maintaining focus on the exhibits. These insights could be applied to the design of remote meeting interfaces—for instance, by visualizing where others' attention is directed or by structuring the interface so that discussion, material viewing, and chat are spatially related. Such designs could help participants manage their attention more effectively and support smoother meeting progress.

6 Conclusion

This study examined how traces left by others and by oneself are utilized during free exploration. The results showed that traces of others, especially areas with many or darker footprints, were primarily used as cues to judge which exhibits were interesting or deserved closer attention. Behavioral analyses also revealed significant differences compared to the control group. Such traces helped participants plan their exploration when they were unsure where to look, and the absence of traces sometimes sparked curiosity about exhibits. However, they also carried the risk of creating excessive expectations or reliance. In contrast, participants' own traces were utilized in more diverse ways. Participants used their footprints not only as cues to recall past behaviors but also to deliberately explore places they had not visited previously or to try different routes. Traces of others provided a social context within the space, functioning as guides or triggers of interest in unfamiliar environments or situations with too many choices. Meanwhile, one's own traces appeared to facilitate reflection on exploration and motivated new discoveries not made during prior visits. Future work should consider additional indicators of attention beyond dwell positions and dwell times. It will also be important to explore how to adjust the amount of trace information presented according to the intended use, thereby refining methods for presenting traces. We also provide an online lightweight version of our VR museum system for readers to experience firsthand: https://vrmuseumothertrace.netlify.app.

Acknowledgments. This work was partially supported by JSPS KAKENHI Grant Number JP22H03635 and 23K24891.

References

1. Albarrak, L., Metatla, O., Roudaut, A.: (Don't) mind the step:investigating the effect of digital social cues on navigation decisions. In: Proceedings ACM Hum.-Comput. Interact. vol. 5, ISS, Article 492(November 2021), p. 18 (2021). https://doi.org/10.1145/3488537
2. Dalton, R.C., Holscher, C., Montello, D.R.: Wayfinding as a social activity. Front. Psychol. **10**(2019), 142 (2019). https://doi.org/10.3389/fpsyg.2019.00142
3. Dieberger, A., Dourish, P., Hook, K., Resnick, P., Wexelblat, A.: Social navigation: techniques for building more usable systems, interactions **7**(6), 36–45 (2000)
4. Wexelblat, A., Maes, P.: Footprint: History-Rich Tools For Information Foraging, CHI99, pp. 270- 277(1999)
5. Wong, Y.L., Zhao, J., Elmqvist, N.: Evaluating social navigation visualization in online geographic maps. Int. J. Hum. Comput. Interact. **31**(2), 118–127 (2015). https://doi.org/10.1080/10447318.2014.959106
6. Baumer, E.P.: Reflective informatics: conceptual dimensions for designing technologies of reflection. In: Proc. CHI '15, pp. 585–594 (2015)
7. Fleck, R., Fitzpatrick, G.: Reflecting on reflection: framing a design landscape. In: Proc OZCHI, pp. 216–223 (2010)
8. Li, I., Dey, A., Forlizzi, J.: A stage-based model of personal informatics systems. In: Proc CHI, pp. 557– 566 (2010)
9. Monastero, B., McGookin, D.K.: Traces: studying a public reactive floor-projection of walking trajectories to support social awareness. In: Proceedings of the 2018 CHI Conference on Human Factors in Computing Systems, vol. 487. ACM (2018)
10. Hirsch, L., George, C., Butz, A.: Traces in virtual environments: a framework and exploration to conceptualize the design of social virtual environments. IEEE Trans. Visual Comput. Graph. **28**(11), 3874–3884 (2022). https://doi.org/10.1109/TVCG.2022.3203092
11. Hirsch, L., Haller, A., Butz, A., George, C.: What a mess!: traces of use to increase asynchronous social presence in shared virtual environments. In: 2022 IEEE Conference on Virtual Reality and 3D User Interfaces Abstracts and Workshops (VRW), pp. 598–599. Christchurch, New Zealand (2022). https://doi.org/10.1109/VRW55335.2022.00150
12. Albarrak, L., Metatla, O., Roudaut, A.: Exploring the design of history-enriched floor interfaces for asynchronous navigation support. In: Proceedings of the 2020 ACM Designing Interactive Systems Conference, pp. 1391–1403 (2020)
13. Shirai, Y., Owada, T., Kamei, K., Kuwabara, K.: Optical stain: amplifying vestiges of a real environment by light projection. In: HCI International 2003 (2003)
14. Frost, J., Smith, B.K.: Visualizing health: imagery in diabetes education. In: Proceedings DUX, pp. 1–14 (2003)
15. Malacria, S., Scarr, J., Cockburn, A., Gutwin, C., Grossman, T.: Skillometers: reflective widgets that motivate and help users to improve performance. In: Proceedings UIST, 321–330 (2013)
16. Jones, J., et al.: Visualizations for self-reflection on mouse pointer performance for older adults. In: Proc ASSETS, pp. 287–288 (2012)

Systems for Supporting Discourse and Understanding

A System for Extracting Discussion Topics Worth Deeper Exploration

Yoko Nishihara[1(✉)], Kosuke Fujishima[2], Megumi Yasuo[3], Junjie Shan[1], and Tetsuo Yoshimoto[4]

[1] College of Information Science and Engineering, Ritsumeikan University, Osaka, Japan
nisihara@fc.ritsumei.ac.jp
[2] Graduate School of Information Science and Engineering, Ritsumeikan University, Osaka, Japan
[3] Ritsumeikan Global and Innovation Research Organization, Osaka, Japan
[4] College of Business Administration, Ritsumeikan University, Osaka, Japan

Abstract. People have discussions in idea generation. Discussion support systems are widely studied. For example, some systems visualize discussion contents by automatically generating transcriptions. Other systems provide participants with summarized discussion content. However, few studies focus on systems that extract discussion points that have not been sufficiently discussed. Identifying such insufficient discussion points allows participants to explore them more deeply. The discussion result will be sufficient, and make participants obtain well-considered ideas from the discussion results. This paper proposes a system that extracts topics that have not been sufficiently discussed, and provides them to participants for deeper exploration. The proposed system firstly clusters the utterance texts in a discussion. Then, the system extracts topics worth exploring deeply using cluster's density. We hypothesize that one cluster expresses one discussion topic, and a low-density cluster indicates that the topic has not been discussed enough. The proposed system extracts low-density clusters as topic aspects worth deeper exploration and visualizes them using representative utterance texts. The discussion participants refer to these extracted topics for in-depth discussion, aiming to achieve more comprehensive results. We conducted evaluation experiments with participants. The experimental results showed that discussion results were characterized by high originality, validity, and efficiency when using the proposed system.

Keywords: Discussion support · Topic extraction · Topics for deeper exploration · Density-based clustering

1 Introduction

People think up new ideas to solve their problems in various fields, such as new product development within a company, addressing social issues in politics, and so on. Ideas often come up from discussions. People share their opinions during the discussion and summarize the results. The results are used to make new ideas. Discussion support systems therefore emerged, such as the auto-transcription system of discussion and the summarization system that support participants in continuing their discussion by referring to the system's output [13].

In contrast, few studies have mentioned topics that are not discussed enough or at all. Identifying and providing these under-explored topics can guide participants to explore them further, potentially leading to more sufficient and well-considered ideas.

This paper proposes a system that extracts topics worth exploring in-depth from the discussion data and then presents these topics to the discussion participants. The proposed system clusters utterance texts of discussions and then identifies topics for deeper exploration based on cluster density. The representative utterance texts are provided to the participants as discussion support.

The contributions of this paper are summarized as follows:

1. We propose a method that utilizes density-based clustering to extract topics worth exploring in depth. The method is implemented as a system that supports the discussion participants.
2. We conducted evaluation experiments with the participants. The experimental results showed that the discussion results obtained high originality, validity, and efficiency by referring to the extracted topics.

2 Related Work

Idea generation support methods have been studied for a long time, such as Mind Map [2] and KJ method [17]. These methods are used to visualize the idea seeds and group them to identify common points among them. Mind Map is a method for drawing a figure that visualizes the relationships between keywords and ideas. Users of the Mind Map arrange a theme in the middle of a figure for idea leading. Then, the user connects other keywords and ideas to related keywords in a radial, branching manner. The ideas are interconnected. The resulting figure will help users grasp the information they have in an overview format. KJ method is also a method to support the users in grouping ideas. In the KJ method, users write down ideas on a card. Then, the user groups the cards into clusters, assigning a label to each cluster. The clustering result supports the user in understanding the information structure. These methods also support idea-generation discussions by helping organize the arising ideas and opinions.

Meanwhile, since ideas often occur within discussions, the discussion support methods are also studied. Brainstorming [15] and six-thinking hats method [1] are traditional yet practical methods. Brainstorming is a method of group thinking that encourages discussion participants to think freely and generate many ideas. The users of Brainstorming are prohibited from denying others' ideas. They are encouraged to combine their ideas with those of others. The idea combination becomes a seed of new ideas. In Brainstorming, the number of generated ideas is more important than the quality. Brainstorming helps participants generate diverse ideas. Six-thinking hats method is also a discussion support method that encourages participants to hold multiple viewpoints during the examination of ideas. Users of the six-thinking hats method are required to give opinions that correspond to six pre-assigned viewpoints of the big picture & managing, facts & information, feelings & emotions, negative, positive, and new ideas. The users of six-thinking hats are asked to wear colored hats that correspond to each viewpoint. That is the reason for the method's name. Both of these methods can support users in generating numerous ideas through discussions and evaluating these ideas from multiple viewpoints.

Discussion contents are important in idea generation. Discussion content support methods are also studied, such as auto-transcription methods and summarization methods [7]. Content summarization methods are classified into two types: extractive summarization (for example, TextRank [12]) and abstractive summarization (which often uses neural network-based algorithms [6,8]). These methods support users in grasping the overview of the discussion in a short time and allow them to continue their discussion easily.

The discussion content can be evaluated by previous methods automatically. One of the methods represents a discussion process as network of utterance tags and evaluates the discussion quality based on the network structure [14]. Another method uses a model that identifies the user's development level and thinking ability [11]. If the discussion has a relatively clear task and goal, the discussion can be evaluated by the sufficiency of the task and goal. For example, an existing method can evaluate whether the discussion was conducted on the agenda [5], and fill in missing points and clarify the schema of the knowledge graph possessed by the expert.

On the other hand, idea generation discussions often lack agendas. It may be challenging to identify the lack of discussion using the previous methods. If opinion's features (such as argumentation, specificity, and collaboration) are evaluated, the opinion should be strengthened [9]. However, the method is also not enough to find the lack in discussion. To the best of our knowledge, there are a few methods that extract insufficient points from the discussion. If insufficient points could be extracted and presented to participants, participants would have the chance to engage in more valuable discussions. Therefore, this paper proposes a system that identifies and provides missing points to discussion participants. The users of the proposed system can check for insufficient points in their discussion and discuss them intensively, which will lead to more comprehensive discussion results.

3 Proposed System

Figure 1 illustrates the flow of the proposed system. The input to the proposed system consists of a discussion theme text and a discussion voice recording data file. The input voice record is transcribed into text. The transcription text is formatted with one utterance per line. Each utterance text is embedded as a

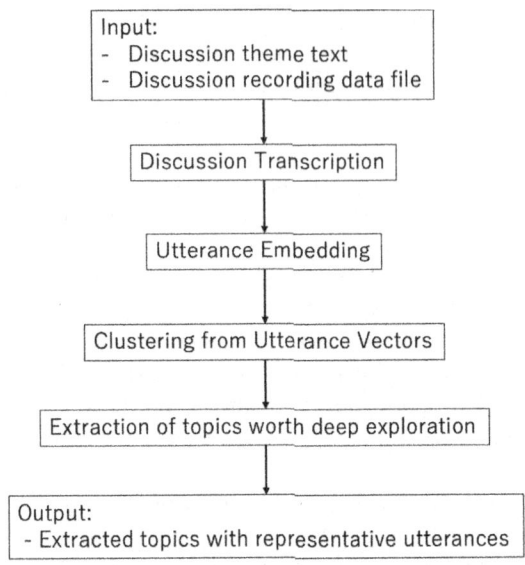

Fig. 1. Outline of the proposed system.

vector. These vectors are then grouped using a density-based clustering method. Each cluster represents a discussion topic. Insufficiently discussed topics are identified as those worth in-depth exploration. Representative utterance texts in the extracted topic clusters are selected and provided to discussion participants. This enables participants to deeply discuss the topics that they have not been noticed as important in depth, and they can obtain new ideas and considerations from the discussion results.

3.1 Input: a Discussion Theme Text and a Discussion Recording File

The proposed system takes a discussion theme text and a discussion recording file as input.

3.2 Transcription of Discussion Recording Data

The input discussion recording data is transcribed into text. The proposed system uses OpenAI's Whisper-large model[1] as an automatic transcription model.

The transcription text is formatted with one utterance per line. Utterances are separated by speakers' turns. Table 1 displays an example of the transcribed text.

---

[1] https://huggingface.co/openai/whisper-large-v3 (22nd May 2025 access confirmed).

The transcribed utterance texts include meaningless utterance, such as fillers, that do not convey opinions. These utterance texts may be noises in topic clustering, so the proposed system removes those texts. In this paper, if an utterance text is shorter than 10 Japanese characters, it will be considered as a noise and removed by the proposed system.

Table 1. Example of discussion data. The utterance texts were translated by authors from Japanese into English.

	Utterance text
1	About the place, I do not like crowds
2	You do not like crowds. So, Tokyo disappears from your options
3	is there some quiet place to work? A quiet place...
4	I might be on that side. I like a quiet place
5	You are on that side too
6	Uh, I prefer to somewhere in between. I would like to live in the suburbs where I can go anywhere that is fun
7	You are talking about a living place
8	I also like living in a quiet place
9	Workplace can be in crowds
10	I prefer not too urban, not too rural

3.3 Embedding of Utterance Texts

The utterance texts are embedded as vectors. The proposed system utilizes Sentence-BERT[2] [16], based on a pre-trained Japanese BERT model published by Tohoku University[3], for embedding utterance texts. The dimension of an/each embedded utterance text is 768.

3.4 Clustering of Embedded Utterance Texts

The embedded utterance texts are grouped by a clustering method. First, Principal Component Analysis (PCA) is performed on the set of embedded vectors to determine the maximum number of dimensions that can achieve a cumulative contribution higher than a specified threshold during dimension compression. The threshold value is set to 80% in the proposed system. Second, dimensionality compression is conducted by using Uniform Manifold Approximation and Projection (UMAP) [10]. The cosine distance is used as a measure of distance.

The dimension-reduced utterance vectors are clustered with the HDBSCAN [3] method to obtain topic clusters of the discussion. The challenging

---

[2] https://huggingface.co/sonoisa/sentence-bert-base-ja-mean-tokens-v2 (16th May 2025 access confirmed).
[3] https://huggingface.co/tohoku-nlp/bert-base-japanese-whole-word-masking (16th May 2025 access confirmed).

aspect of clustering discussion topics is determining the optimal number of clusters. The number of clusters required varies depending on the discussion content. It is challenging to use methods that require determining the number of clusters before clustering, such as K-means. Therefore, the proposed method employs a density-based clustering approach to mitigate this issue.

A well-known density-based clustering methods is DBSCAN [4]. DBSCAN conducts its clustering to achieve a result where every cluster has nearly equal density. This characteristic (requiring uniform density) can be problematic when discussion topics have varying levels of granularity or density. Therefore, the proposed system utilizes HDBSCAN to handle various density clusters. Fig. 2 illustrates the example of the clustering result. Note that the figure only shows data compressed into 2-dimension for visualization on a flat image.

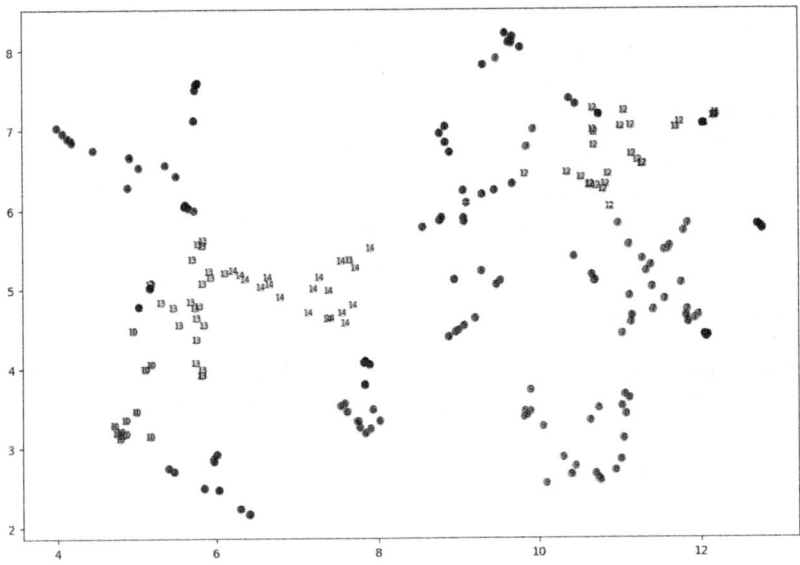

Fig. 2. Example of a clustering result with HDBSCAN. Numbers with dots denote the cluster's index.

3.5 Extraction of Topics Worth Deep Exploration

The proposed system extracts topics worth deep exploration from the clustering result. A topic worth in-depth exploration is defined as one that has not been sufficiently discussed. Each cluster comprises similar utterance texts, representing a distinct topic within the discussion. There are differences in the discussion sufficiency between topics, which is reflected in the density of topic clusters. We hypothesize that a low-density cluster, which behaves as sparsely distributed utterance texts, indicates an insufficiently discussed topic. If a cluster has a low-density, it means that utterances in the cluster has few related utterances. If few related utterances exist, it suggests that the topic of cluster has not yet been fully discussed. The cluster would be the cluster that expresses a topic worth deep exploration. Therefore, the proposed system identifies low-density clusters as those worth exploring in depth. Cluster's density is evaluated as the inverse of the average distance of all vectors in a cluster.

3.6 Output: Topics Worth Deep Exploration

The proposed system outputs topics worth deep exploration to the discussion participants. The topics are provided as utterance texts representing those clusters. The proposed system evaluates cosine similarity between utterance texts (from extracted low-density clusters) and the discussion theme text that are input to the proposed system. The utterance texts with a high cosine similarity are presented as topics worth exploring deeply. The number of visualized utterance texts is $N = 15$.

4 Evaluation Experiment

We conducted evaluation experiments to evaluate the effect of topic visualization on discussion results.

4.1 Experimental Procedures

The procedures were as follows.

1. Participants were recruited and organized into groups. The experimenter assigns a discussion theme to each group. The participants have a 30-min group discussion about the assigned theme (called the 1st discussion).
2. Use the proposed system to extract topics worth deeper exploration from the 1st discussion's transcription. Participants then engaged in a second 30-min discussion (the 2nd discussion) based on the system-extracted topics.
3. After the discussion, the participants were asked to answer a questionnaire survey.

The participants were 18 graduate and undergraduate students majoring in information science. The participants were divided into six groups of three.

The experimenter prepared two discussion themes of (a) travel plan for one week and (b) desirable workplace. These discussion themes were selected because they are easy to evoke opinions for discussion. Each group had a two-turn discussion (1st and 2nd) for each theme. The order of assignment was randomly decided. In the 1st discussion, those participants were asked to provide ideas as part of the divergent process. In the 2nd discussion, participants were required to form a result by combining the ideas as a convergent process. The 1st and 2nd discussions were conducted on different days in order to grasp the 1st discussion.

The participants answered a questionnaire survey after discussions. The questionnaire survey consisted of six items.

1. Evaluation on topics extracted by the proposed system (originality, novelty, validity, efficiency, interestingness, relevance to the discussion theme, each item was evaluated with a Likert scale from 1 to 4.)
2. Evaluation on the 1st discussion (originality, novelty, validity, efficiency, and interestingness, each item was evaluated with a Likert scale from 1 to 4.)
3. Evaluation on the 2nd discussion (originality, novelty, validity, efficiency, and interestingness, each item was evaluated with a Likert scale from 1 to 4.)
4. To what degree did you (participants) feel there were insufficiently explored points in the 1st discussion? (It was evaluated with a Likert scale from 1 to 4.)
5. To what degree did the output of the proposed system support your (participant's) 2nd discussion? (It was evaluated with a Likert scale from 1 to 4.)
6. Was the output of the proposed system difficult to understand or use? (It was evaluated with a Likert scale from 1 to 4.)

The results from item 1 were used to evaluate how the extracted topics affected the 2nd discussion. The results from items 2 and 3 were used to evaluate how the discussion changed from the 1st to the 2nd. The items 2 and 3 were about the evaluation of discussion results that were evaluated by the other group's participants instead.

4.2 Experimental Results

Table 2 shows the results of evaluations on extracted topics. The scores are averages among the participants. The high scores were obtained in the evaluation of relevance to the discussion theme, validity, and efficiency.

Table 2. Average Scores of Topics Worth Deep Exploration. Bold values denote that were obtained higher scores.

	Originality	Novelty	Validity	Efficiency	Interestingness	Relevance
Theme (a)	2.75	2.55	3.44	3.30	2.11	3.52
Theme (b)	2.26	2.28	3.05	3.09	2.95	3.41
Averages	2.50	2.41	**3.25**	**3.19**	2.53	**3.47**

Table 3 shows the results of evaluations on the 1st and 2nd discussions. The scores are also averages among the participants. The scores in the 2nd discussion were higher than those in the 1st discussion in the points of originality, validity, and interestingness ($p < 0.05$).

The average score for the questionnaire 4. was 2.27, that for the questionnaire 5. was 3.21, and that for the questionnaire 6. was 1.88.

Table 3. Average scores of the 1st and 2nd discussions. * denotes there is a significant difference found by t-test (p<0.05).

	Originality	Novelty	Validity	Efficiency	Interestingness
Average on the 1st discussion	2.88	2.77	2.72	2.94	3.16
Average on the 2nd discussion	**3.33***	3.11	**3.44***	3.38	**3.27***

5 Analysis on Experimental Results

We analyzed the extracted topics by the proposed system, and we analyze the effect of the proposed system on the discussion result.

5.1 Extracted Topics Worth Deep Exploration

We discuss characteristics of the extracted topics as those worth exploring deeply. Table 4 shows an example of provided utterance texts as topics worth exploring deeply for theme (a). The discussion theme (a) was about travel plan for a week. The provided utterance texts were indeed relevant to the discussion theme (a), so the evaluation of relation to the discussion theme was obtained a higher score.

Table 5 shows a part of discussion utterances in which the participants referred to the topics worth exploring deeply in the 2nd discussion. The first utterance texts in Table 5 refers to the first topic ("Ideally, I would like to go abroad. I wonder if a week abroad would be enough.") provided by the proposed system (shown in the first line of Table 4). The participants found that this topic was not discussed sufficiently ("Oh, surely this topic disappeared in an instant."). Then, they started to explore the topic. The proposed system extracts low-density clusters as topics to be explored deeply. The low-density cluster means that the topic has few utterance texts so that the topic was not discussed sufficiently. Therefore, the provided topics were evaluated as valid by the participants.

We discuss why the extracted topics were evaluated as efficient by participants. We consider that this is because the participants could use the provided topics as hints to know what point should be discussed more in the 2nd discussion. The score of the questionnaire 5, was also higher (3.21/4), which was about the efficiency of the proposed system in the discussions. The comments from the participants were "It gave me a chance to find out where I wasn't speaking." "The undecided was shown." "It was nice to have a visual representation of what discussions were not being made." Providing participants with these topics for deeper exploration appeared to facilitate their 2nd discussion. Therefore, the score of evaluation on efficiency was higher.

5.2 Discussion Result

Table 3 shows that the three items (originality, validity, and interestingness) obtained significant differences in the 2nd discussion than those in the 1st discussion. The proposed system provided the topics worth exploring deeply that supported the participants to discuss the topics sufficiently. Therefore, the originality and interestingness of the discussion were evaluated higher. The topics provided by the proposed system were related to the discussion theme. The participants could explore the topics deeply. Therefore, the validity of the discussion was evaluated higher.

Table 4. Examples of extracted topics worth deep exploration. The discussion theme is (a).

	Topics Worth Deep Exploration
1	Ideally, I would like to go abroad. I wonder if a week abroad would be enough
2	We have a week. If we think it doesn't take that long to move...
3	You can specify the season in this way
4	It takes just one week
5	But does it work really? One week is enough? One week may be long
6	Exactly. It depends on foreign or domestic. One week is the minimum for traveling overseas
7	One week may be long
8	I want to go overseas. But I know domestic places
9	I'd like to go to those places a lot
10	I also toured Shikoku in three days and two nights. It was a very short trip
11	I don't know much about foreign countries, so when I'm asked to plan a week, I can only make a rough sketch
12	It seems like we have been to big cities. Big cities, famous places. I think we can visit anywhere in a week
13	I once traveled around Shikoku, and to be honest, you can get around in five days
14	It's nice to be near the station
15	I've been there once in June and it was really nice. It was usually fine to wear short sleeves.

Table 5. Example of the 2nd discussion about the theme (a).

	Utterance text
1	Topic 1 is "Ideally, I would like to go abroad. I wonder if a week abroad would be enough." Oh, surely this topic disappeared in an instant. Like not enough.
2	Perhaps South Korea
3	Yes, we skipped
4	It is depends on whether it is near or not
5	I do not know. If we spent the almost one week
6	Surely, i would like to go
7	If we accept long hours to travel, we can go England and Africa
8	How long is it? How long do we take travel time by airplane?
9	I am not sure
10	If you think about the time it takes to get to the airport from here, the time waiting for the flight, the time on the plane, and the time after arriving at the other side of the country, you'll probably lose at least one day
11	Perhaps, we spent one day
12	Some airplanes have direct flights. If our destination is far away, we need to make a connection
13	So, if you go somewhere, stay overnight, and then go somewhere else, you lose a day for each trip
14	I thought it would be better to think of it that way
15	We have only five days in the middle of our trip

6 Conclusions

This paper proposed a system that extracted topics worth exploring deeply and provided them to support discussions. The proposed system conducts clustering on the utterance texts in the discussion, identifies low-density clusters, and then extracts representative utterance texts from these clusters. The discussion participants refer to the provided topics to explore them in depth.

We conducted evaluation experiments with the participants. We asked the participants to discuss an assigned theme in a two-turn discussion. The proposed system extracted topics worth exploring deeply from the 1st discussion, and provided them to the participants for reference during the 2nd. Experimental results showed that the provided topics were evaluated as having high validity, efficiency, and relevance to the discussion theme. We also found that the 2nd discussion was evaluated higher in terms of originality, validity, and interestingness than the 1st discussion, which was made by providing the extracted topics.

We will improve the proposed system to provide the extracted topics at an appropriate granularity in future work. The importance of topic should be considered. We also would conduct more evaluations on statistical data of discussion and the difference between the discussions.

Acknowledgment. The research was partly supported by Ritsumeikan Global and Innovation Research Organization (RGIRO) and AISIN CORPORATION. We show our best appreciation.

References

1. de Bono, E.: Six Thinking Hats: An Essential Approach to Business Management. Little, Brown & Company, Boston (1985)
2. Buzan, T., Buzan, B.: The Mind Map Book: How to Use Radiant Thinking to Maximize Your Brain's Untapped Potential. Plume (1996)
3. Campello, R.J.G.B., Moulavi, D., Sander, J.: Density-based clustering based on hierarchical density estimates. In: Pei, J., Tseng, V.S., Cao, L., Motoda, H., Xu, G. (eds.) PAKDD 2013. LNCS (LNAI), vol. 7819, pp. 160–172. Springer, Heidelberg (2013). https://doi.org/10.1007/978-3-642-37456-2_14
4. Ester, M., Kriegel, H.P., Sander, J., Xu, X.: A density-based algorithm for discovering clusters in large spatial databases with noise. In: Proceedings of the Second International Conference on Knowledge Discovery and Data Mining, pp. 226–231 (1996)
5. Ghosh, S., Kundu, A., Pramanick, A., Bhattacharya, I.: Discovering knowledge graph schema from short natural language text via dialog. In: Pietquin, O., et al. (eds.) Proceedings of the 21th Annual Meeting of the Special Interest Group on Discourse and Dialogue, pp. 136–146. Association for Computational Linguistics, 1st virtual meeting (2020). https://doi.org/10.18653/v1/2020.sigdial-1.18, https://aclanthology.org/2020.sigdial-1.18/
6. Goo, C.W., Chen, Y.N.: Abstractive dialogue summarization with sentence-gated modeling optimized by dialogue acts. In: 2018 IEEE Spoken Language Technology Workshop (SLT), pp. 735–742 (2018). https://doi.org/10.1109/SLT.2018.8639531
7. Kumar, L.P., Kabiri, A.: Meeting summarization: a survey of the state of the art (2022). https://arxiv.org/abs/2212.08206
8. Li, M., Zhang, L., Ji, H., Radke, R.J.: Keep meeting summaries on topic: abstractive multi-modal meeting summarization. In: Korhonen, A., Traum, D., Màrquez, L. (eds.) Proceedings of the 57th Annual Meeting of the Association for Computational Linguistics, pp. 2190–2196. Association for Computational Linguistics, Florence, Italy (2019). https://doi.org/10.18653/v1/P19-1210, https://aclanthology.org/P19-1210/
9. Lugini, L., Olshefski, C., Singh, R., Litman, D., Godley, A.: Discussion tracker: supporting teacher learning about students' collaborative argumentation in high school classrooms. In: Ptaszynski, M., Ziolko, B. (eds.) Proceedings of the 28th International Conference on Computational Linguistics: System Demonstrations, pp. 53–58. International Committee on Computational Linguistics (ICCL), Barcelona, Spain (Online) (2020). https://doi.org/10.18653/v1/2020.coling-demos.10, https://aclanthology.org/2020.coling-demos.10/
10. McInnes, L., Healy, J., Melville, J.: Umap: uniform manifold approximation and projection for dimension reduction (2020). https://arxiv.org/abs/1802.03426
11. Meyer, K.: Evaluating online discussions: four different frames of analysis. J. Asynchron. Learn. Netw. **8**, 101–114 (2004). https://doi.org/10.24059/olj.v8i2.1830
12. Mihalcea, R., Tarau, P.: TextRank: bringing order into text. In: Lin, D., Wu, D. (eds.) Proceedings of the 2004 Conference on Empirical Methods in Natural Language Processing, pp. 404–411. Association for Computational Linguistics, Barcelona, Spain (2004). https://aclanthology.org/W04-3252/

13. Misra, A., Anand, P., Fox Tree, J.E., Walker, M.: Using summarization to discover argument facets in online idealogical dialog. In: Mihalcea, R., Chai, J., Sarkar, A. (eds.) Proceedings of the 2015 Conference of the North American Chapter of the Association for Computational Linguistics: Human Language Technologies, pp. 430–440. Association for Computational Linguistics, Denver, Colorado (2015). https://doi.org/10.3115/v1/N15-1046, https://aclanthology.org/N15-1046/
14. Nishihara, Y., Tsuji, S., Sunayama, W., Yamanishi, R., Imashiro, S.: A generation method for the discussion process model during research progress using transitions of dialog acts. Int. J. Adv. Syst. Meas. **14**(1 and 2), 17–26 (2021)
15. Osborn, A.F.: Applied Imagination: Principles and Procedures of Creative Thinking. Charles Scribner's Sons (1953)
16. Reimers, N., Gurevych, I.: Sentence-BERT: sentence embeddings using Siamese BERT-networks (2019). https://arxiv.org/abs/1908.10084
17. Scupin, R.: The KJ method: a technique for analyzing data derived from Japanese ethnology. Hum. Organ. **56** (1997). https://doi.org/10.17730/humo.56.2.x335923511444655

Exploring the Potential of Hackathons as a Means to Promote Understanding of AI Literacy: A Case Study

Cleo Schulten[1](✉), Li Yuan[2], Kiev Gama[3], Alexander Nolte[4,5], and Irene-Angelica Chounta[1]

[1] University of Duisburg-Essen, Duisburg, Germany
{cleo.schulten,irene-angelica.chounta}@uni-due.de
[2] Beijing Normal University, Zhuhai, China
l.yuan@bnu.edu.cn
[3] Universidade Federal de Pernambuco, Recife, Brazil
kiev@cin.ufpe.br
[4] Eindhoven University of Technology, Eindhoven, The Netherlands
a.u.nolte@tue.nl
[5] Carnegie Mellon University, Pittsburgh, PA, USA

Abstract. In this paper, we discuss the potential of using hackathons to promote critical discussions among participants from diverse backgrounds in the context of Artificial Intelligence. Our main objective for this work was to explore the viability of utilizing a one-day hackathon to bring together stakeholders, such as researchers, teachers, students and developers, to share their perspectives on AI literacy while collaboratively designing digital learning materials to promote AI literacy. In the current landscape, awareness and AI literacy have become essential. There is, however, no clear consensus on the definition of AI literacy, the needed target focus for teaching it, or how to design (digital) learning materials and curricula. Our findings show that the participants' mixed backgrounds contributed to a meaningful discussion, and the hackathon outcomes were characterized as relevant and appropriate for teaching AI Literacy. We envision that this work contributes to the discussion about reaching a consensus on the definition of AI literacy, how to design (digital) learning materials and curricula, and who to include when creating these materials, by using a participatory design approach.

Keywords: Hackathons · Computer supported cooperative work · participatory approaches · AI literacy

1 Introduction

In this paper, we explore the potential of hackathons to facilitate critical discussions about cutting-edge technologies and their societal impact. Through their collaborative nature these events can provide fertile ground for information exchange, knowledge building and establishing common ground between participants from diverse backgrounds and different expertise as they strive to create a shareable artifact within a limited time frame [4].

Concretely, we organized a hackathon to promote discussions about Artificial Intelligence (AI) literacy and create (digital) learning materials. AI literacy is a critical topic for the digital era, particularly as the infiltration of AI in multiple aspects of everyday life grows [2]. Several competency frameworks have emerged to support teaching and training AI literacy, such as the UNESCO frameworks [8, 9]. However, related research points out that there is no clear consensus regarding the definition of AI literacy, what the target focus in teaching AI literacy should be or how to design learning materials and curricula [2, 10].

To address these challenges, we engaged stakeholders from different backgrounds – educators, AI experts and students – in a hackathon to co-create digital materials for teaching and training AI literacy. To further study how hackathons can potentially promote common understanding of AI literacy among diverse stakeholders, we formulated the following research questions:

RQ 1: How relevant were the participants' initial pitches in regard to AI literacy, and how did these evolve throughout the hackathon?
RQ 2: What are the results of the event in terms of satisfaction, learning and the participants' intention to continue on their team projects?

The innovativeness of this research lies in using an event format typically associated with rapid prototyping and technology development [1], to support and promote critical discussions among stakeholders with diverse perspectives towards establishing common ground. We envision that this work contributes to the ongoing discussion on fostering diversity and equitable access by employing a participatory design approach to build a shared understanding of AI literacy.

2 Related Work

As AI aspires to revolutionize societal functions, fostering AI literacy emerges as a priority for education [14, 17]. [7] define AI Literacy as *"a set of competencies [...] to critically evaluate AI technologies; communicate and collaborate effectively with AI; and use AI as a tool online, at home and in the workplace"*. AI literacy, thus, encompasses an understanding of AI technologies, their applications, and the ethical implications arising from their use [5] while occupying a pivotal intersection of digital and data literacy [7]. As such, there is a need for interdisciplinary approaches that align AI technologies with classroom practices and educational objectives [16].

To establish a common understanding of AI literacy, frameworks about AI competencies focus on identifying the skills that individuals should acquire to navigate the AI-era such as, the UNESCO AI Competency Frameworks for students [9] and teachers [8], the AICOMP framework [3] or the framework proposed by [7]. However, although these frameworks indeed define the skills that individuals should master, they do not discuss how these should be achieved. Despite the increasing interest on the topic, there seems to be a lack of clarity regarding what should be included when teaching about AI literacy, how to teach AI literacy [15] or how to assess AI literacy [2].

We argue that fostering AI literacy requires a human-centered, interdisciplinary approach involving diverse stakeholders—such as educators, researchers, and students—in participatory co-design practices like hackathons.

Hackathons are time-bounded events and are commonly organized around a specific theme [4]. Teams are formed to work on topics within that theme and create artifacts to be shared at the end of an event, which, at best, will be continued or reused after the event [11]. To support participants, organizers commonly develop scaffolding [1], such as topic-related talks, mentoring [12], or checkpoints where teams present their progress and receive feedback [13].

We aim to design an event format where anyone, regardless of their prior knowledge, can actively participate, and that fosters the development of a shared conception of an issue or concept while retaining the quality of artifact creation.

3 Methodology

We conducted a case study of a hackathon that focused on designing materials for training AI literacy. To that end, we invited senior and early-career researchers as well as teachers and students with a background in AI in Education. The hackathon was attended by 26 participants overall who split into 4 teams during the event based on their personal interests. Except for one team (Team C), all teams had a mix of technology and education backgrounds as well as students, senior researchers, educators, developers and educational technology (Edu-Tech) professionals (overview in supplementary materials).

3.1 Event Design

The hackathon was organized as a one-day event at a major international conference for AI in Education, and was co-organized by the authors of this paper, following the guidelines of the Hackathon Planning Toolkit [1]. Figure 1 presents an outline of the event's structure and the timing of the data collection (a more detailed overview is included in the supplementary materials).

Fig. 1. Overview on event setup indicating the data collection points.

3.2 Data Collection and Analysis

To answer our research questions, we collected data through **pre- and post-questionnaires, artifacts** created during the hackathon – that is pitches, initial team presentations, final presentations and submitted products –, and **semi-structured interviews**; see Table 1 for an overview of the data collection methods and their relation to the research questions. A more detailed overview of the data collection methods can be found in the supplementary materials.

For the *relevance for (teaching) AI literacy* and the *aspects of AI literacy* [7] covered in the collected artifacts, two authors with expertise in AI in Education coded the collected artifacts. They first worked separately, before discussing potential disagreements and revising the codings if needed. The raters had a moderate agreement for the relevance for (teaching) AI literacy ($\kappa = 0.41$) and near perfect agreement for the covered aspects of AI literacy ($\kappa = 0.84$). We determined combined scores for relevance for AI literacy by calculating the mean scores of both ratings and used an AND logic for the addressed aspects of AI literacy (only taking into account the aspects assigned by both coders).

Table 1. Data and methods used in the analysis of the research questions

	Data (Source)	Method
RQ 1	*Relevance to... ...AI literacy*	**Artifacts**: Coding by experts on [1,5] scale
	...teaching AI literacy	**Artifacts**: Coding by experts on [1,5] scale
	Addressed AI Literacy aspects	**Artifacts**: Coding by experts following the categories proposed by Long and Magerko [7]
	prior knowledge	**Interview**: report
	AI Literacy understanding	**Pre- & Post-Quest.**: report, comparison
	impact of talks	**Interview**: report
	personal background	**Observation and interview**: report
	team work	**Interview**: report
RQ 2	*satisfaction*	**Post-Quest. and Interview**: Mean and standard deviation, report
	perceived learning	**Post-Quest. and Interview**: Mean and standard deviation, report
	intention to continue	**Post-Quest. and Interview**: Mean and standard deviation, report

4 Results

4.1 Relevance of Hackathon Projects Regarding AI Literacy (RQ 1)

All four teams followed different approaches regarding the types of materials they designed. Screenshots and details on the teams projects can be found in the supplementary materials. Team A prototyped an app that would use an LLM to teach about AI through text, visuals, and audio. Team B created mock-ups for a web platform explaining AI concepts, differences from human intelligence, and potential issues. Team C drafted guidelines and a platform to help teachers and students integrate AI in the classroom. Team D designed a wireframe and gameplay for an online game to foster critical thinking and human agency.

Table 2. Overview on relevance to (teaching) AI literacy (on [1–5] scale) and covered AI aspects of the artifacts, that is 9 pitches and 4 teams presentations and products

Artifacts	Relevance to AI Literacy			Relevance to teaching AI Literacy			Covered aspects of AI Literacy		
	range	M	SD	range	M	SD	range	M	SD
Pitches	2–5	3.833	1.225	1–5	2.944	1.446	1–3	1.889	0.782
Initial Pres.	2–5	4.125	1.436	1.5–5	4.00	1.683	0–3	2.25	1.5
Products	3.5–5	4.125	0.629	2–5	3.875	1.315	1–4	2.5	1.291
Final Pres.	4.5–5	4.75	0.289	3.5–5	4.50	0.707	2–5	3.00	1.414

Table 2 shows the artifacts' aggregated relevance to AI literacy and training AI literacy as well as the number of covered AI aspects. The mean values increased over time, from pitches to final presentations, although the final products ranked lower than the final presentations. Similarly, the number of AI literacy aspects covered in the artifacts is rising from pitches to final presentations.

In the pre-questionnaire, 9 participants (of 25) chose the intended **definition of AI literacy** (option 1, see questionnaire in supplementary materials). The most popular answer (12 participants) was option 6. In the post-questionnaire, one person corrected their answer from option 6 to 1, and 4 maintained their previous responses (1 with option 6 and 3 with the intended option 1).

For the **items falling under AI literacy** 2 participants gave 50% correct replies, 10 participants gave 66.7% corrects replies, 6 gave 83.3% correct replies and 8 participants matched the intended response 100%. These findings indicate that even among participants who work on AI in Education, the relevant topics for AI literacy can be ambiguous.

The Interviewees report a *"more or less"* (I1) common understanding of AI literacy in their team, stating that *"[i]t all comes from different perspectives"* (I2).

Tasks within the teams were distributed based on prior knowledge or experience: *"[members] were taking initiative to do [tasks] as they were coming up"* (I1). I2 – who has an educational background – explained that they joined their team because of another team member who *"also comes from the conceptual part"* and was *"ask[ing] deeper questions, not just the technical ones. [Such as] 'But what do we actually want to achieve?'"*. Regarding the work mode, they said that *"the computer scientists were discussing"* more practical aspects. While the two with educational background *"tried to initiate this discussion on the learning outcomes and the potential long-term consequences of this game [...] But I think our provocative questions were also accepted and discussed."* (I2).

4.2 Satisfaction, Learning and Continuation Intentions (RQ 2)

In the post-questionnaire the participants *somewhat agree* with being satisfied with their projects ($M = 1.05, SD = 0.3$), which was also apparent in the interviews: *"I'm very happy with the product [... and] the dynamics of the team"* (I1) and *"This was great. And the discussions that we had were also very provocative"* (I3). The interviews highlighted that critical discussions about AI literacy fell short: *"I am not very satisfied in terms of the discussion on the impact of AI. And it's a bit concerning that even in the event where you have the whole day, and [...] are meant to discuss things, you still have no time to do that"* (I2).

Participants reported having learned something about AI literacy in general ($M = 1.5, SD = 0.577$), a bit about how to teach AI literacy ($M = 0.5, SD = 1.732$) and creating teaching or learning materials ($M = 0.25, SD = 1.5$). Additionally, aspects like communication, project management and game development were mentioned in the post questionnaire and the interviews: *"I learned a bit about collaboration"* (I4). Learning was reportedly similarly inhibited by the time constraints: *"there was not enough time for me to know more [...] mainly there was time to build upon what I already knew"* (I1).

Participants were disinclined to continue with their projects ($M = -0.083, SD = 0.877$). The interviews highlighted that while participants may be interested – *"I'd love to."* (I1) – they either do not have the time or see re-connecting with their group members as a hindrance: *"I don't know if [the other team members] want to continue the idea"* (I3). One participant took aims to *"have some kind of workshop [...] internally"* (I4) at their place of work.

5 Discussion

Concerning the relevance of the hackathon projects for AI literacy (RQ 1), the expert assessments and their agreement scores suggest that AI literacy is not yet thoroughly defined. This is also apparent in the projects' various outcomes (e.g. pitches, presentations, and deliverables). Our findings reflect different perspectives among the stakeholders regarding the definition of AI literacy and their priorities regarding the competencies involved when training for AI literacy [2]. In other words, the plurality of perspectives is depicted in the teams' outcomes. This may indicate that hackathons allow expressions of diversity while at the same time foster common understanding.

Regarding the participants' satisfaction with the hackathon and their continuation intentions (RQ 2), participants were overall positive, although they wished for more time so that they could achieve more and have time for in depth discussions. Still, the majority of participants did not intend to continue with their projects due to other responsibilities, lack of time, or difficulties connecting with team members. This indicates the need for stable structures, opportunities, and incentives for continuation. Continuation after the hackathon is an established research direction [11], indicating that continuation after hackathons is low in general even with participants intending to continue [4].

5.1 Theoretical and Practical Implications

We envision that our work has several implications for research and practice regarding the use of hackathons as participatory forums for facilitating critical discussions. We found that the heterogeneity of the teams was beneficial to the teams' brainstorming process and team members benefited from the diverse input of their teammates. For future events, this could be replicated through guided group formation or event participant selection [4].

The hackathon was overall well received, based on participation numbers, retention, satisfaction, and feedback. However, participants expressed that they would have liked to have more time for *discussion* and to *deliver* finished products. To address this, we suggest that hackathons of this format can be used iteratively to define, communicate and align goals while preparing for prototyping. This setup could for example be utilized as a kick-start brainstorming event for a collaboration, either internally or including external participants [6]. This would remove the pressure of completing a working artifact within the time constraints as well as the barrier of availability after the event for continuation. To achieve more within the event, the hackathon could be extended to a two-day (or longer) event. This would allow for a full day of ideation and additional days for implementation of the project. With an extended event however come additional considerations about duration and what weekdays to pick as well as availability of prospective participants [1].

6 Conclusion

Our findings show that we can utilize hackathons to bring together participants with varying prior knowledge or expertise of the hackathon theme and have a productive discussion. However, we found that with the event's limited time frame came certain shortcomings, concretely reduced time for discussions in favor of producing an artifact and not enough time to produce complete products.

We acknowledge that this research is subject to limitations. Our focus on launching a prototype of the proposed event resulted in a small hackathon and thus a small data sample that was tightened by the few responses to post-questionnaire and interviews. This limits the generalizability of our findings and could have contributed to an interpretation bias. For further investigation, the organization of additional and potentially larger events is needed.

Based on our findings we suggest refinement of the format for future iterations. Concretely, prioritization of ideation and discussion, and an extension of the time-frame to provide room for creation of products. As such, the goals of the event need to direct the setting and should be communicated clearly.

Acknowledgments. The authors would like to thank Wayne Holmes and Tore Hoel, the AIED 2024 Organizers and the hackathon participants for their contributions.

Disclosure of Interests. The authors have no competing interests to declare that are relevant to the content of this article.

References

1. Affia-Jomants, A.a.O., Gama, K., Herbsleb, J.D., Nolte, A.: How to organize an in-person, online or hybrid hackathon – A revised planning kit (2025). https://doi.org/10.48550/arXiv.2008.08025
2. Casal-Otero, L., Catala, A., Fernández-Morante, C., Taboada, M., Cebreiro, B., Barro, S.: AI literacy in K-12: a systematic literature review. Int. J. STEM Educ. **10**(1), 29 (2023). https://doi.org/10.1186/s40594-023-00418-7
3. Ehlers, U.D., Lindner, M., Sommer, S., Rauch, E.: Aicomp - future skills in a world increasingly shaped by AI. Ubiq. Proc. (2023). https://doi.org/10.5334/uproc.91
4. Falk, J., et al.: The Future of Hackathon Research and Practice (2024). https://doi.org/10.1109/ACCESS.2024.3455092
5. Holmes, W., Persson, J., Chounta, I.A., Wasson, B., Dimitrova, V.: Artificial intelligence and education: a critical view through the lens of human rights, democracy, and the rule of law. Council of Europe (2022)
6. Linnell, N., Figueira, S., Chintala, N., Falzarano, L., Ciancio, V.: Hack for the homeless: a humanitarian technology hackathon. In: IEEE Global Humanitarian Technology Conference (GHTC 2014), pp. 577–584 (2014). https://doi.org/10.1109/GHTC.2014.6970341
7. Long, D., Magerko, B.: What is AI literacy? competencies and design considerations. In: Proceedings of the 2020 CHI Conference on Human Factors in Computing Systems, CHI '20, pp. 1–16. Association for Computing Machinery, New York (2020). DOI: https://doi.org/10.1145/3313831.3376727
8. Miao, F., Cukurova, M.: UNESCO (2024). https://doi.org/10.54675/zjte2084
9. Miao, F., Shiohira, K.: UNESCO (2024). https://doi.org/10.54675/jkjb9835
10. Ng, D.T.K., Leung, J.K.L., Chu, K.W.S., Qiao, M.S.: Ai literacy: definition, teaching, evaluation and ethical issues. Proc. Assoc. Inf. Sci. Technol. **58**(1), 504–509 (2021). https://doi.org/10.1002/pra2.487
11. Nolte, A., Chounta, I.A., Herbsleb, J.D.: What happens to all these hackathon projects? Identifying factors to promote hackathon project continuation. Proc. ACM Hum.-Comput. Interact. **4**, 1–26 (2020). https://doi.org/10.1145/3415216
12. Nolte, A., Hayden, L.B., Herbsleb, J.D.: How to support newcomers in scientific hackathons-an action research study on expert mentoring. Proc. ACM Hum.-Comput. Interact. **4**(CSCW1), 1–23 (2020)
13. Schulten, C., Chounta, I.A.: How do we learn in and from hackathons? A systematic literature review. In: Education and Information Technologies, pp. 1–32 (2024)
14. Southworth, J., et al.: Developing a model for AI across the curriculum: transforming the higher education landscape via innovation in AI literacy. Comput. Educ. Artif. Intell. **4**, 100127 (2023). https://doi.org/10.1016/j.caeai.2023.100127
15. Sperling, K., Stenberg, C.J., McGrath, C., Åkerfeldt, A., Heintz, F., Stenliden, L.: In search of artificial intelligence (AI) literacy in teacher education: a scoping review. Comput. Educ. Open **6**, 100169 (2024). https://doi.org/10.1016/j.caeo.2024.100169
16. Stolpe, K., Hallström, J.: Artificial intelligence literacy for technology education. Comput. Educ. Open **6**, 100159 (2024). https://doi.org/10.1016/j.caeo.2024.100159
17. Tuomi, I.: The impact of artificial intelligence on learning, teaching, and education: policies for the future. JRC Sci. Policy Rep. (2018)

Supporting Time-Constrained Student Sports Journalists: Smartwatch Flagging and Match Visualization for Better Interview Questions

Ai Hagihara(✉) [id] and Satoshi Nakamura [id]

Meiji University, 4-21-1 Nakano, Nakano-ku, Tokyo 164-8525, Japan
a.haag004@gmail.com

Abstract. University student sports journalists often face time constraints during post-match interviews, as they are responsible for photography, live updates, and reporting with limited support. As a result, they have little time to take notes or prepare thoughtful questions, which often leads to vague or superficial interviews. Through interviews with student journalists and evaluations involving athletes, we found that questions focusing on specific plays and tactics were perceived more positively by both groups. To address this challenge, we developed a smartwatch-based system that allows journalists to flag important scenes during matches. These flags can later be reviewed using a prototype interface that displays both match videos and time-series information. We conducted two user studies to evaluate the system. The first study confirmed that journalists could successfully use the flagging function under real match conditions. The second showed that reviewing flagged scenes helped journalists formulate more play-specific and tactic-oriented questions. These findings suggest that the proposed system can support student sports journalists in improving the quality of post-match interviews, even under practical constraints.

Keywords: Sports Journalists · Fencing · Retrospection Support · Interview · Flagging

1 Introduction

University sports journalism plays an essential role in promoting the accomplishments of student-athletes and supporting the broader university sports culture. In Japan, many universities with competitive athletic programs maintain student-run sports media organizations. However, student journalists are often responsible for interviews, photography, and social media updates, which are typically handled by multiple staff members in professional media settings.

This multitasking often forces student journalists to cover entire matches alone, leaving little time to take notes or prepare interview questions. As a result, their post-match questions are often vague or generic and rely heavily on the athletes' responses instead of demonstrating a deep understanding of the match. Although student journalists play a central role in communicating sports performance, their interview process remains understudied, especially in relation to how limited working conditions affect the quality of their interactions with athletes.

To better understand this problem, we conducted interviews with student sports journalists and examined how athletes perceived their questions. This dual-perspective investigation revealed the intense workload student journalists face and highlighted discrepancies between the intentions behind interview questions and how athletes evaluate them. These findings clarified key challenges in student sports reporting and informed the design of our support system.

To address these challenges, we realized the need for a method that enables journalists to reflect on the match based on scenes that caught their attention during the game. Our approach allows journalists to mark such moments while watching the match, and later review them using both video footage and time-series information to support question formulation. To ensure that flagging could be done quickly and unobtrusively during the match, we developed a smartwatch-based system that allows journalists to record scenes without interrupting other tasks.

Based on this system design, we set out to explore the following research questions:

- RQ1: *Can student sports journalists use a smartwatch-based system to flag meaningful moments during matches while managing other reporting tasks?*
- RQ2: *Does reviewing flagged moments with visual feedback help journalists generate more specific and insightful post-match interview questions?*

We conducted two user studies to investigate our research questions. The first field study confirmed that flagging with a smartwatch is feasible during real matches while fulfilling other reporting duties. The second study showed that reviewing flagged scenes through our visualization system helped journalists generate more specific and insightful interview questions.

The contributions of this study are as follows:

- We identified the practical challenges faced by student sports journalists through interviews and found that questions focusing on specific plays were rated more positively by both journalists and athletes.
- We proposed and implemented a smartwatch-based flagging and visualization system that enables journalists to efficiently review the match and prepare questions within a limited post-match timeframe.
- We conducted two user studies that demonstrated both the feasibility of in-match flagging and the effectiveness of the system in supporting the formulation of high-quality, play-specific interview questions.

2 Related Work

2.1 Interview Question Content

Several studies have analyzed the content of interview questions posed by journalists. Research analyzing interview cases across various countries points out that questions often lack focus or a clear scope, and there's a deficit of follow-up questions based on active listening [3]. Furthermore, studies highlight biases in question content due to stereotypes; for instance, questions to Caucasian athletes often emphasize character and intelligence, whereas those to black athletes frequently focus on physical prowess and strength [12]. Also, gender stereotypes contribute to content bias, with male athletes often receiving more performance-focused questions than female athletes [5]. This study aims to support the creation of well-focused questions by helping journalists extract specific scenes from a match and explore them in greater depth. It also implicitly encourages focusing on in-game performance, regardless of stereotypes.

2.2 The Influence of Media on Athletes

In interviews, both the questions posed by journalists and the resulting media coverage can affect an athlete's mental state. A survey of 200 players in Iran's football league revealed a significant correlation between media coverage and stress, and between stress and player performance [13]. Conversely, a case study of Saudi Arabia's 2022 World Cup football team revealed media's positive influence on player performance. An online survey of football fans indicated strong agreement that media coverage positively influenced the team's performance [1]. Therefore, ensuring that interview questions closely reflect match events may contribute to better interview experiences for athletes.

2.3 Support for Journalists

Although there is limited research directly supporting the writing and interviewing processes of journalists, several notable studies have been conducted. Franks et al. [4] developed INJECTs, a search tool designed to help journalists generate new ideas for articles by recommending tangential information during their research. Their work demonstrated that this system broadened the scope of journalists' articles. Similarly, Pamudyaningrum et al. [11] proposed a gamified approach to teach interviewing methods, focusing on aspects like question selection and ethical considerations. Their experiments showed that interactivity enhanced enjoyment and engagement. While these studies aim to foster the professional development of journalists, our research specifically aims to support journalists who face difficulties in current interview environments by providing direct assistance during real interview situations.

2.4 Fencing Play Data Analysis

Numerous studies have been conducted on the acquisition and analysis of fencing play data. Kevin et al. [17] proposed FenceNet, a system for automatically classifying footwork techniques. By inputting 2D pose data, the system performs action classification. Using a fencing footwork dataset, they trained and evaluated FenceNet, achieving an accuracy of 85.4% in classification. Nita et al. [9] measured the angular velocity of athletes' bodies during play and revealed the potential to distinguish advanced players from beginners based on their ability to control their movements. Furthermore, by providing real-time visual and tactile feedback using lamp colors and smartwatch vibrations to indicate imbalances, they demonstrated the effectiveness of such feedback in enhancing athletic performance [10].

Other studies have also focused on acquiring and analyzing various play data in fencing, including joint angles [8], sword tip movements [6], and joint loads [2], which are expected to contribute to coaching beginners and providing feedback during training. In addition, many studies have explored visualizing play information, such as real-time visualization of sword tip trajectories superimposed on broadcast footage [14], and analyses of technical and tactical characteristics through graphical representations of footwork and other player movements [16].

While these studies demonstrate various methods for analyzing fencing play, their focus lies primarily on athletic performance analysis and coaching support, often relying on specialized equipment like multiple cameras. These data acquisition methods are not practical for journalists, especially university student journalists who often work alone and manage both photography and real-time social media updates. This gap highlights a critical need for a support system that minimizes the operational burden on journalists, allowing them to effectively capture relevant match information without disrupting their primary interviewing duties.

2.5 Flagging Methods Using Wearable Devices

Many studies have explored flagging methods, particularly in the context of Experience Sampling Methods (ESM), where wearable devices are often utilized due to their continuous wearability.

In a comparative study examining ESM logging using smartphones and smartwatches, it was found that participants recorded more entries when using smartwatches than smartphones. Additionally, the response time between receiving a notification and responding was shorter with smartwatches [15]. Another study involving smartphones, smartwatches, and smart glasses revealed that smartwatches received the highest ratings in terms of comfort. However, due to the limited screen size, some participants noted difficulties with precise touch operations, especially those with larger fingers. In terms of response rate, both smartwatches and smart glasses outperformed smartphones, which showed the lowest response rate. Furthermore, the response time following notifications was significantly shorter for smartwatches and smart glasses compared to smartphones [7].

These findings highlight the advantages of using smartwatches for data input in dynamic environments, particularly their ability to reduce the delay between intention and action, as well as their overall comfort [7,15]. Such characteristics make smartwatches a highly suitable platform for developing flagging systems designed for journalists operating in demanding, multitasking scenarios. This review thus reinforces the rationale for utilizing smartwatches as the input device in our proposed system.

3 Identifying and Validating Interview Difficulties in Student Sports Journalism

3.1 Interview Challenges of Student Sports Journalists

To better understand the working conditions of Japanese university student journalists, we conducted interviews with one member from each of four university sports newspaper organizations. The results revealed that, due to chronic staffing shortages, journalists are often required to take on multiple roles simultaneously, such as photography and interviewing or writing articles. In fact, two of the four interviewees reported consistently working alone because their organizations lacked sufficient personnel. In addition to photography, some groups were also responsible for tasks such as real-time social media updates and video recording for platforms like YouTube.

As a result, many journalists said they were only able to document minimal information during matches, such as score changes. Some even noted they took no notes at all in order to focus fully on capturing high-quality photos. These findings suggest that, under current conditions, student journalists often lack sufficient reference material to ask meaningful post-match interview questions.

We also asked about the time available to prepare interview questions. Journalists who conducted interviews immediately after a match reported that the time between the end of the match and the start of the interview was too short to ask well-thought-out questions. During this period, they must manage various logistical tasks such as moving within the venue, packing up camera equipment, and posting social media updates, leaving little time for review or reflection.

This lack of breathing room means journalists often enter interviews without a clear grasp of what occurred during the match. In particular, same-day interviews suffer from limited preparation time and reference material. These insights highlight a need for support systems that enable quick and easy review of matches and key plays within the limited timeframe before interviews.

3.2 Interview Question Survey with Journalists and Athletes

To explore what kinds of interview questions are perceived as good or bad by journalists and athletes, we conducted a question evaluation survey involving both. Fencing was selected as the target sport, as the first author has four years of experience covering fencing and possesses relevant knowledge about play styles, match characteristics, and tactics.

The evaluation involved 109 interview questions created by two university student sports journalists while watching pre-recorded fencing matches on a PC. These questions were evaluated by the two journalists who created them and by three fencing athletes who participated in the corresponding matches. Journalists rated their confidence in each question on a 5-point scale. Athletes rated each question based on four criteria: ease of answering, clarity of meaning, perceived understanding of their play, and emotional response to being asked the question.

For analysis, the average score across all items was calculated. Scores of 1.0 or higher were considered high evaluations, while scores below 1.0 were considered low evaluations.

Based on this classification, we compared athlete and journalist evaluations. Among the 109 questions, athletes gave high evaluations to 55% of the questions, while journalists gave high evaluations to 44%. Table 1 summarizes the distribution of high and low evaluations from both groups.

Table 1. Distribution of Question Evaluations by Players and Journalists

	Player High Evaluation	Player Low Evaluation
Journalist High Evaluation	48	9
Journalist Low Evaluation	28	24

1) High Evaluation from Both Groups (48 questions): These questions typically addressed general tactical principles (e.g., "The first point is crucial; what were you focusing on?"), referred to previous matches or interviews (e.g., "You won this tournament last year; how do you feel about losing in the semifinals this time?"), or explored specific plays in depth (e.g., "On the 19th point, it looked like you skillfully dodged your opponent's attack and landed a hit; what are your thoughts on that?"). Such questions were perceived as meaningful and well-targeted by both athletes and journalists.

2) Low Evaluation from Both Groups (24 Questions): These included vague or overly abstract questions (e.g., "What are your thoughts looking back on the match?"), or incomplete questions that assumed implicit follow-up (e.g., "You were scoring smoothly up to the 44th point, weren't you?"). Both sides found them difficult to engage with.

3) High Evaluation from Athletes, Low from Journalists (28 Questions): These were often broad or general questions that were easy to answer (e.g., "How was your condition today?") or addressed plays not seen as central to the match by journalists. Athletes still appreciated being asked about those moments.

4) Low Evaluation from Athletes, High from Journalists (9 Questions): These questions often focused on negative performance (e.g., "Why did your opponent score three consecutive points?") or asked for reflection on pressure situations (e.g., "What was your mindset with a 13-point lead?"). While journalists found these analytically useful, athletes found them difficult or uncomfortable.

The analysis revealed the following insights:

- Questions that explored specific plays or tactics were consistently rated highly by both athletes and journalists.
- Athletes' evaluations were influenced not only by the question content itself but also by how well they performed during the referenced plays.
- Journalists' evaluations were shaped not only by the question content but also by whether the answers aligned with the themes or storylines they intended to highlight in their articles.

4 Proposed Method

We propose a match review method that presents match videos alongside time-series play information to support university student sports journalists in formulating deeper interview questions immediately after a match. To enable effective review within the limited post-match time window, the method allows journalists to mark key moments during the match that they wish to revisit. These marks are recorded as "flags" and later used as anchors for retrospective analysis. Figure 1 shows the prototype system interface used in this study.

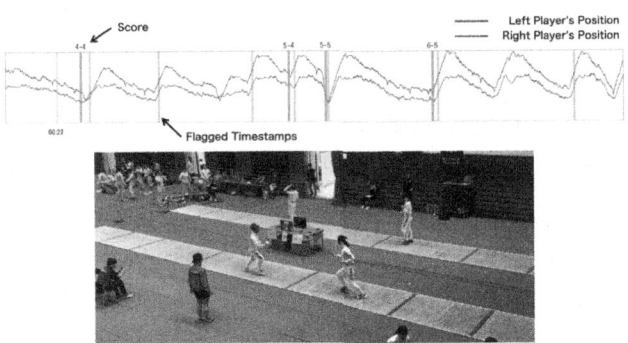

Fig. 1. Prototype interface displaying match video and time-series information. For fencing, the system visualizes player positions on the piste, which is critical for performance analysis.

Photography is one of the most demanding in-match tasks for student journalists and often involves using a DSLR camera with a telephoto lens. As a result, operating handheld devices such as smartphones is impractical during matches. Moreover, requiring visual attention to input flags increases the risk of missing critical moments, such as highlight plays or important reactions. Therefore, the flag input mechanism must support eyes-free operation and provide immediate confirmation through feedback.

To meet these requirements, we developed a smartwatch-based flagging application. The Apple Watch is worn on the wrist, allowing journalists to flag moments with a simple tap, without interrupting other tasks. The system offers both haptic and auditory feedback to confirm successful input. Journalists carry a paired iPhone during the match, which handles data storage and later access. The flagging application was implemented in Swift, along with a companion iOS application for managing and exporting flagged timestamps. Figure 2 illustrates the flag input and data management interfaces.

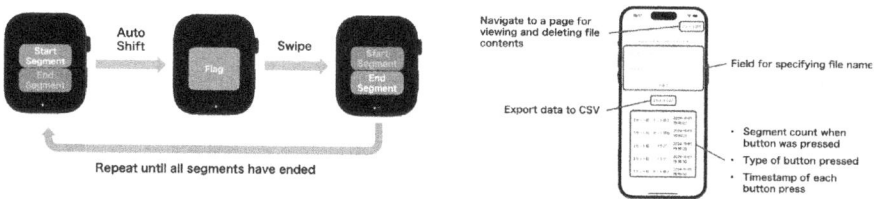

(a) Apple Watch: Flag Input Screens   (b) iPhone: File management interface

Fig. 2. Flag Input and Data Management System

The prototype system for post-match review (Fig. 1) was developed using Processing. Player position tracking was implemented in Python using the YOLOv8 object detection framework. The tracked positions are visualized as a line graph, where a player's rightward movement on the piste corresponds to a downward shift in the graph, supporting quick spatial interpretation of play dynamics.

5 Field Studies: Real-World Validation at Fencing Tournaments

5.1 Overview of the Field Study

This field study aimed to evaluate whether flag input could be performed alongside regular journalistic duties during real matches, thereby testing the practicality of the proposed method. As in the survey conducted in Sect. 3.2, fencing was selected as the target sport. We conducted flagging field studies during both team and individual matches in which members of the Meiji University Athletic Association women's épée fencing team participated.

Two members of the Meiji University sports newspaper organization, each with three years of experience covering the Meiji University fencing team, participated in the field study. Due to their availability, the field studies were conducted individually in two separate sessions. The first field study was conducted during the 76th Kanto Intercollegiate Fencing Championships, held in Tokyo in

October 2024, which included both individual and team events. The second field study was conducted during the 2024 All Japan Intercollegiate Fencing Championships, held in Kyoto in November 2024, which included only team events. The Meiji University women's épée team achieved excellent results in these competitions, as summarized in Table 2. A total of six team matches and seven individual matches were used in the field studies.

Table 2. Major Fencing Competition Results

Competition	Result
Kanto Intercollegiate Fencing Championships (Individual)	1st, 2nd, 3rd, 30th place
Kanto Intercollegiate Fencing Championships (Team)	1st place
All Japan Intercollegiate Fencing Championships (Team)	1st place

Table 3. Predefined Questions for the Semi-Structured Interviews

ID	Question
Q1	In what types of scenes did you input flags?
Q2	Was it possible to input flags while taking photos?
Q3	Did you feel that having only one type of flag was sufficient?
Q4	What aspects do you usually focus on when watching matches?
Q5	Are there any questions you would like to ask at this point?
Q6	Were the flags used merely for recordkeeping?
Q7	Which matches do you feel are worth revisiting?
Q8	Were there any matches you felt did not require review?
Q9	Did your criteria for flagging change as you became more familiar with the system?
Q10	Were there any scenes you now feel should have been flagged?
Q11	Were there any scenes you feel did not need to be flagged?

5.2 Basic Procedure of the Field Study

Before the match, participants were instructed to input flags during scenes they felt they might want to revisit later. During the matches, participants performed their regular journalistic duties as usual, with no instructions given regarding tasks other than flagging.

After each field study, we conducted semi-structured interviews to gather feedback on system usability and how participants performed the flagging. The interview questions are listed in Table 3. During the first field study, only Q1 through Q5 were prepared. Based on the results of the first session, additional questions Q6 through Q11 were added for the second field study.

5.3 Field Study 1: Kanto Intercollegiate Fencing Championships

As shown in Table 4, the number of flags added during each match indicates that the participants were able to input flags without any issues. However, in the individual matches, approximately half of the bouts were between two Meiji University athletes. All matches used in this field study followed a tournament format, and in bouts between athletes from the same university, one athlete was inevitably eliminated. Consequently, once the likely outcome became apparent, participants tended to flag scenes based on the perspective of the athlete who was likely to lose.

Table 4. Number of Flags and Match Results per Round

Competition	Round	No. of Flags	Match Result
Kanto Intercollegiate Women's Épée Individual	Round 2	3	15–10
	Round 2	6	15–12
	Round 3	7	15–14
	Round 4	2	15–7
	Round 4	0	15–8
	Semifinal	7	15–10
	Final	5	15–13
Kanto Intercollegiate Women's Épée Team	Round 2	4	45–21
	Semifinal	9	45–36
	Final	8	45–36
All-Japan Intercollegiate Women's Épée Team	Round 2	4	45–32
	Semifinal	6	45–34
	Final	10	45–32

According to the semi-structured interview results, the response to Q2 indicated that participants were able to perform flag input without any problems while carrying out their regular tasks such as photography. Although flag input took a few seconds, prioritizing photography did not interfere with their regular journalistic duties.

On the other hand, several usability issues were identified in the application. During actual match observation, participants often forgot to press the "Start segment" or "End segment" buttons. This led to frustration and negative impressions of the system. As a result, for Field study 2, we decided to remove unrelated features such as segment management.

5.4 Field Study 2: All-Japan Intercollegiate Fencing Championships

Previously, a segment management function was included to help participants identify which segment a flag was associated with. However, since segment boundaries could be determined using video and chronological information, and because participants frequently forgot to press the "Start segment" or "End segment" buttons in Field study 1 (as described in Sect. 5.3), this function was removed. As a result, the system was simplified so that only the central screen of the application, shown in Fig. 2a, was used.

According to the results, the number of flags per match is shown in Table 4, and all flag inputs were completed successfully. The semi-structured interview results from Field study 2 also supported the findings from Field study 1. Based on responses to Q2, the participants were able to perform flag input while carrying out their normal duties, such as taking and reviewing photographs. Although they reported a subjective delay of about five seconds in inputting flags, they commented that this was not an issue since they could take the delay into account when reviewing the scenes using the chronological information system. In addition, the removal of the segment management function eliminated the negative opinions observed in Field study 1.

These findings confirm that smartwatch-based flagging is feasible in real match settings. These findings suggest that RQ1 can be answered positively.

5.5 Post-Study Analysis

We analyzed the flags recorded during the two field studies, focusing on input patterns and flagged scene types. Many matches involved decisive wins, which may have limited the diversity of match developments.

When and Why Flags Were Placed. We analyzed when and why journalists placed flags during the two field studies. Since many matches ended in dominant victories, the variety of match developments was limited.

In team matches (Table 4), both journalists placed fewer flags during the second round, where the focal team built large early leads and won by over 13 points. These one-sided matches, common in tournament formats, may have reduced the need for detailed review. When outcomes seemed certain, journalists may have shifted their attention to later rounds. As one participant commented in Q8, "I would never review the first match. I might ask something like 'How did you feel in the first match?' but I would focus on the semifinal or final instead."

Fencing team matches consist of nine segments, which we divided into three phases: early (segments 1-3), middle (4-6), and late (7-9). For Journalist 1 (Table 5), most flags in the final were placed in the early phase, when the score was close and shifted frequently. In the semifinal, however, more flags appeared in the late phase, likely reflecting a successful rally after a temporary comeback.

Journalist 2 placed more flags in the final's late phase, often tied to each athlete's final appearance or visible emotional responses from the bench. In the second round and semifinal, flags were concentrated in the early phase when the outcome was still unclear.

Responses to Q1 confirmed that flags were often added during key moments, such as major shifts in score like comebacks or ties, sequences of consecutive points scored or lost, the resumption of play after interruptions, movements that differed from usual patterns, visible expressions of emotion such as fist pumps or shouting, and reactions from the bench or audience.

These results indicate that flagging was largely influenced by score developments and emotional intensity. Such moments often become central topics for interview questions. However, not every dramatic moment was flagged. Journalists relied on their own judgment to select scenes they considered meaningful.

Because the participants had no personal experience with fencing, they often evaluated the importance of a scene based on how the athletes or audience reacted. This suggests that their sense of significance was shaped more by social cues than by technical understanding (Table 6).

Table 5. Number of Flags per Phase for Journalist 1

Round segment	Round 2			Semifinal			Final		
	1–3	4–6	7–9	1–3	4–6	7–9	1–3	4–6	7–9
No. of Flags	2	2	0	1	3	5	5	1	2

Table 6. Number of Flags per Phase for Journalist 2

Round segment	Round 2			Semifinal			Final		
	1–3	4–6	7–9	1–3	4–6	7–9	1–3	4–6	7–9
No. of Flags	3	0	1	3	1	2	1	1	8

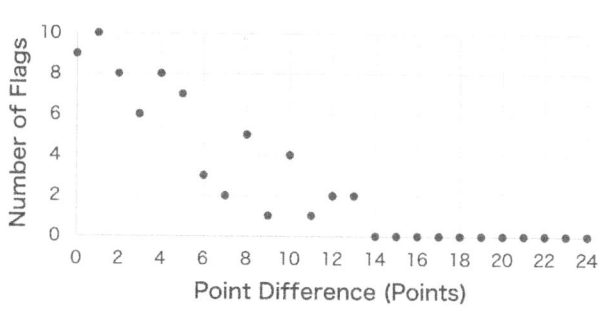

Fig. 3. Relationship between the Score Difference and the Number of Flags

Relationship Between Score Difference and Number of Flags. We also analyzed the relationship between score difference and flag frequency. Figure 3 shows that flags were recorded more often when the score difference was small. The correlation coefficient ($r = -0.88$) indicates a strong negative relationship.

Although journalists saw 5–10 point leads as decisive, flags were still placed, suggesting other factors like emotional reactions influenced decisions.

6 User Study: Exploring Question Generation with Flag-Based Review

6.1 User Study Overview

This section reports on a user study exploring how our flagging system influences the content of interview questions.

Since a fully automated real-time video analysis system has not yet been implemented, the study was conducted using pre-recorded and pre-analyzed match videos viewed on a PC through the prototype system. The participants were the same two student journalists from Sect. 3.2. To evaluate the effectiveness of the proposed method, which presents both match videos and chronological information, we included two baseline conditions for comparison. One was a traditional method based solely on the participants' handwritten notes, and the other was a video-only method that showed only the match footage.

During the study, participants first watched three match videos, each featuring a different athlete, and then formulated interview questions for each athlete. A time limit of two minutes was set for creating questions per athlete, during which participants used the system to review the match and generate questions. After the task, we conducted a follow-up interview survey. Each participant experienced all three methods. Journalist 1 followed the order of traditional method, proposed method, and video method. Journalist 2 followed the sequence of proposed method, video method, and traditional method.

6.2 Results of the User Study

To focus on the effectiveness of the proposed method, we excluded questions that referred to matches where a different method had been used for question generation. The analysis covered a total of 98 questions. To examine whether the content of the questions varied across different methods, we analyzed which elements were included in each question. Table 7 summarizes the results.

We analyzed five key elements found in the questions. These were: Location (player's position), Time (elapsed time), Method (how points were scored), Score (including point differences), and Win/Loss (match outcome). The table shows the proportion of questions that included each of these elements. For example, a question such as "It looked like you were playing defensively for the first minute, but with the score at 8 to 10, what was your approach?" would be categorized as including Location, Time, and Score.

Table 7. Proportion of Questions Containing Each Element

	Location	Time	Method	Score	Win/Loss
Traditional Method (40)	0.04	0.02	0.37	0.27	0.27
Video Method (28)	0.25	0.07	0.24	0.35	0.35
Proposed Method (30)	0.34	0.04	0.38	0.23	0.17

The results show that the proposed method led to more questions that referred to player positioning compared to the other two methods. Although the proportion of questions about attack methods was similar between the proposed and traditional methods, the content differed. The traditional method often used vague phrases such as "aiming for a counter," whereas the proposed method yielded more detailed descriptions of attack methods, such as "dodging the opponent's blade and targeting the hand." The number of questions mentioning win/loss outcomes was lowest in the proposed method.

6.3 Discussion of the User Study

In total, the two participants generated 98 valid questions for three athletes during 18 min of question writing. In actual fencing interviews conducted by the author, the number of questions per athlete is typically no more than ten, indicating that a sufficient number of questions were created. Analysis of the participants' review behavior showed that they frequently focused on the time segments just before and after flagged moments, suggesting that the flags played a key role in enabling efficient review and question generation.

The increase in questions referring to player positioning when using the proposed method is likely due to its visualization of player positions. The video-only method also led to more such questions than the traditional method, suggesting that positions can be somewhat understood through video alone. The proposed method had the lowest proportion of outcome-related questions, indicating that it encouraged participants to focus on subtler aspects of the match and reduced reliance on outcome-based questions.

Questions referring to player positions or detailed attack methods reflect a deeper understanding of the match and were rated highly by both journalists and athletes (Sect. 3.2). Their increase when using the proposed method suggests that the system can improve the quality of post-match interviews, supporting a positive answer to RQ2.

7 Limitations and Future Work

In this study, we conducted a two-stage study. First, we carried out a field study to examine whether journalists could collect subjective flags while carrying out their regular reporting duties. Then, in a laboratory setting, we investigated the effectiveness of using these flags for retrospective question generation. We consider this approach an appropriate step prior to full system implementation. In the future, we plan to develop a system that enables immediate post-match review using both time-series information and match video. With this system in place, we aim to conduct on-site studies during actual post-match interviews to examine both the method's overall effectiveness and its impact on communication between journalists and athletes. Furthermore, the current study was conducted with a limited number of participants, specifically two journalists and three athletes, and employed a qualitative user study approach. In future work, we plan to broaden the participant base and conduct a larger-scale study to quantitatively assess the effectiveness of the proposed method.

At present, real-time video analysis has not been fully automated. The current implementation requires users to manually select targets. archiveTracking frequently fails when athletes cross paths or leave the frame, which makes manual re-annotation necessary. For future development, we aim to achieve real-time video analysis by adopting more robust techniques. These may include leveraging sport-specific features, such as the tendency in fencing for athletes to return to their starting positions after a point is scored.

This study focused on fencing, as the author has domain knowledge and prior reporting experience in the sport. In the future, however, we plan to explore the application of the proposed method to other sports. The types of time-series information that need to be presented vary depending on the sport, and therefore the visualization method used in this study may not be directly transferable. Nevertheless, we believe the core idea of our approach–allowing journalists to flag moments they find subjectively meaningful and later refer to these moments during question formulation using match videos and play data–is broadly applicable to a variety of sports.

8 Conclusion

This study began by identifying key challenges faced by university student sports journalists. Interviews revealed that they often carry a heavy workload during matches and have little time to prepare meaningful interview questions. Evaluations by both athletes and journalists showed that questions focusing on specific plays and tactics were consistently rated more highly.

To support the generation of such questions, we proposed a match review system that combines match videos with time-series data. The system enables journalists to flag noteworthy scenes even while performing other duties. A field study confirmed that flagging is feasible in real-world conditions and tends to increase when the score difference is small. In a user study with a prototype display system, the number of questions referencing player positioning and detailed attack methods increased. These results suggest that our method can enhance the depth and quality of post-match interviews.

In future work, we plan to implement real-time analysis and integrate the system into actual sports reporting workflows. We will also examine the system's broader impact on journalistâĂŞathlete communication.

References

1. Alhuzami, N.: Changing the score: The impact of media coverage on Saudi football team's performance in the 2022 world cup from the perspective of audience. Pakistan J. Life Soc. Sci. **22**, 11882–11895 (2024). https://doi.org/10.57239/PJLSS-2024-22.2.00847
2. Błażkiewicz, M., Borysiuk, Z., Gzik, M.: Determination of loading in the lower limb joints during step-forward lunge in fencing. Acta Bioeng. Biomech. **20**, 3–8 (2018)
3. Eljand-Kärp, V., Harro-Loit, H.: Journalists interviewing elite athletes: Dumb answers or bad questions? Catalan J. Commun. Cultural Stud. **12**(1), 79–97 (2020)
4. Franks, S., et al.: Using computational tools to support journalists' creativity. Journalism **23**(9), 1881–1899 (2022)
5. Fu, L., Danescu-Niculescu-Mizil, C., Lee, L.: Tie-breaker: using language models to quantify gender bias in sports journalism. In: Proceedings of the IJCAI Workshop on NLP Meets Journalism (2016)
6. Grontman, A., Horyza, Ł., Koczan, K., Marzec, M., Śmiertka, M., Trybała, M.: Analysis of sword fencing training evaluation possibilities using motion capture techniques. In: 2020 IEEE 15th International Conference of System of Systems Engineering (SoSE), pp. 325–330. IEEE (2020)
7. Hernandez, J., McDuff, D., Infante, C., Maes, P., Quigley, K., Picard, R.: Wearable ESM: differences in the experience sampling method across wearable devices. In: Proceedings of the 18th International Conference on Human-Computer Interaction with Mobile Devices and Services, pp. 195–205 (2016)
8. Kim, T., Choi, S.: Analysis of the upper and lower limbs movement in elite fencing attack skills. Korean J. Sports Sci. **32**(3), 445–453 (2021)
9. Nita, V., Magyar, P.: Smart IoT device for measuring body angular velocity and centralized assesing of balance and control in fencing. In: 2023 International Symposium on Signals, Circuits and Systems (ISSCS), pp. 1–4. IEEE (2023)
10. Niţă, V.A., Magyar, P.: Improving balance and movement control in fencing using iot and real-time sensorial feedback. Sensors **23**(24), 9801 (2023)
11. Pamudyaningrum, F.E., et al.: UI/UX design for metora: a gamification of learning journalism interviewing method. In: E3S Web of Conferences, vol. 188. EDP Sciences (2020)
12. Peña, V.: All the right questions: exploring racial stereotypes in sports press conferences. Sociol. Sport J. **1**(aop), 1–9 (2024)
13. Shamansouri, E., Khosro, T.: The role of media on athlete's performance and stress. In: 19th Conference of the European Association for Sport Management, pp. 333–334 (2009)
14. Takahashi, M., Yokozawa, S., Mitsumine, H., Itsuki, T., Naoe, M., Funaki, S.: Real-time visualization of sword trajectories in fencing matches. Multimed. Tools Appl., 26411–26425 (2020). https://doi.org/10.1007/s11042-020-09249-y
15. Volsa, S., et al.: Development of an open-source solution to facilitate the use of one-button wearables in experience sampling designs. Behavior Research Methods, pp. 1–24 (2024)
16. Zhang, M., Chen, L., Yuan, X., Huang, R., Liu, S., Yong, J.: Visualization of technical and tactical characteristics in fencing. J. Visualization **22**, 109–124 (2019)
17. Zhu, K., Wong, A., McPhee, J.: Fencenet: fine-grained footwork recognition in fencing. In: Proceedings of the IEEE/CVF Conference on Computer Vision and Pattern Recognition, pp. 3589–3598 (2022)

Structural Analysis of Rebuttals to Evaluate Argumentative Interaction in Parliamentary Debates

Masahiro Fukui[✉][iD] and Satoshi Nakamura[iD]

Meiji University, 4-21-1 Nakano, Nakano-ku, Tokyo 164-8525, Japan
onedanijo11@gmail.com

Abstract. This study introduces a structural framework for evaluating the quality of argumentative interaction in parliamentary debate. We proposed four hypotheses about rebuttal structures and defined corresponding features (Distance, Interval, Order, Rally). From a corpus of 20 English debate rounds with 1,573 ADUs and 679 rebuttal relations, we compared these features with human and LLM ratings. Regression analysis revealed a moderate correlation (r = 0.609), with Rally emerging as the most important predictor of interaction quality, followed by Distance and Interval, while Order showed limited explanatory power. To apply these insights in practice, we developed DebaTube, a visualization system that maps rebuttal structures to debate videos. A user study with experienced debaters confirmed that the system helps identify effective rebuttal patterns and improves exploration efficiency.

Keywords: Parliamentary debate · Rebuttal structure · Dialogue

1 Introduction

Parliamentary debate is a turn-based, impromptu format in which two teams argue for (proposition) or against (opposition) a motion to persuade judges. It is not only a competition but also a valuable educational practice where participants develop critical thinking and learn how to argue constructively [4]. However, due to the complexity of parliamentary debate, debaters often focus excessively on details of individual rebuttal and talk past each other. Nevertheless, most existing methods for debate analysis only evaluate the quality of individual rebuttals. Ruiz-Dolz et al. [6] pointed out that most prior research has focused on short-text debates and tends to oversimplify argumentative dynamics by isolating individual arguments. To address this, they and Hsiao et al. [3] have attempted to model rebuttal structures.

However, while these computational approaches have advanced the modeling of debate dynamics, they primarily focus on predicting debate winners, which provides only a limited view of argumentation quality. In parliamentary debate, this approach cannot fully capture the quality, as teams often win due to opponent mistakes or unconstructive arguments rather than substantive engagement.

Furthermore, this winner-prediction-based evaluation overlooks the dialogic and educational nature of parliamentary debate. Therefore, it is essential to evaluate debates not only by which team wins, but also by how effectively debaters engage with and build upon each other's arguments, which we term "argumentative interaction" in this paper.

In this study, we address the following research question: *What structural features of rebuttals indicate high-quality argumentative interaction in parliamentary debate?*

To explore this question, we propose a novel approach for evaluating the quality of argumentative interaction based on the rebuttal structures. Our analysis builds upon the concept of argumentative discourse units (ADUs), commonly used in argumentation analysis as elemental textual segments that serve specific argumentative functions. We introduce four hypotheses grounded in the structural dynamics of rebuttal relations between ADUs.

The main contributions of this paper are as follows:

1. We constructed a manually annotated corpus of 20 English parliamentary debates with 1,573 ADUs and 679 rebuttal relations.
2. We proposed four structural features and, through expert–LLM combined evaluation, showed they moderately predict interaction quality ($r = 0.609$), with *Rally* as the strongest indicator.
3. We developed *DebaTube*, a visualization system linking rebuttal structures with debate videos, and confirmed its usefulness in a user study.

2 Modeling Rebuttal Structure

2.1 Key Terms and Hypotheses on Rebuttal Structure

To analyze rebuttal structures, we first define key terms. Following prior work in argumentation analysis [8], we adopt the concept of ADUs. Each ADU represents an argumentative unit that contains either a claim with reasons or a standalone claim. Here, Point of Information (POI), which is a question posed during opponents' speeches, is treated as an ADU since they typically present a single claim due to time constraints.

We define a rebuttal as a statement that responds to a specific argument made by the opposing team. Anticipating an opponent's claim or presenting a conflicting stance without reference to a particular statement is not considered a rebuttal. In our model, rebuttals are represented as directed edges between ADUs, forming a graph where nodes are ordered chronologically.

To investigate our research question, we propose four hypotheses grounded in prior argumentation studies, which show that temporal proximity between arguments and argument order [3], and the chains of counter-attacks [1,6] are important factors in debate quality. While these studies primarily focus on winner prediction for either monologues or short-text debates, we extend their insights by adopting a more dialogical perspective and tailoring our approach to the specific characteristics of parliamentary debate, where multiple topics are addressed simultaneously and well-organized arguments are particularly crucial. Based on these theoretical foundations, we propose the following hypotheses:

- **H1**: Rebuttals that target arguments from two or more speeches earlier tend to overlook recent content and create fragmented exchanges. A higher frequency of such distant rebuttals suggests lower interaction quality.
- **H2**: When rebuttals to the same point are spread across a speech with large intervals between them, the coherence of the exchange weakens. Larger intervals between repeated rebuttals indicate unproductive interactions.
- **H3**: Rebuttals that follow the original order of the opponent's arguments within a topic indicate more coherent and productive dialogue.
- **H4**: Longer and more frequent rebuttal rallies, sequences of multiple counter-rebuttals, reflect deeper engagement and higher interaction quality.

2.2 Definitions of Structural Features of Rebuttals

Based on the four hypotheses described in Sect. 2.1, we define structural features that quantify rebuttal characteristics for each debate round: *Distance*, *Interval*, *Order*, and *Rally*. Each corresponds to our hypotheses H1 to H4. We compute these features as follows:

- **Distance (H1)**: This feature calculates the proportion of rebuttals that target ADUs from at least two speakers earlier in the opposing team.
- **Interval (H2)**: For each ADU rebutted multiple times from the same speech, we calculate the interval between the first and last rebuttal, counting both endpoints (e.g., the first to second ADU counts as 2, the first to third ADU counts as 3). We then normalize this by the number of ADUs in the speech minus two (the maximum possible interval), where two is the minimum interval. This feature is the sum of all normalized gaps.
- **Order (H3)**: This feature measures rebuttal pairs from the same speech that either share the same source or have crossing edges. Here, a crossing is defined as when a later rebuttal targets an earlier ADU than the target of a preceding rebuttal (See Fig. 1). The feature returns total rebuttals divided by crossing count.
- **Rally (H4)**: This feature counts pairs of rebuttals where one rebuttal's target is another rebuttal's source, then normalizes by dividing the count by the product of total rebuttals and total speeches.

3 Empirical Study: Structural Features and Argumentative Interaction Quality

3.1 Corpus Construction

We collected 20 videos of two-team parliamentary debates featuring experienced student debaters in practice rounds and tournament preliminaries. All speakers

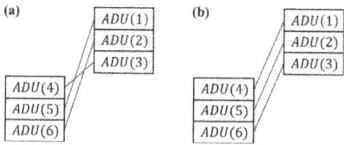

Fig. 1. Illustration of crossing edges in the Order calculation. Black blocks represent ADUs numbered chronologically, with ADUs 4–6 belonging to the same speech, and red lines indicate rebuttal relations. In (a), the rebuttal pairs (4→3, 5→1) and (4→3, 6→2) cross, resulting in a crossing count of 2. In (b), no crossings occur, so the crossing count is 0. (Color figure online)

were Japanese high school or university students debating in English, following worldwide parliamentary debate rules. We specifically chose intermediate-level debates because they contain both strong and weak arguments. This variety allows us to analyze various argumentation characteristics.

The videos were transcribed using whisper-large-v2. The transcripts were then manually segmented into ADUs and annotated with rebuttal relations by the first author, an experienced parliamentary debater, as automated rebuttal detection methods for competitive debate have not been established. As a result, we constructed a corpus of 1,573 ADUs and 679 rebuttal relations.

3.2 Evaluation Method and Inter-rater Reliability

To evaluate the structural features defined in Sect. 2.2, we assessed the quality of argumentative interaction in each round with three raters: a human expert (10+ years of judging experience), a human non-expert (3+ years of debate experience without judging experience), and a large language model (LLM). While acknowledging that LLMs have limitations such as biases toward later speeches, recent studies show that LLMs are sufficiently capable for debate evaluation [5], which we consider acceptable given the exploratory nature of our study. For the LLM rater, we used OpenAI o3[1].

All raters reviewed videos of each debate round and evaluated the statement "Both teams demonstrated high-quality argumentative interaction throughout the debate" using a four-point Likert scale: Agree (4), Rather agree (3), Rather disagree (2), and Disagree (1). For LLM ratings, we generated five outputs per round and used the mode as the final rating, with 90% of rounds achieving consistency in at least 3 out of 5 ratings. Raters also provided open-ended comments for qualitative insights.

To establish our evaluation method, we assessed inter-rater reliability by calculating Cohen's Kappa using binary classifications (positive: scores 3–4; negative: scores 1–2). This preliminary check revealed moderate agreement between the expert and LLM ($\kappa = 0.490$, with 60% perfect agreement on the four-point scale), while the non-expert showed poor agreement with both the expert ($\kappa =$

---

[1] Details of the prompts used are available at: https://osf.io/ceugp.

Table 1. Performance comparison of regression models

Model	RMSE	MAE	Correlation Coefficient
Multiple Linear Regression	0.509	0.409	0.609
Ridge Regression	0.562	0.447	0.508
Lasso Regression	0.511	0.412	0.589

Table 2. Regression coefficients and feature importance

Feature	Multiple Linear	Ridge	Lasso	Importance (%)
$Distance$	−1.172	−0.530	−0.915	28.8
$Interval$	−1.030	−0.611	−0.914	25.3
$Order$	0.216	0.007	0.000	5.3
$Rally$	1.656	0.671	1.319	40.7

0.175) and LLM ($\kappa = -0.056$). Thus, we used the average of expert and LLM rating as our final quality score, excluding the non-expert rating.

3.3 Correlation Between Structural Features and Argument Quality

We verified the hypotheses by calculating features of rebuttal structures in Sect. 2.2 and examining the relationship between features and raters' evaluation through regression analysis. To ensure robust evaluation of model generalization performance, we employed leave-one-out cross-validation on our dataset of 20 samples. The feature values were normalized by dividing each value by the maximum feature value in the 20 rounds.

As Table 1 shows, Multiple Linear Regression achieved the best performance with RMSE of 0.509 and MAE of 0.409. The correlation coefficient between predicted and rater evaluation was 0.609, indicating a moderate positive correlation. Given an SD of 0.688, an RMSE/SD of 0.74 suggests practically acceptable predictive performance for subjective evaluation tasks.

Regarding feature importance, Table 2 shows that the $Rally$ feature demonstrated the highest importance at 40.7%, followed by $Distance$ (28.8%), $Interval$ (25.3%), and $Order$ (5.3%) features. Multiple linear regression showed particularly strong coefficients for $Rally$ (1.656), $Distance$ (1.172), and $Interval$ (1.030). Additionally, both Lasso and Ridge regression eliminated the $Order$ feature (Lasso: 0.000, Ridge: 0.007).

3.4 In-depth Analysis on the Accuracy of Models

As for model's accuracy, results described in Sect. 3.3 show that H4 (related to $Rally$) is strongly supported with the highest importance at 40.7%. Moreover, H1 (related to $Distance$) and H2 (related to $Interval$) are moderately supported with 28.8% and 25.3% importance, respectively. In contrast, H3 (related

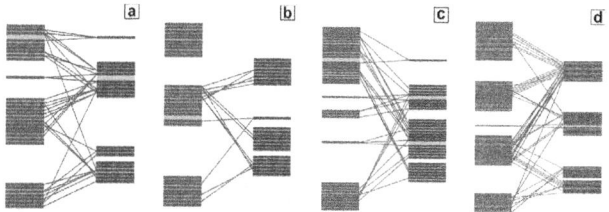

Fig. 2. Visualization of rebuttal structures with the (a) largest *Rally* (b) smallest *Distance* (c) largest *Distance* (d) third-largest *Order* value.

to *Order*) showed limited support with only 5.3% importance and was completely eliminated in Lasso regression.

To understand these results, we provide an in-depth analysis of these structural features through visualization of rebuttal structures. Throughout this paper, we employ the visualizing format where block nodes represent ADUs and line edges represent rebuttals, with red indicating proposition's components and blue indicating opposition's components.

First, *Rally* demonstrated the strongest alignment with H4, suggesting a tendency for the hypothesis to be supported. The round in Fig. 2a shows a round with the largest *Rally* value that received a rating of 3.0 out of 4, despite having the worst *Interval* and *Order* scores. This suggests that long rally indicates meaningful dialogue even when rebuttals are not well-organized.

Second, *Distance* tends to moderately support H1. Figure 2b presents a notable case with the smallest *Distance* and highest rating (3.5) though first opposition speaker did not rebut at all. This suggests continuous counterarguments are important. Furthermore, the feature also captures argumentative flaws. Figure 2c shows the round with the largest *Distance* value (rated 2.5), where the second proposition speaker barely spoke, forcing the opposition to concentrate rebuttals on the first speaker, collapsing the dialogue. Thus, *Distance* reflects both positive and negative aspects of dialogue.

Third, *Interval* demonstrated moderate alignment with H2. For instance, the round with the smallest *Interval* received good rating (3.0) despite average *Rally* value. This suggests that when teams concentrate their multiple attacks on the same argument, it compensates for unremarkable exchange frequency.

Last, *Order* showed minimal alignment with H3 and was eliminated by regularized methods. The model was less effective because individual speeches with many crossings disproportionately lowered the overall score. For example, the round in Fig. 2d received the highest rating (3.5) but had the third-worst *Order* score, as strong early speeches with few crossings (especially 1st opposition and 2nd proposition) were overshadowed by later speeches with many crossings. Weighting crossings per speech could address this issue.

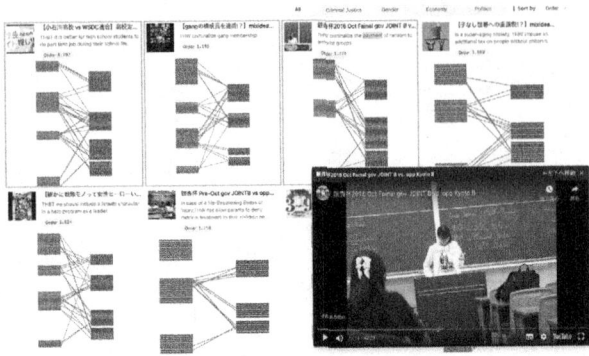

Fig. 3. User Interface of DebaTube. Users can sort rounds by features and pin the round and click any ADU node to jump to the scene.

3.5 Short Summary

Our empirical analysis revealed that structural features of rebuttals, particularly *Rally* and *Distance*, can serve as reliable indicators of argumentative interaction quality. The predictive performance of our model suggests that debate quality can be captured through quantifiable structural patterns. Interestingly, while argumentative interactions may seem complex to quantify, simple structural metrics proved sufficient for evaluation. This indicates that beyond the detailed content of arguments, structural patterns provide useful cues for assessing debate quality. The quantifiable nature of these patterns raises the possibility of making them more accessible through visualization.

4 Application and User Study

Our empirical findings demonstrated that structural features can effectively indicate argumentative interaction quality. To explore how these insights about rebuttal structure can support debate learning in practice, we developed DebaTube[2], an interactive visualization system that leverages our structural features. While previous work has shown the value of argument visualization for understanding political debates [7] and improving discussion skills [2,9], our system specifically targets parliamentary debate education by combining rebuttal structure visualization with video exploration.

DebaTube allows users to visually explore debate patterns using the rebuttal graph and navigate directly to specific argumentative exchanges by clicking ADU nodes, enabling debaters to overview features of many debate rounds at once and efficiently identify and study rounds with desirable argumentative patterns before watching the corresponding video segments (Fig. 3).

We conducted a user study with five experienced debaters to evaluate how structural visualization aids debate exploration. Participants used our system to

---

[2] https://debatube.nkmr.io.

find instructional rounds for four scenarios (e.g., covering struggling teammates, balancing rebuttal targets). Results indicated that some participants tended to compare same speaker positions across rounds, while others carefully examined the visualization before watching the videos. Results show our visualization helps users recognize effective rebuttal patterns and improves exploration efficiency.

5 Conclusion

This study introduced structural features of rebuttals as indicators of high-quality argumentative interaction in parliamentary debate. We proposed four features that describe how rebuttals are distributed, sequenced, and exchanged, offering an alternative to traditional winner-prediction-based methods. This research establishes a structural framework for evaluating argumentative interaction quality by analyzing all rebuttal relations throughout rounds and capturing dialogic dynamics.

Future work will address current limitations: recruiting multiple judges to establish more reliable ground truth and testing how the findings from this paper can be applied to argumentation in various formats, such as political debates and group discussions. Through these, we aim to not only enhance the educational value of competitive debate but also expand argumentation education more broadly by supporting learners' understanding of rebuttal structures.

References

1. Dung, P.M.: On the acceptability of arguments and its fundamental role in nonmonotonic reasoning, logic programming and n-person matches. Artif. Intell. **77**(2), 321–357 (1995)
2. Guerraoui, C., et al.: Teach me how to argue: a survey on NLP feedback systems in argumentation. In: Proceedings of the 10th Workshop on Argument Mining, pp. 19–34 (2023)
3. Hsiao, F.H., Yen, A.Z., Huang, H.H., Chen, H.H.: Modeling inter round attack of online debaters for winner prediction. In: Proceedings of the ACM Web Conference 2022, pp. 2860–2869 (2022)
4. Jodoi, K.: The effects of parliamentary debate as a pedagogy for argumentation in l1 and l2 contexts. Argumentation **39**, 147–163 (2024)
5. Liu, X., Liu, P., He, H.: An empirical analysis on large language models in debate evaluation. In: Proceedings of the 62nd Annual Meeting of the Association for Computational Linguistics, vol. 2, pp. 470–487 (2024)
6. Ruiz-Dolz, H.G.: Automatic debate evaluation with argumentation semantics and natural language argument graph networks. In: Proceedings of the 2023 Conference on Empirical Methods in Natural Language Processing, pp. 6030–6040 (2023)
7. South, L., Schwab, M., Beauchamp, N., Wang, L., Wihbey, J., Borkin, M.A.: Debatevis: visualizing political debates for non-expert users. In: 2020 IEEE Visualization Conference (VIS), pp. 241–245 (2020)
8. Stab, C., Gurevych, I.: Parsing argumentation structures in persuasive essays. Comput. Linguist. **43**, 619–659 (2017)
9. Xia, M., Zhu, Q., Wang, X., Nie, F., Qu, H., Ma, X.: Persua: a visual interactive system to enhance the persuasiveness of arguments in online discussion. Proc. ACM Hum.-Comput. Interact. **6**, 1–30 (2022)

Author Index

A
Adaji, Ifeoma 107
Adani, Muhammad Dias 55
Ando, Masayuki 3
Aurelvia, Arinza 55

C
Chounta, Irene-Angelica 244

D
Dan, Hiroshige 179
Ding, Yaofei 161

E
Echigo, Hiroki 212
Egi, Hironori 20, 39

F
Fujishima, Kosuke 231
Fukui, Masahiro 268

G
Gama, Kiev 244

H
Hagihara, Ai 252
Hernández-Leo, Davinia 29
Hirata, Keiji 90
Hori, Jotaro 3

I
Ieiri, Yuya 179
Ihara, Masayuki 73, 212
Iida, Sora 123
Imagawa, Taketo 73
Inoue, Tomoko 144, 161
Iso, Kazuyuki 73, 212
Izumi, Tomoko 3

K
Kawashima, Hayato 39
Kobayashi, Minoru 73, 212
Kodaira, Masaki 20
Kurokochi, Atsuto 73

L
Liang, Changhao 135

M
Martha, Ati Suci Dian 55
Miura, Hiroya 90

N
Nakamura, Ryosuke 39
Nakamura, Satoshi 123, 252, 268
Negishi, Ayaka 212
Nishida, Takeshi 204
Nishide, Shinya 204
Nishihara, Yoko 195, 231
Nishimura, Ryunosuke 39
Nolte, Alexander 244

O
Ogata, Hiroaki 135
Okpanachi, Linda 107
Okutani, Ryo 179
Otsu, Kouyou 3

R
Rodríguez-Pérez, Gema 107

S
Salma, Soraya Haidar 55
Sánchez-Reina, J. Roberto 29
Sasaki, Kosuke 144
Schulten, Cleo 244
Shan, Junjie 195, 231
Shimizu, Ryohei 20
Shingu, Kaito 195

T
Takegawa, Yoshinari 90
Theophilou, Emily 29

W
Widowati, Sri 55

Y
Yamamoto, Kimitaka 90
Yamaura, Kazuho 195
Yan, Yu 135
Yanagii, Koki 73
Yasuo, Megumi 195, 231
Yoshie, Osamu 179
Yoshimoto, Tetsuo 231
Yuan, Li 244

Made in the USA
Monee, IL
03 May 2026

49438507R00162